Will Storr is an award-winning writer. [the] *Guardian*, *Sunday Times*, *New Yorke* He is the author of six critically acclaimed books, most recently the *Sunday Times* bestseller *The Science of Storytelling*.

@wstorr
willstorr.com

'Will Storr is one of our best journalists of ideas . . . *The Status Game* might be his best yet' James Marriott, Books of the Year, *The Times*

'[*The Status Game*] challenged the way I think about the role of status in my own life . . . I can't stop thinking about it'
Sean Illing, Vox

'Moving . . . Scholarly . . . Storr showcases a rare skill – the ability to use technical academic scholarship in solving a real-world problem'
Helen Dale, CapX

'*The Status Game* brims with deep insights into one of the most universal motives of humans everywhere. It is superbly written and anchored in the best science. From the perks of status gained to the pain of status lost, *The Status Game* unpacks the underlying psychological machinery that drives us all' David M. Buss, author of *The Evolution of Desire*

'Will Storr is a master at this art. His book *The Status Game* could not be more timely and provides a missing piece for understanding where we are, and how to get out of this mess. He seamlessly combines cutting edge research with surprising and gripping vignettes, data, and insights from some of the world's best thinkers. I can't recommend it highly enough'
Greg Lukianoff, co-author with Jonathan Haidt
of *The Coddling of the American Mind*

'I haven't finished reading *The Status Game* because I've only read it once. There's so much in this dazzling book I will be revisiting over and over again' Daniel Finkelstein, author of *Everything in Moderation*

ALSO BY WILL STORR

FICTION
The Hunger and the Howling of Killian Lone

NON-FICTION
Will Storr vs. The Supernatural
The Heretics
Selfie
The Science of Storytelling

The Status Game

WILL STORR

WILLIAM
COLLINS

William Collins
An imprint of HarperCollins*Publishers*
1 London Bridge Street
London SE1 9GF

WilliamCollinsBooks.com

HarperCollins*Publishers*
Macken House, 39/40 Mayor Street Upper,
Dublin 1, D01 C9W8, Ireland

First published in Great Britain in 2021 by William Collins
This William Collins paperback edition published in 2022

4

Copyright © Will Storr 2021, 2022

Will Storr asserts the moral right to be identified
as the author of this work in accordance with the
Copyright, Designs and Patents Act 1988

A catalogue record for this book is available from the British Library

ISBN 978-0-00-835467-1

Typeset in Granjon by Palimpsest Book Production Ltd, Falkirk, Stirlingshire

Printed and bound in the UK using 100% renewable electricity at CPI Group (UK) Ltd

MIX
Paper | Supporting
responsible forestry
FSC™ C007454

This book is produced from independently certified FSC™ paper
to ensure responsible forest management.

For more information visit: www.harpercollins.co.uk/green

For Jones, my lovely boy

'O Athens, can you possibly believe what dangers
I undergo to win good repute among you?'

Alexander the Great
(356–323 BC)

CONTENTS

PROLOGUE

LIFE IS A game.

There's no way to understand the human world without first understanding this. Everyone alive is playing a game whose hidden rules are built into us and that silently directs our thoughts, beliefs and actions. This game is inside us. It *is* us. We can't help but play.

Life takes this strange form because of how we've evolved. Like all living organisms, humans are driven to survive and reproduce. As a tribal species, our personal survival has always depended on our being accepted into a supportive community. Powerful emotions compel us to connect: the joy of belongingness and agony of rejection. But once inside a group, we're rarely content to flop about on its lower rungs. We seek to rise. When we do, and receive acclaim from our people, we feel as if our lives have meaning and purpose and that we're thriving. In ways small and large, the conditions of life begin to improve. Back in the Stone Age, increased status meant greater influence, access to a wider choice of mates and more security and resources for ourselves and our children. It still does today. So we're programmed to seek connection and rank: to be accepted into groups and win status within them. It's part of our nature. It's the game of human life.

No matter where you travel, from the premodern societies of Papua New Guinea to the skyscraper forests of Tokyo and Manhattan, you'll find it: humans forming groups and playing for status. In the developed world, we play political games; religious games; corporate games; sports games; cult games; legal games; fashion games; hobby games; computer games; charity games; social media games; racial, gender and nationalist games. The variety feels infinite. Within these groups, we strive for individual status – acclaim from our co-players. But our groups also compete with rival groups in status contests: political coalition battles political coalition; corporation battles corporation; football team battles football team. When our games win status, we do too. When they lose, so do we. These games form our identity. We become the games we play.

Our need for status gives us a thirst for rank and a fear of its loss that deforms our thinking and denies us the possibility of reliable happiness. It's why, even as we raise ourselves so high above the other animals we appear to them as gods, we still behave like them – and worse. Always on alert for slights and praise, we can be petty, hateful, aggressive, grandiose and delusional. We play for status, if only subtly, with every social interaction, every contribution we make to work, love or family life and every internet post. We play with how we dress, how we speak and what we believe. We play with our lives – with the story we tell of our past and our dreams of the future. Our waking existence is accompanied by its racing commentary of emotions: we can feel horrors when we slip, even by a fraction, and taste ecstasy when we soar. Up and down and up and down and up and down we go, moment by moment, day by day, from childhood to the grave. Life is not a journey towards a perfect destination. It's a game that never ends. And it's the very worst of us.

But it's also the best. We wouldn't have raised ourselves above the other animals in the first place if it wasn't for the peculiar and particular ways we play at life. There are various strategies by which we can earn status. Humans strive for success: to be the best hunter, the best builder, the best cook, the best technologist, the best leader, the best creator of wealth. The game compels us to scheme and to innovate; to push ourselves to new limits in order to win. When we succeed, dozens, hundreds or even millions of others might benefit from our play. Humans strive, too, to be virtuous: to win urgent moral battles, to rescue the imperilled, to lift strangers in distant continents out of poverty or violence, to create vaccines that'll defend the lives of people who'll be born long after we're gone. All such endeavours are accompanied by the game's racing commentary of emotions: the shame and the pride, the plummet and the high. This is why, I've come to believe, we make a fundamental error when we reflexively categorise our desire for status as shameful.

A greater understanding of what helps drive us on our good days and bad must surely be useful. Digging beneath the flattering stories we like to tell of ourselves can help us see more clearly how we can become better, but also how easily we become tempted into delusion and tyranny. By understanding what human life is actually doing when it goes wrong, we can be smarter about avoiding its traps. Likewise, by understanding what we're doing when it goes right, we can make a better future, increasing fairness, wealth and quality of life for all.

This book has been written in a time of rage and fear in the Western world. It didn't seem long ago that our central complaint about the political parties of left and right was that they were too similar. What was the point in voting, we asked, when all you got were slightly different versions of 'neoliberal' capitalism? We don't ask this anymore. The first decade of the twenty-first century has seen the Global Financial Crisis, the invention of the smartphone and the rise of social media. The right lurched rightwards, towards Brexit and Trump, fuelled by pro-nationhood agendas; the left lurched leftwards towards identity politics and its new lexicon of insult: gammon, cis, bro, Karen, TERF, mansplainer, manspreader,

3

white, privileged, pale-male-stale. Families argued, friends broke up, wrong-thinking citizens, celebrities and academics were mobbed and toppled, global corporations sprouted political opinions, reading the news came to feel like swimming through nettles, and then war returned to Europe. What was happening?

Part of the reason we keep making the same mistakes, and tipping into groupish conflict, is that we play life as a status game. Our brains continually, and in countless ways, measure where we sit versus other people. They automatically layer them and the groups they belong to into hierarchies. Most of these processes are subconscious, and hidden from us. Crucially, whilst we subconsciously play life as a game, our conscious experience of it takes the form of a story. The brain feeds us distorted, simplistic and self-serving tales about why *they* are above us and *they* are beneath. In this way, complex truths become reduced to cartoonish moral struggles between good and evil. We're all vulnerable to believing such narratives. They form our experience of reality. They make us feel better about ourselves; they motivate us to strive to improve our rank. But they're delusional. They're responsible for much of the hubris, hatred and hypocrisy that stalk our species. They can even drive us to kill.

What follows is an investigation, based on research spanning psychology, anthropology, sociology, economics and history, into the hidden structure of human life. In order to reveal its secret patterns, we're going to travel back to our evolutionary roots and to the Soviet Union, the Republic of Niger and an island community in Micronesia where they grow enormous yams. We're going to discover what Nazi Germany, the British Industrial Revolution and the USA's Satanic Panic of the 1980s have in common. We're going to climb into the minds of anti-vaccination conspiracy theorists, misogynist spree killers, cult members, online mobbers and racists. We'll discover a new way of defining tyranny – of what happens when status games go bad. We're going to recount the story of the world in an unusual manner:

one in which self and culture change as the rules of status games are rewritten, mostly accidentally. We're going to define three different forms of the status game – the dominance game, the virtue game and the success game – and ask how certain kinds of play can lead us into a fairer, wealthier tomorrow. Finally we'll attend to some practical advice that seeks to assist us in playing our personal games of life.

The arguments in this book are predicated on the simple idea, now well-supported by researchers, that status is a fundamental human need. If it is fundamental, it naturally follows that we'll find evidence of it all over the place: in our actions, in our history and hiding behind many of our thoughts and convictions. In the chapters that follow, as I attempt to reveal it wherever I can, it might feel as if I'm proposing a grossly reductive view of our shared nature. But my focus on one human need shouldn't be taken to imply that others, which aren't the subject of this investigation, don't count. We're obviously driven by a great many impulses – and usually several at once. An inventor may be motivated by insatiable curiosity and the joy of problem-solving and desire to pay their mortgage, for example, as well as by the urge to impress their peers. Status is what researchers call an 'ultimate' rather than a 'proximate' drive: it's a kind of mother-motivation, a deep evolutionary cause of many other downstream beliefs and behaviours that's been favoured by selection and is written into the design of our brains.

So nothing in this book should be taken as my arguing that life is solely driven by status. We are, it should go without saying, driven by a multitude of desires. We want power. We want sex. We want wealth. We want to change society for the better. But it's also true that the status game is deeply implicated in these great human hungers. If you want to rule the world, save the world, buy the world or fuck the world, the first thing to pursue is status. It's the golden key that unlocks our dreams. And your subconscious mind knows this. This is why, as psychologist Professor Brian Boyd writes, we

'naturally pursue status with ferocity: we all relentlessly, if unconsciously, try to raise our own standing by impressing peers, and
naturally, if unconsciously, evaluate others in terms of their standing'.

The Status Game builds on two of my previous books. *The Heretics*
(published in the U.S. as *The Unpersuadables*) asked how intelligent
people end up believing crazy things. I concluded we're especially
vulnerable to irrationality when the 'facts' in question serve to boost
or threaten the heroic story we tell of ourselves. *Selfie* was a journey
into the self and the ways in which evolution, culture and economy
shape who we are. It proposed (in an argument briefly reprised here
in chapter 25) that our highly individualistic neoliberal economy has
thrown the West into an unhealthy 'age of perfectionism'. In the
pages that follow, I'll bring these threads together and tie them into
something new.

If you've arrived from my preceding book, *The Science of
Storytelling*, you'd be forgiven for wondering if you're about to tumble
into a gigantic contradiction. I went to some lengths to persuade you
that your brain is a storyteller and now, here I am, insisting it's a
game player. But as I hope will become clear, this is actually a parallel
argument investigated at a deeper level. If the conscious experience
is organised as a story, this book concerns the subconscious truth that
lies underneath.

In the years it's taken me to research this subject, I've come to
understand so much more about other people and why they can be
so enraging, dastardly, confusing and wonderful. They, and I, are
no longer quite so mysterious. My hope is that by defining human
life more precisely, we might be better able to meet its challenges,
defend ourselves from its terrors and, in the end, be just a little more
certain about how to live lives of meaning, safety and happiness.
What follows is a tentative journey through the status game. You'll
recognise it, of course, having already been a lifelong player.

I

The Life and Afterlife of Ben Gunn

A S HE RAISED a wooden chair leg in the air and brought it down onto the head of his new friend, Ben's life began. It was just after 7 p.m. on 9 April 1980 on a school playing field in Brecon, Wales. 'My life started then,' said Ben. 'Everything before that is irrelevant.'

Ben was 14. His victim, Brian, was 11. Earlier that day, they'd escaped from their care home. In the grounds of an empty school they'd discovered a pile of broken furniture and had a play fight. When they were finished, Ben accidentally let slip a secret. He couldn't believe what he'd said. If his confession was revealed he felt sure he'd be rejected by all of society, spat on in the street, rendered utterly worthless. 'There was no thought process. I just knew I'd told him and he'd tell the world. I was overwhelmed by emotion. Within a second, I was hitting him with a chair leg because I knew I'd destroyed myself.'

Ben ran to a phone box and dialled 999: 'I've killed a boy. I hit him with a stick and I think I strangled him.' Brian was found with a piece of his skull missing. He died, three days later, at Cardiff Royal Infirmary. Ben only discovered he was dead when his solicitor told him, 'Well, you know it's going to be murder now. Did nobody tell you?' When they sentenced him to an indefinite term at Her Majesty's pleasure he was wearing his school uniform. They took him down before the judge had even finished his summing up: *'You killed a boy without rhyme or reason. You brought his life to an end without any motive in circumstances which you know amounted to murder . . .'*

In prison, they treated him as if he was worthless. During an early cell search, 'they piled everything on the floor, all my clothes, bedding, everything I owned, then just marched out'. Ben was outraged. He refused to tidy up and slept on the floor for three nights. A direct order was issued. He still refused. They sent him to solitary confinement. There he sat alone in a cold cell. This was his world now. He was a child murderer, the lowest of the low. He had nothing. He was no one.

Ben attempted escapes. He tried to starve himself to death. At his first parole hearing, ten years into his sentence, he was denied release. They denied him again and again. Twelve years, fifteen years, twenty years and then twenty-five, Ben remained in prison. Then, in the summer of 2007, he fell in love with Alex, a visiting teacher. 'He wore khaki and had a beard down to here,' she told me. 'He looked like a cross between Osama bin Laden and Rasputin, and carried this dirty water jug filled with coffee. I asked, "Who's that?" They said, "That's Ben Gunn. Keep out of his way."'

But Alex and Ben began flirting. They had sex in a stationery cupboard. They'd communicate in secret, with Alex typing into Ben's computer, so it looked as if she was helping with his classroom studies, but the words were of love and desire. They'd swap hundreds of Post-it notes and voice recordings on memory sticks. Ben would call her on a contraband mobile phone at 12 p.m., 4.30 p.m. and 9 p.m. every day.

By 2010, Ben had been in prison for thirty years, three times longer than his minimum tariff demanded. He should've been released decades ago. But every time an opportunity for parole came up, he managed to supply the prison service with a new reason to deny it. The MP Michael Gove, who'd been campaigning for his release, told *The Times* newspaper he thought there was, 'perhaps a self-destructive element in his make-up, because the prison authorities always have a misdemeanour to report, some serious (never violent), some trite, to prevent parole being granted'. To encourage him out, Alex would paint him pictures of the things they'd be able to enjoy together on the outside: the cottage in the country, the fire in the winter, the cat. She couldn't understand it: he could have her and everything else he wanted. All he had to do was behave. Why was he refusing?

Then one day Ben told her straight: 'I want to stay.'

* * *

If life is as we imagine it, this doesn't make sense. It was all there waiting for Ben: freedom, love and a beautiful cottage in the Cotswolds. This was a religious parable, a Hollywood ending, the archetypal story of heroic redemption. He'd atoned for his sins and here was his final destination, his glorious reward. But Ben didn't want it. He preferred to stay in prison.

What had happened to make him cling to life inside? How had he rescued himself from the psychological depths of attempting suicide by starvation? When you take a human and strip them of all the esteem they desire, when you lock them in a dismal building with criminals and a prison staff that treats them with bullying contempt, how can they save themselves? How does a brain, with hundreds of thousands of years of evolution built into it, respond to such a situation?

It builds a life for itself. A characteristically human life.

Years earlier, Ben had started to study. He read up on zen Buddhism, military history, politics and physics. He gained a degree in politics and history, a master's in peace and reconciliation, began a PhD in criminology and was appointed general secretary of the Association of Prisoners. 'I became known as the subversive, the political animal, the jailhouse lawyer.' He also became a vegan. 'Not so much a moral thing as being a pain in the arse.' (One lunchtime, to annoy him in return, the prison service presented him a meal of mashed potato and boiled potato with a baked potato on the side.)

Ben made a life for himself by playing a game he thought of as 'resisting abuses of power'. He came to excel at it. In all his time inside, he only ever met one prison governor he considered knew the rules as well as he did. Ben would help other prisoners fight the system, sometimes tying officers up for months with densely argued appeals to the most trivial misdemeanour charges. He became notorious with the officials. The parole board declared him a 'fully paid-up member of the awkward squad'. He was a success. 'He was someone in prison,' Alex told me.

'And I knew that would change as soon as I got out,' said Ben. 'I'd go from being a medium fish in a small pond to being just another ex-con.'

To coax him out, Alex encouraged him to write a blog. The first post on PrisonerBen was published on the 31 August 2009. Readership grew to over 20,000. In 2011 it was nominated for a prestigious Orwell Prize. And, finally, Ben changed his mind. On 23 August 2012, aged 47, prisoner 12612 GUNN was released. Before he left, a member of the prison staff gave him a warning, 'You're going to lose what status you have in here.'

'What did he mean by that?' I asked.

'As a lifer you have a particular place in the prison hierarchy and as a jailhouse lawyer, you do too,' he said. 'All these things give you status and I knew, as soon as I walked out, they'd be irrelevant.'

As far as I could tell, those officers had been right. Since his release, Ben had been struggling. Thin, pale, shaven headed, rolling narrow cigarettes and sitting in the sunny garden room of Alex's Cotswolds cottage, he'd vividly described his collapse into despair. 'On some unconscious level it was deeply disturbing being released. I was sitting on the floor for two weeks rocking back and forth. I could see where I was in prison. I knew who I was and what I wanted to be. Now I'm completely lost. I'm imploding.' And yet when I enquired as to whether the officers were correct in predicting he'd suffer from a precipitous drop in status, he denied it.

When asked why we do the things we do, we rarely say, 'It's because of status. I really love it.' It can be distasteful to think of it as any kind of motivating force, let alone a vital one. It contradicts the heroic story we like to tell of ourselves. When we pursue the great goals of our lives, we tend to focus on our happy ending. We want the qualification, the promotion, the milestone, the crown. These motivations, that tend to spring to mind immediately, are known by researchers as 'proximate'. They're absolutely real and valid but they have other upstream 'ultimate' causes. Ultimate causes are often subconscious and so hidden from us: they're the reason we want the qualification, the promotion, the milestone, the crown, in the first place. They're an essential impulse that's been selected by evolution and laid down in the wiring of our brains. As the evolutionary biologist Professor Nichola Raihani writes, 'Ultimate explanations help us to understand *why* we feel the motives we do, and *why* brains are designed the way they are.'

If our need for status is fundamental, this discomfort we feel about admitting it may seem surprising. But we tend to believe the brain's heroic story, not the subconscious realpolitik of the game. To admit to being motivated by improving our rank risks making others think less of us, which loses us rank. Even admitting it to ourselves can make us feel reduced. So our awareness of our desire for status eats itself. We readily recognise it in rivals and even use it as a method of insult – which, ironically, is status play: an attempt to downgrade others and thereby raise ourselves up.

Because it has a canny way of hiding itself like this, let's drag our quarry from its guilty corner. Status isn't about being liked or accepted: these are separate needs, associated with connection. When people defer to us, offer respect, admiration or praise, or allow us to influence them in some way, that's status. It feels good. Feeling good about it is part of our human nature. It's in our basic coding, our evolution, our DNA. And it doesn't require a stupendous achievement like scoring a goal in the World Cup or blowing up the Death Star. We can feel the velvet touch of status repeatedly throughout the course of a single conversation or in the glance of a passing stranger.

Whenever we're in the presence of humans, consciously or unconsciously, we're being judged, measured. And their judgements matter. Wherever psychologists look, they find a remarkably powerful link between status and wellbeing. One study of more than sixty thousand people across 123 countries found people's wellbeing 'consistently depended on the degree to which people felt respected by others'. Attainment of status or its loss was 'the strongest predictor of long-term positive and negative feelings'. Elsewhere, an extensive review of the scientific literature concluded that 'the importance of status was observed across individuals who differed in culture, gender, age, and personality . . . the relevant evidence suggests that the desire for status is indeed fundamental'.

Ben's story is a profound lesson in how to live. It shows us that it's possible to survive everything being taken from us. We can become despised by society, classed a child murderer, and have a brutal force such as the prison service ranged against us. We can hit such depths of torment that we refuse to eat for forty-three days, starving until we feel our eyeballs drying out. And yet out of these circumstances of grotesque debasement, we can flourish. Ben built a life of meaning and purpose and he did it by plugging himself into a set of like-minded brains and playing a game in which the goal was to earn status. His rank as a lifer and jailhouse lawyer gave him deference and respect. He became useful to his co-players in their conflicts against the prison staff. He grew to be admired and valuable. He invested all the efforts of his days, months and years into the playing of this game. He created a world of meaning for himself. Then, after prison, he collapsed. When freedom means expulsion from the meaning you've spent your life making, then freedom is hell.

2

Getting Along, Getting Ahead

I F BEN CAN thrive in prison, we can hope to thrive too. There can't be many of us who find ourselves as lacking in agency and opportunity as he did. How easy it should be! Open the door, step out of it, and there it is: the world in all its hustle and wonder. The story we're often told is that, with sufficient application of self-belief and effort, we can do anything we want; be whoever we want.

But it's not so easy. The world isn't as it seems. On the other side of that door you won't find a simple pathway to happiness that you can march up heroically for seven or eight decades. Everyone out there is playing a game. That game has its own hidden rules, traps and shortcuts. And yet almost nobody alive is fully conscious of its form, despite being active daily participants. So let's attempt to wake ourselves up to the great game. Let's try to define more precisely what human life is and what it's trying to be.

Humans are a species of great ape. We survive by belonging to highly co-operative groups that share labour. We've been living in settled communities for around five hundred generations. But we existed in mobile hunter-gatherer bands for far longer than this – at least one hundred thousand generations. Our brains remain programmed for this style of life. We are today as we've always been:

tribal. We have instincts that compel us to seek connection with coalitions of others. Once we've been accepted into a group, we strive to achieve their approval and acclaim.

If we're to flourish, this approval and acclaim is critical. Researchers find that in the kinds of premodern communities our brains evolved in, 'social status is a universal cue to the control of resources', writes psychologist Professor David Buss. 'Along with status comes better food, more abundant territory, superior health care.' It leads to greater access to preferred mates and 'bestows on children social opportunities' that youngsters in lower ranking families miss out on. When researchers analysed 186 premodern societies around the world, they found men of higher status 'invariably had greater wealth and more wives and provided better nourishment for their children'. This was, and remains, the secret of maximising our capacity for survival and reproduction: the higher we rise, the more likely we are to live, love and procreate. It's the essence of human thriving. It's the status game.

Evolution has programmed us to seek groups to join and then strive for rank within them. But, especially in the modern era, we're not limited to one group. For those of us not in prison, a typical life involves the playing of multiple games. Wherever we connect with like-minded others, the game will be on: at work, online, on the sports field, at the volunteer centre, in the club, park or activist collective – even at home. The minimum requirement for play is connection. Before we can be rewarded with status, we must first be accepted into the group as a player.

Psychologists find that simply connecting with others and feeling accepted by them can be profoundly good for us. But equally revealing is how our minds and bodies react when we fail to connect. A wide range of research finds people with depression tend to belong to 'far fewer' groups than the rest of the population. Studies across time suggest the more a depressed person identifies with their group – the more of their own sense of self they invest in it – the more their symptoms lift. Failure to connect can even make us physically ill. Numerous studies find it's possible to predict mortality by observing the extent to which someone has meaningful contact with others. One survey of nearly seven thousand residents of Alameda County in California found 'the people most likely to survive to old age were those with solid face-to-face relationships', writes psychologist Susan Pinker. Their social relationships, or lack of them, 'predicted mortality, independently of how healthy, well-to-do, or physically fit' they were.

Disconnection is a fearsome state for a social animal to find itself in. It's a warning that its life is failing and its world has become hostile: where there's no connection, there's no protection. Isolation damages us so profoundly it can change who we are. It can force us into a 'defensive crouch', writes psychologist Professor John Cacioppo, in which we seek to fend off the threat of further rejection. Our perceptions of other people become warped. They start to appear 'more critical, competitive, denigrating, or otherwise unwelcoming'. These faulty interpretations 'quickly become expectations'. We can become scrappy, bitter and negative, a mindset that 'leads to greater marital strife, more run-ins with neighbours, and more social problems overall'.

When this happens, we can become even more isolated and vulnerable to yet further varieties of antisocial behaviour. Rejected people are more likely to issue punishments and less likely to donate money or help strangers. They can engage in self-damaging habits. In one study, participants were told they were taste-testing chocolate chip cookies. Before the test began, they were asked to mingle with other tasters then choose two they'd like to work with. Some were told (falsely) that nobody had picked them; others that everyone had. The first group, who'd been socially rejected, went on to eat an average of nine cookies more than the non-rejected: nearly twice the number. Most of them even rated the taste of the cookies more highly, implying their rejection actually altered their perceptions of the sugary food.

When our lives begin to fail, then, our minds and bodies fail too: we can become sick, angry, antisocial and increasingly isolated. We are, writes Cacioppo, 'creatures shaped by evolution to feel safe in company and endangered when unwillingly alone'. But connection itself doesn't make for a successful life. We're rarely content to linger on the lowest social rungs of our groups, likeable but useless. We desire worth, acclaim, to be of value. There's an itch to move up. In the oft-quoted words of psychologist Professor Robert Hogan, humans are driven to 'get along and get ahead'. Or, from the perspective of our current investigation, to be accepted into status games and to play well.

If rejection from the game can make us sad, angry and sick, the effects of failing to win status can be deadly. The epidemiologist Dr Michael Marmot has exposed the extraordinary power the status game has over our physical wellbeing. He spent decades analysing the health of members of the British civil service. 'Britain was and is a stratified society', he writes, 'and no part of it is more exquisitely stratified.' This made it 'an ideal "laboratory" in which to discover how subtle differences in social ranking can lead to dramatic differences in health, in people who are neither very poor nor very rich'.

Marmot was surprised to discover precisely how high a civil servant climbed in the game of the civil service predicted their health outcomes and mortality rates. This was not, as you might reasonably assume, to do with the wealthier individuals leading healthier and more privileged lifestyles. This effect, which Marmot calls the 'status syndrome', was entirely independent: a wealthy smoker just one rung below the very top of the status game was more likely to fall ill, as a result of their habit, than the smoker one rung above them.

And these health differentials were extremely significant. Workers 'at the bottom of the office hierarchy have, at ages forty to sixty-four,

four times the risk of death of the administrators at the top of the hierarchy'. This remained true with every step you took up or down the game. The lower you dropped, the worse your health and the earlier your death. 'The group second from the top has higher mortality than those above them in the ranking.' These remarkable and telling findings have been confirmed in men and in women. They've even been found in baboons. In the lab, monkeys were fed diets high in cholesterol and fat until they developed dangerous levels of atherosclerotic plaque. The higher the monkey was in their troop's status hierarchy, the less likely they were to fall ill as a result of their nasty diets. When researchers conspired to alter the hierarchy, each monkey's risk of illness changed in lockstep with their change in status. 'It was the new position, not the one they started with, that determined the degree of atherosclerosis they developed,' writes Marmot. And 'the differences were dramatic'.

Tentative clues as to how this might happen come from the new science of social genomics, which examines how our social worlds affect our genes and the ways they function. The basic idea is that, when we're not doing well in the game of life, our bodies prepare for crisis by switching our settings so we're readied for attack. It increases inflammation, which helps the healing of any physical wounds we might be about to suffer. It also saves resources by reducing our antiviral response. But when our inflammation is raised for too long, it can damage us in myriad ways. It increases susceptibility to neurodegenerative disease, promotes the spread of plaque in the arteries and the growth of cancer cells. According to a world leader in this field, Professor Steve Cole, 'several studies have related objective indicators of low social status to increased expression of pro-inflammatory genes and/or decreased expression of antiviral genes. Being beaten down in the rat race naturally changes what you expect from tomorrow, and that does seem to filter down into the way your cells prepare for tomorrow.'

It's probably not a surprise to discover that feeling deprived of status is a major source of anxiety and depression. When life is a game we're losing, we hurt. One review of the scientific literature found that 'perceiving oneself as having low rank compared to others is consistently linked to higher depressive symptoms'. Some psychologists argue that when we become depressed we 'mentally withdraw from the competition for higher status'. This keeps us off 'high-status individuals' radars' and conserves energy, helping us cope with the 'reduced opportunities imposed by low status'. Frequent defeat in the status game has us scuttling off to the grey safety of the back of the cave. In the sanctuary of those shadows, our inner monologue can turn on us, becoming hypercritical in a process known as self-subordination. We talk ourselves down in an onslaught of insult, convincing ourselves the fight is useless, that we belong at the bottom, that we can only ever fail.

When we're chronically deprived of status, the mind may even turn against itself and cause its own destruction. Although the causes of suicide are many and complex, lack of status is a known common driver. Tellingly, it's sudden movements down the game that can be most dangerous. Suicide 'concentrates among those who experience an increase in their social inferiority' and occurs mostly 'when people fall below others', writes sociologist Dr Jason Manning, who adds, 'the greater and faster the downward mobility, the more likely it is to trigger suicide'. Those who decide to end their lives, finally quitting the game that's caused such agony, might have experienced a recent financial loss, or have been made unemployed. They might've lost reputation. They might simply have stayed still whilst others have accelerated away from them: 'suicide is encouraged not just by falling, but by falling behind'.

This game that we play is deadly serious. It's only by surveying the damage that failure can do that we begin to grasp that status isn't merely a nice sensation, like the nice sensation of clean sheets or toffee apples. We need it. Status is an essential nutrient found not in meat or fruit or sunlight but in the successful playing of our lives. When we feel chronically deprived of it, or disconnected from the game, our minds and bodies can turn against us. To our brains, status is a resource as real as oxygen or water. When we lose it, we break.

3

An Imagined World of Symbols

WE DON'T FEEL like players of games. We feel like heroes in stories. This is the illusion the brain spins for us. It makes us feel as if we are the hero at the centre of the universe, orbited by a cast of supporting characters. The goals of our lives are the plots that consume us, as we overcome obstacles and strive nobly towards happy endings. This brain-generated story is self-serving, motivating and convincing in its tiniest details. It feels real because it's the only reality we know. But it's a lie.

Nobody knows how this experience of 'consciousness' is generated. But neuroscientists and psychologists agree it's a fantastically simplistic and altered impression of true reality. It seems as if we have untrammelled access to the exterior world, that we look *out* of our heads at the space that surrounds our bodies. But this is not correct. We don't look out, we look *in*. Information from around us is picked up by our senses and encoded into billions of electrical pulses. The brain reads these pulses like a computer reads code, and uses them to conjure our perception of reality. The disturbing truth is that all of this takes place *inside* the cramped bone vault of our skull. Life is a three-dimensional picture show, a story that we watch inside our heads.

We hallucinate our world into being. Writes the neuroscientist Professor David Eagleman, 'What we call normal perception does not really differ from hallucinations, except that the latter are not anchored by external input.' This anchoring of our perception into reality is the job of our senses. But our senses are not to be trusted. Ears, eyes, tongues, skin and noses don't supply sounds, colours, tastes, touches and smells to the brain, but 'a chattering stream of electrical pulses racing up the thick bundles of data cables we call nerves'. The experiences the brain makes of these pulses are acts of creation.

Much of what seems inarguably real and true, in the space around us, is not. The actual world is monochrome and silent. Sounds, colours, tastes and smells exist only in the projection in our heads. What's actually out there are vibrating particles, floating chemical compounds, molecules and colourless light waves of varying lengths. Our perceptions of these phenomena are special effects in a brain-generated movie. And our senses can only detect the tiniest fraction of what's out there. Our eyes, for instance, are able to pick up less than one ten-trillionth of the available light spectrum.

So the brain creates our experience of the world. Next it conjures us, the self at its centre. It is a hero-maker, manufacturing both the illusion of self and its gripping narrative, framing our life as a journey towards a hopeful destination. The story it tells even has a narrator, an inner voice that chirrups away, performing a live improvisation of our autobiography. Neuroscientist Professor Michael Gazzaniga calls it the 'interpreter module'. Its job, he writes, is to provide 'the storyline and the narrative' of our life. It 'generates explanations about our perceptions, memories and actions and the relationships among them. This leads to a personal narrative, the story that ties together all the disparate aspects of our conscious experience into a coherent whole: order from chaos.' This story 'may be completely wrong'. It often is. 'That "you" that you are so proud of is a story woven together by your interpreter module to account for as much of your behaviour as it can incorporate, and it denies and rationalises the rest.'

A psychologically healthy brain excels at making its owner feel heroic. It does this by reordering our experiences, remixing our memories and rationalising our behaviour, using a battery of reality-warping weapons that make us believe we're more virtuous, more correct in our beliefs and have more hopeful futures in store than others. For psychologist Professor Thomas Gilovich, the evidence is 'clear and consistent: we are inclined to adopt self-serving beliefs about ourselves, and comforting beliefs about the world'. The most powerful of these weapons is thought to be the moral bias. No matter what we do, and how dishonestly we play, the brain nudges us to conclude we're ultimately a better person than most. In one study, participants guessed what percentage of time they exhibited a range of virtuous behaviours. Six weeks later, they were asked again, but this time they were also shown the average ratings of other people. On the vast majority of behaviours, they rated themselves as much more moral than these normals. What they didn't realise was the 'average ratings' for others were, in fact, *their own ratings from six weeks earlier*. Another study, comparing people's self-image on a range of traits found that 'virtually all individuals irrationally inflated their moral qualities'. The researchers wrote, 'most people strongly believe they are just, virtuous, and moral, yet regard the average person as distinctly less so'. Moral superiority, they concluded, is a 'uniquely strong and prevalent form of positive illusion'.

Culture conspires in this dream of human life. Cultures are built out of billions of brains: billions of neural storytellers working in concert. They fill their religions, novels, newspapers, screens, speeches, gossip and ideologies with simplistic stories of moral heroes and evil villains; actors battling odds and fighting evil on their journeys towards promised lands. We all live the dream of the mind.

To reveal the hidden structure of human life, we must burrow beneath the illusionary story of consciousness and into the subconscious, an incomparably more powerful place. It's in these mysterious deeps that the vast majority of the computation of life actually takes place. Despite how it feels, consciousness is 'not at the centre of the action in the brain', writes Eagleman, 'it is far out on a distant edge, hearing but whispers of the activity'. The subconscious circuits that generate this hallucinatory story-world were 'carved by natural selection to solve problems that our ancestors faced during our species' evolutionary history'.

The human brain is specialised for the games we evolved to play. Neuroscientist Professor Chris Frith writes that it 'represents the world as a reward space'. It's coded to discover 'the valuable things in the world and what actions we need to take to get them … everything around me exerts a push or a pull because my brain has learned to attach value to them'. As we've learned, humans value connection and status. In order to earn the resources essential for our survival and reproduction, we seek to bond with our co-players; in order to secure *more* of those resources we seek rank. But how do we gauge this rank? How do we tell how we're doing in this game of life?

We do it, in part, by assigning values to objects. A Cartier watch is worth *this* much status; a Casio watch is worth *that*. These 'status symbols' tell us, and our co-players, how we're performing. We pay obsessive attention to them. We need to: unlike in a computer game, there's no definitive scoreboard in human life. We can never see precisely where players sit versus us in the rankings. We can only sense it from symbols to which we've attached particular values. In order to manage this process, the subconscious has a 'status detection system' that includes mechanisms that read 'relevant cues in the environment to assess status'.

This system is astonishingly sensitive. It doesn't only use inanimate objects as status symbols, it can project value onto virtually anything, including people's appearance and behaviours. Status symbolising acts in one study of office life included 'always carrying a folder', 'walking in a purposeful manner even if only to the water cooler' and 'displaying multiple clocks'. When all the vice presidents at a US corporation were issued with single-pen desk sets, 'one vice president shortly moved to a two-pen set, and within four days all vice presidents had worked their way up to three-pen sets'. People have been seen to become preoccupied with 'trivial' phenomena they interpreted as symbolic of their status, such as the relative quantity of orange juice poured in their glass and 'negligible' differences in clothing. In the luxury attire game, the general rule is the larger the logo, the lower the status and therefore price. One analysis found 'an increase in logo size of one point on a seven-point scale translates to a $122.26 price decrease for Gucci handbags and a $26.27 price decrease for Louis Vuitton handbags'. The logo on Bottega Veneta's $2,500 Hobo bag isn't visible. They put it on the inside.

These apparently trite symbols matter. In one test, when participants were shown photos of people wearing 'rich' or 'poor' clothes, they automatically assumed those in wealthier looking outfits were significantly more competent and of higher status. This effect remained when they were warned upfront of the potential bias, when they were informed the clothing was definitely irrelevant and when they were told all the people worked in sales at a 'midsize firm in the Midwest' and earned around US$80,000. It even remained when the participants were paid money to make an accurate guess. And all it took for their status detection systems to make these extraordinarily stubborn judgements was a single flash of each photo, lasting 129 milliseconds.

The status detection system continually reads symbolic information from the voice and body language of our co-players. It registers facial markers for dominance or submission in forty-three milliseconds and calculates the quality and quantity of eye contact we're receiving (more is better) and it does so constantly, unconsciously and 'with numerical precision'. High-status people tend to speak more often and more loudly; are perceived to be more facially expressive; achieve more successful interruptions in conversation; stand closer to us; touch themselves less; use more relaxed, open postures; use more 'filled pauses' such as 'um' and 'ah' and have a steadier vocal tone (although some of these symbols may vary culturally). When researchers took candid photos of ninety-six pairs of co-workers interacting, cut them out and stuck them against a white background to remove contextual information, people were 'exceedingly accurate' in their estimates of who had higher status. Merely by glancing at a still image of them talking, they could tell who was on top.

The status detection system even reads symbolic information in sounds we can't consciously hear. When speaking, we emit a low-frequency hum at around 500 hertz. When people meet and talk, their hums shift. The highest-status person in the group sets its level and the rest adjust to match. This hum is thought to be an 'unconscious social instrument' that helps sort us into status hierarchies. Analyses of interviews on *The Larry King Show* found the host deferentially changed his hum to match Elizabeth Taylor whilst Dan Quayle adjusted to him.

The status detection system is highly evident in the behaviour of youngsters. Around three-quarters of arguments between children aged 18 and 30 months are over possessions, a figure that rises to 90 per cent when just two toddlers are present. For developmental psychologist Professor Bruce Hood, possession is a 'means to establish where you are in the nursery pecking order'. The moment a toy is claimed by one child, other preschoolers want it. 'Owning stuff is all to do with status amongst competitors. These early disputes are a taster for later life in the real world.' Just like the adults they'll become, these young status-strivers are hypocritical. Children are 'sensitive to inequality', writes the psychologist Professor Paul Bloom, 'but it seems to upset them only when they themselves are the ones getting less'. Infants become upset when handed fewer sugary treats than others. 5-year-olds seek relative advantage, often choosing to reject equal payouts of two prize tokens for everyone, preferring one token for themselves if it means others get none. Even in children, 'the inequality associated with relative advantage is so appealing that it overrides both a desire for fairness and a desire for absolute gain'.

What starts as fights over playroom toys grows into the great battles of adulthood. We're used to thinking of money and power as principal motivating forces of life. But studies suggest that, unlike status, the desire for power over others is not fundamental in humans. Unlike status, it doesn't strongly predict wellbeing. Moreover, unlike status, the desire for power is quenchable. 'After acquiring a moderate amount of power, most people become less interested in gaining even more,' writes sociologist Professor Cecilia Ridgeway. 'But not so status.'

Likewise, the desire for wealth is not fundamental. Status is the original form of currency, and the one that matters more. Studies show a majority of employees would accept a higher-status job title over a pay rise: one survey of 1,500 UK office workers had around 70 per cent choosing status over money, with creative assistants preferring 'chief imagination officer' and file clerks opting for 'data storage specialists'. Those data storage specialists were onto something. Assuming we have enough money to live, it seems relative status makes us happier than raw cash.

This has been found many times, with one study using data from twelve thousand British adults concluding 'the ranked position of an individual's income predicts general life satisfaction, whereas absolute income and reference income have no effect'. Elsewhere, economists find people's happiness goes down if others living nearby earn more than they do. And it drops most of all for those who spend time socialising in their neighbourhood. The effect is strong: 'An increase in neighbours' earnings and a similarly sized decrease in own income each have roughly about the same negative effect on well-being.'

This meets our understanding of how the brain works. It has to judge our status relative to everyone else's, because that's how it perceives. For neuroscientist Professor Sophie Scott, 'perception has no ground zero. There's not an absolute truth about the world that we compare everything else to, so it's all relative.' The status detection system, therefore, works in contest mode. Researchers find our reward systems are activated most when we achieve *relative* rather than absolute rewards; we're designed to feel best not when we get more, but when we get more than those around us.

Some argue this is also true on the national level. As a country's average earnings go up, they say, average happiness doesn't. By the logic of the game, this makes sense: if everyone's getting richer at once, your extra pennies haven't bought you superior status. But the argument has been controversial. This is partly because nations are so complex it's hard to cleanly isolate the link between economic growth and happiness. Some data, using cross-country evidence, does appear to show rising national income correlating with rising national happiness. But, according to happiness researcher Dr Christopher Boyce, the increase is weak. 'That data just shows that economic growth is correlated (albeit very weakly, and not causally related) with higher life satisfaction. Statistically, whether it's across countries or across people living within the same country, there is nearly always an effect of having more money on happiness, yet the effect is not large at all. And so whilst money can buy happiness, much of the time it doesn't or the effect is negligible.' Meanwhile, academics at the University of Oxford's Wellbeing Research Centre find that, as you might expect, the less rich countries do see increases in happiness as the general standard of living improves. But for the already wealthy nations, over the long term, money makes surprisingly little difference. Between 1965 and 1990 the US economy grew by a healthy 1.7 per cent a year, whilst Japan saw an impressive annual jump of 4.1 per cent. In both nations, happiness barely budged.

Money is many things, of course: we need it to survive and it provides a dazzling array of life's pleasures. But, like power, we also use it as a status symbol – as we do the size of a logo on a handbag and the amount of orange juice poured in a glass. They are Pac-Man cookies in the game of human life. Humans are extraordinarily imaginative creatures who can turn almost anything into status symbols. In 1948, the anthropologist Professor William Bascom published an analysis of a status game on the Micronesian island of Pohnpei based on yams. Life there was like life everywhere: stratified into rankings. At the top were chiefs, with those beneath ordered along hereditary and political lines. Promotion to the upper ranks was difficult, but there was one rapid route to ascension. Men who brought yams to feasts hosted by the chiefs could win significant status. But the yam had to be big: 'a man cannot win prestige by bringing a large number of small yams to a feast', noted Bascom. The owner of the largest yam at a feast would be publicly declared 'Number One' by his rivals and praised by the chief for his generosity.

Bascom found the men of Pohnpei in a state of symbolic war as they all competed to be Number One. Each man would raise around fifty yams a year, purely for feasts, growing them in secret, remote, overgrown plots they'd creep out of bed at two in the morning to tend to, lining the pits with soil and fertiliser until dawn. A single yam could take ten years to grow, reach over four metres in length, weigh over ninety kilograms and require as many as twelve men to carry into the feast using a special stretcher on poles. 'That Ponapeans are able to grow yams of enormous size cannot be doubted,' Bascom wrote. 'The reputation has spread at least as far as Truk, where yams are of minor importance.'

A delicate system of etiquette bloomed into life around these yam wars. 'It is impolite to look at another man's yams, and anyone caught doing so will feel the shame of gossip and ridicule,' wrote Bascom.

Pohnpeians go so far as to 'pretend to ignore even the yams growing near the house' which were only there to be eaten. When a man is named Number One at a feast, 'he must not act proudly or boast openly about his achievement. When others discuss the merits of his yam, he pretends not to listen.' This show of humility is partly a game-playing strategy. 'The man who is acclaimed "Number One" does not dare to ridicule or laugh at the man with the second largest yam, or even the man who has brought the smallest one, for fear that they may bring larger yams than he does to the next feast . . . and if the challenger has not brought larger yams himself, he is publicly shamed.'

The yam game of Pohnpei might sound ludicrous, but it's no different to the games any of us play using orange juice, watches or fast walking in the office to symbolise status. In the 1950s, shortly after Bascom wrote his paper, vehicle manufacturers succeeded in persuading the US public that very long cars were a status game symbol. In one Dodge radio commercial a man exclaimed, 'Boy, you must be rich to own a car as big as this!' Rivals Plymouth produced a print ad in which a family grinned by its extra-long vehicle, 'We're not wealthy . . . we just look it!' Ford's advert highlighted their engorged taillights, which 'let the people behind you know you are ahead of them!' Such appeals worked all too well. American cars became longer and longer. Great steel whales of the road began choking city traffic. Parking meters were torn up and spaced out at ever greater lengths. City governors beseeched manufacturers to make cars short again. Robert Wagner, the mayor of New York, declared they'd be buying no more Cadillacs until they were shrunk, only to be defied by his own City Controller who defended himself thusly: 'The top officials of the city, for the dignity of their offices, should have Cadillacs.'

The status detection system never switches off. The game never pauses. This is why, especially in the public sphere, we can find ourselves playing hyper-local status games that are often fleet-ingly transient and can be between just two people. We might find ourselves playing a hyper-local game in a hotel lift that lasts forty-eight seconds: who's an employee and who's a guest? Who's getting out at the plush top floors? Who's that person not giving me the respect I'm due by crowding into me? Who's got the flashiest luggage? Hyper-local games pop up anywhere that people with a broadly agreed set of symbols gather. Australia's Bondi Beach is a status game with hyper-local rules, as is a self-help class, a nightclub, a queue for the bus and a gang of friends sharing a meal.

The anthropologist Professor Robert Paul writes that our pursuit of symbolic status 'has to do with the fact that human social life inherently depends on there being a public arena in which symbols can be made available to perception and shared by many people'. People who have connected 'share in the perception of these symbols, and incorporate them into their own thinking, feeling, and identity', which 'means that they experience their consociates as "kin"'.

It's in this way that we exist as a tribe, a culture, a people. We come into being as a collective when we connect with like-minded others whose brains process reality in similar ways; who dream the same dream of life. We recognise the same symbols; play the same game. As we do, we become the source of each other's status, the people of the yam. We see the yam, we know what it means, we experience a profound sense of connection with those who perceive this reality as we do. We play the yam game as a single organism, feeding one another status when we judge it's been earned. Over decades of worry, strategy and toil we pursue it, using shared symbols to build great kingdoms of meaning. These kingdoms – these virtual, connected, brain-generated hallucinations of reality – are the realms in which we exist. Our status game is a place. It's our neural territory, our world.

4

An Imagined World of Rules

L IFE IS NOT as it appears. As neuroscientist Professor Chris
Frith writes, 'our perception of the world is a fantasy that
collides with reality'. The dream state we exist in is founded on
objective truth – we're alive on a planet, breathing air under skies.
But on these foundations we build an infinite variety of imaginary
games. Groups of people gather together, agree what symbols they're
going to use to mean 'status', then strive to achieve it. These symbols
might take the form of money or power or a plastic dumper truck
in a kindergarten toy box. They might be a luxury logo or some sexy
abs or an academic prize or a gigantic yam. The dream of the mind
projects value onto these symbols – so much value we can be driven
to fight and die for them. It tells us a story that says they're of glorious
importance: that our gods are real and our pursuit of them is holy.
It makes us feel, not like players of games, but heroes on journeys
towards destinations of wonder. We believe this story. It's woven
into our perception of reality. It feels no less real than the planet, air
and sky. But the truth of human life is that it's a set of hallucinatory
games organised around symbols. These games are an act of shared
imagination. They come into being in the neural realms of those
with whom we choose to play – our kin, our tribe, our people. These

are the ones who truly understand us, who scratch the same meanings as we do into the walls of the world.

And yet this description of life remains incomplete. If our days only consisted of groups of people lunging madly at prizes, civilisation couldn't function. Monopoly players play for symbolic Monopoly money and locations on a board and plastic houses and hotels. But you can't just grab at them. Players must adhere to precise codes of behaviour. The status game is no different. It requires rules that players agree to. And, just like its capacity for processing status symbols, the brain has an extraordinary capacity for learning and following rules.

The rules by which we play at life are impossible to count. Most of the time, we're not even consciously aware we're following them: we just behave in ways we've learned are correct and judge ourselves and others – measuring, removing and awarding status – by how well they're followed. These rules were invented by our ancestors, both recent and ancient. We know how to live successful lives today because we've inherited instructions from humans who've lived before us. Their rules tell us how we must act and who we must be in order to win. They're stored in two separate places: as the anthropologist Professor Robert Paul writes, there are 'two separate channels of inheritance at work in human life'. Each channel contains its own set of instructions. The first set was laid by our ancestors who spent millions of years living in mobile, tribal bands. This was the era in which our brains did much of their evolution. Everyone alive today is still coded to play hunter-gatherer games. These rules are stored in our DNA.

Hunter-gatherer rules were designed for a specific purpose: to help keep our tribes functional and their members working together peacefully and well. A game was created in which prosocial behaviour that benefitted the group was incentivised. Roughly speaking, the more you put the tribe's interests before your own, the more you'd earn status and the better your conditions of life would become. These rules were essential because humans can often be greedy, dishonest and aggressive. One survey of sixty premodern societies uncovered seven common rules of play that are thought to be universal: help your family; help your group; return favours; be brave; defer to superiors; divide resources fairly; respect others' property. These elemental rules dictate the ways humans keep their tribes working well. They tell us basically how to play: deferring to superiors means 'being deferential, respectful, loyal or obedient to those above you in a hierarchy, using appropriate forms of address and etiquette'; returning favours includes 'repaying a debt, forgiving people when they apologise'; dividing resources includes 'being willing to negotiate, compromise'.

These DNA rules are the outlines of human behaviour. They're our basic instructions for life. They're common to us all and represent our shared humanity. They're why, if you put an Eritrean stuntwoman, an Inuit shaman and a Slovakian chess master in a New York hotel room, they'd be able to cooperate on a rudimentary level and then, after a while, an unstable hierarchy would likely construct itself, with one on the top and the others slotted beneath. This is just what happens when you connect humans into groups. The game emerges unbidden.

The second set of rules comes from people who've been around more recently. They're encoded in culture. Every culture has a distinct set of rules by which it wants its members to live. We're judged by others, as we judge ourselves, by how well we play by them. Like the ancient DNA rules, they become so embedded into our perception that we barely know they're there, unless someone violates them.

Consider the pub. Most English people who go to the pub enjoy themselves without thinking about what they're actually doing. But pubs have myriad hidden rules. Anthropologist Professor Kate Fox has noted some of them. She writes, for example, that the 'bar counter of the pub is one of the very few places in England where it is socially acceptable to strike up a conversation with a complete stranger'. An extension of this 'sociability rule' applies to a 'limited extent' near the dartboard and pool table, 'but only to those *standing* near the players: the tables in the vicinity of these games are still private'. Other rules obvious to the English, but not so to strangers, include 'one or two people, not the whole group, go up to the bar to buy drinks'; once at the bar 'there is an invisible queue, that both the bar staff and the customers are aware of'; there's a 'strict etiquette involved in attracting the attention of bar staff: this must be done without speaking, without making any noise and without resorting to the vulgarity of obvious gesticulation'; regulars are permitted to break this rule but only in a bantering style; thanks or 'cheers' must be said to the barperson 'when the drinks are handed over, and again when the change is given'; the 'First commandment' of pub chat is 'thou shalt not take things too seriously . . . even sticking to the same subject for more than a few minutes may sometimes be taken as a sign of excessive seriousness'. And so on.

Around the world, there are gigantic shifts in the ways status games are played. These shifts can create some radical differences in self as brains form around local rules. Among the most studied are the differences between East and West. Westerners tend to see status-pursuit as primarily the job of the individual. This moulds their strategies for playing the game. Psychologists find that Westerners generally like to stand out and feel unique, tending towards conceited self-views and rating themselves better than average at all kinds of traits including healthy habits, immunity to bias and driving skills. In one study, 86 per cent of Australians rated their job performance as 'above average'; in another, 96 per cent of Americans described themselves as 'special'. East Asian games tend to be more collective. In countries such as Japan and China, status-pursuit is more commonly seen as the responsibility of the group.

They're more likely to feel raised up when they serve the collective, winning status by appearing humble, conformist and self-sacrificial. In the East, it's often the status of the group above all. This is a game plan that might sound worthy and wonderful until you consider its ramifications for individual human rights.

It can also mean cultural tension. When we travel to different continents, we sometimes experience 'culture shock' as the behaviours we've been taught should achieve acceptance and status begin to fail. Westerners who pride themselves as being straight-talking, high-achieving and unique can be seen as immature and uncivilised by people in Asia. Over there the concept of 'face' is an essential component of the status game. Sociologist Professor David Yau Fai Ho has defined three ways it's possible to lose face: when 'one fails to meet others' expectations associated with his/her social status'; when 'one is not treated by others as respectfully as his/her face deserves'; and when one's in-group members (e.g. family members, relatives, immediate subordinates) fail to meet their social roles'. The Asian group-centred game can be radically different to that played in the West. There, if an employee is singled out for praise, their team can experience a loss of face. The praised employee feels not elated but shamed and motivated to reduce their performance, deliberately doing a worse job so harmony and the group's face can be restored.

Rules shift as you travel in geographic space but also as you travel around in time; different people in different eras would've grown up playing radically different games. Their variety can be found in popular books of etiquette that have been written through the ages. In 1486, Dame Juliana Berners laid out what kinds of birds it was appropriate for those of varying status rank to use when hawking: a yeoman could have a goshawk; a lady a merlin; an earl a peregrine; a prince a falcon; a king a gerfalcon and an emperor an eagle. In 1558, Florentine etiquette writer Giovanni della Casa recommended to those sharing a bed with a stranger that 'it is not a refined habit, when coming across something disgusting in the sheet, as sometimes happens, to turn at once to one's companion and point it out to him. It is far less proper to hold out the stinking thing for another to smell, as some are wont, who even urge the other to do so, lifting the foul-smelling thing to his nostrils and saying, "I should like to know how much that stinks".' *The Chinese Book of Etiquette and Conduct for Women and Girls*, first published in the West in 1900, but many centuries older, says to:

> Honour greatly your father-in-law;
> Before him, let neither gladness nor sorrow
> Show forth in your face.
> Dare not even to walk behind him,
> Stand not before him when you speak,
> But to one side or behind him.
> And hasten his every command to obey.
> When your mother-in-law sits
> You should respectfully stand;
> Obey quickly her commands.

These were playbooks for the game of life. And the rules that were codified in their pages would've felt as real and true as ours do today. *Of course* you should never walk behind your father-in-law; *of course* a yeoman can't fly a gerfalcon; *of course* you can't strike up conversations with strangers sitting at tables in an English pub. Knowing and following these rules would signal your position as a superior person; flouting them would mark you down.

The brain begins learning these rules in infancy. As 2-year-olds, we have around one hundred trillion connections between our brain cells, double that of an adult. This is because, when we're born, we don't know *where* we're going to pop out. Baby brains are specialised for many environments, many games. At this age, we're better than adults at recognising faces of other races and can hear tones in foreign languages that grown-ups are deaf to. But then our brain begins to carve itself to its local environment. Connections start being culled at a rate of up to one hundred thousand per second. We begin to take the form of a player of our particular time and place.

As we grow into childhood, these cultural rules and symbols are pressed into us by teachers and parents, with repetitive rounds of punishments and praise: 'good boy! good girl!' When we do the 'right' thing, we feel ourselves soar; when 'bad', we fall. We develop a conscience, with its dreadful currents of shame, embarrassment, guilt and regret, but that also allows us to surf joyful waves of pride. Our conscience provides us with a 'social mirror', writes the anthropologist Professor Christopher Boehm. 'By continually glancing at it, we can keep track of shameful pitfalls that threaten our reputational status or proudly and virtuously chart our personal progress.'

Up and down and up and down and up and down we go, as we play at daily life. The rules and symbols of our time and place direct our beliefs, thoughts and behaviour. They define us. We begin offering status to other people when we judge them to be playing well by our own internalised sets of rules. When they fail, we withdraw it. We perform the game, acting it with our muscles, beaming it from our eyes and singing it in our tone of voice. As well as being inside us, the status game is now outside us too, as we connect with other humans-like-us and together create a world of meaning in which to play.

There's no opting out of the game. It's written into our brain and the brains of everyone we'll ever meet. Some try to cure themselves of status-striving with meditation. But meditators can become notably pleased with themselves. A study of around 3,700 who'd practised specifically to 'reduce attachment to the personal self and ego needs such as social approval and success' found they scored highly in measures of 'spiritual superiority', agreeing with statements such as

'I am more in touch with my senses than most others', 'because of my background and experiences, I am more in touch with my body than other people' and 'the world would be a better place if others too had the insights that I have now'. Study leader Professor Roos Vonk found the self-views they developed were 'the exact opposite of enlightenment'.

The only feasible way to opt out of the game is to seek an empty room and stay in it. In Japan, more than half a million adults suffer 'social withdrawal syndrome', refusing to leave their bedrooms unless absolutely compelled to. These 'hikikomori' are 'incapable of following the rules of society', the sociologist Professor Teppei Sekimizi has said. They find connection and status too difficult to reliably achieve, strongly agreeing with statements such as: 'I cannot blend into groups' and 'I am anxious about what others might think of me.' Many stay locked up for years. Some die alone. And this, ultimately, is the choice facing each one of us: hikikomori or play.

5

The Three Games

STATUS COMES IN many forms. We might earn it from something as simple as our age: young wins by the hotel pool; old wins on the train. Those lucky enough to be beautiful earn it from their looks. A major review of the psychological literature found attractive people are judged and treated more positively than the unattractive, 'even by those who know them'. Much of the rest of human life is comprised of three varieties of status-striving and three varieties of game: dominance, virtue and success. In dominance games, status is coerced by force or fear. In virtue games, status is awarded to players who are conspicuously dutiful, obedient and moralistic. In success games, status is awarded for the achievement of closely specified outcomes, beyond simply winning, that require skill, talent or knowledge. Mafias and armies are dominance games. Religions and royal institutions are virtue games. Corporations and sporting contests are success games.

It's important to note that these games aren't strictly categorical. There are probably no completely pure games, only blends of dominance, virtue and success. One mode of play, however, will usually become sufficiently prominent that it comes to define its game, like a flavour in a soup. A street fight can be reasonably described as a dominance game but there also tend to be rules of virtue in such contests (no hair pulling, no crotch kicking) and their outcome depends on competence as well as strength. Similarly, the tech company Apple plays a success game when innovating, but also a virtue game when advertising its brand values and a dominance game when suing rivals for patent infringement. The games played by boxers and chefs in Michelin-starred kitchens are fascinating for their being relatively equally weighted combinations of dominance, virtue and success: they're often brutally fierce, bound by tradition and strict codes of behaviour, and winners are celebrated for achieving acts of extreme competence.

The same is true for us as players. The three varieties of game tend towards three general varieties of human: we can be Idi Amin, Mother Theresa or Albert Einstein. But everyone contains elements of all three archetypes. Humans have the capacity to source status from acts of dominance, virtue and competence and, crazed as we are, we're going to use any strategy we can: a scientist, a princess and a cartel boss will all use shifting modes of dominance, virtue and success as they play their games of life. We're all a sometimes uncomfortable, often contradictory mixture of these three routes to the great prize.

The story of how human life took this form is the story of our species. More than two and a half million years ago, we were specialised for dominance games, being frighteningly aggressive prehumans about the size of chimpanzees. Our bones were thicker, our teeth longer and our jaws wider, we had dense brow ridges jutting over our eye sockets and had as much as double the muscular strength of today. Dominance is how animals frequently play status games. When hens are brought into each other's company they peck at each other until a pecking order is established; crayfish circle each other before launching into a savage limb-tearing attack, the victor strutting around in apparent triumph as the loser scuttles away.

Although violence wasn't the only way we gained status – in several primate societies, including our close relative the chimpanzee, nurturing relationships with allies and maintaining peace among subordinates is also critical – there's little doubt we were far more savage then. Males would've had murderous tempers that were easily triggered by rivals. 'Reactive aggression would have dominated social life in the same way as it does in most social primates,' writes anthropologist Professor Richard Wrangham. Evidence, including that of our once 'massive faces', suggests we most likely 'continued to physically fight, one on one, until at least the Mid-Pleistocene' – roughly between 770,000 and 126,000 years ago.

We shifted away from fist and fang when we began playing games with symbols in the communal imagination. Accounts of how and why this happened can only be speculative and are debated hotly. Some believe that, after we came down from the trees, the threat from predators huddled us into protective groups. As living became denser, males found themselves with more rivals to fight off, so began shifting their mating strategy towards one of pair-bonding, in which they'd offer meat and protection to females in return for preferred sexual access. These emergent families became extended, with grandparents, uncles and aunts building sustained relationships and sharing childrearing responsibilities. When women pair-bonded with males from different families, loose tribes or clans formed. Close-living meant close-learning and the ability for rules and symbols to be communicated down the generations.

For biologist Professor Edward O. Wilson our use of campsites, beginning perhaps a million years ago, was another critical event. He describes them as human 'nests' and observes that all animals 'without exception' that have achieved the intense mode of survival-through-cooperation of which we're capable have lived this way. Like them we 'raised young in the nest, foraged away from it for food, and brought the bounty back to share with others'. Nested life meant dividing labour, sharing resources, defending our nests in teams and launching raids on the nests of others.

In this communal, nested world, brute ferocity by alpha males was unwelcome and unuseful. Getting along and getting ahead meant winning the cooperation of others. Hyper-violent males who attempted to dominate the tribe would increasingly find themselves ostracized or executed. More peaceable and socially intelligent men began to gain status. Slowly, a novel breed of human came into being, one that had subtly different patterns of hormones and brain chemistry regulating their behaviour. Our skeletons changed, our brains changed and our ways of living changed too.

We still had our ancient predisposition to self-organise into ranks: our ancestors had 'clearly defined status hierarchies', writes psychologist Professor David Buss, 'with resources flowing freely to those at the top and trickling slowly to those at the bottom'. These hierarchies would've naturally divided into young and old, and male versus male, as they competed for females, and female versus female, as they competed for males. In a possible hangover from our alpha male dominated prehuman days that would have some dreadful consequences for women we're still battling today, men were often automatically granted higher status. But newer subdivisions also emerged, as we learned to specialise in tasks that were necessary to keep the group functioning.

And so our status games began shifting into the realm of shared imagination. What mattered increasingly was not how brutal we were, but what our co-players thought of us. We could earn this kind of prestige-based status by showing we were useful to the group. We could do this in two ways. Firstly, by being *successful*, demonstrating knowledge and skill that benefitted others. We could tell great stories, accurately predict the future, be an excellent hunter, sorcerer, toolmaker, tracker or honey-finder. In Panama, members of the Kuna tribe play success games by keeping a lifetime record of their tapir kills, those with the highest number receiving heightened status. Similarly, the best turtle hunters among the Meriam people of the Torres Strait earn respect from village elders and have their opinions disproportionately supported in public meetings and private disputes.

Secondly, we could earn prestige-based status by being *virtuous*: by demonstrating beliefs or behaviours that served the group's interests. This kind of status is awarded to those who show concern for the public good, display commitment to the group or enforce its rules. They'll also rise up the rankings if they're thought of as being courageous or generous towards their co-players. In Tanzania, Hadza hunters who share meat widely 'gain great social status – prestige that can be parlayed into powerful social alliances, the deference of other men, and greater mating success', writes Buss. People engage in 'competitive altruism', battling to be 'seen by others as great contributors to the group'. Of course, status is awarded to the altruistic in more modern societies too: studies show those who donate to charity, for example, experience 'a dramatic boost in prestige in the eyes of others'.

In order to be able to play the two varieties of prestige game, our brains had to develop an unusual ability. Prestige games are symbolic. Unlike physical dominance contests, they're not played with our actual selves, but with our reputation. We can think of our reputation as a symbolic version of us that exists in the minds of others. Human brains required the capacity to store these highly detailed symbolic selves. Our neural worlds are crowded with hallucinations of others so vivid they can almost be summoned at will. We all walk around with everyone we know crowded inside our heads.

Additionally, we needed to be able to talk. We might've stored the reputations of others in our brains, but those reputations lived and died in the stories we told of them. The current dominant theory says this is why we evolved speech – to gossip. If others in the tribe spoke well of us, we'd be rewarded with a prestigious reputation and its glittering dividends; if bad, we'd sink in the rankings and risk punishment. We could also gain status from gossiping. Who we gossip with can itself be a status symbol: swapping tattle with high-ranked others implies we're of high rank too. Furthermore, one of gossip's critical purposes was to demonstrate the rules of the tribe and what happened if you broke them. By gossiping we demonstrate our knowledge of the rules, and our loyalty to them, and this can also earn status. Gossip has been described as 'an activity that is attention seeking, promoting self-interest and self-image through social comparison, and the discrediting of others'. It's universal and essential to our gameplay: children start to gossip almost as soon as they can speak.

As well as in gossip, a tribe's rules and symbols would've been encoded in myths and legends told by elders, in rituals and ceremonies and the dress and behaviour of others. As we grew up, we'd internalise these rules and symbols, developing a conscience, a kind of imaginary tribe that would judge us and warn us when we'd erred. Breaking the rules by failing to share meat, say, or performing incorrectly in a ritual, 'meant facing reputational damage, diminishing mating prospects, ostracism and, in the extreme, execution by the group', writes biologist Professor Joseph Henrich. 'Natural selection shaped our psychology to make us docile, ashamed at norm violations, and adept at acquiring and internalising social norms.'

As the ways we played for status changed, we slowly transmuted into the weird, strutting, mind-haunted, jewel-sparkling animals we'd recognise today. We began indulging in status-seeking activities such as painting, playing musical instruments, wearing elaborate jewellery and making, trading and displaying covetous objects. In Germany, a 40,000-year-old figurine of a lion-man has been discovered that it's thought would've taken over four hundred hours for a skilled artisan to make. In the Ukraine, the remains of four monumental structures built from vast interlocking mammoth bones have been found, with some of the skulls in the buildings weighing at least one hundred kilograms. Thought to be over twenty thousand years old, they housed treasures such as amber ornaments and fossil shells, some of which had been brought, and probably traded, from over five hundred kilometres away.

We were becoming more vain and also more virtuous. Our shift from playing dominance games to reputation games led to our being incredibly tolerant when dealing with members of our own group, compared to our primate relatives. Physical aggression between humans happens at a frequency of less than one per cent compared to chimpanzees and bonobos. Chimpanzee troops have been found to be 'several hundred to a thousand times' more aggressive than even the most violent human societies. We don't need to tear each other's limbs and genitals off and drink their blood for status, as chimpanzees do, when we can earn it by raising our prestige and displaying our ranking with ivory lions and glittering shells.

Games of prestige are played everywhere from the jungles and savannahs of premodern societies to the avenues and skyscrapers of the glittering cities. It was once assumed only humans used prestige but it's since been detected in other animals, such as when a wise old elephant leads her herd to water. But no species has taken it anywhere near as far as us. Prestige is our most marvellous craving. It's a bribe that induces us into being useful, benefitting the interests of the tribe. It's enabled us to master the art of co-operative living. We pursue goals, and tackle problems, as members of collaborative groups because we're programmed to care deeply about what our co-players think of us: we revel in the reward of status they supply. When we strive to earn a good, prestigious reputation using either of the two available strategies – by being virtuous or successful – we progress. This is the secret of our success as a species and has enabled us to dominate the planet. As anthropologist Dr Jerome Barkow has written, 'Without symbolic prestige, it's difficult to see how complex societies could have developed.'

But there are downsides. Because our brains value reputational status so fundamentally, its loss can feel unbearable. In some societies, such as that of the Lepcha in the Himalayas, loss of reputation is the most common reason people take their own lives. This is also true in modern nations such as Ghana, where one 32-year-old was documented drinking pesticide after villagers caught him having sex with a sheep. Accusations of sexual crimes against children are associated with 'drastically elevated' rates of suicide: one survey found 53 per cent of Americans saying they'd prefer instant death than the reputation of a child molester; 70 per cent opted for the amputation of their dominant hand over a swastika tattoo on their face; 40 per cent preferred a year in jail to the reputation of a criminal.

In each status game we play, we have a reputation. In its details, that reputation will be different within the mind of every player. We exist in varying degrees of depth and varying degrees of fairness in all these minds. Whenever others think of us, they'll overwrite us with their own status information. Are we moral or immoral? Expert or useless? How do we look? How do we talk? What job do we do? Do we make them feel loved or hated? Fancied or repulsed? Pitied or admired? It's this distorted and partial avatar we play at life with, not our whole self. Nobody ever truly knows us. They never will.

6

Prestige Games

B Y STUDYING THE two prestige games of virtue and success, researchers have uncovered many hidden rules of human life. They've made sense of some of the more bizarre behaviours of our species. For instance, why is it that some people gather others around them as if they're magnetised? Why do their adoring fans behave so giddily and embarrassingly in their presence? Why do they begin copying how they dress, how they talk and what they read?

Whenever a person shows they're valuable to their game, by being conspicuously virtuous or successful, it's registered by their co-players. Subconsciously, they'll see this person's winning behaviour as a chance to win themselves. They'll desire to learn from them, so they too can rise up in the rankings. This means being near to them as much as possible. As a reward for all their valuable time and knowledge, they offer them symbolic status: they lavish them with eye contact and defer to them in conversation; they might maintain a hunched, subservient posture; bare their teeth in submissive displays known as 'fear grimaces' in apes and 'smiles' in humans; fetch them food, drink or other gifts; walk behind them; hold doors open; seat them in a special location or use honorific titles to address them. The prestigious player will luxuriate in these signals of status. These people clearly think they're *marvellous*. But as lovely as it feels, it's often a trick, a strategy, a game plan.

These game-playing instincts are a component of our universal human nature. In their hot desire to learn from prestigious players, people often copy them blindly: dressing like them, eating what they eat, talking as they talk, reading books they recommend, absorbing their beliefs, behaviours and mannerisms. These lower-ranked players can come to seem virtually possessed. The circuitry that's driving them has been present for millions of years: monkeys also copy high-status associates. But our evolutionary cousins don't take the copying instinct anywhere near as far as we do. Studies comparing infant humans to chimpanzees show both species copy a prestigious individual's actions, such as when they skilfully retrieve a treat with a stick – but only humans copy *all* the actions. Chimpanzees judiciously identify and edit out any pointless parts of the procedure, copying only what's necessary to get the treat. Humans copy everything.

This is thought to be the basis of the concept of faith that features in many status games, from religions to corporations. It can somehow just *feel right* to copy beliefs and behaviours of high-status people even if they don't make rational sense. It's in this way that children in countries such as India overcome the pain of eating spicy foods. Mimicking the actions of high-status people is so desirable, it's argued, their brains reinterpret the pain signals as pleasurable. Children are thought to teach themselves to enjoy spice-burning foods using automatic prestige-driven imitation. They rarely have to be forced.

Much of our mimicking behaviour is subconscious. We don't realise we're doing it, or why. But how do we choose who to copy? How do we identify potentially useful co-players? We're born with a natural ability to seek them out. We unconsciously scan our game for various 'cues' that someone's worth learning from. And it begins early. Professor Joseph Henrich, a world expert in the psychology of status, writes that, 'by age one infants use their own early cultural knowledge to figure out who tends to know things, and then use this information to focus learning, attention and memory'.

The brain is coded to seek four main cues that, once detected, trigger their focus. Firstly, we look for the *self-similarity* cue. We make the assumption we're most likely to learn useful lessons from *people like us*. We have an inbuilt preference for those who match our age, race and gender. We attend to them, and thus offer them status, preferentially. This is a deep source of much of the cliquish-ness and prejudice that pollutes so many status games. Sadly, it seems automatic. Even very young infants defer to strangers who share their mother's dialect.

Next we look for 'skill cues'. Who, in our game, seems particularly able? Research suggests we start mimicking people who display competence at tasks at around 14 months. We also seek out 'success cues' – status symbols such as an experienced hunter's necklace of teeth; a tribal chief's larger hut; a PhD; a pair of Manolo Blahnik's Lurums. Our desire to signal success in this way is the cause of the 'conspicuous consumption' that occurs across the world. The global luxury market is worth around $1.2 trillion per year, with $285 billion being spent on goods, much of it in Asia. Members of the Amazonian Tsimane' tribe who earn more money than others burn up a greater percentage of it on flashy goods such as watches; over in the West, if you want to, you can buy a Franck Muller Aeternitas Mega 4 watch for $2.7 million.

Finally, we look for 'prestige cues': we analyse the body language, eye movements and voice patterns of our co-players to see who they're deferring to. We detect similar clues in the behaviour of prestigious people themselves. Then, we start paying attention to them. These processes are potent and ancient and designed to operate in small groups, not the colossal modern environment of global media and internet. Today it's not uncommon for millions to pay attention to one person simply because millions of others are paying attention to them and for this to become a feedback loop, sending a relatively unremarkable individual into the distant upper reaches of planetary status. Academics call this 'The Paris Hilton Effect'.

Anyone who fancies changing the world would be well advised to study the power of these cues to influence human behaviour. The subconscious *copy-flatter-conform* behaviours they trigger can be extraordinarily effecting. The English explorer Captain James Cook used prestige cues to compel his men to eat the sauerkraut that was an experimental remedy for scurvy, the disease known as 'the plague of the Sea, and the Spoyle of Mariners' that was responsible for roughly two million deaths of sailors between 1500 and 1800. In 1769, Cook set sail for the South Pacific with 7,860 pounds of the pungent fermented cabbage on board and ordered it be served only at the 'Cabbin Table' and not to the crew. This was a prestige cue. 'The moment they see their superiors set a value upon it, it becomes the finest stuff in the world,' Cook noted in his journal. Sure enough, the lower ranked players began requesting it. Before long, sauerkraut had to be rationed. The number of men that died from scurvy on that expedition was a record-breaking zero.

Prestige cues haven't only improved the diets of sailors. For generations, Britain had the justifiable reputation of having some of the worst food in Europe and perhaps the world. In the 1970s and 1980s, many of its highest-status chefs were actually French (when Albert Roux arrived in England in the 1950s olive oil was for sale only in chemists as a treatment for ear wax) whilst its TV cookery stars – Delia Smith, Madhur Jaffrey, Keith Floyd – were not especially statusful, embodying the middle-aged homeliness of Sunday afternoon in the cul-de-sac. That changed in January 1987 when a working-class chef from Leeds began leading the kitchen at a new restaurant, Harvey's, in south London. Marco Pierre White won his first Michelin star within a year and his second the next. The 25-year-old quickly became famous.

Not only was White astonishingly talented, he was beautiful, charismatic and dangerous, developing a reputation for passionate fury both in the kitchen and on the restaurant floor, where he'd sometimes eject diners. In 1988 a TV series, *Marco*, was made about him and, in 1990, *White Heat* was published. A luxurious book of black and white photographs taken at Harvey's, it showed White as a rock star, posing topless, smoking, cleaver slashing, dark curls tumbling to his shoulders. In and out of the world of chefs, it was a sensation. 'I don't know if I can adequately convey to you the impact that *White Heat* had on me, on the chefs and cooks around me, on subsequent generations,' wrote the New York chef-author Anthony Bourdain. 'Suddenly, there was life pre-Marco, and post-Marco . . . This book gave us power. It all started here.'

White became the youngest chef in history to win three Michelin stars. Finally Britain could take some pride in the culinary scene that had long been a source of international shame. Members of the elite filled the icon's tables and they put him in their newspapers and on their television channels. A nation's prestige cognition began twitching as fine dining became a significant symbol of status. White also helped make food-work itself statusful: a new generation of Britons saw the chef game as one that could offer major prestige – and there was now an emerging market waiting for them.

On his way up, White played the status game with intensity. 'Marco only came to steal my recipes,' wrote Chef Pierre Koffmann, at whose London restaurant, La Tante Claire, he'd trained. 'But he's one of the best chefs I ever had in my kitchen – always looking, always listening, wanting to absorb as much as possible as quickly as possible.' But when White himself became prestigious, he paid it back and more. Working under him in the tiny kitchen at Harvey's were several young chefs who'd earn their own Michelin stars in Britain, not least a boyish Gordon Ramsay, who White would describe as, 'One of the most competitive people I've ever met in my life . . .

Gordon wants to catch more fish than Marco, Gordon wants to catch a bigger fish than Marco.' In many ways a mini-Marco, Ramsay would earn sixteen stars at various restaurants and train much of the next century's elite: Clare Smyth, Angela Hartnett, Mark Sargeant, Marcus Wareing, Jason Atherton and more.

Marco Pierre White was a one-man status generating machine. The awards, the fame, the beauty, the TV series, the book: these were prestige cues, signalling major success-based status. They triggered a generation and helped change a culture. Excellent food became a status symbol, and this value spread through cities, towns, farms and farm shops, specialist retailers and supermarkets. It was expressed on television, in magazines, newspapers and, eventually, on social media. Of course, other factors were also critical, not least a healthy economy, and White was undoubtedly not the only gale behind the wave. But his contribution to Britain finding its culinary pride was enormous. This is how cultures often progress. At the core of the process is our individual tendency to mimic prestigious people in the hope that we'll become prestigious ourselves.

It works the opposite way too. If people we consider significantly beneath us begin copying us, we're likely to drop the behaviours that earned us status in the first place. When the fashion brand Burberry's signature check design was adopted by football fans and working-class celebrities, who displayed it on bikinis, umbrellas and prams, they felt it necessary to claw back numerous licensing deals in order to staunch the carotid bleed of upper-class customers. Similarly, researchers find African Americans tend to abandon clothing and slang that's adopted by whites.

Whole societies can drop habits for the same reason. Starting in the Renaissance, duelling was long a popular method by which 'men of birth and quality' in Europe and the USA settled disputes. Hundreds of thousands lost their lives to these contests that were often triggered by the pettiest of status slights. A typical duellist would 'prefer to die by a bullet or stab wound than allow unfavourable ideas about him to remain lodged in the mind', writes Alain de Botton, who records a man in Paris being killed after describing his rival's apartment as 'tasteless', a man in Florence dying after accusing his cousin of 'not understanding Dante' and a duel over possession of an Angora cat.

Duelling was widespread for hundreds of years. In the eighteenth century David Hume complained it had 'shed much of the best blood in Christendom'. It's argued that one reason it fell from fashion in the early 1800s was its being copied by the lower orders, leading the upper classes to abandon it. This signalled it was no longer prestigious, and so everyone gave up. One contemporary British parliamentarian described the process: 'I remember that some linen-drapers' assistants took it into their heads to go down one Sunday morning . . . and they began fighting duels; and that as soon as the linen-drapers' assistants took to duelling, it became very infamous in the eyes of the upper classes . . . Now nothing would be so ridiculous as any nobleman or gentleman thinking of resenting an insult by going out and fighting a duel about it.'

More recently, the eating of shark fin soup has declined significantly in China, due in large part to a successful programme of prestige-signalling. The largely tasteless and nutrition-free dish was known as an elite delicacy in Imperial China, and was eagerly copied in the new economy, where the monied elite used it as a status signaller at weddings and banquets. Around seventy-three million sharks were killed for soup every year. A public information campaign was launched, headed by prestigious celebrities including basketball star Yao Ming. Importantly, China's president removed the dish from all their official banquets. Between 2011 and 2018 consumption in China fell by 80 per cent.

Essential to the operation of these status dynamics is influence. When we identify prestigious players our subconscious *copy-flatter-conform* programming is triggered and we allow them to alter our beliefs and behaviour. Status games run on powerlines of influence and deference that crackle up and down their hierarchy. This is why, of all the countless status symbols that exist in human life, influence is probably the most reliable. We often assume money or fancy possessions are the most certain symbols of a person's rank, but the highest-status monk in the world may have less wealth, and fewer Hermès ties, than the most junior banker on Wall Street. Influence is different.

Of course, it's not a perfect signal of status; someone low-ranking could influence others with gossip, flattery or lies. But it is an immediate and predictable result of it. Even in small-scale societies, a person's status is commonly expressed in their capacity to influence: they 'tend to be more prominent in group discussions, to make their opinions known and their suggestions clear, and to articulate the consensus once it is determined'. The outsized influence that high-status players exert can also be measured in how much they talk. One study of premodern societies found top-ranking members spoke fifteen times more frequently than those at the bottom, and almost five times more than those one rank beneath them.

Influence is a useful signal in dominance games, in which it manifests as power, and also in the two prestige games where it's willingly offered by co-players. Wherever you track trails of influence – of people deferring, altering their beliefs or behaviour to match those of the people above them – you'll find status games being played and won. We frequently measure our own level of status by our capacity to influence. Our status detection systems monitor the extent to which others defer to us in the subtlest negotiations of behaviour, body language and tone.

This is one reason we can take it so personally when our ideas, tastes or opinions are rejected. If human life was strictly rational, we'd be likely to feel blank when disagreed with, or perhaps worried a suboptimal decision was being made. We might even feel pleased about it, taking the disagreement as a signal of the group's rigour. But when our attempts at influence fail – especially in public, especially in the witness of higher-status players – we can become preoccupied, livid, bitter and vengeful. When this happens, we often slip into a more primitive mode of play in which status is not earned in displays of usefulness, but grabbed in acts of dominance.

7

Dominance Games

Easter Sunday 2018, a routine traffic stop in Tenafly, New Jersey. Police officers spotted an out-of-town car that had part of its licence plate obscured as well as tinted side windows, which were forbidden in the state. Having pulled the vehicle over, the officers found three young adults, including a driver who failed to produce valid insurance or registration. They impounded the car, ordering it to be collected when the correct documents could be produced. One of the passengers called her mother to arrange for her to come pick them up.

That's when it all went weird.

60 years old, narrow and imposing in tight black athleisure wear and a burgundy gilet, she strode in, pushed her sunglasses up onto her forehead and, with an outstretched hand and a business card, announced, 'I'm Caren Turner.'

'That's fine,' said the first police officer, glancing at her card. 'I don't need that.'

'Ok fine. I'm Caren Turner,' she said again.

'You're just here as a ride, right?'

'No I'm not. I'm here as a concerned citizen. And a friend of the mayor. And I've been in Tenafly for twenty-five years and I take full

56

responsibility for them. What was the reason they were pulled over?'

'The driver has all the information. He'll tell you.'

'No-no-no-no-no,' she said, the no's coming at him like little nubby bullets. 'I need to know.'

'No, you don't need to know. You're not involved here. You're picking them up.'

'No-no-no, I'm involved. Trust me. I'm very involved.'

During the encounter, which was captured on a police dash-cam, Turner repeatedly attempted to get the officers to tell her why they'd pulled the car over. The officers repeatedly advised her to ask the driver. Turner showed her business card again and was again rebuffed – 'We don't need to see credentials' – but then she whipped out a gold badge.

'I'm the commissioner of the Port Authority and I'm heading up over four thousand police officers. Ok? So. If there's a problem—'

'There's no problem,' said the second officer. 'It's an unregistered vehicle.'

'Now why were they pulled over, first of all?'

'Miss—'

'No, don't call me Miss. I'm Commissioner. Thank you.'

Turner's attempt at getting an answer to her question continued to fail. It failed when she told them she was an attorney. It failed when she told them the passengers included people 'attending Yale graduate school, a PhD student'. It failed when she repeated her demand: 'I need to know.' The second officer explained his refusal to give her what she wanted: 'It's more of the way you approached me and your demeanour.' As Turner became more aggravated, she began holding her arms away from her body, gesticulating with a jabbing finger and standing closer to the second officer – and closer and closer, pinning him against his car. 'Step back,' she was told. 'Take a step back from me. I can't move back any further.'

About seven minutes into the encounter, she berated the men. 'I'm very disappointed in the way you two are acting.' When the second officer suggested she take the youngsters home she placed her hand on her hip and scolded him, 'That's pathetic. And you are a disappointment.' She turned to the other officer. 'And you're just following him. So you're also a disappointment.'

'You may take them now,' said officer two.

'You may not Tell. Me. When. To. Take. My. Child,' she said, her head pecking side to side with each staccato syllable. 'You may shut the fuck up and not tell me when I may take my kid and her friends, who are PhD students from MIT and Yale. You may tell me nothing because you've told me nothing. Shame on both of you. I will be talking to the chief of police and I will be speaking to the mayor . . . I've got all your details, sweetheart.' Eventually Turner left. Then she came back. When one officer admitted he was 'a little disappointed' in her she snapped back, 'You don't get to be disappointed in me.' She told them, 'The police have all been in my home and my second home and in the third home in Tenafly.'

'I don't see how that's relevant to this situation,' said officer one.

The video found its way online and into the media. A week later, Turner resigned her position at the Port Authority of New York and New Jersey, where she'd also been chair of the ethics committee. In a statement she regretted letting 'my emotions get the better of me' and her 'off-colour language'. But she denied using her position to seek special treatment and finished with this delicious flourish: 'I encourage the Tenafly Police Department to review best practices with respect to tone and de-escalation, so that incidents like this do not recur.'

What happened, on that bright Saturday afternoon in March, was an argument about a question. Caren Turner wanted to know why her daughter and friends had been pulled over. The officers requested she ask the driver, who was standing perhaps three metres away and in possession of all the answers. Beneath the surface (not far beneath the surface; less than a half a millimetre beneath the surface) this was a status battle, a dispute over who had superior rank. Caren Turner played a dominance game. She lost.

Whenever our sense of status is challenged, like this, we can easily slip into a different state of being. We employ primeval neural coding that was written millions of years ago, in the prehuman era of dominance. Whilst the prestige games of virtue and success have made us gentler and wiser animals, these superior modes of playing haven't completely overwritten our bestial capacities. As psychologist Professor Dan McAdams writes, 'the human expectation that social status can be seized through brute force and intimidation, that the strongest and the biggest and boldest will lord it over the rank and file, is very old, awesomely intuitive and deeply ingrained. Its younger rival – prestige – was never able to dislodge dominance from the human mind.'

The beast is still in us. It is our *second self*. Many of us shade between these states multiple times a day, often without realising we're morphing from one self into another. And they really are different modes of being. Prestige and dominance behaviours are 'underpinned by distinct psychological processes, behaviours and neurochemistry which were selected for distinct evolutionary pressures'. We tend to hold ourselves differently when inhabited by each version of us: when in a dominant, second-self mode we take up more space, hold our arms away from our bodies, smile less often and maintain a downwards head tilt; when in a prestigious state we embody our status in subtler ways, expanding our chest, pushing our torso out, tilting our head upwards. Studies show even children younger than 2 can differentiate between players using strategies of dominance and prestige.

Both work. Dominant and prestigious players alike have more influence over co-players. Dominant men, like prestigious men, have greater reproductive success. One meta-analysis of over thirty studies found dominance to be one of the 'most robust predictors of leader emergence, outperforming myriad others including conscientiousness and intelligence'. This is despite the fact that dominant-style leaders are usually less effective than the prestigious, being more likely to put their own interests before the group, less likely to seek advice and tending to respond to criticism with 'ego defensive aggression'. They're also overbearing, like to publicly credit themselves with the success of the group, tease and humiliate subordinates and are manipulative, compared to prestigious leaders who are more likely to be self-deprecating, tell jokes and publicly attribute success to the team. Tellingly, we're especially prone to raising up dominant leaders when the status of our game is under threat. In studies, men and women have picked silhouettes of tall, bulky people with thin eyes and lips and a strong jawline as ideal leaders in times of war; in peacetime those with narrower frames were more popular.

The critical difference between dominance and prestige is that we don't give status freely to second-self players. Typically, dominant players take it from us. Psychologists describe dominance strategy as entailing the 'induction of fear, through intimidation and coercion, to attain or maintain rank and influence'. They force deference from co-players by inducing 'fear of their ability to inflict physical or psychological harm' using 'acts of aggression, coercion, threats, derogation, debasement, and manipulation'. Second-self players can use violence and the fear of it to claw their way up the rankings, then, but they can also exploit varieties of pain that are marked not by blood and bruises, but by tears, shame and despair.

These modes of dominance are one of the most easily observable differences between men and women. It's not unusual for either sex to act with hostility in defence of their status. Almost half of males and females, in one study, gave 'status/reputation concerns' as the primary cause of their most recent act of aggression. But still, today, men have a propensity for physical status contests built into their minds, muscles and bones. They're overwhelmingly the perpetrators of murder, and comprise most of their victims, with around 90 per cent of global homicides being committed by males, and 70 per cent being their targets. In the majority of cases, killers are unemployed, unmarried, poorly educated and under 30. Their sense of status is fragile. In most places, the leading reasons given for killing are 'status-driven', writes conflict researcher Dr Mike Martin, 'the result of altercations over trivial disputes'.

Professor James Gilligan, who's spent more than three decades using prisons and prison hospitals as 'laboratories' to study the causes of criminal violence, finds that 'time after time' men give the same answer as to why they assault or kill: '"because he disrespected me" or "he disrespected my visitor [or wife, mother, sister, girlfriend, daughter, etc.]." In fact, they used that phrase so often that they abbreviated it into the slang phrase, "He dis'ed me." Whenever people use a word so often that they abbreviate it, it is clearly central to their moral and emotional vocabulary.' Gilligan once believed muggings and armed robberies to be motivated primarily by greed or need. 'But when I actually sat down and spoke at length with men who had repeatedly committed such crimes, I would start to hear comments like "I never got so much *respect* before in my life as I did when I pointed a gun at some dude's face."'

The causes of female violence are little different. One study into working-class 16-year-olds in Britain found theirs was commonly triggered by insults, often to do with intelligence, delinquency or sexual behaviour. But serious violence among women and girls is comparatively rare. For psychologist Professor Jonathan Haidt, 'girls and boys are equally aggressive but their aggression is different. Boys' aggression revolves around the threat of violence: "I will physically hurt you" . . . but girls' aggression has always been relational: "I will destroy your reputation or your relationships".' Researchers argue female aggression tends to be 'indirect'. Rather than assault an antagonist's physical body, face-to-face, they'll attack their avatar. They'll attempt to secure their enemy's ostracization, severing their connections to games, and use mockery, gossip and insult to strip them of status. Of course, these are average differences. Reputation-attacking strategies are also widely exploited by men, although the nature of insults can vary: one analysis of online conflict found 'women derogate other women's promiscuity and physical attractiveness on social media more than men do, while men derogate men on their abilities more than women do'. Likewise, plenty of women use face-to-face dominance, as our encounter with alpha female Caren Turner shows.

Dominance behaviour is more likely to be triggered when the relative status of the protagonists is murky. If the hierarchy doesn't clearly show who's in charge, there's a greater temptation to use aggression to secure supremacy. During the traffic stop, Turner appeared to believe her position as Port Authority Commissioner, attorney, friend of the mayor, associate of the Chief of Police, host of Yale and MIT PhD students and owner of three houses in Tenafly clearly symbolised her superiority. But to the police officers she was 'just here as a ride'. This is true of purely verbal disputes and it's true of those that turn physical. For sociologist Professor Roger Gould, 'the more ambiguous the relation is with respect to who should be expected to outrank whom, the more likely violence is'.

The disagreement between Turner and the officers was ostensibly about a question: 'why did you pull them over?' The question was reasonable. Their refusal to answer was petty. But this is often the way with such disputes, including those that become so aggressive they end in murder. When people have an outburst over something trivial – an unanswered question, a tiny debt, a perceived lack of gratitude, a minor discourtesy on the road – they often justify themselves by saying it's about the 'principle' of the matter. For Gould, those who talk of principle mean 'the other party has arrogated to himself or herself a dominant role that has not previously characterised the relation'. In life, even the subtlest interpersonal events can be symbolic. They're all too easily read by the status detection system as 'fuck you'.

When this happens, we're often guilty of forcing our way back on top with aggression or the threat of it. This sits uncomfortably with the image we tend to prefer of ourselves as a moral hero. So we deny our behaviour. We tell a story that blames circumstance or the devil or our villainous antagonists: those dreadful officers with their triggering tone and failure to de-escalate. These brain-spun visions blind us to the full reality of who we are. We're players in games using strategies that have worked for millions of years. We all have that beast within us. We're all Caren Turner.

8

Male, Grandiose, Humiliated:
The Game's Most Lethal

Elliot was 11 years old and playing happily at summer camp when he accidentally bumped into a pretty and popular girl. 'She got very angry,' he recounted later. 'She cursed at me and pushed me.' He froze, shocked, completely lost as to how to respond. Everybody was watching. 'Are you okay?' asked one of his friends. Elliot couldn't speak or move. He felt humiliated. He barely talked for the rest of the day. 'I couldn't believe what had happened.' The experience made him feel like an 'insignificant, unworthy little mouse. I felt so small and vulnerable. I couldn't believe this girl was so horrible to me, and I thought it was because she viewed me as a loser.' As he grew into his teens, continually rejected and bullied by the cool school elites, Elliot never forgot the incident. 'It would scar me for life.'

Ted was a gifted scholar, arriving at Harvard University at age 16. One day, he applied to take part in an experiment led by the prestigious psychologist Professor Henry Murray. Ted was instructed to spend a month writing an 'exposition of your personal philosophy of life, an affirmation of the major guiding principles in accord with which you live or hope to live' and an autobiography containing deeply personal information about subjects including toilet training, thumb sucking and masturbation. What Ted didn't know was that Murray had a history working on behalf of secretive government agencies. This would be a study of harsh interrogation techniques, specifically the 'effects of emotional and psychological trauma on unwitting human subjects'. Once he'd detailed his secrets and philosophies, Ted was led into a brightly lit room, had wires and probes attached to him, and was sat in front of a one-way mirror. There began a series of what Murray called 'vehement, sweeping, and personally abusive' attacks on his personal history and the rules and symbols by which he lived and hoped to live. 'Every week for three years, someone met with him to verbally abuse him and humiliate him,' Ted's brother said. 'He never told us about the experiments, but we noticed how he changed.' Ted himself described the humiliation experiments as 'the worst experience of my life'.

Ed grew up with an abusive mother. She was alcoholic and paranoid and 'extremely domineering'. She'd berate him in public and refuse him affection for fear it would turn him gay. Large for his age, when Ed was 10 she became obsessed with the idea he'd molest his sister, so she locked him in the basement to sleep. He spent months down there, the only exit a trapdoor under the space where the kitchen table usually stood. She'd frequently belittle him, telling him none of the smart, beautiful young women at the university where she worked would go near him. His was a childhood of rejection and humiliation. 'I had this love-hate complex with my mother that was very hard for me to handle,' he said. This 'hassle' with his mother made him feel 'very inadequate around women, because they posed a threat to me. Inside I blew them up very large. You know, the little games women play, I couldn't play [or] meet their demands. So I backslid.'

Ed backslid. He really did. He killed his grandmother, 'because

I wanted to kill my mother'. Then he killed his mother. He cut off her head and had sex with it, then buried it in the garden, eyes facing upwards because she always wanted people to 'look up to her'. He also killed eight other women, having sex with some of their corpses and eating others. Ed Kemper remains one of America's most notorious serial killers. Elliot Rodger, meanwhile, became a spree killer, killing six young people and then himself at the University of California, Santa Barbara, in 2014. And Ted? That's Ted Kaczynski. The Unabomber.

If so much of life is a status game, what happens when all our status is taken from us? What happens when we're made to feel like nothing, again and again and again? Humiliation can be seen as the opposite of status, the hell to its heaven. Like status, humiliation comes from other people. Like status, it involves their judgement of our place in the social rankings. Like status, the higher they sit in the rankings, and the more of them there are, the more powerful their judgement. And, like status, it matters. Humiliation has been described by researchers as 'the nuclear bomb of the emotions' and has been shown to cause major depressions, suicidal states, psychosis, extreme rage and severe anxiety, 'including ones characteristic of post-traumatic stress disorder'. Criminal violence expert Professor James Gilligan describes the experience of humiliation as an 'annihilation of the self'. His decades of research in prisons and prison hospitals, seeking the causes of violence, led him to 'a psychological truth exemplified by the fact that one after another of the most violent men I have worked with over the years have described to me how they had been humiliated repeatedly throughout their childhoods'.

The logic of the status game dictates that humiliation (and to a lesser degree shame, which can be seen as the private experience of humiliation, the sense of being judged appalling by the imaginary audience in our heads) must be uniquely catastrophic. For psychologists Professor Raymond Bergner and Dr Walter Torres humiliation is an absolute purging of status and the ability to claim it. They propose four preconditions for an episode to count as humiliating. Firstly, we should believe, as most of us do, that we're deserving of status. Secondly, humiliating incidents are public. Thirdly, the person doing the degrading must themselves have some modicum of status. And finally, the stinger: the 'rejection of the status to claim status'. Or, from our perspective, rejection from the status game entirely.

In severe states of humiliation, we tumble so spectacularly down the rankings that we're no longer considered a useful co-player. So we're gone, exiled, cancelled. Connection to our kin is severed. 'The critical nature of this element is hard to overstate,' they write. 'When humiliation annuls the status of individuals to claim status, they are in essence denied eligibility to recover the status they have lost.' If humans are players, programmed to seek connection and status, humiliation insults both our deepest needs. And there's nothing we can do about it. 'They have effectively lost the voice to make claims within the relevant community and especially to make counterclaims on their own behalf to remove their humiliation.' The only way to recover is to find a new game even if that means rebuilding an entire life and self. 'Many humiliated individuals find it necessary to move to another community to recover their status, or more broadly, to reconstruct their lives.'

But there is one other option. An African proverb says, 'the child who is not embraced by the village will burn it down to feel its warmth'. If the game rejects you, you can return in dominance as a vengeful God, using deadly violence to force the game to attend to you in humility. The life's work of Professor Gilligan led him to conclude the fundamental cause of most human violence is the 'wish to ward off or eliminate the feeling of shame and humiliation and replace it with its opposite, the feeling of pride'.

Of course, it would be naive to claim Ed, Ted and Elliot were triggered solely as a response to humiliation. If the cauterisation of status was a simple mass-killing switch, such crimes would be common. Various further contributory factors are possible. All three were men, which dramatically increases the likelihood they'd seek to restore their lost status with violence. Elliot Rodger was said to be on the autism spectrum, which might've impacted his ability to make friends and girlfriends; a court psychiatrist claimed Ed Kemper had paranoid schizophrenia (although this remains contested); and Kaczynski's brother said Ted once 'showed indications of schizophrenia'. But none of these conditions are answers in themselves, because the vast majority of those that have them don't burn down their villages.

And that's what happened. All three attacked the status games from which they felt rejected, asserting their dominance over their degraders. Ed Kemper's mother would taunt her son with her belief that the high-status co-ed girls at her university would never date him. He began killing those girls, becoming the 'Co-Ed Killer', before finishing with his mother: 'I cut off her head and I humiliated her corpse.' He then pushed her voice box into the food disposal unit. 'It seemed appropriate as much as she'd bitched and screamed and yelled at me over so many years.' Kemper's psychological profiler at the FBI, John Douglas, writes: 'He was a man on a mission who'd had humiliating experiences with women and was now out to punish as many as he could,' adding he was 'someone not born a serial killer but manufactured as one'.

Ted Kaczynski, who'd been humiliated by a prestigious scientist at Harvard, became the 'Unabomber', the 'un' standing for the universities that were partly his target. His brain took his feelings of debasement and resentment and magicked them into a story in which he was the hero. He went to war against smart people and the world they'd made, writing that the technological age and its consequences have 'been a disaster for the human race' and have 'made life unfulfilling, have subjected human beings to indignities, have led to widespread psychological suffering'. His bombing campaign was the start of a revolution, aimed at freeing the masses from slavery by 'the system'. He sought and received, in return for a promissory cessation of violence, the extraordinarily statusful experience of having his 35,000-word exposition on modernity's evils published by the *Washington Post*.

And Elliot Rodger? This is what he had to say in the novel-length autobiography he distributed prior to his spree: 'All those popular kids who live such lives of hedonistic pleasure while I've had to rot in loneliness all these years. They all looked down upon me every time I tried to join them. They've all treated me like a mouse . . . If humanity will not give me a worthy place among them, then I will destroy them all. I am better than all of them. I am a god. Exacting my retribution is my way of proving my true worth to the world.' Acute or chronic social rejection has been found to be a major contributory factor in 87 per cent of all school shootings between 1995 and 2003.

But there's one final factor that ties together this triumvirate of destroyers. Not only did Rodger, Kemper and Kaczynski experience severe humiliation, they also had an immense psychological height from which to fall. All were intelligent – Kemper had an IQ of 145, near genius level – and all were markedly grandiose, with Kaczynski hoping to spearhead a global revolution and Rodger's autobiography greasy with entitlement and narcissism, including descriptions of himself as a 'beautiful, magnificent gentleman'. Kemper gloried in his notoriety: during a long drive with police officers following his arrest he paraded himself at rest-stops, showing his handcuffs, and speculated excitedly about press coverage. It's even been suggested his confessions of cannibalism and necrophilia were status-seeking untruths. All three had a need for status that was unusually, perhaps pathologically fierce, and so the humiliations they suffered would've been all the more agonising. Writes mental health expert Professor Marit Svindseth, 'even the slightest disagreement or slur from a person of similar or higher-status rank might be enough to humiliate the narcissist'. Feeling entitled to a place at the top of the game, they were driven to depravity by life at the bottom.

This pattern – male, grandiose, humiliated – is also evident in those who commit nonviolent acts of destruction against their game. From an early age Robert Hanssen dreamed of being a spy. He loved James Bond and bought himself a Walther PPK pistol, a shortwave radio and even opened a Swiss bank account. But Hanssen's father was abusive, belittling him and inflicting strange punishments. 'He forced him to sit with his legs spread in some fashion,' his psychiatrist reported. 'He was forced to sit in that position and it was humiliating.' Such degradings also happened outside the home. Whenever his best friend's mother encountered his father, there was 'always something belittling about Bob. No matter what Bob did, it wasn't right. I've never seen a father like that. He would never have a kind word to say about his only child.' Even after Hanssen was grown and married, the degrading continued. When his parents came round for dinner, he'd be too frightened to come downstairs. 'He would get sick to his stomach and could not face his father at the table. [His wife] Bonnie finally said, "If you are under this roof, if you cannot be respectful to Bob, then you are not welcome to come."'

But Hanssen's need for status was strong. He became an 'ultra-religious, devout, zealous' member of the Catholic Church, a part of the elite group Opus Dei that was the Pope's personal prelature. He joined the FBI in 1976 where he hoped to live a life of statusful excitement as a counter-intelligence operative but was repeatedly turned down for such prestigious roles. According to his biographer, he kept finding himself in back rooms, 'watching from afar as others performed more exciting work'. Hanssen was seen as 'very, very smart' with strong technical skills, but he came off as superior and difficult, carrying a 'wry expression on his face. He just didn't suffer fools gladly. Why should I have to reduce myself to this level?' In 1979 Hanssen contacted the Soviet Union and offered to spy for them. He wasn't arrested until 2001, by which time he'd passed thousands of top-secret documents to the KGB and compromised many of their assets, some of whom were executed. Hanssen is considered the most damaging spy in US history. Following his trial his psychiatrist said, 'If I had to pick one core psychological reason for his spying, I would target the experience he had in his relations with his father.'

Humiliation is also a principal cause of honour killings. They involve a family conspiring to murder someone they believe has brought humiliation upon their family by breaking the rules and symbols of their game, usually with behaviours related to sexuality or being 'too Western'. In some Muslim, Hindu and Sikh niches it's felt the only way to restore the family's lost status is to kill those perceived to be at fault. Victims might have refused arranged marriage, had premarital sex or an affair, or sought a divorce. They might've wanted to renounce their faith entirely. Some killings happen as a result of being a victim of rape or wearing jewellery. The victims are almost always women, sometimes gay men, and the perpetrators surprisingly gender diverse. One albeit small study of thirty-one killings across Europe and Asia, by Emerita Professor of Psychology Phyllis Chesler, found women were 'hands-on killers' in 39 per cent of cases and co-conspirators in 61 per cent. The exception was India, where women were the killers in every case. Chesler writes that these families who kill are often viewed in their communities 'as heroes'. Statistics vary, but the UN estimate of around five thousand such deaths a year is conservative.

One danger of surveying extreme cases is that us normals can feel exempt from their lessons. But in their looming shadows, thoughtful readers might detect their own silhouettes. Surveys hint at how gruesomely painful episodes of humiliation can be to ordinary people, and are suggestive of their ability to summon demons, with one finding 59 per cent of men and 45 per cent of women admitting to homicidal fantasies in revenge for them. Others might object entirely to attempts at understanding such reprehensible acts, as if doing so somehow permits them. The language of blame and forgiveness might be suitable for courts, churches and those directly affected, but by allowing moral talk to arrest our thinking, we become less useful; less able to identify risks and preventatives.

In 2014, in the aftermath of Elliot Rodger's killing of four men and two women and his injuring of fourteen others, people began looking for the cause of his barbarity. What demonic power could've derailed Rodger's journey of life with such force? Commentators from Glenn Beck on the right to *Vice* magazine on the left soon identified his obsession with the computer game World of Warcraft. 'Please listen to me, you've got to get the video games out of your child's hand,' said Beck. 'They cannot handle it. This is not the same as Pac-Man. These are virtual worlds where they live.' Similarly, *Vice* pointed to 'the addictive cycle of gaming' that takes players 'ever further away from nurturing human contact, love, and social ambition'. But there's a problem with these stories, evident in Rodger's 108,000-word autobiography.

My Twisted World: The Story of Elliot Rodger is an extraordinary document. Gripping and appalling, it recounts in bracing detail his descent from 'blissful' early childhood to a young adulthood of rejection, hatred and homicidal madness. His grandiose need for status is present from the start: we learn his father hails 'from the prestigious Rodger family' whilst his mother was 'friends with very important individuals from the film industry, including George Lucas and Steven Spielberg'. Life was essentially happy, aside from his parents' divorce, up until he realised he was becoming shorter and weaker than his classmates. 'This vexed me no end.'

The ages between 9 and 13 were Rodger's 'last period of contentment'. In his social life he began to notice 'there were hierarchies, that some people were better than others . . . At school, there were always the "cool kids" who seemed to be more admirable than everyone else.' He realised he 'wasn't cool at all. I had a dorky hairstyle. I wore plain and uncool clothing, and I was shy and unpopular . . . on top of this was the feeling that I was different because I am of mixed race.' Following this realisation, nothing would be the same. 'The peaceful and innocent environment of childhood where everyone had an equal footing was all over. The time of fair play was at its end.'

As a boy, he'd practised being 'cool' by learning to skateboard. Now he was older, the rules had changed: 'The "cool" thing to do now was to be popular with girls. *How in the blazes was I going to do that?*' Rodger found himself shunned and bullied. 'I was extremely unpopular, widely disliked and viewed as the weirdest kid.' But he found succour in the online computer games he'd meet with others to play, sometimes hanging out at an internet cafe until 3 a.m.: 'I was having so much fun outside of school with my friends at Planet Cyber that I didn't really care about getting popular or getting attention from girls.' When he discovered World of Warcraft, a game that allows players to team up online and pursue missions, 'it really blew my mind. My first experience with WoW was like stepping into another world of excitement and adventure . . . it was like living another life.' It became an obsession. 'I hid myself away in the online World of Warcraft, a place where I felt comfortable and secure.'

Meanwhile the budding of his sex drive was proving hellish. Terrified of females and yet desirous of their approval, Rodger's teenage years were spent in rejected, dumbfounded agony. He begged his parents not to send him to a mixed gender school. His peers mocked him, threw food at him and stole his belongings. He spent every possible moment in World of Warcraft, achieving the extraordinary status of its highest level, a 'huge and important accomplishment'. The three local boys with whom he'd play online were 'the closest thing I had to a group of friends'. But then Rodger made a grievous discovery. Those friends would often meet up in secret so they could play without him. 'Even in World of Warcraft, I was an outcast, alone and unwanted.' He began to feel 'lonely even while playing'. He'd break down in tears in the middle of games. 'I began to ask myself what the point was in playing it.' So he stopped.

And then something switched. Up until this point, Rodger had presented as confused, miserable and bitter. He was also hateful: his fear of women had curdled into a powerful misogyny, his loathing extending to the 'cool' men they chose to date. But angry misogynists, sadly, aren't rare. Only when his source of connection and status was lost did absolute pandemonium let loose in his thoughts. 'I began to have fantasies of becoming very powerful and stopping everyone from having sex,' he wrote. 'This was a major turning point.' On his final day of playing World of Warcraft, he described to his last remaining friend his 'newfound views' that 'sex must be abolished'.

Rodger's brain had taken his feelings of debasement and resentment and magicked them into a story in which he was the hero. It said his suffering was the fault of women, who 'represent everything that is unfair with this world' and who 'control which men get [sex] and which men don't'. By always choosing 'the stupid, degenerate, obnoxious men', they were going to 'hinder the advancement of the human race'. He dreamed up an 'ultimate and perfect ideology of how a fair and pure world would work'. Sex would be outlawed. Women would be destroyed, with some remaining to procreate via artificial insemination. He took these hideous visions to be evidence of his superiority. 'I see the world differently than anyone else. Because of all the injustices I went through and the worldview I developed because of them, I must be destined for greatness.' In the brain-spun dream in which he'd become lost, his misogyny was righteous. 'All I ever wanted was to love women, and in turn to be loved by them back. Their behaviour towards me has only earned my hatred, and rightfully so! I am the true victim in all of this. I am the good guy.'

Rodger was 17. For the next five years until his killing spree, besides sporadic returns, his online game-playing ceased. At the same time, his misery, loathing and madness caught fire. World of Warcraft had been the only place he'd felt of value. It was a status game and one he'd excelled at. Far from being the cause of his madness, it was more likely the last thing keeping him sane.

9

Change the Rules, Change the Player

WHY DO PEOPLE run very fast? Like, Mo Farah – what's the point? And why do people invest a significant amount of money, time and discomfort in watching these very fast runners? Staring and screaming from their plastic bucket-seats in those awful concrete arenas, they seem to care a lot about how many milliseconds faster this one ran than that one. Why? And while we're at it, what's the point of football? What's the point of chess? What's the point of computer games? All those hours wasted in bedrooms pressing clicky buttons. How is that making you a better person? How is that moving you on in life's heroic journey? Like Elliot Rodger – why did he become obsessed with World of Warcraft? Was it because he loved killing things? Was it because he was a monster?

World of Warcraft is a status generating machine. The game conjured for Rodger an alternative reality in which an avatar of his self could play. He built a life in there. He played games of dominance and success. He thrived. This is how all the games people play for fun function: by exploiting the neural circuitry that evolved to play the status game, which is the original game, and the greatest game of all. Athletes, boxers, swimmers, players of basketball, chess and football and participants in reality TV competitions compete for status in imagined worlds of rules and symbols. Solitary games, such as crosswords, are played before the imaginary audience that live in our heads, our conscience groaning and cheering as we fail or succeed.

To amplify their excitement, the games we make for pleasure have clever tweaks made to their rules. They're usually time-limited, either by a set period of play or a mission or battle to complete; they're overtly 'zero sum', with a specific named goal to be reached at the expense of other competitors, and they're formally ranked, with the position of each player or team precisely scored and announced for everyone to see. Often, the games we play in daily life don't have these qualities. They tend to be open-ended: they last as long as our relationships with our co-players continue. And our position, as it shifts from minute to minute, day to day, is neither fixed in a precisely defined rank nor declared publicly. Instead, it's sensed. The status detection system reads it from clues in the world of symbols we're immersed in. This means it's possible to attend a work meeting as a relatively low-ranked team member, contribute a fantastically useful idea, receive symbolic rewards of attention, praise and influence, and leave feeling on top of the world. We might not be number one, but we feel like we are. Even though we have a job title and a pay grade, these don't represent a precise and inarguable judgement, like the position on a sports arena's scoreboard. If business meetings were like this, with one winner's spot for everyone to fight over, and performance rankings announced in bright lights for everyone to see – well, you can imagine.

Naturally occurring status games don't require such tweaks to function. We can be motivated, and urged into greater feats, by symbolic rewards from co-players, our promotion to higher ranks being valued more as a recognition of our worth than as a signal we've vanquished many enemies. These positive feelings from the group are key: in team tugs of war, when individual performance is hidden, people pull about half as hard as when working alone, but ramp up their efforts when a crowd cheers them on. The same is true of runners and cyclists who also perform better with an appreciative audience.

One of the most successful status games I've come across is that of the internationally popular health regimen CrossFit. Founded in the U.S. in 2000, it brilliantly uses the desire for connection and status to drive its members sometimes to near-addiction. CrossFitters attend sessions at a local 'box' where they take part in the prescribed 'Workout of the Day' (or 'WOD'). WODs – always-changing combinations of high-intensity activities – are adapted to each member's fitness level. This means CrossFitters don't have to compete with each other (although they can if they wish), but instead push themselves to beat their own previous bests. Crucially, they do this surrounded by their fellow CrossFitters who track each others' progress and cheer each other on. At CrossFit, status is not jealously guarded by individuals fighting over a zero-sum place on a single leader board, but lavished at any player who strives.

Studies find CrossFitters have 'higher levels of social bonding and community belonging' than traditional gym users. A 2021 paper found them to be highly motivated by the 'social capital' and 'camaraderie' their sessions provide, with one respondent explaining they 'complement each other on achievements and all those types of things. I like the fact that if one person is struggling to finish their workout or having a bad day or it's just a tough workout for them, then you've got people cheering them on all the time.'

In the past, these superbly managed status game-dynamics have worked perhaps too well. CrossFitters have the reputation of having a cult-like devotion to their groups and for sometimes pushing themselves too far: a popular 'unofficial-mascot' is a cartoon clown called Uncle Rhabdo, who's often depicted ripped and exhausted beside a dialysis machine with his kidney on the floor. 'Rhabdo' is short for Rhabdomyolysis, a potentially fatal condition that can occur when extreme exercise causes the muscle cells to break down. Another mascot-clown, 'Pukie', is shown with a plume of green vomit, caused by over-exertion, firing out of his mouth.

CrossFit groups are also relatively small, typically hosting thirteen to eighteen people. Relative smallness is another property of healthy status games. In the Stone Age, the tribal subgroups in which we spent most of our time numbered perhaps twenty-five to thirty people, many of them extended family members. As we've learned, there would've been divisions even within those: men would've largely competed for status with other men, and women with women. Within the gender divide there would have been further divisions by age and specialist arenas of competence: tracker, healer, storyteller, honey-finder. This is why everyone in the world doesn't feel as if they're striving for status against everyone else in the world. If, tomorrow morning, all seven billion of us decided we were personally competing with Michelle Obama or the King of Thailand, we'd likely suffer a global nervous breakdown. Researchers find happiness isn't closely linked to our socioeconomic status, which captures our rank compared with others across the whole of society, including class. It's actually our smaller games that matter: 'studies show that respect and admiration within one's local group, but not socioeconomic status, predicts subjective well-being'.

Our natural propensity to play small, local games is found in combat units during war, in which soldiers tend to be motivated less by the distant aims of their national leader than their desire for connection and respect from their brothers-in-arms and the primal thrill of dominance play. For violence researcher and former British Army officer Dr Mike Martin combat in Afghanistan was, 'hands down, the greatest rush of positive emotions' he'd ever experienced. 'Fighting, when you and a small group of humans are trying to out-shoot and out-manoeuvre another group of humans, and they they you, is the ultimate team sport.' Studies of soldiers usually find their central motivation comes not from king, queen or country, but from their close comrades. For even Nazi fighters, it's been found that 'political values played a very minor part in sustaining their motivation for combat'.

These soldiers don't compete with each other but against a common enemy. Status games don't function best by generating maximal competition between players. Research on this matter is mixed, but moderate levels are thought to increase diligence and productivity. Too much internal competition, however, can be counterproductive. If a hard atmosphere of all-against-all descends, players can be incentivised to stop rewarding each other with status and there'll be a paucity of supply. Life, under such conditions, can reek of stress and misery. It can also contribute to a game becoming corrupted.

In June 2001, *Time* magazine reported on one 'fiercely competitive' US company's 'rank and yank' system by which employee performance was graded by colleagues into various strata, the top 5 per cent announced as 'superior' and the bottom 15 per cent at risk of losing their jobs. The magazine described the process: 'in a typically intense session, as many as twenty-five managers may gather around a conference table in a windowless room with a computer screen filled with employee rankings projected on one wall. Each participant comes armed with notebooks bulging with job reviews. As the discussion proceeds, the managers may shift people from one ranking to another, deciding their fate with the click of a computer mouse.' The reporter worried that 'competitive systems' such as rank-and-yank could 'stir suspicion and discourage teamwork'. One manager defended the arrangement: 'You have to know where you stand, and I believe the system does an excellent job of doing that.' It was hard to deny the company's success: it was the seventh largest in the USA, at its height valued at seventy billion dollars.

Just four months after the *Time* article was published, the company went bankrupt. Several of its executives were prosecuted; one of them, CEO Jeff Skilling, facing charges including conspiracy, securities fraud and insider trading, was eventually jailed for twenty-four years. The company was Enron, sometimes considered one of the most corrupt corporate organisations in history, with its culture of ruthless competitiveness at the heart of its rot.

A better strategy is the promotion of rivalry. Rivalry is distinguished from competition by its focus. Competitions are many-against-many, whilst rivalries tend to be one-against-one – one individual versus another or one game versus another. It emerges over time between parties who've jostled repeatedly and have a history of tight skirmishes, near misses and close calls. Rivalry between companies has been found to be highest when they're competing in the same domain and are most evenly matched. In what feels like an echo of our sometimes bloodily territorial hunter-gatherer past, even being near one another geographically can increase firm-versus-firm rivalry.

The world-altering power of rivalry is evident in the following tale from Silicon Valley. It starts when Apple CEO Steve Jobs encounters a senior executive from Microsoft, a rival technology game with whom Jobs had had a long history of battles and who'd once dominated Apple almost to destruction. The executive was married to a friend of Jobs' wife Laurene, so the men met regularly. 'Anytime Steve had any social interaction with that guy, Steve would come back pissed off,' former Apple executive Scott Forstall has said. 'He came back one time and that guy said Microsoft had solved computing . . . they were going to do tablet computing and they were going to do it with pens. That guy shoved it in Steve's face, the way they were going to rule the world with their tablets with pens. Steve came in Monday and there was a set of expletives and then it was like, "Let's show them how it's really done".' Triggered by the Microsoft man's arrogant behaviour, Jobs set up a team to experiment with a tablet that was operated not with pens, but with fingers. The device they designed became the iPhone then re-emerged as the iPad. 'It began because Steve hated this guy. That's the actual origin of it,' said Forstall, who sagely added, 'it was not good for Microsoft that Steve ever met this guy.'

Success doesn't require being maddened by rivalry, like Steve Jobs, or forced to war after a jealously defended, limited store of status like the employees of Enron. Most of our status play happens nose-to-nose, with co-players immediately around us. Like soldiers at war, we're usually sustained by the prizes that come, not from being at the very top, but from routine play with familiars: colleagues, family members, friends offline and on. We display knowledge of the game's rules and follow them virtuously and with skill; proving ourselves of value to its overall mission. In our daily strivings, we hope our playing is appreciated and admired, just as we're expected to pay that admiration back. But the games we play have extraordinary power over us. All too often, when the rules change, so do we.

10

The Slot Machine for Status

W E'RE BEGINNING TO sense the power of the status game. In discerning the truth beneath the myth of the human condition, we catch a glimpse of its immense capacity for creating joy and havoc. When we earn connection and status, we thrive; when we lose it we can become sick, sad, suicidal and murderous. High-status women and men can mesmerise us, drawing us to theatres, convention halls, cinemas and sports arenas. We can feel ourselves becoming almost possessed by them as our *copy-flatter-conform* mechanisms switch on. But this isn't the only way we can be altered, without our conscious volition, by the game. As the employees at Enron discovered, it's possible for the rules to be altered such that they contribute to our corruption. The strategies by which we earn connection and status shape who we are. To a significant extent, we become the puppets of the games we play.

In recent years, something like this has been happening to the world's 3.6 billion users of social media. Social media is a status game. It can't not be: it's human life, unfolding online. It's all there, the success games of the selfie-takers and humble-braggers; the virtue games of the wellness gurus and political campaigners; the dominance games of the mobbers and the cancellers. But the everyday striving that would've happened naturally, online, has been intensified by technologists who've tweaked their rules and symbols. They've made these games both highly competitive and madly compulsive. A 2019 survey of nearly two thousand US smartphone users found they check their phones an average of ninety-six times a day, about once every ten minutes. This marked a 20 per cent increase from just two years earlier. Another survey, of 1,200 users, found 23 per cent check their phones less than a minute after waking and a further 34 per cent manage to hold out between five and ten minutes. Only 6 per cent managed to wait two hours or more.

This reflects my experience. Despite the fact I only ever posted moderately on Twitter, rarely more than once a week on Instagram and never on Facebook, I still found my smartphone had become a constant companion. I finally quit the device on the realisation that, even on walks with my wife and dogs in the countryside, I couldn't stop myself removing it from my pocket every couple of minutes and opening a social media app, my thumb moving up and down in a repetitive scrolling hook. There'd be no conscious thought: the thing would just appear. Even when I left it at home, my hand would grab for my pocket repeatedly, as if possessed by some alien presence.

That technology is strong magic. Its chief wizard is Dr B. J. Fogg, founder of the Persuasive Technology Lab, which is based out of Silicon Valley's favoured educational institution, Stanford University. Fogg's legend grew in 2007 when he started teaching a class in using his persuasive techniques to build apps on Facebook. By the end of the ten-week course, his students had amassed sixteen million users between them, earning one million dollars in advertising revenue.

Fogg's fascination with controlling behaviour began when, aged 10, he studied propaganda at school. 'I learned names for the various propaganda techniques, and I could soon identify them in magazine ads and TV commercials,' he writes. 'I felt empowered . . . I marvelled at how words, images, and songs could get people to donate blood, buy new cars, or join the Army. This was my first formal introduction to persuasion. After that, everywhere I looked I started seeing what I called "propaganda," used for good purposes and bad.' Growing up with a tech-obsessed father, Fogg wondered about harnessing the power of computers to persuade. At Stanford, he studied how interacting with them can 'change people's attitudes and behaviours'. In 2003 he published *Persuasive Technology: Using Computers to Change What We Think and Do*. Years before the invention of the smartphone, it outlined his vision of our connected tomorrow: 'Someday in the future, a first-year student named Pamela sits in a college library and removes an electronic device from her purse. It's just smaller than a deck of cards, easily carried around, and serves as Pamela's mobile phone, information portal, entertainment platform, and personal organiser. She takes this device almost everywhere and feels a bit lost without it.'

Such devices, Fogg believed, would be 'persuasive technology systems'. They'd be able to change users' thoughts and behaviours with a power that'd never been known in history. 'Traditional media, from bumper stickers to radio spots, from print ads to television commercials, have long been used to influence people to change their attitudes or behaviours,' he wrote. 'What's different about computers and persuasion? The answer, in a word, is interactivity.' This device would interact with its user and its user's life, adjusting its manipulative tactics as their situation changed, communicating with them almost as if it was sentient. 'When you pack a mobile persuasive technology with you, you pack a source of influence. At any time (ideally, at the appropriate time), the device can suggest, encourage, and reward; it can track your performance or lead you through a process.' It could do this with 'microsuasion' elements – notifications, badges or symbols of status: all the nudges with which we're now familiar on social media.

He codified his theory in what he called the 'Fogg Behaviour

Model'. He taught the model at 'Behavior Design Boot Camps' and at the Stanford Persuasion Lab that *Wired* magazine called 'a toll booth for entrepreneurs and product designers on their way to Facebook and Google'. The model said a person is compelled to act when three forces collide in a moment: motivation (we must want the thing); trigger (something must happen to trigger a desire to get more of it) and ability (it must be easy). Take LinkedIn. At its launch, it visually represented the size of a user's professional network with a hub-and-spoke icon. The bigger the icon, the greater the status. People want status (that's the motivation), the icon generates a sudden urge to get more (that's the trigger) and LinkedIn provides an easy solution, in the use of the site to generate more connections (that's ability). 'Even though at the time there was nothing useful you could do with LinkedIn, that simple icon had a powerful effect in tapping into people's desire not to look like losers,' Fogg has said.

But the core of his dark genius lay in one brilliant further insight. It led to a tweak in the way status games are played on social media that would perhaps do more than any other to make them habitual. He described a way of issuing rewards such that they'd encourage compulsive behaviours. If a programmer wanted to create a certain action, in a user, they should offer a symbol of reinforcement after they'd performed the desired 'target behaviour'. But here was the trick: the positive reinforcement would be inconsistent. You wouldn't always know what you were going to get. 'To strengthen an existing behaviour, reinforcers are most effective when they are unpredictable,' Fogg wrote in 2003. 'Playing slot machines is a good example: Winning a payoff of quarters streaming into a metal tray is a reinforcer, but it is random. This type of unpredictable reward schedule makes the target behaviour – in this case, gambling – very compelling, even addictive.'

The story of Fogg's lab is relatively well known amongst those with a backstage interest in social media. The idea of turning phones into slot machines came about before smartphones even existed; it certainly appears to have worked. But there seems to be a missing piece to the theory. It's not clear the technologists are fully aware what their users are actually gambling with. Social media is a slot machine for status. This is what makes it so obsessively compelling. Every time we post a photo, video or a comment, we're judged. We await replies, likes or upvotes and, just as a gambler never knows how the slot machine will pay out, we don't know what reward we'll receive for our contribution. Will we go up? Will we go down? The great prize changes every time. This variation creates compulsion. We just want to keep playing, again and again, to see what we'll get.

The simple act of using social media can be a Fogg-ish trigger, compelling us to play. We all want status and seeing others receive it creates an urgency to grab some for ourselves. If we do well in the game, significant symbols of status may accrue to us: more followers and elite followers including celebrities, some of whom we might even get to know. We may receive a blue tick or the 'verified' marker that's sometimes awarded to top-tier players. A rare few achieve massive success across platforms and become wealthy. In 2020, YouTuber Eleonora 'Lele' Pons was reportedly charging $142,800 for one sponsored Instagram post; fellow YouTuber Zach King was listed at $81,100. They had forty-one million and twenty-three million followers on the photo sharing site respectively. According to the *Washington Post*, top YouTube stars earn between two and five million dollars a year from that platform alone.

But even those who are several galaxies distant from Lele and Zach can find, by investing sufficient time and energy into the game, their avatar may come to hold more status than they do in their 'real' offline life. To these people, the platforms become massive repositories of status, an immeasurably precious resource they'd find agonising to give up. To keep what they have, and earn more, they must keep playing: pulling the arm of that slot machine again and again and again.

Even in 2003 Fogg was aware of his theory's dark power. Notices about ethical concerns were woven carefully through his courses, writing and teaching. As sincere as he may have been, these notes of caution feel, in retrospect, like giving ants to anteaters and saying 'don't eat any ants'. The technologists he taught and inspired have been, at times, less cautious in their messaging. Facebook's former vice president of user growth, Chamath Palihapitiya, once said the site aimed 'to psychologically figure out how to manipulate you as fast as possible'.

This is not, of course, to argue that status is the *only* force driving the spread of social media. As well as being a major money-maker for many, it's a fantastic connection-generating machine. But I don't believe it's possible to understand the astonishing ascendancy of social media without understanding the status game. Its global rise is one of the major societal events of our lifetimes. If we view the human condition from a conventional perspective, a lot of it makes about as much sense as very fast running. Putting pictures of your tanned knees on the internet, why bother? Arguing with strangers over micro-disagreements concerning issues that'll never affect you, what a waste of time. But if we view ourselves not as heroes on journeys but as biological machines designed to play symbolic games of status wherever we go, its success not only makes sense, it feels inevitable.

11

The Flaw

THERE'S NO HAPPY ending. That's the bad news. But this is not how life feels. To be alive, and to be psychologically healthy, is to be vulnerable to the story of consciousness that tells us that with one particular victory, with *that* peak finally climbed, we'll be satisfied. Peace, happiness and delicious stillness will be ours. This, sadly, is a delusion. We'll never get there because partly what we're doing is playing a game for status. And the problem with status is, no matter how much we win, we're never satisfied. We always want more. This is the flaw in the human condition that keeps us playing.

Consider Paul McCartney. As a former member of The Beatles he's spent his life inhaling status like oxygen. Demented fans, the adoration of the opposite sex, the lifelong reputation of a genius and wealth never-ending, he's had about as much of the stuff as anyone in modern history. And yet, even in the midst of it all, he found himself bothered by the fact that, on the sticky labels on his records, and on all the sleeves, the songs he'd co-written were credited to 'Lennon-McCartney'.

Lennon came first.

Why should Lennon come first? How was that fair? It hadn't seemed important when, as bedroom-practising teenagers, they'd agreed the credit no matter which of them wrote what. But now, for some reason, it mattered. So McCartney made a plan. Wherever his contracts gave him wiggle-room, he began switching the names so Lennon came second. His 1976 live album, *Wings Over America*, featured five Beatles songs. He credited them to McCartney-Lennon. Then, prior to the 1995 release of the greatest hits collection *Anthology*, he asked if Lennon could come second on 'Yesterday', a song McCartney had written alone. Yoko Ono said no.

In November 2002 McCartney released another live album. *Back in the U.S.* featured nineteen Beatles songs. And Paul McCartney flipped the names in the credits, every single one. Ono wasn't having it. She instructed her lawyer to release a statement. McCartney's actions, it said, were 'ridiculous, absurd and petty'. Then, apparently no stranger to a bit of ridiculous, absurd and petty herself, she reportedly removed his name from the Plastic Ono Band's most famous song, 'Give Peace a Chance', a credit Lennon granted him as thanks for help with other music. It wasn't until 2003 that Ono and McCartney reached a truce. But even in 2015 he was still grumbling about it.

McCartney has the reputation of a decent man, remarkably undamaged by life in the music elite. And yet, the flipping. The order of the names. It seems he still feels it: that craving, that tension, that disturbance in the blood. It's a flaw that seems to be a fact of human nature. Sociologist Professor Cecilia Ridgeway describes experiments that tried to locate the point at which our need for status, once acquired, stabilises. 'There was no point at which preference for higher status levelled off,' she writes. The researchers thought one reason the desire for status is 'never really satiated' is because 'it can never really be possessed by the individual once and for all. Since it is esteem given by others, it can always, at least theoretically, be taken away.' So we keep wanting more. And more and more and more.

The flaw can be detected in how we feel about money, that shiny symbol we often use as a measure of status. No matter how much we earn, the flaw wants more. And we convince ourselves we're worth it. One survey of more than seventy thousand people found almost two-thirds earning market-rate wages believed they were being short-changed whilst only 6 per cent thought they were getting over the odds. A team led by psychologist Professor Michael Norton contacted over two thousand people whose net worth started at one million dollars and rose to an awful lot more. They were asked to rate their happiness on a ten-point scale, then say how much cash they'd need to be perfectly happy. 'All the way up the income-wealth spectrum,' Norton reported, 'basically everyone says two or three times as much.'

Perfectly happy. They're not going to be perfectly happy. But that's the flaw. It's part of the dream we weave of reality. It tells us there's a destination. But we'll never stop wanting more. And, even though we may suffer wafts of imposter syndrome when feeling out of our depth in specific situations, we're ultimately pretty good at accepting any status that happens to wash back in our direction. This counts, too, for elites at the top of their games. They accept it. They get used to it. They become acclimatised to the myriad ways they measure status: money; power; influence; flattery; clothing and jewellery; mode of transport and allocation of seat therein; holiday and residential locations; numbers of staff; size and luxury of house and workspace; laughter at jokes; eye contact; body language; measures of orange juice poured in a glass. *They've earned it!* Then they want more. They get more. Then *that* becomes normalised. It's in this way that our bosses, politicians and celebrities can become drunk on status, their behaviour growing ever more crazed.

Status drunkenness is extraordinary and ordinary and testament to how the game can intoxicate human cognition. Newspapers abound with tales of reported diva demands: Tom Cruise requesting a restaurant be emptied so he could eat in peace; Kanye West declaring his dressing room carpet 'too bumpy' and insisting it be ironed; Madonna demanding hers be 'stripped of DNA by a sterilisation team' – all exercises of power that symbolise massively elevated status.

Some national leaders are worse. The Czarina, Anna of Russia, insisted her courtiers wore a different suit each time she saw them. Imelda Marcos, former First Lady of the Philippines, had a thirst for success symbols that's legendary: after enjoying a safari in Kenya she flew a menagerie of African mammals into Calauit Island, evicting two hundred and fifty-four families to make way for it; such was her love of building and buying impressive buildings, including several in Manhattan, it was joked she had an 'edifice complex'; after the Marcoses fled their palace, a single receipt from a 1978 splurge in a New York Bulgari store was found for nearly one and a half million dollars. Marcos's brain wove a self-serving dream that said such extravagance was virtuous, her 'duty' to the poor: 'You have to be some kind of light, a star to give them guidelines.' But my favourite national leader is Turkmenistan's Saparmurat Niyazov, aka the 'Father of all Turkmen', who renamed the days of the week, a crater on the moon, a breed of horse, a city, a canal, the months of the year and the word for bread after himself and members of his family. He then had a huge gold-plated statue erected of himself, in the capital, which rotated so he always faced the sun.

Status drunkenness is practically the defining condition of royalty, with its palaces and crowns and compulsory rituals of deference. Prince Andrew was attacked for spending tens of thousands of taxpayer pounds on private flights to watch golf, but his extravagance had nothing on his ancestor George IV. After George's rival Napoleon enjoyed a lavish coronation as Emperor of France, he determined his celebration would be superior. It was marked with a preposterous feast in Westminster Hall that included 80 joints of venison, 80 joints of beef, 400 calves feet, 40 salmon, 40 trout,

80 turbot, 1,610 chickens, 160 vegetable dishes, 160 geese and three-quarters of a ton of bacon. On the drinks menu were 240 bottles of Burgundy, 1,200 bottles of champagne and 2,400 bottles of claret. The first course was escorted in by the Duke of Wellington, Lord Howard and the Marquess of Anglesey, who rode into the dining hall on horseback.

Today's titans of capitalism often ache with the flaw, their shining headquarters being flophouses of status drunkenness. The condition of terrible, gibbering conceit that's befallen some of our leaders of industry and finance was exposed following the global financial crisis. When the CEOs of Ford, Chrysler and General Motors travelled to Washington on a begging mission for public money, they did so in private jets. Over in the UK a household name was made of Fred Goodwin, the CEO who walked the Royal Bank of Scotland into debts of over £24 billion and a taxpayer bailout of £45 billion.

Goodwin's merciless appetite for cost-cutting earned him the title 'Fred the Shred'. But such sacrifices were not for him. In 2005 he oversaw the opening of a £350 million headquarters in which, newspapers reported, he'd had the director's kitchens relocated so his favourite lunch of scallops wouldn't get too cold en route to table. Fresh fruit was flown in daily from Paris. When a tiny stain was spotted in the lobby outside his football pitch-sized office, he ordered its redecoration with £1,000-per-roll wallpaper. One day, Goodwin sent an email threatening disciplinary action after being accidentally served a pink biscuit, subject line: ROGUE BISCUIT.

All of which shows that status drunkenness is real and resentment can be fun. But as pleasurable as listing the excesses of the elites can be, the flaw that leads to them can be damaging to us all, not least when they manifest in the companies for which we work. Research by organisational psychologist Professor Dennis Tourish found people in lower corporate ranks tend to 'habitually exaggerate the extent to which they agree with the opinions and actions of higher-status people as a means of acquiring influence' while critical views are mostly kept quiet. And then the flaw kicks in. Leaders, being human, are vulnerable to believing all this lovely status-boosting news. They often accept praise and agreement uncritically and fail to grow suspicious over the lack of bad news. Those who attempt to deliver it are often punished with a reputation for being difficult, overly negative or not 'team players'. They can ultimately find their careers in jeopardy.

These bosses observe their place in the game and weave a self-serving dream that explains it. Their brains make them the star of a heroic story in which their elevated status is wholly deserved. Stuck in their delusion, any news that flatters feels like truth, just as any counter-news feels like an unjust attack. Reasonable dissenters are cast as villains and penalised. Other players, now fearful, hold their tongue. This situation is not uncommon. One survey found 85 per cent of employees feeling unable to 'raise an issue or concern to their bosses even though they felt that the issue was important'. When Tourish and his team go into companies and report back negative staff opinion, leaders are 'frequently shocked'. Whilst some take it seriously, 'many bitterly contest the findings. They argue that no one has ever brought such issues to their attention before and that the data must therefore be flawed.'

Canny players sense the flaw in their elites and seek to improve their own rank with flattery. And flattery works: Tourish calls it a 'perfumed trap'. A study of 451 CEOs found leaders who were exposed to more frequent and intense flattery and agreement rated their own abilities more highly, were less able to change course when things went wrong, and led firms that were more likely to suffer persistently poor performance. When Tourish warns leaders about such dangers they usually nod in easy agreement. 'During workshops, many have swapped amusing anecdotes that vividly describe the process in action,' he writes. But 'they then mostly go on to assume that they themselves are immune to its effects. In reality, they almost never are.' Tellingly Tourish has found the most successful leaders are usually those with the 'least compliant' followers.

Of course, most of us will never breathe these levels of status. But we can still find warning from the experiences of CEOs, royals and celebrities. We all, to some extent or other, live inside a self-serving story. When we find ourselves spoiled or flattered and fluttered at, we can often fail to question it. We accept it, we enjoy it, and we deserve more. And we're never satisfied with what we get. So we play on, believing the next move or the move after that will make us happy, perhaps even perfectly so.

But status never makes us perfectly happy. In a small but fascinating study, psychologists persuaded fifteen highly identifiable American celebrities, including a top-tier Hollywood actor, a basketball hero and an R&B superstar, to submit to an analysis of what actually happens at the Paul McCartney heights. They described the initial surge of major status as something fantastical. One recalled, 'the swell of people, the requests, the letters, the emails, the greetings on the street, the people in cars, the honking of the horns, the screaming of your name . . . it starts to build and build like a small tornado, and it's coming at you, and coming at you.' Out of nowhere, 'you're worth something. You're important.'

Then comes the brain-story that says they've earned it. 'My life is different in that people kiss my ass and that's not always a good thing because then you start believing that your ass is worthy of being kissed,' said another. 'You have to constantly stay on guard for that. And I think it's very hard. There are times when I exploit that. I take advantage of people sucking up to me, or the power that I wield.' As overwhelming as it is, it's not enough. It's never enough. Said another, 'I've been addicted to almost every substance known to man and the most addicting of them all is fame.'

Then, paranoia. 'I don't think you trust anybody the same way when you become well-known . . . are they laughing at my jokes because they think I'm funny or because it's me saying them?' They start to lose people they love. 'I've lost friends . . . they feel inferior . . . You're special and they aren't. The next thing you know, they'd really rather not have anything to do with you.' Some superstars expressed disillusionment with the game. But it wasn't the status itself that was the problem. Rather they weren't getting the *right kind* of status: they had plenty of the success variety, now they wanted status for their virtue. 'You find out there are millions of people who like you for what you do. They couldn't care less who you are.'

The flaw is a component of the dream we weave around reality. It's a quirk in our cognition that keeps us in the game and playing. If there's any consolation in these stories it's that, paradoxically, it's something of a leveller. The elites, so far above us, will never find what they're looking for. No matter who we are or how high on the scoreboard we climb, life is a game that never ends.

12

The Universal Prejudice

THERE'S A UNIVERSAL prejudice, a bias that unites humanity: we don't like those who swagger about above us in the higher ranks. This is a resentment that transcends politics, class, gender and culture. Its gangrene drips through all of human life. People feel perfectly comfortable being perfectly cruel about celebrities, CEOs, politicians and royalty, as if their elevated rank makes them immune to pain. Some time ago, I caught myself chuckling at a tweet that said, 'These are all real *Telegraph* columnists: Sophia Money-Coutts, Harry de Quetteville, Hamish de Bretton-Gordon, Boudicca Fox-Leonard.' With a pinch of self-reproach I realised I was simply being invited to point and laugh at posh people. At last count, that tweet had been liked 27,000 times.

This discomfort we feel towards conspicuously high-status players stretches back through the millennia and is a wired-in component of our game-playing cognition. Humans have always been incorrigible seekers of rank. Our jostling for position was managed in Stone Age societies with such force that their hierarchies were much shallower than we're used to today, with less inequality between the top and the bottom. One recent study found no evidence of significantly heightened stress in low status women of the 'egalitarian' Hadza tribe of northern Tanzania. It's sometimes claimed hunter-gatherers had no status game at all, and that we evolved in a kind of naive bliss of perfect equality. But it would be a mistake to conclude these shallow hierarchies are evidence we're not programmed to care about status. On the contrary, writes the psychologist Professor Paul Bloom, 'egalitarian lifestyles of the hunter-gatherers exist because the individuals care a lot about status. Individuals in these societies end up roughly equal because everyone is struggling to ensure that nobody gets too much power over him or her.'

These relatively flat arenas of play were made possible by our being highly sensitive to signs of 'big shot' behaviour and hotly policing it. A climate of 'militant egalitarianism' was maintained in which our anti-big shot instincts ensured no single player could grow too grand. In contemporary hunter-gatherer groups, hunters who appear overly proud of their catch are routinely mocked: the anthropologist Dr Elizabeth Cashdan writes that among the !Kung hunters of the Kalahari, 'if an individual does not minimise or speak lightly of his own accomplishments, his friends and relatives will not hesitate to do it for him'. They've been recorded teasing one such man, asking of his kill, 'What is it? Some kind of rabbit?' In Inuit camps, when subtle facial disapproval, open shaming and public ridicule don't succeed in dampening big shot behaviour, the entire tribe gathers around the cocky offender to sing a 'song of derision' in their face. Modern hunter-gatherer gossip remains preoccupied with 'norm violations by high-status individuals'. Studies in the developed world find we too prefer tattle about high-status people, preferably of our own gender – rivals in our games.

Our ill feeling towards high-status players has been captured in the lab. When neuroscientists had participants read about someone popular, rich and smart, they saw brain regions involved in the perception of pain become activated. When they read of this invented person suffering a demotion, their pleasure systems flared up.

Psychologists see this effect cross-culturally, with one study in Japan and Australia finding participants took pleasure in the felling of a 'tall poppy': the higher their status, the greater the enjoyment of their de-grading. The most venomous levels of envy were reported when the poppy's success was in a 'domain that was important to the participant, such as academic achievement among students' – when they were rivals in their games.

And yet, as we've learned, we're also *drawn* to high-status people: we crave contact with the famous, the successful and the brilliant. So our relationship with elite players is thunderously ambivalent. On one hand, we gather close to them, offering them status in order to learn from them and, in the process, become statusful ourselves. On the other, we experience grinding resentments towards them. This, perhaps, is one result of the mismatch between our neural game-playing equipment and the massively outsized structure of modern games. Our brains may be specialised for small tribal groups but today – especially at work and online – we play colossal games in which poppies loom over us like redwoods. Status is relative: the higher others rise, the lower we sit in comparison. It's a resource and their highly visible thriving steals it from us. The exceptions we make tend to be for ambassadors for our groups: artists, thinkers, athletes and leaders with whom we strongly identify. They seem to symbolise us, somehow. They carry with them a piece of our own identity, a pound of our flesh – so their success becomes our success and we cheer it wildly. To our subconscious these idols are fantastically accomplished versions of us: our *copy, flatter, conform* cognition overrides our resentment.

The uncomfortable mismatch that exists between the small games we're programmed to play and the stretched games we actually play is the source of much conflict and injustice. The great stretching of the human game began when we abandoned our campsites for settled farming and herding communities. The old tribal clans that were based around extended-family networks found permanent homes and fields in which to work. They then connected into larger communities. These were often centred around villages, called chiefdoms. These extended-family-based groups began to specialise, arranging themselves around certain games: blacksmiths, carpenters, herders. These became castes. Social status position and occupation became increasingly defined by kin and lineage: you could be born into a weaving, milk-selling or carcass-rendering caste. The class system we have today, in which a person's future status and occupation is strongly influenced by the accident of their birth, is a continuation of a process that stretches back thousands of years, to the dawn of civilisation.

In these ancient communities, one family-based clan would inevitably become wealthier and more powerful than the others. As settled life developed, there grew food surpluses immeasurably greater than that which existed in earlier eras. There was also division of land. For the first time, major wealth began to accumulate in private hands. Most of it floated upwards, to the clan at the top. And how would they explain their rise? By telling a self-serving story which said they deserved to be there: that they were truly special. They'd often forbid intermarriage with lower clans, a move that enabled them to define themselves as a categorically separate, divine class of human. They'd lead the chiefdom, either via a council of elders or a single ruler.

With these new accumulations of status and its symbols, the old method of policing the game began to fail. Human tribes once successfully shrivelled their hierarchies using gossip: big shots and big shot behaviour were punished by the people. But now high-and-mighty rulers were able to emerge. And so our prehuman craving for major status roared forth in reanimated triumph. The status these elites experienced would've felt deserved to them, even god-given, as their brains wove their predictable, self-serving dreams. Then the flaw kicked in: they acclimatised to their levels of status and wanted more. Grabbing greater status meant leading larger groups: more players beneath them meant more influence, more deference and more things that glittered. As populations increased, territories merged and elites sought to expand their domains in acts of invasion; chiefdoms became kingdoms and states and empires. Our fields of play became gigantic, the elites now playing above us at a godlike distance.

As much as the great stretching benefitted those at the top, players on the lowest rungs began to suffer. They grew weaker and sicker. Skeletons from 3,500-year-old tombs in Greece show high-status royals were two to three inches taller than commoners, and had an average of one dental cavity to their three. Over in Chile, elite mummies buried with ornaments and gold hair clips were found to have a 400 per cent lower incidence of bone lesions caused by infectious disease, with commoner women suffering markedly more than their men. Our settling down and claiming the earth triggered a monstrous expansion of the status game from which we've never recovered.

Humans are today as we've always been: ambitious and delusional animals. We're also jealous and resentful. Conspicuous symbols of others' thriving – wealth, possessions, double-barrelled surnames in the *Daily Telegraph* – can alter how we play the game of life. They can change us, making us meaner, harder and less co-operative. Social networks researcher Professor Nicholas Christakis led an experiment in which participants played in three online worlds, the first egalitarian, the second with midrange Scandinavian levels of inequality, the third with enlarged U.S. levels. Each set of players was randomly assigned to be rich or poor and given real money. They then had to decide whether to contribute to the wealth of the group, take advantage for their own selfish ends or defect. Surprisingly, what made the most difference to their behaviour wasn't the level of inequality in their game, but whether or not the inequality was visible. When players' wealth was hidden everyone, including the elites, became more egalitarian. But when wealth was displayed, players in every game became less friendly, cooperated 'roughly half as much' and the rich were significantly more likely to exploit the poor.

Humanity's great stretching also led to another quirk of life that's common and dreadfully consequential. As we've learned, we evolved to play status games informally: whilst our rank, in hunter-gatherer tribes, was sometimes indicated externally in success cues – the hunter's necklace of bones; the chief's safer sleeping site – mostly it would've been sensed. We'd detect it in body language, voice tones and levels of deference. But when we formed settled societies, chiefs, kings, priests, prime ministers and CEOs had their high status confirmed in titles and rituals, acts of enforced deference and splendour. And so two parallel games began to be played: the *formal* game, announced in the grand hierarchies of culture, economy and society, and the informal *true* game, that continued to occur in the minds of the players.

This leads to a phenomenon that might be called the Prince Charles Paradox, in which one person can be simultaneously high and low in status. Prince Charles enjoys superlative amounts of *formal* status, being next in line to the British throne. But he's also relatively low in *true* status, with only around half of his British subjects holding a positive opinion of him. These dynamics can generate wild storms of misery for players when their leaders – be they a paranoid royal or a horrible boss – become insecure about their level of true status and demand of them ever-greater demonstrations of loyalty, subservience and adoration.

Formal games madden us further by offering formal prizes that are zero-sum, with one person's winning meaning another's loss. This is especially true in the modern era. The writing game that authors play is full of such zero-sum battles: limited spots in newspaper review pages; 'new release' displays in book shops; positions in numbered sales ranks and the status of 'lead title' at publishing houses. From our first day at school right up to retirement, most of us find ourselves warring over status-freighted prizes. Life in the tribe would have featured far fewer such contests. Though I can't prove it, I suspect our massively increased exposure to formal zero-sum play is responsible for much of the misery, anxiety and exhaustion we experience as twenty-first-century players. It certainly causes a lot of the hostility we feel towards others.

We didn't evolve to play games formally and we didn't evolve to play games so steep. But we did evolve to feel resentment. A long time ago, this dangerous emotion helped keep our tribes functional and their hierarchies shallow. It would prick us into punishing those we felt were swaggering above us, attempting to claim status that was undeserved. Today we're surrounded by such people. The resentments they trigger can sour the story we tell of the world, populating it with a ceaseless line-up of villains at whom we point and jeer and sing our songs of derision in all our righteousness and envy.

13

Living the Dream

WHEN I WAS 14 I bought a Mötley Crüe T-shirt from the sale bin in Woolworths (Theatre of Pain tour; £3.99). Wearing it in public for the first time made me absurdly proud. I was narcissistic on behalf of my glam metal kin: we were *better* than those idiots who liked boybands or rave. I knew this to be the truth and I knew it totally. And now I was showing it, the imagined status somehow pouring into me as I trotted like a prat up and down the pedestrian precinct. This kind of behaviour, of course, is not unusual. It's a standard component of human life. The social taboo against big shot behaviour doesn't hold for being boastful on behalf of our groups. On the contrary it's considered ordinary, even laudable, to express such feelings.

To understand why, we can travel to the Republic of Niger and the city of Maradi. It is 1974 and the anthropologist Professor Jerome Barkow has encountered a puzzle. Many of Maradi's citizens were descendants of royal refugees from the nearby kingdom of Katsina. Back in the nineteenth century, their families had been forced to flee after their homelands were invaded by Islamic jihadists. These royal descendants were now poor, having never recovered the elite stature of their ancestors. Barkow expected them to harbour a vengeful hatred of the Muslims who'd robbed them of their status. But, to his surprise, the opposite seemed true. 'I was startled to find no hint of resistance to Islam, despite the area's history,' he writes. 'Instead, I found individual after individual who claimed to come from a deeply pious and scholarly family.' Not only had Islam become a powerful force, it was growing.

It didn't make sense. So Barkow began asking questions. He found two direct descendants of Katsina royalty to interview. One had embraced Islam, the other hadn't. Daya had studied with a Koranic scholar since boyhood. By 16 he'd memorised the Koran and could recite it in sections – an achievement entitling him to a prestigious graduation ceremony called a *sauka*. Daya continued to study the Koran for several hours a day. He had two wives, three children and was poor but proud. At that time, Maradi was occupied by the French. Daya resented the countrymen who'd chosen to play the colonials' game, enjoying their Francophile education and gaining status within their systems of power. 'His opinion of the French-educated bureaucratic elite was scathing. His respect was reserved for the Koranic scholars, and he was spending several hours each day with them, and shared much of his income with them.'

Then there was Shida. Like Daya, he too was a direct descendant of Katsina royalty. Like Daya, he hadn't benefitted from the Francophone schooling of the bureaucratic elite. But neither had Shida received a Koranic education. Instead he'd followed a more traditional path, apprenticing himself to a trade, first to a tailor, then a peanut buyer. But apprenticing didn't suit Shida. He kept quarrelling with his mentors and his professional relationships would break down. A close friend blamed his failures on his 'nobleman's heart'. He believed Shida's connection to royalty had made him too proud; he couldn't lower himself to the rank of apprentice peanut buyer. When Barkow met Shida, he was being financially supported by his wife and mother. 'Unlike Daya, who conveyed an impression of energy and self-confidence, Shida seemed physically weak, stooped, and uncertain.'

Both men revelled in their statusful royal backgrounds. Both men had begun their adult lives full of ambition. But only Daya had found a game to play that provided status enough to satisfy his nobleman's heart. Daya had 'based his self-esteem on a conception of himself as a good Moslem'. For him, and for other royal descendants Barkow interviewed, 'only Islamic learning was worthy of prestige. Other kinds of learning, when discussed at all, were disparaged as just a means of getting money. Daya and many like him were privately scornful of the Francophone elite who, however, largely monopolised political power . . . he could evaluate himself as of higher standing than the ruling bureaucrats by using prestige criteria having to do with Islam.'

In order for his status game to work for him, Daya had to have faith in its 'prestige criteria'. And so his brain wove for him a dream that said the game of Islam was not an act of shared imagination, but true. He was a virtuous actor in a god-created reality. This became his neural territory, his world. Its rules and symbols – its 'prestige criteria' – felt unquestionably valid. His memorising of the Koran meant something real. He believed his dream was true and he believed it totally. He had to. The logic of the status game demands we consider our groups to be worthy of high esteem. If we don't think they're inherently statusful, how can we draw status from them? Belief in the dream nourished Daya: it filled his nobleman's heart with 'energy and self-confidence'. He tied himself to its puppet strings. It became his identity. Just as Ben Gunn rescued himself from having his status removed in prison, and Elliot Rodger temporarily rescued himself from bullying and rejection in the World of Warcraft, so Daya rescued himself from having his royal rank removed – by joining the very game responsible for his ancestors' fall. Whilst he thrived, the other man shrivelled. Shida didn't believe in the status game of peanut buying, and that left him 'weak, stooped, and uncertain'.

Within the games we play, we police each other. It's in everyone's interest the game remains fair and stable and that big shots are managed. But no such policing happens in status competitions *between* games. On the contrary, our co-players award us even more status when we behave in ways that boost our game's rank and diminish that of our rivals: when we sneer, for example, that the Francophone elite are only in it for the money. When pricked by status anxiety, we often look at our rival games – the corporations, the religions, the football clubs, the music tribes, the school cliques, the nations – and convince ourselves ours is somehow superior. Even if they're above us in the hierarchy of games, we'll tell stories that say we'd rather be where *we* are. Our game is the one: *our* football team, *our* company, *our* clique, *our* tribe, *our* religion. This grandiosity we feel for our games is highly conspicuous in sports. Even if a football team is low in the league, its supporters can spend much of their social time persuading each other that they're actually somehow superior. They seek out canny arguments to devalue rivals, reframing losses as injustices or near-wins and reliving glories from the past. The more they convince each other, the more their dream thickens up and the more narcissistic they grow on behalf of their games. This is status play. It's dishonest and it's spiteful and it's one of life's great pleasures.

This groupish grandiosity is also conspicuous in nationalism. One study into 'national narcissism' asked thousands of students across thirty-five countries, 'What contribution do you think the country you are living in has made to world history?' Their totals added up to a hilariously impossible 1,156 per cent. Just like sports fans, many citizens draw personal status from that of their nation, even if unconsciously. I don't consider myself nationalistic even slightly but when I moved to Australia I had the dismaying experience of finding myself speaking in an exaggerated English accent in public. I had to force myself to speak normally. It was embarrassing, and actually a terrible strategy for gaining status in Australia. Nevertheless, to some moronic part of my brain, my sense of myself as an English person was clearly important (I'd also get annoyed when they called us 'whingeing poms', even though we are.)

Research into the effects of national status on individual happiness suggests I'm not alone. A study tracking happiness in Britain over the last two centuries, by analysing the language in millions of books and newspaper articles, found the national mood experienced a peak in the 1880s. This might've been an era of widespread poverty, disease and child labour, but it was when Britain was near the top of the global status game, approaching the pinnacle of empire. The pleasure this conjured in ordinary people can be glimpsed in the memory of author Laurie Lee who recalled in his 1920s classroom, 'a wall of maps with all the colonial possessions marked in red and we used to sit there; we were very poor in those days, poor but uncomplaining, we lived on boiled and baked cabbage, the poorest of the poor. And we used to sit there, looking at these maps and thinking, we are the greatest in the world. We own all those pieces of red on that map, on that world map. The whole of Africa, the whole of India, all those islands across the Pacific. Then we'd look at each other as if we were centurions.'

Whether they're nations, religions or football supporters, status games are made out of people. In order to believe our games are superior, we must believe its players are also superior. Psychologists have long known of our primal instinct for thinking better of our playmates. Humans have a bias for their own that's universal, subconscious and triggered at the slightest provocation. As soon as we connect into a group, bound by even the loosest of ties, the unfair status-boosting begins. In one study, 5-year-olds were given a coloured T-shirt to wear and were then shown pictures of various children, some in matching shirts, others not. They knew their colour was random and meaningless and yet they *still* thought more positively of kids wearing the same colour, believing them to be more generous and kind. They also rewarded them unfairly, allocating them more toy coins in a game. They even remained more statusful in their memories: they were better able to recall the positive actions of their shirt-wearing brethren than the equally positive actions of those in different colours.

This is the truth of human nature: we're helpless players of games and are programmed to play unfairly. The brain judges our status in contest mode, by comparing what we have to others. The more our group possesses, and the higher it climbs versus rival groups, the more of the great prize we personally win. Perhaps even more damaging than our tendency towards avarice and shadiness is the fact our brains hide these behaviours from us. They tell a self-serving story in which we're not calculating players of games but moral heroes. It's not us or our co-players who are deluded, greedy and corrupt, it's everyone else. It's the blue T-shirts that are *truly* superior, it's the Islamists, it's the French, it's the British Empire, it's that prat in the precinct who spent four quid in Woolworths and now thinks he's King of Tunbridge Wells.

14

Subjugation, Revolution, Civilisation

OUR TENDENCY TO believe the stories spun by brains and cultures is a source of much of the injustice that's stained human history. Determined as we are to award ourselves and our playmates all the prizes, we excel at perceiving only the self-serving sliver of the truth. Our stories often benefit us, convincing us of the righteousness of our fight, motivating us to play harder for ever-greater rank. But they can sometimes work against us. They can even persuade us to conspire in our own subjugation.

This is a role the great religions have played. The hidden truth of religions is that they're status games: Muslims, Buddhists, Hindus and Christians agree a set of rules and symbols by which to play, then form a hierarchy along which they rise and fall. The dream that's woven over this truth often tells of major status rewards not in this life but the next. Religions, it hardly needs pointing out, are virtue games. This means that to succeed – to earn connection and respect in this life and then heaven or a superior life via reincarnation – a player must be moralistic, faithful, obedient and dutiful. They must do as their gods, priests and sacred texts instruct.

The ultimate purpose of all status games is control. They were designed by evolution to generate cooperation between humans; to force (in the case of dominance) or bribe (in the case of the prestige games of success and virtue) us to conform. It's thought the major religions came about as a way of controlling the unprecedented numbers of people that began living side-by-side in the first 'mega-societies'. Gossip alone couldn't manage hundreds of thousands of disparate people, as it had in the hunter-gatherer era, so we invented moralising gods that tempted and punished us into behaving. At the time of writing, there's a fierce debate amongst academics about whether moralising gods preceded large, complex societies or co-evolved alongside them. Most researchers agree, however, about the fundamental role of 'big religion'. It created a standard set of rules and symbols by which players of different languages, ethnicities and cultural backgrounds could play. And they believed them. They lived the dream of reality they'd been sold.

Theirs was an era dominated by the virtue games of faith, caste and sovereign. A taste of that highly stratified virtue-bound life can be found in the Hindu caste system. At over two thousand years old, it's probably the oldest cultural status game on earth. It's also likely the most complex, with 3,000 castes and 25,000 subcastes organised into five major strata: priests and teachers at the top who were made from the creator god Brahma's head; warriors and rulers that came from his arms; farmers, traders and merchants from his thighs; labourers from his feet; and then, at the bottom, the untouchables. Caste didn't only define a player's occupation but their rights, duties, rituals and codes of behaviour, including what they could own, how they were buried and even their practices of personal hygiene.

Life for the untouchables has been savage for millennia. Early written references to untouchability are found in the Laws of Manu, which date to between the second and third century BC. People expressed 'grave anxiety' and 'horror' at having 'any kind of contact' with untouchables, writes researcher Malay Neerav. If a high-status person touched an untouchable they were required to bathe; if the shadow of an untouchable fell over a teacher's meal, the food would be rendered unclean and destroyed. They lived in separate colonies and didn't share wells. Romantic contact was taboo. In Mehrana, a village near New Delhi, a high-caste 16-year-old girl was caught with her 20-year-old untouchable boyfriend. The village elders held an all-night meeting, debating their punishment. When execution was proposed there were 'no protests'. Around three thousand residents, almost the entire village, watched the lovers being hanged from a banyan tree. That was in 1991. Today there are over 160 million untouchables in India. According to the *National Geographic*, they're still 'relegated to the lowest jobs and live in constant fear of being publicly humiliated, paraded naked, beaten, and raped with impunity by upper-caste Hindus seeking to keep them in their place. Merely walking through an upper-caste neighbourhood is a life-threatening offence.'

How does such a system remain stable? If we're all such relentlessly ambitious players, why have the untouchables cooperated, for thousands of years, with this monstrously degraded dream of life? Many do so because they believe it. Pious untouchables accept they've earned their de-grading by committing sins in a past life; only by following the rules in the present will they win higher status in the next. This is how many major religions have compelled people to conspire in their own subjugation. You win by knowing your place and staying in it, in the expectation of rewards after death. Everything was God-created, went the logic, so people were precisely where God wanted them to be. As the Christian hymn sings it: 'The rich man in his castle, the poor man at his gate, God made them high or lowly, and ordered their estate.'

If a low-caste player in a virtue society such as India did muster the vision to throw for higher rank, their co-players would often conspire to yank them back down. The novelist V. S. Naipaul writes of a businessman who, impressed with the intelligence of an untouchable servant, provided for his education and promotion. But years later, on his return to India, he found him back where he'd started, cleaning toilets. 'He had been boycotted by his clan for breaking away from them; he was barred from the evening smoking group. There was no other group he could join, no woman he could marry. His solitariness was insupportable, and he had returned to his duty.' Explaining this incident, political economist Professor Timur Kuran writes that 'by ostracizing a peer who has taken a better job, the latrine cleaners can protect their own personal and collective reputations. They can signal to the entire community, including groups higher up in the social hierarchy, their willingness to live by the prevailing social rules.' There was status to make by ruining the ambitious man so he was pulled back under by the luckless logic of the game.

In the modern era, not all of India's untouchables fully buy the ancient story that's responsible for their fates. One study found about a third accepting they'd earned untouchability by committing sins in past lives, with others blaming unfairness or believing a more self-serving version of the Hindu dream, claiming 'they never took a true plunge in status, that they were really Brahmans in disguise'. Tellingly, some untouchables seek to restore their sense of relative status by looking down at those even more untouchable than they. In his autobiography, untouchable writer Hazari speaks the words of a true player: 'We consider the untouchables of the Punjab lower than ourselves in the United Provinces; we would not marry with them, or even drink from the same vessel.'

Another major reason a society's hierarchy remains stable, and doesn't continually collapse into warring chaos, is that we're programmed to play local games, nose-to-nose with those around us. The great mass of folk aren't revolutionary or regicidal. Many don't seek complete supremacy. One study found more than 65 per cent of people not wanting the 'highest status rank'. Instead, we're preoccupied with the busy business of ordinary life and the status we expect it to supply. This is even more true in virtue-based societies and eras. Back in the age of kingdom and empire, we might've been ruled by some distant leader in theory, but we'd mostly be concerned with obligations to our tight-knit clan and adhering to its local rules and symbols. Life was small, confined to a small territory and a small group. Playing well with the people immediately around us would've characterised its game.

As long as those games functioned properly, and our group received the rewards it expected, the status quo would likely be maintained. A robust society is one in which the general populace is protected from outside threat and status trickles down in ways that are expected. Even if elite groups – the religious, legal, military, bureaucratic, aristocratic games – get nearly all the rewards, and bottom castes virtually none at all, stability won't usually be threatened. What creates revolutionary conditions isn't the steepness of the inequality but the perception the game has stopped paying out as it should.

This is why poverty alone doesn't tend to lead to revolutions. Revolutions – defined as mass movements to replace a ruling order in the name of social justice – have been found to occur in middle-income countries more than the poorest. Sociologist Professor Jack Goldstone writes, 'what matters is that people feel they are losing their proper place in society for reasons that are not inevitable and not their fault'. The anxiety caused by their games' loss of status reflects that which is found in the depression and suicide research. What goes for ourselves goes for our groups: when we and our people sense our collective status is in decline, we become dangerously distressed.

When a game's status begins to slip, its players can be merciless. But for a revolution to succeed, the games at the bottom of the hierarchy require the help of the elites: 'indeed,' writes Goldstone, 'in most revolutions it is the elites who mobilise the population to help them overthrow the regime.' Examinations of the years leading up to revolutions tend to find 'rulers have become weakened, erratic, or predatory so that many of the elites no longer feel rewarded or supported, and are not inclined to support the regime'. Elites then conspire with games beneath them, 'popular groups' such as peasant communes, workers' unions, professional guilds or youth organisations, who also feel their position is declining and their expected rewards are not being met.

Such dynamics drove Tunisia's 'Jasmine Revolution'. In the twenty-eight days between December 2010 and January 2011 the lower-middle-income country secured the exile of its president of twenty-four years, Zine El Abidine Ben Ali. The Tunisian population had experienced a 'youth bulge'. This led to food shortages and the end of subsidies for education, fuel and food, and a decline in statusful government jobs for graduates. Unemployment soared, especially amongst the educated middle classes, who were denied their expected prestigious careers. Meanwhile, Ben Ali was handsomely rewarding his tight inner circle with gains often taken from the business community from whom he'd demand payoffs.

The nation's games were failing. The president was blamed. Some of the rage was focussed on his increasingly aggressive and corrupt police force. On 17 December street vendor Mohamed Bouazizi set himself on fire in protest at being repeatedly harassed for bribes. He'd apparently been humiliated, that day, by the municipal inspector Faida Hamdy: his family claim she took his weighing scales, assaulted him and insulted his dead father. 'Bouazizi's actions resonated among Tunisians who keenly felt the lack of opportunities and constant harassment under Ben Ali's rule,' writes Goldstone. Crowds gathered. The police fired, killing protestors. Their attempts at censoring the media failed: young Tunisians used Facebook more than youth in any other North African country, which enabled the scenes to spread and, with them, the protests. The revolution was on, crucially supported by 'a remarkable array of organisations'. One, the Tunisian

General Labour Union, organised national strikes, then the army refused to shoot at Tunisian citizens. Games up and down the hierarchy turned on Ben Ali. Just four weeks after Bouazizi's protest, he fled.

Elsewhere, Goldstone finds a predictable precursor to societal collapse to be 'elite-overproduction' – when too many elite players are produced and have to fight over too few high-status positions. A moderate level of overproduction is beneficial, as it creates healthy competition and increases the quality of the elites that do end up occupying its most prestigious positions, in government, media, the legal world, and so on. But too much overproduction leads to resentful cadres of failed elites forming their own status games in opposition to the successful. They begin warring for status, attacking the establishment, which contributes to its destabilisation. Goldstone finds these dynamics in the years leading up to the English Civil War, the French Revolution and crises in China and Turkey. Once again, we find chaos and history being made in the aftermath of the game's expected rewards failing to pay out.

Even when societies don't fall to revolution or elite overproduction, those who rule them can become tamed and toppled by status play. This is true for civilisations that have endured for centuries. When a status-hungry imperial force conquers a people, they establish themselves as elites. As the generations pass, indigenous people, seeking status, increasingly play the empire's games, adopting its rules and symbols: speaking its language, worshipping its gods, working for its institutions. Eventually, desiring full and unprejudiced membership of the elites, they demand equal status and often do so with aggression in the form of civil disobedience, legal challenge or violence. Thus begins the fall of the empire's founders. Historian Professor Yuval Noah Harari describes this as the 'imperial cycle' by which conquered cultures are 'digested' by imperial games that continue to 'flourish and develop' even after its founders are long ejected.

These dynamics have unified regions such as China and India, creating vast civilisations. In India, the British brought oppression, murder, and exploitation, but they also stitched together what had been a 'bewildering mosaic of warring kingdoms, principalities and tribes', founded the judicial system, built the railways essential for the economy and an administrative structure that remains relied upon today. During the Raj, 'many Indians adopted, with the zest of converts, Western ideas such as self-determination and human rights, and were dismayed when the British refused to live up to their own declared values by granting native Indians neither equal rights as British subjects or independence', writes Harari. This pattern of status-striving has repainted the world. Most humans alive today are playing by the rules and symbols of their long-vanquished overlords.

The hidden rules of the status game have helped drive human history. Over hundreds and thousands of years our endless strivings have led to invasion, subjugation, revolution, oppression and civilisation. This should come as no surprise. After all, history is made by people and people are born to play.

15

Making a Player

IN MODERN WESTERN societies, we live inside a story that says, if we want it badly enough, we can do anything. Open the door, step outside, *go for it*. This cultural myth tells us to shoot for the moon. But the reality of shooting for the moon is that it requires years of training, millions of dollars, the support of a major space agency and a rocket. Without that, you'll fall to earth and break your back. It takes a certain kind of person, with a certain kind of background, to successfully shoot for the moon. And you're probably not it.

The sad fact is, the human world doesn't actually resemble a bazaar crammed with games we can select at will. The reasons we find ourselves playing the games we do are several, not random, and frequently out of our control. They tend to form between people who have aspects of character and personality in common: teachers, soldiers, politicians, comedians, competitive cat groomers and astronauts tend to be coalitions of like-minded people. Nobody gets to choose exactly what kind of mind they have – whether they're confident, shy, a genius, extroverted, or love boxing or literature or smoking weed or the politics of left or right. These things mostly happen to us depending on how our brains develop and what kinds of experiences we have.

Three major forces conspire to push us in certain directions: genes, upbringing and peer group. We've already learned how, especially in childhood, the brain draws information from the culture that surrounds it and shapes us to its contours. But the process of honing begins before even this. The brain's roughly 86 billion neurons are made in the womb, as are major components of our hormonal and neurochemical systems. This is the biological equipment through which we'll process reality – and its design is unique to us. How it's wired up is directed partly by random biological events and partly by instructions encoded in genes we inherit from our parents. This genome strongly influences the ways we perceive and respond to the games of life. For instance, how anxious we are is thought to depend partly on a brain region called the amygdala and a hormone called serotonin. Just as nobody has exactly the same fingerprints, nobody has exactly the same amygdalae or serotonin system. Some people happen to be wired with an increased sensitivity to threat: their alarm is triggered more easily. They're likely to be more neurotic, more cautious and more sensitive to criticism. They may also struggle socially.

This personality difference can have a significant effect on the games they'll end up playing. Someone high in anxiety may be attracted to different games than a natural taker of risks. When I interviewed personality psychologist Professor Daniel Nettle, he predicted that, as a writer, I'd be high in the traits of neuroticism and openness to experience: I took a personality test and discovered he was correct. Researchers find 'the jobs in which we spend a large portion of our lives and the prestige and income that comes from those jobs are at least partly influenced by the genes we inherit from our parents'. For geneticist Professor Robert Plomin, the contribution our genes make to our becoming who we are is 'not just statistically significant, it is massive'.

Our genes also influence how successful we'll be. People wired to experience greater feelings of thrill and reward when they win are more likely to become wealthy. Most billionaires become billionaires, in part, because they're monstrously competitive. They may be extroverts who, writes Nettle, 'tend to be ambitious' and 'are prepared to work very hard in pursuit of fame or money'. Even more successful are those with a stellar capacity for self-control. This is associated with a trait known as conscientiousness, which is the 'most reliable personality predictor of occupational success across the board'.

So we're born with inherited tendencies, a set of predilections, a groove that guides our development. But genes don't spell destiny or doom. During our formative years, our brains continue being wired up by the rules and symbols of our time and place. Early life experiences steer us, one way or another, into becoming specific types of people with specific suites of beliefs, interests and attitudes about the world. These help define our modes of play. Anthropologist Professor Adrie Kusserow has made a fascinating investigation into how social class impacts parenting. She spent time with white parents in three New York City area communities: impoverished Queenston where she 'could never wear sandals because of all the broken crack vials littering the streets'; patriotic, blue-collar Kelley, its residents of mainly Irish, German and Italian heritage, a 'safe and neat community' with a 'great deal of pride'; and finally, Parkside, a wealthy district in Manhattan.

Poor and blue-collar children were taught the game was tough and success required resilience. Qualities not tolerated in youngsters included: 'spoiled', 'fresh', 'whiny', 'weak-minded', 'prissy', 'soft', 'mushy' and 'pushover'. One Queenston mother told Kusserow, 'you shouldn't pay too much attention to any emotion and you shouldn't baby them too much, give them too much praise. You don't want them to be too soft.' During one interview, a 4-year-old spilled her grape juice, causing her mother to yell, 'That's great, Laura, just great. Clean it up before I smack you one.' Kids in Queenston and

Kelley were also taught respect for the fundamental parent–child status hierarchy. 'Examples of the child's lower status were manifested in the child not having access to all parts of the house or pieces of furniture (for example, the parent's bedroom, the dining room for guests, a father's chair) and the child having to use a respectful tone of voice in talking with parents.'

In both these groups, status was awarded for being maximally resilient. But the parents differed profoundly in their reasons for making this such an important rule. In Queenston, resilience was required to give children the strength of character to protect themselves from absolute destruction at the game's bottom. Queenston parents 'saw themselves as holding their own in a jungle of violence and corrupt youth'. In Kelley, resilience took a more optimistic form. There, it was required to break through into better status games. They wanted their young to have the mettle to: 'try things out', 'stand out', 'get a lot more out of this world', 'break away', 'go for your dreams'. One parent told Kusserow, 'I want my kids to definitely strive for everything they can possibly get – not take it, but work for it.'

But in wealthy Parkside Kusserow found a radically different type of player being built. There, children were seen not as tough warriors of the game but as fragile buds that needed to be 'opened out into the world, into a successful career'. Parents emphasised 'the delicacy of the child's self, the extreme care, resources, wide canvas and gentle touch needed in helping this unique self to "flower" and open up to its full potential'. One mother, on reading a story in which a 12-year-old was admonished for not saying 'thank you' for her birthday party, shuddered at the notion. Her own daughter 'would be so struck with a deep sense of guilt that I wouldn't do that to her. We have such power over our children especially at these ages when they are so vulnerable.'

Rather than respecting a parent–child status hierarchy, Parkside youngsters were encouraged to see themselves as equals. One mother said treating her daughter as an adult 'gives her a certain status in the family, makes her feel like she's on an equal footing, her feelings are as important as anyone else's'. Kusserow noted various techniques that encouraged this thinking, including: children calling teachers by their first names; consulting the child on the solving of family problems; allowing them to 'teach the parent' and adults asking, 'How can I help you get what you want?' One father said of his daughter, 'My basic feeling is that I have no right to discipline her . . . I'm conscious of the power differential and I don't feel just because I'm bigger and stronger and know more that I have the right to push her around because we disagree on something.' His daughter was 3.

Mothers and fathers in every area wanted the best for their children, but Parkside parents wanted *the* best: 'I'm not interested in the normal, I'm interested in the best,' said one mother. 'My daughter is extraordinary at chess and ice skating, for which I pay through the nose for her to be extraordinary at.' Ironically, however, Kusserow found the children who were treated as the delicate, precious equals of their elders could show less stability. 'What seems lacking for some Parkside children is the sense of security, protection, respect and humility that can arise from knowing that one is *not* at the top of the hierarchy,' she wrote. These children were told they were delicate and so they felt delicate, but at the same time automatically deserving of an elite position. Kusserow's research was published in 2004. The striking mix of fragility and entitlement she found seems characteristic of the status-striving of some of our most privileged young adults today.

In the early years of childhood, our status-striving often takes the form of dominance as we demand what we want and, when thwarted, attempt to force our will with tears, tantrums and teeth. It's in adolescence that we begin to play adult games. We leave the hierarchy of the family for the contests of the outside world. This is our time of joining.

At least in the developed world, the games we join in adolescence usually take the form of a clique or peer group – a set of people with whom we can comfortably play. This begins to happen in adolescence partly as a result of alterations to a region of the brain that makes us much more sensitive to the judgements of others. We start to desire the reward of social approval and dread rejection. This sudden sensitivity to reputation makes teenagers highly prone to self-consciousness and embarrassment. Between the ages of 11 and 14, writes neuroscientist Professor Sarah-Jayne Blakemore, they 'become increasingly aware that others have the capacity to evaluate them, and as a result may overestimate the extent to which this actually occurs'.

As their brains continue to change, they begin to feel the presence of an 'imaginary audience' of others, constantly watching and judging them, a feeling that 'remains quite high even in adulthood'. Unlike younger people, teenagers are likely to take the evaluations of their peers to be a true indication of their self-worth – or lack of it. As their self-esteem shifts from being based on how they feel in the moment to how they imagine their peers are evaluating them, they begin to crave their approval. Their chase for status can become all consuming. 'By the time we are thirteen,' writes psychologist Professor Mitch Prinstein, 'it seems as if there is nothing more important to us than this type of popularity. We talk about who has it. We strategise how to get it. We are devastated when we lose it. We even do things we know are wrong, immoral, illegal, or dangerous merely to obtain status, or to fiercely defend it.'

In order to gorge on the status they so desire, teenagers connect into status games and play them. We've joined our tribes at about this age for at least tens of thousands of years. In premodern societies, adolescence is thought to have been a 'critical window for acquiring status', much like the window we have in early childhood for acquiring language. This emergence into adulthood has sometimes been marked with agonising initiation ceremonies: teeth are yanked out; little fingers removed; drugs or poisons swallowed; skin whipped, sliced, burned or tattooed. Initiates into the Bimin-Kuskusmin tribe, of Papua New Guinea, have their septum pierced with a cassowary bone dagger and have scalding fat dripped down their arms as they 'struggle and shriek as large blisters form'. Young initiates 'may be terrified', writes anthropologist Professor Alan Fiske, 'but they are typically proud to have reached the status of prospective inductees ... usually, they go willingly to be initiated, or even eagerly request it'. Such tortures are designed to mark the person's body with a tribal identifier, thus 'the mutilated individual is removed from the common mass of humanity'.

Inductions don't only take place in traditional societies, and not all are violent. Some religious groups require adolescents to formally accept or reject the game they were raised in: Catholics and protestants call this confirmation, the Amish rumspringa; they happen around age 14. Jewish mitzvahs, at 12 or 13, mark the passage into full accountability under their game's rules.

But in other contemporary groups the violence remains. Young men joining street-gangs or armies are sometimes 'beaten in' ('all those sticks that you were beaten with put into you another ideology,' remarked one Mai-Mai militia inductee in the eastern Congo). In the USA, rituals of 'hazing' as entry into elite college sororities or sports teams are said to remain despite clampdowns. Students can be kicked in their sleep, tattooed, assaulted with paddles, urinated on or sexually humiliated. Fiske quotes one member's rationalisation: 'The claim to belonging to a superior "elite" must have some justification, and hazing forms part of that. It separates those who have undergone it from the larger groups of people around them, a separation that the former initiates of hazing see as lifting them over those less, unhazed people.'

Even if we're not required to humiliate or break ourselves, we still find ourselves proudly displaying our membership of games with clothing, cultural tastes, beliefs or attitudes. This game we've joined has rules and symbols we adopt as our own – often to our parents' horror – and, when we do, we lock into a neural territory. Our co-players become our people, our tribe, our kin, they a source of our status, and we a source of theirs.

This brain-directed emergence into adult games usually happens around the time we start secondary school. Adolescent students learn a harsh lesson of human life: not only are there hierarchies of status *within* games, the *games themselves* form a hierarchy, with some nearer the top, and others lower down. Elite cliques are formed by players who are naturally better at making friends. 'Social mammals are status seeking, that is, interested in befriending powerful, appealing, or popular individuals,' writes Professor Nicholas Christakis, an expert in social networks. 'Those desirable partners tend to be connected to other desirable partners because they get to choose who they are friends with. Partly as a result, less popular individuals wind up being friends with less popular individuals.' It's this type of sorting that results in our 'status-based society'.

In the mid-nineties, a team led by anthropologist Professor Don Merten captured teens discovering the rough realities of the status game at a middle-class junior high in a suburb of Chicago. With their game-playing cognition fully coming online, new arrivals found themselves being automatically sorted into a hierarchy of status games, with 'trendies', 'jocks' and 'preppies' at the top and 'nerds', 'burnouts' and 'mels' at the bottom. 'They're judging you this year, and that's what I don't like,' said one interviewee. 'Because they never used to judge you last year . . . this year they're judging you on what you look like, what clothes you wear, what kind of friends you hang out with. Like if your friend is a burnout, then you're a burnout.'

Status games also formed around after-school activities that existed in an 'informal hierarchy' that was 'generally agreed upon by the students'. The most prestigious game for boys was the basketball team whilst for girls it was the cheerleader squad (the rank of the 'Creative Stitchery Club' remains sadly unrecorded). The year Merten's team visited, around fifty girls tried out for just eight cheerleader spots that were usually filled exclusively from a clique of 'socially prominent' girls. The elite few who made it found it 'difficult to contain their exhilaration' but yet instinctively felt moved to disguise their big shot feelings. One was documented saying she'd never wear her cheerleader uniform to school again after her friends cheered when she walked into PE all decked out in it. This made her 'terribly embarrassed', she insisted. Except, noted the ethnographer, 'you could tell that she loved the whole thing'.

That year, the cheerleaders were in for a shock. It would be their next harsh lesson in the status game. One of the lowest games at the school, just above the mels, were the burnouts. Unlike the groomed, polished and socially oiled preppie elite, the burnouts had a reputation for scruffiness, rebellion and the casual enjoyment of drugs, alcohol and sex. Some of them wore bandanas. Of course, no burnout could *ever* be selected as a cheerleader. Except that's what happened. One cheerleader explained to the researchers the magnificent agony they endured as a result of burnout 'Jackie' joining their game. 'It was really hard in the beginning because they would say the names [of the cheerleaders] over the speakers as we walked down the hall. Everyone would go, "Oh god, how come all the losers made it this year?" . . . I would be like almost crying. Paula told me that Rod went on the bus and he goes, "We are not coming to any of the games any more because our cheerleaders are losers."'

They turned on Jackie in rehearsals. A friend reported, 'If Jackie did one thing wrong, they jumped on her back just because that gave them reason to be mad at her. I didn't like that. I mean, if it's something as little as that, like she didn't do a jump or something at the right time and she was two seconds late or something, they'd get really mad at her.'

The second harsh lesson those cheerleaders learned was that status leaks. Prestigious games and individuals can find their position threatened by proximity to those of lower rank. But this particular story's ending seems a happy one, because the opposite is also true: lower-status people can use the proximity principle to move up. Burnout Jackie saw her rank rise. When one cheerleader was asked if people saw Jackie differently, following her selection, she said, 'Well, I guess that they don't think of her as a burnout too much any more, or a real slutty person. I don't know. She is going out with Mark Williams. Everyone is like, "Mark Williams? Why is Mark going with her?"'

After school the games of true adulthood await. As we discovered in the darkly competitive world of Enron, the games we join have the power to corrupt us. This process has been captured in an extraordinary paper by Patrick J. Schiltz – former big-firm attorney, Associate Professor of Law at Indiana's prestigious Notre Dame Law School and present-day judge. Addressing a cadre of incoming law students, he wrote: 'If you go to work for a big firm, you will probably begin to practice law unethically in at least some respects within your first year or two in practice. This happens to most young lawyers in big firms. It happened to me.'

Those who yearn to become big-firm lawyers are, he writes, a 'remarkably insecure and competitive group of people'. They've spent their entire lives competing through the education system to get where they are. 'Now that they're in a big law firm, what's going to happen? Are they going to stop competing? Of course not. They're going to keep competing – competing to bill more hours, to attract more clients, to win more cases, to do more deals. They're playing a game. And money is how the score is kept in that game.' Their fever for lucre is exacerbated by regular trade press articles on how much this or that big shot is making. Lists of lawyers' incomes are published biannually and 'pored over by lawyers with the intensity that small children bring to poring over the statistics of their favourite baseball players'.

This is how youthful idealism stales and grows mould. They arrive at their big firm to discover a new set of rules and symbols, a new game to play: they must compete using wealth as a symbol of status. Their indoctrination will be delicate but emphatic: 'the culture will pressure you in many subtle ways to replace your values with the system's'. During a lawyer's first month, a senior partner will invite them to a barbecue. They'll travel up a long drive, park by ranks of luxury cars and walk up a long verdant drive towards an enormous house. Someone in a black bow tie will answer the door. In a perfect, huge garden, they'll be served pâté, shrimp, miniature quiches and cocktails. A caterer will grill swordfish. And in the corner they'll glimpse 'the senior partner, sipping a glass of white wine, holding court with a worshipful group of junior partners and senior associates. The senior partner will be wearing designer sunglasses and designer clothes; the logo on his shirt will signal its exorbitant cost; his shorts will be pressed. He will have a tan – albeit a slightly orange, tanning salon enhanced tan – and the nicest haircut you've ever seen.'

In this and 'a thousand other ways' they'll begin absorbing the lawyer's game. 'It is very difficult for a young lawyer immersed in this culture day after day to maintain the values she had as a law student. Slowly, almost imperceptibly, young lawyers change. They begin to admire things they did not admire before, be ashamed of things they were not ashamed of before, find it impossible to live without things they lived without before. Somewhere, somehow, a lawyer changes from a person who gets intense pleasure from being able to buy her first car stereo to a person enraged over a $400,000 bonus.'

But there's a problem: if these young lawyers are already working as hard as it's possible to work – and they are – how can they get the edge? In order to win, they'll begin to cheat in ways that seem, at first, excusable. They'll bill a client for ninety minutes for a job that took an hour, but promise to repay them that half an hour another time – it's not stealing, it's borrowing. And they'll do it, they'll repay. But then they'll stop repaying. They'll tell themselves they did such good work that their client should 'pay a bit more for it'. They'll start lying to get an edge too: an excuse over a missed deadline here, a document that's unhelpful to their client getting 'lost' there.

A couple of years in and they won't notice they're continually lying, cheating and stealing. 'You will still be making dozens of quick, instinctive decisions every day, but those decisions, instead of reflecting the notions of right and wrong by which you conduct your personal life, will instead reflect the set of values by which you will conduct your professional life – a set of values that embodies not what is right or wrong, but what is profitable, and what you can get away with. The system will have succeeded in replacing your values with the system's values, and the system will be profiting as a result.'

As we grow into adults, that system – that game – gains enormous power to shape who we become. We mould ourselves to its rules and symbols. As we move through our days, our identity shifts depending on which game we happen to be playing. We can be an architect at work, a mother at home, a campaigner online, an authority on Charlotte Brontë at the book group, a restorer of rocket launchers in the shed – and in each case, we can hope to feel *good* at these roles: competent, better than him and her and getting better still. Our sense of self attaches to each game, an alien funnel implanting itself into an organism of many and sucking out what it needs. Our individuality merges with the game and becomes blurred at the edges, our moral behaviour and perception of reality deranging itself in its service. This is what our adult identity adds up to. We are the sum of the games we play.

16

Believing the Dream

THE STORY WE like to tell about humanity speaks of a heroic journey of progress. It's the arrow of history, the footsteps in the sand, the holy fate of us all. There's evidence for this view everywhere: in rapidly advancing science, technology and living standards. In the last 500 years, we've been through a scientific revolution and an 'enlightenment': great intellectual movements that led to the wonders of modernity and showed the irrational beliefs of old to be false. There's no reason, anymore, to cling to mad ideas. So why do billions still cling? Why do we remain superstitious, gullible and religious? The persistence of irrationality is a puzzle. But the status game suggests an explanation. Humans aren't heroes on wondrous journeys of progress, we're players programmed for games. To succeed in these games, we seek high-status allies. When we find them, our *copy-flatter-conform* circuitry switches on. We mimic not just their behaviour but their beliefs. The better we believe, the higher we rise. And so faith, not truth, is incentivised.

It's by this process that we come upon many of our most deeply held convictions. It can feel like we choose our beliefs as a cook chooses a recipe, carefully considering an array of options before making a selection. But usually, we believe what our groups believe, obediently copying the perceptions of our elites and accepting the world as they define it. This is how status games are played and how human culture has to work. We can't be expected to test for ourselves every fact on which we have to rely, so instead we look upwards for guidance. We have faith. We believe. And sometimes we end up believing crazy things.

Maranda Dynda knows this. In 2012 she was an 18-year-old mother-to-be in rural Pennsylvania and hoping for a home birth. It wasn't easy to find a suitable, available midwife. It took months. But when Maranda finally found one, she was everything she'd hoped for. On the day they first met, she came into the house laden with bags, books, papers and a stethoscope and was friendly but no-nonsense, sitting herself on the old wooden rocking chair Maranda had bought at a yard sale. With the professional experience of a decade and eight children of her own, she was someone for an expectant Mom to look up to. 'She felt safe and smart,' Maranda remembers. She asked a series of standard questions – How far along are you? How've you been feeling? Have you put any thought into cribs? – and then she asked, 'Have you considered not vaccinating?'

'I didn't know what she meant,' Maranda told me. 'Vaccinating is just a thing you do. You go to the doctor, you get your shots. It's like paying your electric bill or putting gas in your car. So this was like her saying, "Have you ever not put gas in your car? Have you thought about doing that?"'

'I don't know what you're asking me,' she told the midwife.

Maranda sat and listened as a wild new dream of reality emerged in front of her, right there in her living room. The midwife said after she'd vaccinated her first child it was like night and day – bam! – he got vaccinated and he was autistic. The light just left his eyes. And did Maranda know vaccines could give kids diabetes? And they can make it appear that you've beaten them up? That's one of the side effects. Child abuse, it looks like. So child services might take your baby away. 'Anyway,' she finished. 'You should make up your own mind. It's totally up to you. There's some great information on Google.'

After the midwife left, Maranda investigated. She used Google because that's what she'd been told. She typed: 'Why not vaccinate?' And there it all was: breakdowns, from A–Z, on the ingredients in vaccines and why they're dangerous; blogs detailing how children developed epilepsy and died following vaccinations; videos about 'big pHARMa' and the cash premiums doctors are paid for poisoning babies. She clicked on the website of Dr Joseph Mercola, a '*New York Times* Bestselling Author' and winner of the Ultimate Wellness Game Changer Award. It looked professional. Serious. MERCOLA: TAKE CONTROL OF YOUR HEALTH. At the time of writing, its main story announced: 'Kids Given Vaccines Have 22 Times the Rate of Ear Infections, 32 times the rate of sinusitis, 4x allergies, 2x asthma, 4x hayfever, 3x ADHD and 19 times higher odds of Autism based on this 7,850 person survey. Yet 98% of parents give it to their children.'

Then Maranda looked on Facebook. 'Facebook was the big one,' she said. 'You find a Facebook group, join it and it sucks you in.' One of the groups was Great Mothers Questioning Vaccines. She made her first comment, announcing herself as 'vaccine hesitant'. It didn't take long. The group massed around her like a slug on an earthworm. 'I was bombarded: "I was a nurse and I saw vaccines do harm"; "I have five kids, I vaccinated the first one and they're like this"; "I've been doing research for thirty-five years."' Maranda felt fascinated and horrified by their stories. But she also felt good. As an 18-year-old whose friends were all at college, she had no mothers to talk to, besides her own. 'It felt warm and cosy.'

But Maranda's seduction into the group didn't only take the form of the rewards of connection. 'I tend to really respect strong, confident women,' she said. 'I grew up in a family of women. And I thought, look at all these mothers, these experienced women I'm surrounded by! They're so much smarter than me. I don't know what I'm doing and they all know what they're doing. It was like – imagine you're a little kid who wants to be a firefighter and you visit a fire station and you see all the big, strong firefighters and they're really good at it. You think, *I want to be just like them.* I wanted to be a cool, strong Mom who takes this knowledge I've suddenly gained and uses it for my benefit, my child's benefit, the world's benefit.'

Her indoctrination was rapid. She played that slot machine for status and kept on winning. 'You're socially rewarded for going with the group,' she said. 'It's Facebook likes, it's comments like "yeah way to go Mom, you're so strong, you're so smart, you're doing the best thing" – going to a young Mom from women who are sometimes older than my Mom.' She found the experience 'captivating. There was also the thing of – this is happening and we need to do something about it. So we were rallying the forces. It felt political.'

Soon, Maranda was out in the world, playing a virtue game, evangelising her new beliefs. She told her mother and her cousins. She began looking for any reason to raise the topic socially. 'You want to bring it up with people you can argue with, because you want to be like, *I'm smarter than you, I know more than you do, look at this thing I know that you don't.* It's really embarrassing to think about now. I thought I knew it all. I thought, *that's going to show them, they're going to really regret arguing with me.*'

I asked Maranda if part of the point was to go back to the group and report in, for status rewards. 'That's absolutely accurate,' she said. 'And that went for everybody: "I went to the doctor's today and boy did I show them." "I went to my cousin's today and I was spittin' fire." You were rewarded for that. The louder you were, the more unmovable you were, the higher you moved up socially. You became someone for other people to try to strive to be like. You'd look at them and you'd think, *they're so confident in everything they're saying, they believe it so strongly, they're willing to do anything. I need to become this.* I think it's an unconscious thing. Humans want to be revered. They want to be on top of the group.'

After she gave birth, Maranda refused to vaccinate her daughter. 'Please respect my opinions,' she told her doctor. 'Thank you very much.' But over the next two years, she began to feel discomfited by some of the other fringe beliefs expressed by her co-players. She'd always prided herself on being rationally minded and would read science textbooks for fun as a child: 'I'd always loved and trusted science with everything in my being.' It was this rebellious counter-identity that would save her. She'd believed her anti-vax stance was based on evidence. But she learned some of the mothers thought the only reason people were gay was because of vaccines. Then someone said AIDS didn't exist. Then someone warned they were all going to be put in FEMA death camps. 'Every time I saw these comments I thought, *what the hell is that?*' she said. 'It took me a long time. But eventually I thought, *Why am I taking one of these things and saying "this is totally true" and the others I'm going "that's kind of crazy?"* Especially when it came from someone who'd given me information I'd used.'

Maranda Googled again. This time, she purposefully looked for information that countered her biases. She also considered the role mainstream medicine played in her life. 'I have asthma, my father's disabled, there are medical issues rampant in my family. I would've died from asthma if not for medicine. I was suddenly putting the pieces together.'

She quietly left her Facebook groups. She arranged for her daughter, who was then 2, to be vaccinated. When she signed up to the pro-vaccines page, Voices for Vaccines, they asked if a blog could be written about her experience. This is how her former co-players learned of her betrayal. 'The blog blew up. It was one of their most read posts ever. It was getting shared around anti-vaccine groups.' And so, as inevitable as night, came the hate. 'The same people who'd told me I was the best Mom in the world told me I was a piece-of-garbage Mom. There were women who'd supported me so strongly during my very difficult birth who then were like, "you should've died in labour."' Elite figures with whom she'd never communicated sent messages saying her daughter would grow up to hate her and become 'retarded'.

She could imagine what they were saying back on the Facebook group. 'It was common to make posts about people like me and say "wow what an idiot". They'd all mob up in mutual hate for them.' They found it impossible to understand why anyone would leave them: in their brain-generated fantasy of reality, they were obviously just *better* than everyone else. 'They think they're smarter. They think everyone else is in the system and they're beating the system. They think they love their children more.' And why not? Who wouldn't want to be one of the Great Mothers Questioning Vaccines? Who would want to harm their children?

Maranda was seduced into irrationality by a coalition of high-status Moms who pulled her into their dream of life with their rewards of the great prize. She became possessed by the game, evangelising it to all who knew her, risking her baby's health. Her desire to be a good mother came to depend on the belief that vaccines were harmful. Achieving the former meant believing the latter, playing their game and winning, *for my benefit, my child's benefit, the world's benefit*. Maranda was going to be an amazing Mom and she was going to help save the world. The status on offer was bountiful. When she turned her back and rebelled, she wasn't permitted to simply vanish. They took the time to let her know: all that status she'd been awarded had been revoked. She was nobody. Worse than nobody. It would be better if she were dead.

Maranda's experience isn't unusual. She wasn't being stupid, she was being human, playing the game of life exactly as she's designed to.

During the Stone Age, it didn't matter if the stories we told about the world weren't true. Faith in the myths and prejudices of our tribe served to bond us together, co-ordinate our behaviour and motivate us to fight harder against enemies. But in the twenty-first century environment, in which we exist side by side in multiple intertwined and overlapping groups, the human tendency to credulously accept the wild dreams of our game leads all too frequently to error, mistrust, division, aggression, hubris and catastrophe. And the tendency is strong.

Psychologists have amassed a sizeable literature that demonstrates how even our closest convictions are often absorbed from our games. This is true of our political beliefs. In one study, researchers who altered the apparent policies of the Republicans and Democrats found voters changed their support for harsh or lavish welfare programmes accordingly. Not only did they not realise they were being manipulated, they found good reasons to support their altered beliefs and could readily explain how they'd come to them. Psychologist Dr Lilliana Mason writes, 'more often than not, citizens do not choose which party to support based on policy opinion; they alter their policy opinion according to which party they support. Usually they do not notice that this is happening, and most, in fact, feel outraged when the possibility is mentioned.'

Our brain has various tricks that nudge us into accepting our game's story of the world and believing what it's supposed to: it tells us the members of our group are more intelligent than others; it finds it harder to reason logically over arguments that contradict our group's beliefs; it processes opinions we already agree with as if they're facts; it often automatically assumes those who hold different beliefs are stupider, more biased, less moral and less trustworthy than we are, making it all too easy to dismiss them.

And intelligence is no inoculation. On the contrary. When brilliant people are motivated to find evidence to support their group's false beliefs, they're brilliant at finding it. Their superior intelligence simply makes them better at reaffirming their bent story of reality. When psychologists study how people's religious, political and social identities affect their beliefs, they find that the more educated, numerate and intelligent they are, the more likely they are to endorse the fringe ideas of their groups. This goes for deniers of climate change, vaccination and evolution – the smarter a player is, the greater the likelihood they'll reject scientific consensus. We're all vulnerable to believing what our coalition wants us to believe. For anthropologist Professor John Tooby, 'Coalition mindedness makes everyone, including scientists, far stupider in coalitional collectivities than as individuals.'

Needless to say, we're not entirely gullible. When the facts of a matter are strong and we devote sincere conscious effort to understanding them, we can be perfectly capable of rationality. Personal experiences can throw us out of our bubble. There are also categories of beliefs we can accept without a struggle, many of them objectively measurable and devoid of status value, such as the length of the Mississippi River. If we don't endlessly debate these kinds of facts, it's because we don't have any of our status invested in them. But, when we do, our thinking can rapidly become deranged.

In the places where status is won and lost, we can be vulnerable to believing almost anything. Billions play games in the fantastic dreamworlds conjured by the great religions: Christians believe evil was introduced to the world as a punishment from God after a woman ate an apple; Muslims believe angels were created on a Wednesday and walk the earth noting down believers' good and bad acts; Jews believe they're a chosen people selected by God to be a 'light unto nations'; Hindus believe eternal souls travel through cycles of birth and rebirth that only cease when a state of perfection is achieved; Jehovah's Witnesses believe it's better to die than receive blood transfusions, which are against God's will; Buddhists believe there are thirty-one planes of existence, including the 'realm of hungry ghosts', through which the reincarnated ascend, depending on how well they play their game; Sikh men wear special pants to control their lust and believe hair is God's creation so must never be cut.

Of course, not all modern adherents believe such stories. Some take their more incredible details as metaphorical whilst accepting their underlying supernatural claims. But that 84 per cent of the world's population identifies as religious shows the game's capacity to flood our minds with strange notions: our compulsion to seek schemes that make connection and status and weave wild dreams around them. And there's no reason for unbelievers to feel superior. Atheists are often born and educated in a place where their particular values are considered pre-eminent, and their particular icons deferred to. What's true for them is true for everyone. Most of the time, we don't check for ourselves what's true, we check with our elites. We believe what we're supposed to.

This even counts for the most precious of our beliefs, the ones we categorise as 'moral'. The moral reality we live in is a virtue game. We use our displays of morality to manufacture status. It's good that we do this. It's functional. It's why billionaires fund libraries, university scholarships and scientific endeavours; it's why a study of 11,672 organ donations in the USA found only thirty-one were made anonymously. It's why we feel good when we commit moral acts and thoughts privately and enjoy the approval of our imaginary audience. Virtue status is the bribe that nudges us into putting the interests of other people – principally our co-players – before our own.

We treat moral beliefs as if they're universal and absolute: one study found people were more likely to believe God could change physical laws of the universe than he could moral 'facts'. Such facts can seem to belong to the same category as objects in nature, as if they could be observed under microscopes or proven by mathematical formulae. If moral truth exists anywhere, it's in our DNA: that ancient game-playing coding that evolved to nudge us into behaving co-operatively in hunter-gatherer groups. But these instructions – *strive to appear virtuous; privilege your group over others* – are few and vague and open to riotous differences in interpretation. All the rest is an act of shared imagination. It's a dream we weave around a status game.

The dream shifts as we range across the continents. For the Malagasy people in Madagascar, it's taboo to eat a blind hen, to dream about blood and to sleep facing westwards, as you'll kick the sunrise. Adolescent boys of the Marind of South New Guinea are introduced to a culture of 'institutionalised sodomy' in which they sleep in the men's house and absorb the sperm of their elders via anal copulation, making them stronger. Among the people of the Moose, teenage girls are abducted and forced to have sex with a married man, an act for which, writes psychologist Professor David Buss, 'all concerned – including the girl – judge that her parents giving her to the man was a virtuous, generous act of gratitude'. As alien as these norms might seem, they'll feel morally correct to most who play by them. They're part of the dream of reality in which they exist, a dream that feels no less obvious and true to them than ours does to us.

Such 'facts' also change across time. We don't have to travel back far to discover moral superstars holding moral views that would destroy them today. Feminist hero and birth control campaigner Marie Stopes, who was voted Woman of the Millennium by the readers of *The Guardian* and honoured on special Royal Mail stamps in 2008, was an anti-Semite and eugenicist who once wrote that 'our race is weakened by an appallingly high percentage of unfit weaklings and diseased individuals' and that 'it is the urgent duty of the community to make parenthood impossible for those whose mental and physical conditions are such that there is well-nigh a certainty that their offspring must be physically and mentally tainted'. Meanwhile, Gandhi once explained his agitation against the British thusly: 'Ours is one continual struggle against a degradation sought to be inflicted upon us by the Europeans, who desire to degrade us to the level of the raw Kaffir [black African] . . . whose sole ambition is to collect a certain number of cattle to buy a wife with and . . . pass his life in indolence and nakedness.' Such statements seem obviously appalling. But there's about as much sense in blaming Gandhi for not sharing our modern, Western views on race as there is in blaming the Vikings for not having Netflix. Moral 'truths' are acts of imagination. They're ideas we play games with.

The dream feels so real. And yet it's all conjured up by the game-making brain. The world around our bodies is chaotic and confusing. But the brain must make sense of it. It has to turn that blizzard of noise into a precise, colourful and detailed world it can predict and successfully interact with, such that it gets what it wants. When the brain discovers a game that seems to make sense of its felt reality and offer a pathway to rewards, it can embrace its rules and symbols with an ecstatic fervour. The noise is silenced! The chaos is tamed! We've found our story and the heroic role we're going to play in it! We've learned the truth and the way – the meaning of life! It's yams, it's God, it's money, it's saving the world from evil big pHARMa. It's not like a religious experience, it *is* a religious experience. It's how the writer Arthur Koestler felt as a young man in 1931, joining the Communist Party:

'To say that one had "seen the light" is a poor description of the mental rapture which only the convert knows (regardless of what faith he has been converted to). The new light seems to pour from all directions across the skull; the whole universe falls into pattern, like stray pieces of a jigsaw puzzle assembled by one magic stroke. There is now an answer to every question, doubts and conflicts are a matter of the tortured past – a past already remote, when one lived in dismal ignorance in the tasteless, colourless world of those who *don't know*. Nothing henceforth can disturb the convert's inner peace and serenity – except the occasional fear of losing faith again, losing thereby what alone makes life worth living, and falling back into the outer darkness, where there is wailing and gnashing of teeth.'

17

Goldrush!

THE GREAT MOTHERS Questioning Vaccines formed themselves around an idea: that vaccines were harmful. Securing
connection was as easy as believing. But to earn status, a player had
to do more than merely agree. They had to become possessed by the
belief, defending it, evangelising it, acting it out in their life. The
more they allowed the belief to take them over, the higher they
climbed. Much of the groupish tumult we see in the world is fuelled
by these dynamics. And status is a fuel like no other. Whereas coal,
gas and oil are costly to produce and in limited supply, status just
goes on and on and on – yet is hardly less flammable. When status
games form around an irrational belief they can grow breathtakingly
large, spreading gibberish, mayhem and agony across the continents.

During the 1980s, status games began mining rewards for players
in the belief that there were secret, powerful networks of satanic
paedophiles running daycare centres in the USA. This was an era
that had seen the spectacular rise in the status games of the psycho-
therapists and social workers, especially those focussed on child abuse.
Previous decades had been dominated by Freudian theories that
tended to dismiss adult recollections of abuse as fantasies. As such,
its appalling realities were often ignored. By the early 1980s that had

changed. The public learned child abuse was real, and it seemed terrifyingly widespread. Everyone knew child-abusing monsters looked like perfectly ordinary mothers and fathers – and perfectly ordinary mothers and fathers were *everywhere*.

And so began a golden age for abuse-fighting games. The gossip networks of mass media bulged with outrage-making dread. Popular dramas and made-for-TV movies ran child abuse storylines; maga-zines and newspapers spruiked panicky reports; celebrities revealed childhood experiences in emotional, status-getting interviews; books were published with titles such as *Father's Days*, *Daddy's Girl*, *I Never Told Anyone*, *Kiss Daddy Goodnight*. One of their authors, feminist activist Louise Armstrong, has since written of the 'staggering array of clinicians and counsellors and therapists and researchers and authorities and experts' that emerged at the time, 'all with their careers sighted on one aspect or another' of child abuse.

The 1980s also saw the ecstatic resurgence of conservative Christian games, following the ideological beatings they'd taken during the 1960s and 1970s, as the sexual revolution and equality-focussed second-wave feminists attacked their ideas about the central impor-tance of traditional family life. The election of Ronald Reagan helped them rediscover their power as a dominant cultural force. And, to their horror, by the start of the 1980s, 45 per cent of American women were working outside the home, many dropping their children off to be looked after by near-strangers at daycare centres. To the conserv-ative Christians, these were the victories of Satan.

The Christians' war on Satan and the therapists' war on child abuse were to come together in unholy conjugation in 1980, in the pages of a bestselling book. *Michelle Remembers* was a supposedly true account of childhood satanic ritual abuse, written by the victim's psychiatrist, Dr Lawrence Pazder. Amongst other things, Michelle claimed to have been raped by satanists, smeared with blood and excrement and forced to assist in the murder of another child with a crucifix; doctors who were members of the cult took the then-infant Michelle to an operating theatre and surgically implanted horns and a tail onto her body. The abuse culminated in an eighty-one-day ritual in which Satan himself turned up, only for Jesus, Mary and Michael the Archangel to arrive and conveniently remove the physical scars left by her abuse. Pazder told journalists, 'In the beginning I wondered if she had made things up. But if this is a hoax, it would be the most incredible hoax ever.'

Pazder's book earned $342,000 in advance money alone and was publicised with full-page newspaper advertisements. It set him on a thirty-nine-day publicity tour of America. He became a superstar in the wildly blooming abuse-busting therapeutic world, travelling up and down the nation educating mental health clinicians and law enforcement officers about the threat satanists posed. It was at an early event, during a presentation to the prestigious American Psychiatric Association, that Pazder introduced the term 'ritual abuse'.

The Satanic Panic was fuelled by status games. They were formed wherever believers gathered, in conferences, seminars, training sessions and organisations such as the Preschool-Age Molested Children's Professional Group, Children's Institute International and the National Center for Child Abuse and Neglect. A survey of more than two thousand psychologists, psychiatrists and social workers who worked with ritual abuse cases found they 'had a very high rate of attending lectures, seminars or workshops concerned with ritualistic crime or ritualistic abuse'. Newcomers would have their ancient tribal coding switched on as they experienced wonderful feelings of connection to the game. They'd then sit gripped as the Satan-hunters wove a new dream for them to live in, and taught them how to earn status within it.

Sessions would often start with horrific, outrage-building testimony. Next, trainee players would be lured with the promise of major virtue status by their battling of what psychiatrist Dr Roland Summit described as, 'the most serious threat to children and to society that we must face in our lifetime'. They were taught rules like the 'Rule of P's' – professions most likely to harbour satanists included providers of daycare, physicians, psychiatrists, principals and teachers, police, politicians, priests, public officials and pall-bearers. Elite players would then lead group discussion sessions during which stray doubters were dealt with; impediments to consensus made quiet.

At training sessions, they'd have further lessons in playing the Satan-hunting game. Rule number one was 'believe the children'. According to Summit, 'the more illogical and incredible' the testimony of a child, the 'more likely' it was to be true. And if they changed their mind and told you, actually, they made it all up, that's 'the normal course' and exactly to be expected: such denials were evidence of the satanists' genius for mind control. Indeed, 'very few children, no more than two or three per thousand, have ever been found to exaggerate or to invent claims of sexual molestation'. Believe the Children became a sacred belief for the Satan-hunters; the rule that defined their game. They wore it on lapel badges; activist parents formed the Believe The Children Organisation. It 'became the banner of that decade', writes sociologist Professor Mary de Young, 'and those who marched under it were of a single mind that no allegation of sexual abuse was unbelievable [and] no retraction or denial was acceptable'.

Special methods were taught for gathering evidence from children. Clues that ritual abuse had been inflicted included: fear of the dark; fear of dying; poor attention span; fear of aggressive animals and low self-esteem. Children would have their anuses examined with a 'wink response test': a swab was touched near the anus, if it spontaneously opened, that meant abuse. Infant girls would have a magnifying camera called a colposcope inserted into them, with which an examiner would seek out the tiniest scars, abrasions, and blood vessel disturbances, as well as minute variations in the size and shape of their hymens. These were 'microtraumas', said the Satan-hunters. Even though invisible to the naked eye, microtraumas were evidence of abuse.

Other evidence came from interviews with children. Methods were taught by experts from Children's Institute International, who conducted hundreds of them, charging $455 a time. CII members such as Astrid Heger and Kee MacFarlane earned major prestige for their work. They were invited to speak at national and international conferences, interviewed by journalists, made guest appearances on nationally syndicated television shows and were widely consulted on abuse cases. Their videotaped interviews were not only often highly suggestive and leading, they also resorted to coercion that could shade into bullying. In one, Heger told a young girl, 'I don't want to hear any more "no's". Every little boy and girl in the whole school got touched like that.' MacFarlane similarly refused to accept the repeated and clear denials of a boy called Keith. Their conversation, enacted via hand-puppets, had MacFarlane saying, 'Are you going to be stupid, or are you going to be smart and help us here?' and 'Well what good are you? You must be dumb.' In another, a 5-year-old boy repeatedly told MacFarlane he never saw the accused daycare staff do anything 'bad'.

'You're just afraid,' she told him.

'No I'm not.'

'You're just a scaredy cat. How come you won't tell me?'

As this case suggests, interviewers exploited children's natural desire for status to persuade them to give the 'right' answers. One was encouraged by being told, 'You're an absolute trooper, I think you're almost a man.' In another MacFarlane said to a girl named Kristie, 'We know there were naked games at your preschool.' She looked at the girl's hand-puppet. 'Do you remember that, bear?'

When the girl shook the bear's head to say 'no', MacFarlane said, 'Oh, bear! Maybe you don't have a very good memory. Your memory must not be as good as Kristie's friend's memories.' One former interviewee recalled being rewarded with praise for lying about being abused by his father. 'If I brought something that seemed like it was moving things forward, or affirming something, I definitely felt like something was accomplished, for sure. I didn't want to be the idiot kid who couldn't remember anything. And then they tell you, "You're doing a good job".'

Having been taught the game at conferences, seminars and work-shops, many hundreds of mental health professionals returned to their communities to begin playing at finding their own evidence of ritual abuse. Adhering to the sacred rule of *believe the children*, no claim proved too insane. Children had had their eyes stapled shut, been buried in airless coffins and watched a lawyer slaughter hundreds of animals. Others had been: sexually abused by a flock of elderly nuns; thrown from boats into schools of sharks; flushed down toilets into underground abuse chambers; taken to graveyards to kill baby tigers; shut in basements filled with roaring lions; watched coffins being dug up and their corpses removed and stabbed; found themselves in secret tunnels, aeroplanes, gyms, mansions, car washes and hot air balloons. All these abuses somehow took place when the children were at daycare, only to be returned smartly to their parents at the end of each day showing no signs of the horrors they'd endured.

The demented dreams of the professional Satan-hunters began to infect concerned parents, who read about this new and terrifying form of child abuse in books and articles, and were introduced to it by therapists. 'Abundant with clinical terms and concepts, sparse on empirical data, bereft of theory,' writes de Young, it helped parents 'make sense' of their children's behaviour. One mother testified at trial that these ideas helped her realise that her child's repeated denials anything bad had happened were actually signals that it had.

Status flooded into these games by many routes, not least proximity to prestigious governmental bodies and glittering rivers of cash. In 1984 the Justice Department financed a four-day conference that brought together eighty-five elite names. Following congressional hearings the same year, which included testimony from players such as superstar child interviewer Kee MacFarlane, Congress doubled its funding for child protection programmes to $158 million over four years, to which $25 million was quickly added for training for day-care staff, so they could better detect and prevent abuse. In 1984, NCCAN's budget more than quadrupled and included a $146,000 payment to Kee MacFarlane for a set of child interviews. By 1985 its annual budget for research and demonstration grants had grown to nearly $14 million. They awarded one grant to an employee of a state mental health department, to study children at a preschool in Niles, Michigan. The kids had apparently been abused in a church and in tunnels, been buried in the ground, engaged in blood rituals, had objects inserted into their genitals and been threatened with sharks. NCCAN's payment to the researcher for a 'followup study' on the children was $449,000.

The law enforcement establishment were also incentivised to believe the movement's dreams to be credible and true. These included ambitious, often conservative-Christian district attorneys, who'd been elected on promises to prioritise child protection and zealous police officers who'd been tempted into the game at the same events as the therapists and social workers. These cops, writes former officer Robert Hicks, 'attend a few cult seminars, return to their departments, and organise portfolios of satanalia so that they themselves can give seminars to teachers, parents, and enforcers; they join informal networks of other cult cops, then parade their own consciousness-raising seminars'. With their status being engorged by active belief in these allegations, police and prosecutors proved no less credulous than the mental health workers. In one single case, in

Wenatchee, Washington, forty-three adults were arrested on more than 29,000 charges.

These games were swollen and accelerated by national fame. Superstars such as Sally Jessy Raphael and Oprah Winfrey ran specials on ritual abuse, interviewing their elite figures. Winfrey introduced her ten million viewers to a guest who was, 'used in worshipping the devil, participated in human sacrifice rituals [and] cannibalism'. At the time of its broadcast, Geraldo Rivera's special, *Devil Worship: Exposing Satan's Underground*, was the highest-rated televised documentary ever. A reporter for the *Los Angeles Times*, David Shaw, would go on to win a Pulitzer Prize for his exposé of the widespread failures of journalism that took place in the period, including by his own newspaper.

The communities that were affected ran hot with gossip. In Manhattan Beach, California, one daycare centre was pelted with eggs, had its windows smashed and was set on fire, its outer walls graffitied: ONLY THE BEGINNING and DEAD. Parents dug in its grounds searching for a secret labyrinth of tunnels. When unsuccessful, the district attorney hired a firm of archaeologists to assist. When they too were unsuccessful, the parents hired their own archaeologists. Nobody found any tunnels. Nevertheless a survey of that community found 98 per cent thought one of the accused, Ray Buckey, was 'definitely or probably guilty' with 93 per cent thinking the same of Peggy McMartin-Buckey; 80 per cent had 'no doubt' of their guilt. When she was bailed, following twenty-two months of pretrial detention, Peggy was shunned, received late-night telephone death threats and was verbally and physically assaulted.

Their case alone cost $15 million dollars to bring and was, at the time, the longest and most expensive criminal trial in US history. They were ultimately acquitted. Meanwhile, those closely involved with the accusations, writes de Young, 'took to the national conference, lecture, consultancy and expert testimony circuit' where they 'recruited others who, in turn, went on to find cases of daycare ritual abuse in their own communities and then trained others still to do the same in their communities'. And so the game continued to reproduce itself, its unholy dream captivating more and more people. Most recruits to the Satan-hunting game 'trace their interest . . . to this small cadre of moral entrepreneurs'.

During this period, 190 people were formally charged in ritual abuse cases and at least eighty-three convicted. One man was convicted almost entirely on the testimony of a 3-year-old. Many spent years in prison. Frances and Dan Keller of Austin, Texas, were accused of forcing children to drink blood-laced Kool-Aid and watch the chainsaw dismemberment and graveyard burial of a passerby. The same children claimed they'd been flown to Mexico to be sexually assaulted by soldiers and then returned home in time for their parents to collect them, as if nothing had happened. The Kellers spent twenty-two years in prison.

Perhaps the most astonishing thing about these charges and prosecutions is the lack of physical evidence in support of them. It should've been everywhere: the blood, the scars, the DNA, the witnesses, the flight records, the tunnels, the robes, the corpses, the sharks, the dead baby tigers. Instead, police and prosecutors relied upon debunked and invented tests for winking anuses and micro-traumas and the coerced and literally unbelievable testimony of children. These events, writes de Young, constituted a 'triumph of ideology over science'. And the role that the status games of conferences, seminars and training sessions played in it all 'may actually be difficult to overestimate'.

If the small original cadre of Satan-hunters had been motivated to solve the problem of ritual abuse, they'd have played a success game. In success games, status is awarded principally for displays of competence. They make for a culture of analysis, experimentation, practice, research, testing, revision, data and open debate. A success game approach to the riddance of secret sex-satanists could be expected to start with a useful assessment of the problem. This would've led to the realisation it didn't exist. The consequence? Not much status for the Satan-hunters.

Instead, they played a virtue game. Virtue games often do weave a story around their striving that says they are motivated by the solving of some critical problem – frequently in the form of some evil, high-status enemy – but the truth is betrayed by their mode of play. Virtue games tend to be focussed mostly on the promotion of the game itself, with maintenance of conformity, correct beliefs and behaviours being of heightened importance. The hunters' core beliefs were often challenged by children in interviews and their virtue play is evident in their magicking of these denials into further evidence that their diseased perception of reality was correct. They were willing to 'believe the children', but only when the children confirmed their beliefs. The consequence? Status beyond their wildest dreams.

Of course, it's not impossible that some of these cases could've had abuse at their core. Political scientist Dr Ross Cheit has even gone so far as to argue most defendants were probably guilty. But Cheit's thesis has come under serious criticism from academics and journalists who accuse him of omissions and distortions. For instance, Cheit believes there was 'substantial evidence' against the Kellers, including the testimony of Dr Michael Mouw, who told the court he'd found physical evidence of abuse in a 3-year-old girl. However, this evidence appears to belong to the dubious category of the microtrauma: in 2013 Mouw testified he'd since learned more about female genitalia and now had 'no doubt' her hymen was normal. 'Sometimes it takes time to figure out what you don't know,' he said. 'I was mistaken.' Cheit also cites the corroboration of other child witnesses, despite its being secured by intense and often highly suggestive questioning.

Even if we allow the possibility that some abuse occurred, we can be sure the allegations of ritual abuse were preposterous. It should've been obviously true these children weren't having their eyes stapled shut and being tossed at sharks. It seems barely possible that so many people had their lives ruined by the magnificently wacky dream the Satan-hunters wove. But to the vaguely interested onlooker, following the events mostly via headlines and talkshows, some measure of credulity is understandable. After all, the people making the allegations were high-status figures who spoke at conferences and wrote for newspapers and authored academic papers and were interviewed by Oprah. They knew what they were talking about. Their claims were supported by other high-status figures, such as police officers and prosecutors, and numerous convictions had been won. Everyone knew child abuse was the most urgent moral crisis facing America, and that all those poor suffering children had, for so long, been ignored. Who could be against believing the children? Who could be against fighting abuse?

The greater puzzle sits with the warrior evangelists who drove the events, and invested a significant measure of their personal status in their being true. When the tale is recounted as briefly as this, it's easy to miss that some of these cases lasted years and were worked on intensely by any number of professional adults. Police forces diligently and repeatedly searched for secret tunnels, sacrificed babies and mutilated animals. Checks and balances, both institutional and in the individual intelligence of those involved, failed and failed and kept on failing. Most of the players who conspired to take the innocent carers down – psychiatrists, therapists, doctors, social workers, police officers, journalists – ought to have been incentivised to find the facts. And yet they were not only often utterly credulous, but rigidly insistent of their truth, evangelising it all the way to the slamming of the cell door.

The standard account of human life struggles to make sense of this. Either these warriors were brave heroes striving to make the world a better place or they were lying, scheming villains gladly sacrificing the innocent. Neither option is credible. The Satan-hunters were simply doing what nature had programmed them to do. Their brains detected a game that offered fantastic rewards: connection with like-minded others and status in the form of influence, acclaim, cash, fame, proximity to the prestigious games of law, media and government and the reputation of an avenging angel, defending the lives of America's children. And so they played. They believed the dream and they believed it sincerely. Of course they did. They were only human.

Events like these are often described as moral panics. Whilst this is surely correct in some cases, our investigation suggests an alternative possibility: that much of their explosive energy can derive not from panic, but desire for acclaim. They happen when games suddenly find ways of generating outsized volumes of status for their players. When a rich seam is discovered, more and more individuals are attracted to the game, with a precondition for play being acceptance of its beliefs, no matter how unlikely. Status is earned with *active belief*. As the games grow, and suck in satellite games around them, their beliefs come to seem increasingly mainstream. More players playing means more status being generated, and so the game's sucking power becomes more monstrous still, and so on and so on in a runaway process, the whole thing becoming self-sustaining, self-expanding, with it eventually becoming sufficiently massive to be felt right across the culture. In such scenarios, the status on offer can become vast and almost irresistibly seductive. Individual players transmute from being ordinary people living ordinary lives to becoming mighty and noble changers of worlds.

If there's a warning from this, it's that we should be suspicious of any idea, such as 'believe children' or 'vaccines are harmful', that allows connection into a game. We should be yet more suspicious when status, in that game, is earned by active belief in it. This is what happened during the Satanic Panic and it's what Maranda Dynda experienced in the world of the vaccine deniers and it's what drove the men of Pohnpei to devote their lives to the growing of massive yams. When people accept a core belief and act on it, as the price for earning connection and status, they allow themselves to become possessed. That belief is now a status symbol. As their hallucination of reality bends itself around it, they become its host and crusader, deranged and impossible to reason with. In short, their belief has become sacred.

There are many definitions of what 'sacred' means, but from the perspective of this investigation, something is sacred when it becomes symbolic of our status game. As we've learned, the entire world as we experience it inside our brains is built out of symbols. This is the virtual interface on which we play the game of life. A Casio and a Cartier watch are both symbolic, signalling different volumes of status. But some phenomena can become symbolic not just of an amount of status, but of a status game itself. They might be flags, buildings, battle sites, uniforms, gang colours, ceremonies, books, songs, phrases, or the images, remains or birthplaces of elite players, living or dead. Leaders can become sacred. Perhaps the ultimate sacred symbol is the monotheistic God: the all-powerful creator and referee of his status game.

Beliefs can become sacred too. They frequently do. This is why our reasoning about our sacred beliefs can become so impaired. 'When a group of people make something sacred,' writes the psychologist Professor Jonathan Haidt, they 'lose the ability to think clearly about it.' Beliefs are like my Mötley Crüe T-shirt, only infinitely more dangerous.

Sacred symbols can be seen as physical carriers of our status: when someone attacks them, they attack our game and our co-playing kin;

they degrade all that we've earned and all that we value. They scorn our dream of reality, our lived experience, and the ways we think and act in it in order to feel superior. This is why beliefs can make us irrational and violent. It's why they can send us to war.

18

War Games

IT ALL BEGAN over lunch by the beach in La Jolla, California. That afternoon, in the autumn of 1984, a counterculture businessman named Larry Brilliant tried to hustle a publisher, Stewart Brand, into using his online conferencing technology. Brand was famous for publishing *The Whole Earth Catalog*, a magazine and product guide for people who lived communally. Apple co-founder Steve Jobs called the catalogue 'one of the bibles of my generation', describing it as 'like Google in paperback form, thirty-five years before Google came along'. That day, Brilliant tried to convince Brand to have a presence online. Readers of the original catalogues and their successor, the *Whole Earth Review*, could connect via their computers, over modems and phone lines, and chat. How about that? They could create a kind of virtual hippy commune. Who knows what would happen? Wouldn't it be interesting to find out? Brand agreed. He named this experimental community 'The Whole Earth 'Lectronic Link' – 'The Well' for short. It was launched to the public in 1985, on April Fools' Day.

Before The Well, there'd been online bulletin boards and suchlike, relatively closed spaces in which academics and tech nerds could communicate. But there'd never been anything quite like this. All of today's social media platforms are built on the bones of The Well. The contemporary model it resembles most closely is Reddit. Users of The Well would join 'conferences', analogous to Reddit's 'subreddits', arranged around various subjects and chat either publicly or via direct messages known as 'sends'. Writes Well historian Katie Hafner, 'The idea was just about as simple as it could be: Find a bunch of people who are associated by something as random as the age of their children or their preference in wine or their taste in music, who would take that association seriously; give them the means to stay in continuous communication with each other; and step back and see what happens.'

What happened was people gathering around these 'random associations' and forming status games. Players were mostly of a certain type. Hafner describes them as 'baby boomers in their late thirties and early forties, smart and left-leaning without being self-consciously PC, mostly male, many with postgraduate degrees'. These like minds 'found something of a club' in their online forums: they'd discuss their lives and expertise, showing off what they knew. But then, about a year after its launch, when user numbers approached five hundred, someone different arrived. His log-in was Grandma, his name Mark Ethan Smith. Unlike his relatively privileged co-players, Smith had been homeless for around twenty years and was living in near-poverty in Berkeley. And he was angry. He hated men. He came to despise the 'white male clan' he believed characterised The Well.

Smith would start brutal 'flamewars', making outrageous assertions or attacks on people on the forums, in direct messages and multi-hundred-line emails – even on the phone ('Smith had a knack for finding people's home telephone numbers,' writes Hafner). Men were 'penis bearing morons', the designers of the platform were 'the same kind of guys who take time off from developing nuclear weapons to molest children or harass women but are mostly incapable of human relationships'. Those arguing back were told: 'Somebody has to defend the rapists, incestuous fathers, abandoners, batterers, non-payers of child support, discriminatory employers, harassing co-workers and other bums, why not you?' He threatened to track down and sue his adversaries for damages: 'sadists and bigots will not stop torturing people and violating their rights unless they are forced to'. He allegedly wrote that gay men should 'Suck AIDS and DIE!' User after user was triggered; epic threads were created as people argued back. One complained Smith was being 'patently offensive for the sheer pleasure of raising the blood pressure of others'.

Mark Ethan Smith was the world's first internet troll.

He was also biologically female. He wasn't trans, he was gender non-conforming – 'I never became a man, nor do I wish to be known as a man, or, for that matter as a woman,' he wrote. 'In the 5,000 year history of patriarchy, I may be the first individual to exist as a person, without regard to sex.' He objected to having a female name and pronouns he considered 'diminutive', insisting on the 'right to equal terms' with men. His demands to be referred to as 'he' – unusual at that time – were respected by many women of The Well and a few of the men. But more found it preposterous. One wrote: 'According to Mark, you have to call me by a name or pronoun of my choice. In the future please refer to me as: "THE GRAND PUBA, MASTER OF ALL HE SEES OR THE ENTIRE UNIVERSE WHICHEVER IS BIGGER".'

It didn't take long for the organism to begin moving against Smith. As one former member has recalled: 'The more defined The Well became as a community, the more it became aware of itself, and the more it became aware that there were others that were not of it, and the more hostile it became toward them.' When reason didn't work, Smith was abused and insulted. 'You are a sick individual and should be locked up in a mental institution forever,' wrote one. 'Give us all a break and go jump off the Golden Gate Bridge.' Some tried to introduce special code to filter out his posts (it didn't work). Appeals were made to administrators to have him banned. The site's then-director, Doug McClure, refused: 'Just because [he] was obnoxious and had strange ideas didn't mean that [he] shouldn't get to play.' But then McClure left. In October 1986, Smith was told by a new manager his account was suspended indefinitely. According to Smith, hundreds of thousands of his words then vanished.

To anyone who's spent time online, all of this probably sounds familiar. It was all there, back in the 1980s, during the first eighteen months of social media: the status-striving, the groupishness, the trolling and the banning. They were even arguing about pronouns. One of Smith's supporters, an original Well member, described his foes as a 'mob', writing, 'when I saw my fellow Well denizens boiling the virtual tar, and gathering the virtual feathers, I felt pity for their narrowness'. In an undated essay reflecting on his experience, Smith seems most upset at the loss of his contributions. 'If The Well establishment disagreed with my opinions, they could have done so without censoring me.'

Why did all this happen? When Smith presented ideas they didn't believe in, why didn't they simply ignore him? And when he abused them, why couldn't they ignore it? Then, when he was banned, why did they feel the need to erase his work? Why not ignore it? Just forget about it. Why not? Ignoring should be easy, it should be the default: it's literally doing nothing. But in these situations we hardly ever ignore. Because it's not actually effortless. When we encounter people whose beliefs contradict our own, we can find it acutely uncomfortable. We become preoccupied and hateful and flip into dominance state. Our beliefs can even drive us to war.

Such behaviour can be difficult to understand. What's the point in getting so emotional about a stranger being wrong? It doesn't make sense. Especially since, as is so often the case, we become furious over issues that have no real-world effect on the lives of us or anyone we know. Of all the things we could be doing with our energies, being angry at the internet seems a worse than pointless choice. So why do we have this reflex? It only makes sense if we adjust our conception of the human condition. Life is a game played with symbols, and beliefs can be no less symbolic than an invader's battle flag.

Our status games are embedded into our perception. We experience reality through them. So when we encounter someone playing a rival game, it can be disturbing. If they're living by a conflicting set of rules and symbols, they're implying *our* rules and symbols – our criteria for claiming status – are invalid, and our dream of reality is false. They're a sentient repudiation of the value we've spent our lives earning. They insult us simply by being who they are. It should be no surprise, then, that encountering someone with conflicting beliefs can feel like an attack: status is a resource, and they're taking it from us. When neuroscientist Professor Sarah Gimbel presented forty people with evidence their strongly held political beliefs were wrong, the response she observed in their brains was 'very similar to what would happen if, say, you were walking through the forest and came across a bear'.

When this happens we're often compelled to take comfort in the presence of our like-minded kin. We tend to the wounds that have been torn into our hallucination of the world with frantic conversation, medicated with status talk: our foes are *ignorant, insane, Nazis, feminazis, white supremacists, TERFs, bros, wokes, gammons, Karens, SJWs, arseholes, cunts, dicks, tits, crisp packets blowing in the wind*. We jab our fingernails into every crack we find in their dream of reality and, with each one discovered, the threat of their rival claim to status diminishes as ours is reaffirmed. And so our bloodied understanding of life and how it operates is healed; our belief in our game and our criteria for earning status is restored, and the thick evening sunlight of self-satisfaction is allowed to return.

But the dream is now becoming dangerous. It takes the differences between us and our rivals and weaves over them a moral story that says they're not simply wrong, they're evil. This permits further vilification. Our perception warps and bends as we vindictively examine the actions of our foes, searching for any evidence to justify our slide towards dominance. Studies have found this in benign situations: in one neuroscience lab, participants who were offered more points for discriminating blues over reds were, within minutes, better able to see blues. But it also seems common when we're engaged in judging our rivals. Psychologists had participants decide if protestors in a video were breaking various laws. In one version, they were said to be protesting an abortion clinic; in another, it was military recruiting. The participants' judgements of the legality of their behaviour depended to a significant degree on whether or not they appeared to share their moral beliefs. 'Our subjects all viewed the same video,' wrote the researchers. 'But what they saw depended on the congruence of the protestors' positions with the subjects' own cultural values.'

This vindictive mindset is exemplified in the account of the Communist Dai Hsaio-Ai who recalled the bullying that children of former bourgeoisie parents would receive at school: 'Any mistake, whether related to politics or not, was certain to be interpreted in terms of their social class standing. For example, a foul committed on the basketball court might become "another manifestation of the rich peasant mentality".' We can always find new reasons to justify our hatreds when our diseased dream of reality keeps imagining them into being.

Our hatreds are further justified by the belief that our status game is not an act of shared imagination that's local to our kin, but real. And if our criteria for claiming status are real, that means *everyone* should abide by them. We have a spiteful and snobbish habit of judging all people by our rules, whether they're playing with us or not. It's by this logic that an American can look down on a Chinese person who spits in a street, whilst a Japanese person can look down on that American for blowing their nose. If they're not playing by the imagined rules *we've* decided are important and true, we give them a plummeting. Psychologist Professor Sam Gosling finds this when his students cluster into personality groups: 'the extroverts don't disguise their disdain for the uncommunicative introverts, who selfishly refuse to keep the discussion alive; they cannot fathom why their mute colleagues don't do their bit to carry some of the conversational load. At the same time, the introverts have nothing but contempt for their garrulous counterparts; why not, they wonder, wait until you've got something worth saying before opening your mouth?'

We take our foe's adherence to their own game as proof of their disgrace. When they defend themselves, our brains fight off their rival dream of reality by warping ours further, such that it becomes impossible for them to win. If they present counter arguments, we often demand unreasonably high evidence for their claims just as we accept unreasonably low evidence for ours. We like to find any excuse to dismiss their strongest arguments and simply forget those that disturb us most. We adopt harsh double standards, extending them none of the patience, understanding and empathy we lavish on our own. As accusation and outrage builds, our co-players supply us with ever more reasons why *we're* right, helping us calm any dissonance generated by our wanting to feel virtuous whilst wanting to cause them pain. We begin to see the individual players who make up their game as an indistinguishable stain, judging them all as identical and identically contemptible. Look at them: they deserve it, *they're asking for it*. We attack as a blameless, heroic David fighting the cruel monster Goliath. Our kin play their part, cheering us on with every perceived victory, flooding us with boosted status until we're giddy.

We think of morality as unquestionably good: how could it be otherwise? But the moral rules we abide by are a component of our status game, the dream world in which we exist. This dream can all too easily become a nightmare, tricking us into believing our acts of barbarity are holy. As psychologists Professors Steve Reicher and Alex Haslam write: 'People do great wrong, not because they are unaware of what they are doing but because they consider it to be right. This is possible because they actively identify with groups whose ideology justifies and condones the oppression and destruction of others.' Elsewhere anthropologists Professors Alan Page Fiske and Tage Shakti Rai find that 'when people hurt or kill someone, they usually do so because they feel they ought to: they feel that it is morally right or even obligatory to be violent'. When the victim is 'perceived as a potential threat or contaminant to the in-group', such acts are seen as 'morally praiseworthy'.

Most of the time, we don't fight with violence. Instead we engage in battles of belief. For humans, ideology is territory. Our species has an astonishing capacity for fighting wars over the content of other people's minds. This is evident in rare premodern societies whose traditions happen to curtail biological reproduction. The Marind of South New Guinea believed semen to be a magical source of strength and fertility; they used it as an ointment for body and hair and mixed it in their food; when spread onto spears, bows and fishhooks the semen guided the weapons to their targets. Mostly, this magic semen couldn't be harvested via masturbation. It had to be mixed with vaginal fluid following ritual sex. The women of the Marind engaged in extremely frequent sexual intercourse, and not only for this purpose: on her wedding night, a woman would have sex with all the men of her new partner's subclan – often as many as a dozen – before getting to her husband. She'd do the same following childbirth. These practices were intended to increase fertility. Instead, notes anthropologist Professor Robert Paul, they likely 'had the opposite effect'. The combination of frequent sperm harvesting from the men and inflammation of the cervix from 'excessive copulation' in the women meant fertility rates were low and falling.

And yet both their population and territory were expanding. They'd achieve this by launching raiding parties into neighbouring lands and kidnapping children to raise as their own. This is how the Marind kept their game alive. They may not have been reproducing genetically but they were 'certainly reproducing themselves by producing successors, heirs, and bearers of the cultural symbolic system passed on to them by their adoptive parents', writes Paul. For the Marind, these stolen children were 'real descendants – just as real as if they had been biological offspring'.

Societies like the Marind's thrive because human identity is fluid and creative. It's not basic markers such as sex, race or nationality that ultimately define us, it's our imagined games. Of course, we can play those kinds of games, and often do, but they're not compulsory. It's even possible to play status games in opposition to our born identity. In recent years a number of white people in the US have been caught playing ethnic minority identity games, earning status by 'passing' dishonestly as black. In 2020, a white associate professor of African history, Jessica Krug, resigned from her job having admitted assuming 'identities within a Blackness that I had no right to claim' for the 'better part' of her adult life. Krug's status play included anti-white beliefs. During the ensuing scandal, an Afro-Latino man she'd briefly dated told reporters, 'I have never met anyone more racist than her. It was all F whites, F the police, F capitalism, all of that stuff. You could not believe the look on her face when I revealed I had friends of all races. I feared she was ready to fistfight me if I challenged any of her views.'

Krug was showing her date who she was, which game she was playing and by what criteria she was claiming status. When we defend our sacred beliefs, like this, we're defending our experience of the world and our perceived value within it. But we don't only *defend* our positions from attack. We go on the offensive. You might have had the experience of meeting someone new and having them pepper their initial conversation with ambiguous remarks about politicians, say, or controversial news events. When this happens, you're usually being tested. The speaker is asking, *what game is this person playing? Are they kin? Are we going be a source of status for one another? Or is this an opponent, playing a rival game?* In their use of these tender prods, they're prowling the edge of your neural territory, on high alert for any clue that might betray whether you're playmate or enemy.

The extent of our warlike nature has been controversial. It's been argued humans have a biological switch that, when activated, means our games automatically attack foes with violence. Most scholars now think this isn't true. Some even claim life in the Stone Age lacked war pretty much entirely. This seems incorrect for a number of reasons. One of the first major cross-cultural studies of intergroup conflict among hunter-gatherers found that, while some groups were peaceful, 90 per cent fought wars more often than 'rarely or never', with the majority fighting regularly. Most systematic studies support the argument that warfare was common. Whilst intergroup violence might not be automatic, it is an undeniable human tendency. In the modern era, it can be found at all scales of society, from gang violence to religious sectarianism to state terrorism to civil and international war. The sad fact is, for all the astonishing levels of nonviolence we extend towards our kin, when it comes to the aggression of game-versus-game we remain, according to anthropologist Professor Richard Wrangham, 'exceptionally' violent.

But it's only when we expand our conception of war to encompass battles over ideological territory that we truly see what monstrously aggressive animals we are. People everywhere crusade on behalf of their sacred beliefs. When we go on the attack, like this, we're reaching into the minds of others and attempting to rearrange them such that they start playing *our* games, dreaming our dreams instead of theirs. Every convert's theft is transmogrified into a gift: they go from stealing status from us to offering it. And it feels good. We're all so many neural imperialists, fighting to expand our territory by making incursions into the minds of others.

Our thirst for these kinds of psychological conquests is evident in the history of white colonialists in Canada and Australia who prevented indigenous populations from speaking their language and practising their religion. It's evident in the nearly four hundred re-education camps in which the Chinese have held hundreds of thousands of Uighur Muslims. It's evident in the Communist regime of Enver Hoxha in which Albanians were imprisoned for wearing Western-style flared trousers or having an 'imperialist haircut'. It's evident in the more than two hundred thousand souls incarcerated by the East German Stasi, most of them psychologically tortured, some physically brutalised and shot in prison basements, the most common offence being an alleged wish to leave Communist East for Capitalist West. In thirteenth-century France, when the Cathars refused to convert, the Catholics who burned them alive were so afraid that their slightly different beliefs about God and Satan would somehow reanimate, and start conquering psychological territory, they dug up their bones and burned them again.

For political psychologist Dr Lilliana Mason, part of the reason we continually attempt at warring for victory is that 'people are compelled to think of their groups as better than others. Without that, they themselves feel inferior.' At a 'very primal level' players are motivated 'to view the world through a competitive lens, with importance placed on their own group's superiority'. Humans love to become superior: to win. Researchers find groups tend to prefer the simple fact of winning against other groups even if it means fewer benefits for its players. Sociologist Professor Nicholas Christakis writes, this finding 'depresses me even more than the existence of xenophobia'. We want a lot for our groups, of course, but of even greater importance is creating a yawning distance of victory between us and our rivals. 'What seems to be important to people is how much more members of one's own group get compared to members of other groups, not how much one's group has,' he writes. 'Not only must one's group have a lot, it must have more than other groups.'

This goes, too, for wars of belief. We don't just seek to win arguments with our ideological foes, we seek domination, as the citizens of The Well showed in their treatment of Mark Ethan Smith. They couldn't ignore him because he was stealing status from them; for the same reason, Smith couldn't ignore them. They couldn't even bring themselves to use his preferred pronoun – an act that, symbolically, meant deference to his rules and symbols, thus defeat. So he responded with threats and de-grading abuse; they responded with insult, ostracization and censorship. They couldn't simply live with one another's claims to status. One party had to win.

This is an inevitable, terrible consequence of the game of life we play. We're wired to love being above. We continually seek to rearrange the world such that our game is on top, all the while telling self-serving stories about the immaculate virtue of our behaviour. The lesson many will find impossible to accept is this: never believe groups who claim they just want 'equality' with rivals. No matter what they say, no matter what they believe, they don't. They weave a marvellous dream of fairness for all, but the dream is a lie.

19

The Tyranny of the Cousins

STATUS GAMES ARE potent organisms. They sometimes appear to be in possession of their own intelligence; to have a will that can overwhelm that of their players. The Satan-hunters became the puppets of their game, absorbing its wild dream then going out into the world to fight on its behalf. By their dutiful service, the game they belonged to grew in power. Similarly, when the Great Mothers Questioning Vaccines turned on Maranda Dynda, and the men of The Well turned on Mark Ethan Smith, they did so in obedience to the organism. No single player had the ability to switch these mobbings on or off. It was as if the game's immune system fired up in the minds of its players. Under its strange authority, the group moved as one in rejection of the foreign object.

A game's command over its players strengthens when it flips into a mode of war. Connections between players *tighten*. These effects have been shown in numerous studies. An analysis of social ties between World War II veterans found individuals who experienced combat with one another maintained stronger personal connections even forty years later. Their bonds were intensified yet further if their units had suffered deaths, suggesting, 'the more intense the social threat, the greater the social bonding'. Elsewhere, Chinese participants having their brains scanned whilst reading about a threat from the Japanese showed 'higher neural synchrony' with each other. This tightening up – the thickening of the connections between them – helped them coordinate faster in group tasks. Tighter games work better together: the dominion of the individual recedes, that of the group swells, and it becomes better able to defend itself from attack.

But this super-cohesive war mode is also triggered when there's status to win. We can see this in goldrush movements such as the Satanic Panic whose mad energy seemed to derive principally from the prizes on offer. Studies confirm that groups can thicken up in this manner – offensively as well as defensively. In one, cohesion and in-group preference were found to increase when one group was awarded the prize of a transistor radio. The 'opportunity to acquire resources' was found to be 'a powerful context for triggering group cohesion'. It's also consistent with the different ways human groups have always made war. We defend ourselves from raids *and* we launch raids on others; both are highly co-operative endeavours that benefit from this super-cohesive mode of play.

When a game thickens, individual players begin to merge with one another and its dream becomes more powerful. We become increasingly lost in it and devoted to serving it. But no single player is in control of this tightening up. Eerily, it just happens. We begin coercing ourselves and each other. This happens as a result of one of the most counter-intuitive facts about status games and the premodern groups they grew out of: no one person is truly in charge of them. In this era of presidents, queens, popes, celebrities, superstar activists and CEOs, it's easy to assume leadership is a natural feature of human life. But this is not the case. Although they were organised around hierarchies, hunter-gatherer communities weren't very often ruled by a lone 'big man' figure. Writes anthropologist Professor Christopher Boehm, 'sometimes a wise individual may be accorded the status of temporary or permanent band leader. However, that person is expected to behave with humility, for the accepted leader-ship style permits nothing more assertive than carefully listening to everyone else's opinion and then gently helping to implement a consensus – if this spontaneously forms. Such decisions may involve a band's next move or the group's taking action against a serious deviant, but such leaders by themselves cannot settle on an outcome; this is a decision for the entire group.' And it would be that group, not the individual, that held final authority.

It's thought we evolved like this partly as a way of dealing with dominant players. For hundreds of thousands of years, when indi-viduals (usually men) repeatedly tried to force their way up the rankings with aggression and threats of it, we've killed them. But executing unwanted players creates a new problem. We can't play a game whereby one player is able to simply denounce another for dominant behaviour and take their life. Far from ridding us of the nuisance of dominant play, this would incentivise it, as players could just accuse rivals of malfeasance and take them out. So instead, the game itself made the decision. Players would come together as an organism of thought and, only after consensus was achieved, would a killing be permitted. In our tribal, kin-based games it was our tribal kin who'd decide collectively whether unwanted players lived or died.

For the vast majority of our time on earth, then, humans haven't been subject to the tyranny of leaders. Instead, we lived in fear of what anthropologists call the 'tyranny of the cousins'. These 'cousins' weren't necessarily actual cousins. They'd usually be clan elders that, in these shallow hierarchies, passed for the elite. Whilst they're thought to have almost always been men, both genders could take part in the act of deadly consensus-making. Writes Boehm, 'when a band coalesces to bring down a tyrant, the females may be as active as the males in the political dynamics involved'. Some accounts even show men and women symbolically sharing responsibility for an execution: in one, a man was beaten by a band of males who then fired poison arrows into his body until he 'looked like a porcupine'. When he was dead, the women stepped forward and stabbed his corpse with spears.

This might sound fair enough, if harsh. If a player attempts to dominate a game through terror, that player is taken out. Execution is the ultimate humiliation; a rejection by the game that's physical as well as psychological, not to mention final. But unfortunately for the history of the human race, it's not quite as straightforward as this. The problem is, there aren't two separate and easily identifiable forms of player – tyrants and non-tyrants. We *all* contain the capacity for tyranny. Who's the tyrant and who's the victim can often be difficult to tell. The cousins themselves could be brutal.

Indeed, the same hunter-gatherer groups that came together to bloodily cancel tyrants also used deadly force against those who broke many other of their game's rules. Players could be executed for theft and hoarding of meat, for malicious sorcery, for unauthorised viewing of the magic trumpets and for 'treading on the men's secret path'. The games we evolved to play could be oppressive and terrifying. Anthropologist Professor Richard Wrangham describes us as having lived in a 'social cage of tradition' in which players 'lived or died by their willingness to conform'. The power of these cousins was 'absolute. If you did not conform to their dictates, you were in danger.'

We've encountered these dynamics in Mehrana, India. When the high-caste girl was caught with an untouchable boy, the village elders held an all-night meeting, proposed their being hanged from a banyan tree and encountered no protests from three thousand villagers. Wrangham describes a similar account of deadly consensus-making amongst the Gebusi people in New Guinea. A member of the tribe had become seriously ill and malicious sorcery was blamed. At a meeting, a medium conducted a ritual with magic leaves that indicated a relative of the patient was the culprit. Now under threat, the accused had to strategise. He couldn't risk appearing unrepentant by outright denial. Instead, he flirted desperately with confession: 'I don't know anything about it. He's my own relative, too, I couldn't make him sick. I don't know . . . I might have been a little angry from not eating enough fish lately, but I certainly wouldn't make my own relative sick like that.' In the days following the meeting, the man's accuser went about the community quietly building support for deadly action. During a night-time meeting, the cousins grew 'more and more enthusiastic about the idea that the alleged sorcerer was responsible for the death', writes Wrangham. 'Consensus is reached. All decide the accused is guilty. At dawn, they stage an ambush. They kill with clubs or arrows. Sometimes there is torture first. Then they butcher and cook him.'

The impression of consensus, in our groups, was vital. It didn't have to be a technical consensus. What counted was the general sense of the group, as an organism, supporting the action. It was often built in a boiling atmosphere of gossip and the recounting of past sins that would generate plumes of moral outrage, directed at the accused. As well as executions, the group could exact punishments of shame: these could begin as simple 'social aloofness' as targets weren't greeted. They could also be ignored, mocked and humiliated. When a member of the Mbuti in the Congo was caught cheating during a hunt, men and women began gossiping about him, insulting him behind his back, detailing past misdemeanours. His reputation was monstered as consensus on the corruption of his character grew. On his return to camp he was ignored: nobody, not even the children, offered him a seat as was proper. When he tried taking one by force he was told, 'animals lie on the ground'. When he was accused of cheating publicly, he first tried lying then wept in apology, clutching his stomach saying he would die because he wasn't respected.

The cousins were terrible and powerful and we still carry a deep dread of them within us. They make their presence known in the enormous literature that shows how naturally we can conform to the perceptions of our groups: an iconic 1951 experiment by psychologist Professor Solomon Asch had participants making simple and obvious assessments as to which of three lines was the nearest in length to another. When seven fake participants voiced a different majority view, 32 per cent of people conformed to their judgement. No overt pressure was applied to these participants. That nearly a third of them were prepared to deny the clear evidence of their eyes when the power of the group was so weak, and the stakes so low, hints at the extent to which humans are likely to conform to the dreams of a group when it's 1938, say, and you're living in Moscow or Berlin. We fear the cousins; we're compelled to play obediently by their social cage of rules.

But the cousins are also inside us. We all contain the capacity for tyranny. 8-month-olds prefer to play with a puppet they've seen punishing a transgressor in a puppet show. Children start enforcing rules spontaneously at around age 3. A study into the reasons school-children, aged between 5 and 7, reject playmates found a tendency to do so when their behaviour became a threat to the status of themselves or their clique. Psychologist Professor Francisco Juan García Bacete has said, 'what actually leads to rejection are the rejecters' interpretations of the child's behaviour, and whether they think it will have a negative impact on themselves or their social group'. Elsewhere, brain scans show the mere anticipation of a transgressor being punished for rule-breaks is experienced as pleasurable.

We don't like to think of ourselves this way. The story we prefer removes oppression and hatred from our essential game-playing human nature and blames it on corrupted leaders and their evil schemes. We can see this mode of naivety in the pioneers of internet and social media who predicted that connecting millions of humans together online would create a kind of utopia. In 1996, a former member of The Well, John Perry Barlow, published a 'Declaration of the Independence of Cyberspace' in which he announced a new 'civilisation of the Mind' was being created in which the old hierarchies of power were not welcome. 'I declare the global social space we are building to be naturally independent of the tyrannies you seek to impose on us . . . We are creating a world where anyone, anywhere may express his or her beliefs, no matter how singular, without fear of being coerced into silence or conformity.'

But that's not how it turned out. Today, even seemingly innocuous comments on social media can lead to a group coalescing in screeching outrage. Online mobs play virtue-dominance games: status is awarded to players who enforce their rules to those both inside and outside their groups. They're also tight: the players involved are highly conformist. These mobs throb with the horrible power of the cousins. Their attacks are often deleted or Swiss-cheesed after they've occurred. But occasionally some survive. One such case is that of Karen Templer, the mobbing of whom ranged across multiple platforms, including YouTube and Instagram, but also in comments beneath her blog which she declined to erase, 'as I don't believe in editing the historical record'.

Templer is a knitter and owner of the knitting website Fringe Association (tagline: Knit and Let Knit). In January 2019 she uploaded a blog called 'My Year of Color' in which, amongst other things, she looked forward to a trip to India. Templer had once found the prospect of foreign travel 'daunting' but now wanted to 'be a person who says yes more'. India's literature and history had been a 'lifelong obsession'. The family of a childhood friend, who was Indian, once offered to take her: 'To a suburban midwestern teenager with a severe anxiety disorder, that was like being offered a seat on a flight to Mars. It was fun to think about, but are you kidding me?' When a new opportunity came along, she found the courage to say yes. 'I felt like the top of my head was going to fly off, I was so indescribably excited.'

At first, the comments were supportive. 'Right on!' wrote Christine Lindop. 'This is the direction that those orange sandals have been pointing you in.' Similar posts soon piled up:

Eastlondonknit: That is very awesome about India!!

Tina M Bury: This has brought me so much joy and warm fuzzies today! Yes!!

Cheryl Ortwein: YAHOOOO

Miss Agnes: You go girl!

Deepa: The US is now my home in every sense (20 years!) and my heart is here, but my soul will always be in India. I tell people it is like no other place on earth, truly. It is everything you have heard about it and yet it will surprise you in every way.

Diane: Best. Post. EVER!

Mala Srikanth: I live in the Indian Himalayas . . . You will have a wonderful time.

Narangkar: Ooh, exciting! India will always be special to me because I grew up there.

Marie Carter: You are even more inspiring than I thought

Duni: Congratufuckinglations!

But then there arrived an ominous post: 'I came across an interesting review of the article on instagram and despite being priviledged [sic] and [a white?] person myself, I agree with the critics – we have to be careful about how we communicate colour. Language is so powerful and some of the statements are questionable and very inconsiderate.'

Templer was worried. 'I have[n't] seen whatever criticism you're referring to or agreeing with,' she wrote. 'What is it that you find inconsiderate in what I've said here?'

'Karen,' wrote Alex J Klein, 'I'd ask you to re-read what you wrote and think about how your words feed into a colonial/imperialist mindset toward India and other non-Western countries. Multiple times you compare the idea of going to India to the idea of going to another planet – how do you think a person from India would feel to hear that?'

Of course, at least three people ostensibly from India responded to Templer's post with statements of joyful encouragement. 'What I said is that, as a teenager, India felt as far away and unattainable to me as Mars,' Templer wrote, 'that it was impossible to contemplate actually being able to go to either place. I'm not sure how that's imperialist but will give it some thought.' She noted the positive feedback from Indian friends and readers. 'I'll have to see if anything I said offended them.'

'Instead of asking your Indian friends to perform more emotional labor for you and assuage your white women's tears,' Klein replied, 'maybe do some reflection on how your equation of India with an alien world reinforces an "other" mindset that is at the core of imperialism and colonialism.'

Other attackers soon flapped in and landed, including Caroline who thanked Klein for his intervention – 'I second your comment whole-heartedly' – and Sarah, who added, 'Romanticizing other lands and cultures is a dangerous thing to do.' Templer apologised. She attempted once more to explain herself: 'The only way in which I was equating India and Mars, as I just said to Alex above, is that they would have seemed equally far away and out of reach to my teenage self.'

'Rather than being defensive,' wrote Caroline, 'I ask you to truly listen to what people have said to you here and on instagram. Also, you clearly need to go read up on POC [people of colour] emotional labor if you think it's not emotional labor to ask your Indian friends to weigh in on this. While you're at it, you should read about white fragility and intent vs. impact. Regardless of what you intended by this post, the impact has been completely different for many people. You need to go educate yourself.'

'To everyone I offended by what I've written here, I want to say I hear you and I am sorry,' wrote Templer.

'You're sorry people are offended?' wrote Rachel. 'That's not an apology for your deeply racist and reductive statement. Please rethink this trip. Don't force the people of India to deal with you and your colonializing mindset.'

Some of Templer's readers voiced support, but others began turning against her. Marie Carter, who'd previously written, 'You are even more inspiring than I thought ♥', now wrote: 'I am ashamed to say that I failed to consider the impact of this post on all of us non-white people . . . my heart hurts and I won't be able to live with myself unless I acknowledge the pain to me and others like me of the words used. I am no longer going to say nothing.'

'Same here,' replied Liz N who described reading 'thousands of comments' about her post on Instagram.

Templer relented. In a follow-up blog entitled 'Words Matter' she confessed to being 'insensitive' and 'horrible' and 'careless' for treating India like a 'backdrop for white people' and perpetuating 'the harmful notion that Indians (and POC in general) are "other," or even to be feared'. She ended by apologising yet again, 'profusely to everyone I hurt, and to everyone who has taken any kind of heat for calling me out on it. I was wrong, and the women who took the risk to speak out were right.'

It's haunting to witness the parallels between what anthropologists find in premodern societies and what we see, here, in the twenty-first-century tribal battlegrounds of social media. Templer's initial response to her accusers recalls the account from the Gebusi, in which the accused worriedly flits between defence and confession: *'He's my own relative, too, I couldn't make him sick. I don't know . . . I might have been a little angry from not eating enough fish lately.'* It's in the sense, if not the reality, of a ferociously growing consensus against the deviant. It's in the gossip, the social distancing, the shaming. It's in the extremely local weirdness of the accusations. For players living inside the accusers' dream, it was apparently obvious how their target had transgressed the rules. But to those outside it, her crime was obscure: Templer had viewed the magic trumpets. For her sin the cousins had coalesced for attack and were building consensus against her, in all their righteousness and thirst.

In the end, she saved herself. At the time of writing, Templer's company still exists, as does her blog. By conforming to the tyrannical cousins, and the frenzy spreading across the gossip networks of social media, she avoided being 'cancelled' – which is what we call it when internet mobs, unsatisfied by mockery, denunciation and humiliation meted out online, attempt at having their target de-graded as much as possible in the physical world. The effects of a cancellation can be as mild as the loss of limited amounts of work or as severe as the destruction of livelihood and reputation – or worse. Examples are numerous and easy to find. In recent years, academics have been denounced and had papers retracted and honorifics removed; public intellectuals have been 'de-platformed' from events; journalists, editors, agents and business leaders have been fired or forced to resign; athletes and authors have lost contracts; businesses including a food truck and a yoga studio have shut down; British journalist Helen Lewis had her computer game voiceover removed in a software update; drag queen Vanity von Glow was banned from performing at various London venues; Tabitha Moore-Morris, a Kentucky hospital worker, lost her job of twenty years; brilliant Silicon Valley technologist, Austen Heinz, lost his reputation and committed suicide.

These mobs don't seek to win over their victims and turn them into allies. They seek the maximal removal of their status and any of its symbols; ideally, reputational death. In a world dominated by games of prestige, this is how we do killing. The ultimate target of cancellation is not the human, but their belief. Mobs are performative. They say to their many onlookers, 'if you express this opinion, you too can expect a call from the cousins'. No single person is in charge of these mobs just as no single person can stop them. They just happen, usually when someone expresses a view that contradicts a game's sacred symbolic beliefs. The tyrannical group can accept no challenge to their criteria for claiming status. When their mob grows into a status goldrush, a massive blast of vindictive energy gets directed at the victim. Attracted by the prizes, more and more ambitious players pile in and the game becomes an animal of attack, glorying in the ecstasy of dominance.

To understand how this form of status play is affecting society, we can travel to northern Iraq. It's the summer of 2014 and a group of selfie-taking activists, predominantly millennials, are on their way to the city of Mosul. They are ISIS and they're playing a dominance-virtue game. Their social media uploads show them black-clad and heavily armed and include videos of the nightmarish torture and execution they'd inflict on captured enemies – all under the hashtag #AllEyesOnISIS. This became the top-trending hashtag on Arabic Twitter. ISIS had nearly fifty digital hubs in different regions, each targeting content to different demographics. They increased user engagement by asking how captives should be executed: 'Suggest a way to Kill the Jordanian Pilot Pig'. They also piggybacked onto other trending topics. During the World Cup one fighter posted a gruesome photograph with the comment: 'This is our football, it's made of skin #WorldCup'.

Ten thousand Iraqi soldiers had stood in defence of Mosul. But ISIS's social media campaign had everyone 'consumed with fear', write researchers P. W. Singer and Emerson Brooking. Their hashtag 'took on the power of an invisible artillery bombardment, its thousands of messages spiralling out in front of the advancing force. Their detonation would sow terror, disunion and defection.' As they approached Mosul, thousands of Iraqi soldiers fled, many leaving weapons and vehicles behind. By the time they arrived at the outskirts, 'only a handful of brave (or confused) soldiers and police remained behind. It wasn't a battle but a massacre, dutifully filmed and edited for the next cycle of easy online distribution.' ISIS used 'a different sort of blitzkrieg, one that used the internet itself as a weapon' and it was by this method their 'improbable momentum' continued.

Online mobs are like ISIS. They use social media in the same way as the terrorist group. Western cultures have a sacred rule forbidding bigotry. Leaders of corporations and the institutions of government, media and education know that to be suspected of misogyny, racism, homophobia or transphobia is to face reputational death. This is what these mobs threaten. It's not necessary for elites to be directly accused of these transgressions, it's enough to witness the mob's performance. By this method, just like ISIS, activists use the dread machine of social media to gain a level of status – and the influence and power that goes with it – that massively outsizes their numbers.

We can know this through public surveys. The year after Templer's mobbing, one of the largest ever studies of Britain's social psychology was published, containing data from over ten thousand respondents. It found seven distinct opinion groups, describing 'progressive activists' as being the one 'motivated by the pursuit of social justice'. They make for a 'powerful and vocal group for whom politics is at the core of their identity'. The progressive activists believe the game is essentially fixed, that a player's life outcomes are 'determined more by the social structures in which they grow up than by their individual efforts'. Of all the groups, they're the most highly educated and also the wealthiest, with more earning a household income above £50,000 than any other. They're also 'the dominant voice' on social media, a realm in which they play a 'commanding role'. They're six times more likely to post about politics on Twitter and other platforms than any other group. They make more total social media contributions than the rest of the nation combined. And yet, as of 2020, they comprised just 13 per cent of the population. In the USA, a similar study found they numbered 8 per cent.

National surveys reveal how marginal their beliefs and behaviours are. General attitudes in the UK and US seem relatively progressive: in 1958, just 4 per cent of Americans favoured interracial marriage compared to 87 per cent in 2013. Only 3 per cent of Britons believe being 'truly British' requires being white; 73 per cent agree hate speech is an issue; more than half think transphobia is 'somewhat' or 'a great deal' of a problem. And yet many behaviours that characterise progressive activists and their mobs are unpopular. The politically correct policing of speech is largely unwelcome in both nations. Across all US racial groups, 80 per cent believe 'political correctness is a problem in this country'; 87 per cent of Hispanics and three-quarters of African Americans agree. In the UK, 72 per cent believe political correctness has become a problem. A sizeable minority, 29 per cent, agree that Britain is a 'systematically or institutionally racist country'. Polling company YouGov found much lower support for other positions associated with progressive activism: 12 per cent believed it was fair to punish an adult for controversial views they expressed online as a teenager; 10 per cent thought it 'not okay' for non-Japanese people to wear a kimono and only 5 per cent thought the next Governor of the Bank of England should be a woman (3 per cent thought it should be a man; 87 per cent said gender didn't matter).

Of course, progressive activists don't only gain outsized status via their mobs. With their peerless levels of wealth and education, they're also able to insert their elites into many of society's most powerful games. It's important to note, too, that concluding *all* progressive activists approve of mob behaviour would be extremely unfair. But this is the point. Those who play in their mobs are a minority of a minority. And yet too often their commanding voice on social media becomes a commanding voice in our democracies. Like ISIS, they achieve this outsized status partly by the spreading of dread. Their gossip, accusation and merciless fury is designed to weave the illusion of consensus, wake our ancient dread of the cousins and bully us into their social cage.

This is how mobs win.

20

Victims, Warriors, Witches

WHEN A GAME goes to war, it tightens up. It strengthens its dominion over individual players, whose selves increasingly merge in its service. Its dreams turn wilder and darker. Its heroes seem more heroic, its villains more villainous, its moral lessons become purer. Players who tell tales that reaffirm its self-serving narrative are rewarded with status. Their accounts are often those of victimhood that draw their foes as powerful, heartless and dangerous. When actual reality provides a paucity of such accounts, players can simply invent them. In 2013, at the University of Wyoming, an anonymous Facebook page on which students would post about their 'crushes' received an entry directed at a prominent feminist and award-winning blogger: 'I want to hatefuck Meg Lanker Simons so hard. That chick that runs her liberal mouth all the time and doesn't care who knows it. I think its hot and it makes me angry. One night with me and shes gonna be a good Republican bitch.' Lanker-Simons replied, writing it was 'disgusting, misogynistic, and apparently something the admins of this page think is a perfectly acceptable sentiment'. There followed a student demonstration against 'rape culture' at which Lanker-Simons spoke. Following an investigation, police concluded the post had been written by Meg Lanker-Simons.

This wasn't an isolated incident. Recent notorious hoaxes include that of US actor Jussie Smollett who police accused of faking a racist, homophobic assault by Trump supporters because he 'wanted to promote his career', and who was subsequently found guilty of lying about the attack to officers; a campaign of offensive graffiti at Vassar College reportedly including 'Hey Tranny. Know Your Place' that was found to be the work of two students, one of whom, Genesis Hernandez, was a transgender activist and member of the college's Bias Incident Response Team; psychologist Professor Kerri Dunn, described by the *Los Angeles Times* as 'a hero to many students . . . [for] lifting her voice for the oppressed', who, after delivering a lecture on hate speech, found her car smashed, slashed and graffitied with 'Kike Whore', 'N— Lover',* 'Bitch', 'Shut Up' 'Bitch', 'Shut Up' and a half-finished swastika, and who, it was subsequently discovered, committed the vandalism herself. This mode of performative story-making isn't only carried out by players on the left. In 2008 Republican campaign volunteer Ashley Todd faked an attack in which she said an African American knocked her to the ground and scratched 'B' for Barack Obama into her face. Similarly, in 2007, Princeton student Francisco Nava falsely claimed to have been threatened then beaten unconscious due to his membership of the conservative Anscombe Society.

These hoaxers reaffirmed the simplistic moral stories their games told of the world, reassuring them their criteria for claiming status were true. They appeared on television, in newspapers, in lecture halls and at the head of campus demonstrations. In times of war we honour our victims. Their tales are of suffering and of bravery and survival: out of their victimhood they become heroic. They allow their co-players to feel heroic, too, in their coming together in noble defiance of the monsters.

---

* This racial slur was written in full.

Out of this coalition will often emerge a few who possess the courage and ambition to step up and make active war with the enemy. These warriors are usually thirstier for rank than other players. An analysis of warriorship in premodern societies discovered a positive relationship between conflict intensity and the status on offer for fighters. 'Warriors are motivated to participate in warfare because of the possibility of rewards,' it found. These included 'increased status, honorific names or titles, or special insignia'. They're also more likely to be collective narcissists: they believe their game is obviously superior and automatically deserving of deference. Research suggests simple satisfaction and pride in our group, when it's securely felt and not grandiose, doesn't necessarily lead to negative effects, and can even promote tolerance. What makes the difference is that narcissistic dream: the conviction that their game is special and entitled to be treated that way. 'Collective narcissists, preoccupied with the in-group's superiority and its validation by others, are likely to be particularly sensitive to signs of insufficient recognition of the in-group, exaggerate them and experience them as an insult,' according to one paper. Collective narcissism was found to be a 'specific and unique, systematic predictor of hypersensitivity to in-group insult and proclivity for hostile over-reaction'.

Warriors are also likely to strongly identify with their game, believing in it utterly and having more of their personal status invested in it. 'When a group's status is threatened, a strongly identified group member will fight to maintain the status of the group,' writes political psychologist Dr Lilliana Mason. It's their identification with the game that 'drives the group member to take action to maintain positive group status'. In one study, participants watched the film *Rocky IV*, with some seeing a re-edited version in which the American hero loses to the Russian fighter, Ivan Drago. Viewers who most closely identified with being American suffered 'severe hits' to their sense of status, feeling 'very negatively about themselves after watching Rocky lose'. The psychologists then gave them the chance to voice hostile opinions about their rivals, the Russians. Those who did, making 'insulting judgements' about them, felt their injured pride recover.

Warriors – highly identified with their game and often narcissistic on its behalf – can become drunk on the status earned from warring, and seek to make battle almost anywhere. They fight defensively and also offensively, picking opportunistic fights with foes. This kind of virtue-dominance play is conspicuous on social media where warriors play a game of attack, defend and win, earning status for themselves and their group. Their strategies are revealed in analyses of tweets that find those most likely to be retweeted contain more moral words, more emotion, and more moral outrage. A study of seventy million messages on the Chinese platform Weibo found the emotion that 'travelled fastest and farthest through the social network' was anger. Meanwhile, studies of mobbing events on Twitter find shamers increase their follower counts faster than non-shamers.

Historically, the role of the 'cousins' was to enforce a game's norms, whilst warriors went out into the world to fight on its behalf, grabbing resources from rival groups or defending them from raiders. But in the modern world these archetypes often merge. Theoretically, the Great Mothers Questioning Vaccines had cousins within their Facebook group, where they enforced their beliefs, and warriors outside it, where they'd defend and evangelise their criteria for claiming status. But in reality they were often the same person. Participants in online mobs are warriors doing the bidding of their own internal cousins. We all have the capacity to engage in these suites of behaviour: it's in our coding and has been for hundreds of thousands of years. A warning that someone's slipped into this state of tightness is their seeming wholly obsessed with their game's sacred beliefs and their enforcement. They can seem able to think and talk of little else. They find this pleasurable because they're playing a symbolic game of status with them: with every thought, utterance and expression of active belief, they earn prizes.

The British television star Jameela Jamil has arguably achieved greater status for her online warring than for presenting or acting. Focussing on issues around mental health and body image, she's argued that those who don't admit to having their photos retouched are guilty of a 'disgusting crime'. She's publicly attacked elite women such as the Kardashians, Cardi B, Rihanna, Miley Cyrus, Nicki Minaj, Iggy Azelea, Caroline Calloway, Beyoncé and J. K. Rowling. In 2019 she criticised a TV show centred on plastic surgery, presented by Caroline Flack, with whom she engaged in a hostile Twitter exchange. Flack was then subjected to an 'online pile-on' by Jamil's followers, with one asking how she could defend 'a show this toxic and exploitative that you're willingly hosting?' Four months later, when Flack committed suicide following highly publicised issues in her private life, Jamil wrote: 'It was only a matter of time before the media and the prolonged social media dogpile, hers lasted for MONTHS, pushed someone completely over the edge.' A journalist then released a private message he'd been sent by Flack: 'I'm struggling with Jameela. The hate she aims at me.' For her warring, Jamil has won significant status. In 2019, she was selected by Meghan, the Duchess of Sussex, to appear on the cover of *Vogue* magazine as one of fifteen female 'Forces for Change'. She has more than a million followers on Twitter and, on Instagram, over three million.

Naturally there are warriors on the opposing side too. In January 2020, another British actor, Laurence Fox, made headlines following an appearance on the BBC debate show *Question Time* in which he rebutted the charge of being a 'white privileged male' as 'racist'. He later complained the inclusion of Sikh soldiers in the First World War film *1917* was an act of 'forced diversity' before apologising on learning 130,000 Sikhs fought in the war. He then attempted to foment a boycott of the supermarket chain Sainsbury's for their support of Black History Month, which he claimed amounted to 'racial segregation and discrimination'. Before his *Question Time* appearance, Fox had just under fifty thousand Twitter followers. By the end of the year, he'd surpassed a quarter of a million.

Warriors such as Jamil and Fox earn significant status in spite of their errors, reversals and shamings. They're often members of their game's elite: highly visible players, highly identified with the game, seeking to generate major virtue status. Their attacks are frequently enabled by resentful, ambitious low-status players who conspire in the gossiping and mobbing. One investigation found those most likely to circulate 'hostile political rumours' including conspiracy theories and 'fake news' on social media were often 'status-obsessed, yet socially marginalised', their behaviour fuelled by a 'thwarted desire for high status', their aim, to 'mobilise the audience against disliked elites'.

Under these conditions, the dream we weave over reality can become brutish and hysterical. As we saw in the mobbing of Karen Templer, a game's moral positions can shift, morphing into more and more extreme versions of themselves. Templer was targeted after writing her invitation to India felt like being 'offered a seat on a flight to Mars'. In the pathologically tight fantasy world of her accusers, this statement was proof she was a racist, a colonialist, a white supremacist. Researchers Dr Justin Tosi and Dr Brandon Warmke describe the process of 'ramping up' by which status-strivers, trying to outdo one another, push their game's moral positions into ever tighter places: 'Once we hear what others' views are (or at least what they say they are), we have two options. We can either accept that we are morally ordinary and keep our views as they are, or we can ever so slightly shift our views (or at least our presentation of them) to retain our status as the moral exemplar within the group. For many, the latter option is preferable.' When warriors ramp up, in this way, they're 'not trying to arrive at the correct moral claim . . . What drives them is the desire to be the most morally impressive.'

As the game becomes tighter its dream becomes stranger: purer, stricter and made out of more extreme beliefs. Then what do we do, us ordinary players? Risk the wrath of the cousins and their caste of warriors by voicing our doubts? Or keep our heads down and play along? We've already encountered the famous Solomon Asch 'lines study' of conformity, in which a third of participants in a comparatively loose laboratory group denied the clear evidence of their eyes, announcing their beliefs matched those of the majority. A study led by psychologist Professor Robb Willer found similar dynamics. Participants tasted samples of wine and were asked to choose their favourite by rating them on a scale. They weren't told these samples were actually identical, from the same bottle. They were to be the fifth out of six reviewers. When they saw the first four tasters had assessed one sample as greatly superior, just over half the participants agreed with them – a result showing conformity at even greater rates than Asch. And then, the twist. A sixth reviewer came in and told the truth, saying they tasted identical. The participants were then asked to rate the tasters. Who had better palates? The lying first four? Or the truth-telling sixth? When asked privately, they rated the sixth. But those asked publicly not only endorsed the false majority view, they punished the sole teller of truth by downgrading them.

For the researchers, these behaviours are a predictable consequence of a game's becoming dangerously tight. Some players will be true believers, swept up into the dream entirely. Others won't. They'll sense its gathering madness. But, nervous of the power of the cousins, they'll pretend to believe. These false believers still act as if they're loyal players, adhering to the game's rules, symbols and beliefs. But in the secret psychological territory in their skulls, they've lost faith in the dreamed-up story. Because tight groups tend towards irrationality and aggressive conformity, they're frequently populated by both true and false believers. The false believers often attempt to prove their loyalty with active belief, enforcing the rules. They do this 'to demonstrate their sincerity', write the researchers. 'That is, to show that they did not conform simply to secure social approval. This is because, to true believers in the group, mere conformity is insufficient. Those who conform may only be posturing for group approval.'

So who are the true believers? And who are the dangerous hidden deviants betraying our dream of reality from within? The game becomes even tighter as players 'pressure one another in order to cover up their own private doubts'. This makes suspicions increase yet further. The game can then enter what sociologists Dr Bradley Campbell and Dr Jason Manning call a 'purity spiral' in which players 'strive to outdo one another in displays of zealotry, condemning and expelling members of their own movement for smaller and smaller deviations from its core virtues'. They jostle to prove themselves honest by accusing and denouncing others, each desperate to demonstrate their acceptance of the game. Any deviants discovered can be shamed, ostracized or even killed. When a game enters this mode of play, it's started hunting witches.

The European witch-hunts, which were most active between the fifteenth and seventeenth centuries, usually took place in times of severe pressure for the group, when hostile climactic conditions led to crop failures and food shortages. These pressures, writes historian Professor Peter Marshall, contributed to 'a heightened sense of the need for societal purity and uniformity, which manifested itself in action against these most abnormal of deviants'. A diabolical dream was woven around these meteorological events that said they were caused by false believers living among them who had supernatural powers. But witchcraft wasn't easy to prove. When a game descends into this state, it's typical for enforcers to argue they're dealing with an exceptional problem which requires an exceptional relaxation of legal protections. For witch-hunter Henri Boguet, 'Witchcraft is a crime apart . . . Therefore the trial of this crime must be conducted in an extraordinary manner; and the usual legalities and ordinary procedures cannot be strictly observed.' For Jean Bodin, 'proof of such evil is so obscure and difficult that not one of a million witches would be accused and punished if regular legal procedure were followed'. During the century and a half of the most intense witch hunting, at least eighty thousand people were tried, around half of whom were executed. Most were poor women, often widows. In one German town, around four hundred were killed in a single day.

Similar dynamics occurred during the years of the Spanish Inquisition. In 1478, Spain's monarchs approved the introduction of a special court to find out what was happening in the psychological territory of former Jews that, following a period of pressure, had converted to Christianity. The Tribunal of the Holy Office of the Inquisition would investigate claims of secret Jewish belief and practice in these '*conversos*'. They had legal protections for their quarry removed: under canon law, anonymous denunciations had been forbidden, now they were not only permitted but encouraged. 'The records of the Inquisition are full of instances where neighbours denounced neighbours, friends denounced friends, and members of the same family denounced each other,' writes historian Professor Henry Kamen. The motivation for some was sheer greed: accused *conversos* were often removed from their jobs and had property confiscated. 'Very many of those arrested and burnt by the reverend fathers were arrested and burnt only because of their property,' wrote one *converso*. According to another, in the Castile region, 'fifteen hundred people have been burnt through false witness'. And yet the inquisitors declared 'false witness' at their procedures to be extremely rare. Official records of one set of 1,172 trials found just eight cases of perjury. Just like the witch-hunters elsewhere in Europe, the Satan-hunters of America in the 1980s and the online mobbers of the social media age, they played a game that awarded prizes on the discovery of deviants – and they discovered deviants *everywhere*.

As the inquisition's dominance-virtue play was rewarded, their game gained power, their dream of reality darkened and their perception of their enemies became sociopathically vindictive. *Conversos* were prosecuted for the mildest of perceived slights against the Catholic game. One woman was reported for smiling when someone mentioned the Virgin Mary; another for not eating pork and changing her linen on a Saturday (she was tortured on the rack); a man in his eighties was brought before the inquisition for eating bacon on a Friday, traditionally a meat-free day. Simple ignorance, such as not knowing the creed, was accepted as evidence of heretical belief. The atmosphere for those under suspicion could be suffocating. Terrified *conversos* began denouncing themselves. One man, Gonzalez Ruiz, reported himself to the inquisition for saying, during a game of cards, 'Even with God as your partner you won't win this game.' Many felt the terrors of the social cage. In 1538, one *converso* wrote, 'preachers do not dare to preach, and those who preach do not dare to touch on contentious matters, for . . . nobody in this life is without his policeman'.

This is what happens when life gets tight. The power of the tyrannical cousins is uncaged, their warriors fight, witches are burned and the game's neural territory becomes a surreal and suffocating nightmare of dominance-virtue play. There are demands for conformity and purity; there is gossip, fear, paranoia and denunciation; there are calls for the relaxation of legal protections; there are double standards directed at the enemy and fantasy sins prosecuted by unjust means; there is despair, humiliation and misery; there are lives spoiled and sometimes finished. And then there are the winners: proud warriors all, giddily assured of their status as moral exemplars, beaming in victory from their place up above.

21

Lost in a Dream

WHEN A GAME endures a period of major threat, its resulting state of tightness can leave traces for centuries. Psychologist Professor Michele Gelfand studies these effects globally. She finds nations that have suffered events such as disease, famine, natural disaster or conflict have tighter cultures with stronger social norms and less tolerance for deviance than looser nations. 'Groups that deal with many ecological and historical threats need to do everything they can to create order in the face of chaos,' she writes. 'The greater the threat, the tighter the community.'

In tight cultures – that include Pakistan, Germany, Malaysia, Switzerland, India, Singapore, Norway, Turkey, Japan and China – players dress more similarly, buy more similar things and possess superior self-control: they tend to have lower rates of crime, alcohol abuse and obesity. Their citizens are more punctual, and so is their public transport: Swiss trains have an average 97 per cent punctuality rate; in 2014, fourteen trains in Singapore arrived more than 30 minutes late; in 2013, Japan's *Shinkansens* had an average delay of 54 seconds. Even the time shown on public clocks across tight nations is more likely to be in sync.

People raised in tight cultures are also greater respecters of hierarchy and authority. Tight players are more likely to earn status from precisely correct moral behaviour, to a sometimes comical extent. In Germany, where rules mandate certain hours of the week as 'quiet', one resident complained about a barking dog: in court the judge permitted the animal to bark for thirty minutes per day in ten-minute intervals. They're more interested in moral purity, more likely to have the death penalty, less welcoming to outsiders and prefer dominant leaders. Tight players also show a greater vulnerability to believing the wild, sacred dreams of their game. An analysis of tightness-looseness across the US states found a 'remarkably high percentage of religious believers' in the tighter states, including around 80 per cent of adults in Kansas, Mississippi and South Carolina.

Of course, these are generalities. It's obviously not true that every individual in Singapore and Switzerland is more conformist than every citizen of Britain and Brazil. It's also a fact that tightness-looseness isn't a binary setting: it exists on a spectrum. But we all have a sense of what it looks like when a game becomes uncomfortably tight. Its players become 'single-minded', blending into one another as the social cage descends and their dreams of reality more perfectly combine. They grow increasingly obsessed with their game and its sacred beliefs. When their cousins are rampant, we say they're 'brainwashed' and that their groups are like 'religions' or 'cults'.

Cults are the tightest games of all. They maintain their power by being the sole significant source of connection and status for their players. Earning a place in a cult means actively following its belief system and adhering utterly to its game in thought and behaviour, allowing it to colonise your neural territory entirely. A true cult member has one active identity. Players attracted to them are often those who've failed at the games of conventional life. Alienated, injured and in need, their brains seek a game that seems to offer certainty, in which connection and status can be won by following an absolutely precise set of rules.

This was true of many members of a US cult known, for much of its existence, as Human Individual Metamorphosis. Its leader, Bonnie Nettles and her deputy, Marshall Applewhite, wove an incredible dream for their players in which, by following their rules with unwavering precision, they'd find themselves graduating to the 'next level' of existence, the 'evolutionary level above human'. After a period of training, they'd be picked up by UFOs and flown to heaven, a place that was 'real, that can be reached among those who attain to it'.

Nettles and Applewhite, who went by various names including Ti and Do, were seen by themselves and their disciples as the literal incarnations of God and Jesus. They were sacred beings, the living symbols and absolute masters of their game. But when they met, in 1972, both had been alienated from the ordinary games of life. Do's sixteen-year marriage and career as a music professor had ended after accusations he'd had a sexual relationship with a male student; Ti's daughter recalls her mother gazing into the sky wishing a flying saucer would whisk her away: 'Neither one of us felt that we were part of this world. We were always on the outside looking in. We wanted something different.'

They began teaching New Age subjects together and came to believe they were high-status people, no less than the 'two witnesses' described in the Bible's Book of Revelation to whom God says he'll 'grant authority' and will 'prophesy for twelve hundred and sixty days clothed in sackcloth'. They began proselytising; a small community of followers gathered around them. Many seemed disconnected from the games of the conventional world, just like Ti and Do. One recalled feeling, 'alienated, hopeless, incomplete and utterly unsatisfied in this world no matter what I tried'.

For Ti and Do, none of the rules by which other humans played counted. Professor of Religion Benjamin Zeller writes they 'believed that their status as the two witnesses and the importance of their spiritual mission permitted them to violate human laws'. The only valid rules were those they conjured into being. In order for their followers to be fit for entry into the Next Level, they had to 'literally overcome every human indulgence and human need'. This metamorphosis would be 'the most difficult task that there is . . . you have to lose everything. You will sever every attachment with that world that you have.' Players were required to inhabit the game entirely, using its criteria for claiming status to the exclusion of all others. This meant shedding past identities including their jobs, spouses, children, possessions and even their names: each individual was rechristened with a six-letter moniker ending 'ody'.

In 1976, eighty-eight men and women arrived in the remote Medicine Bow National Forest in Wyoming to live and play a game that offered a reassuringly precise path to otherworldly status. Failure to adhere to the rules wasn't tolerated by Ti and Do: nineteen were expelled that year alone. Over the next two decades the game developed its own esoteric language: their home community was the 'craft'; bedrooms were 'rest chambers'; kitchens 'nutri-labs'; laundries 'fibre-labs'; bathrooms 'bath chambers'; the body was the 'vehicle'; a bra was a 'slingshot'; a fart was a 'poofoofus'. Its many hundreds of rules were recorded in 'procedure books'. These dictated correct Next Level behaviours, from what television shows could be watched, to how long you could spend in the bath (six minutes), to how much toothpaste you could use (enough to cover one quarter of the bristles), how men should shave their faces (down, not up), how scrambled eggs should be cooked ('totally dry but not browned') and where you could poofoofus (hold it in and release in the bath chamber). Their schedule was similarly precisely defined: daily vitamins were to be swallowed at 19:22. Gossiping and 'chit chatting' was banned, as was talking in a whisper. Knowingly breaking a procedure counted as a 'major offence', putting a player at risk of expulsion.

A player's neural territory had to be conquered completely by the imaginary game of Human Individual Metamorphosis. Offences included: 'having likes or dislikes'; 'having inappropriate curiosity'; 'having private thoughts' and 'trusting my own judgment – or using my own mind'. If players felt an incorrect thought beginning to form they were to 'put up a blank card' and move their mind to a correct place. Former member Swyody recalls, 'one could identify a type of thought even before it became a thought. Before that, one would hear the beginning of the thought and cut it short so the words actually don't finish in one's brain.' He also recounts being taught by Ti and Do that if 'they saw a tent as polka dotted, even if you disagreed, you would want to believe it is polka dotted and you would have to raise your vibrations to see it as they see it'. Then there was the Eyes Task. 'We each had a clipboard and we were assigned to watch our classmates and if they did or said anything we questioned, or thought Ti and Do would want to know about, or broke any procedure we were to record it. Ti and Do would read these each day.' Contraventions of procedure were announced at regular 'slippage meetings'. Members would sit in a circle and publicly confess their 'slips'. When others would suggest what they could've done better, they had to say 'thank you'. A written report of the confessions was sent to Ti and Do.

For Swyody, the most arduous struggle was the prohibition against sexual activity or thought. Correct procedure had it that players slept with their hands above their waist. When a 'nocturnal emission' occurred during an erotic dream, correct procedure was to clean yourself up with one of the hand-towels specifically reserved for this purpose, each of which had to be signed out, so Ti and Do could be made aware. Ashamed, Swyody sometimes found himself skipping this. Although he became proficient at putting a 'blank card' up to sexual thoughts, and stopping them before he'd had them, this eventually proved impossible: 'when you've been maintaining celibacy of mind and body for years, one can become quite the sensitive time bomb, to where even one thought can instantly cause arousal'.

A solution was suggested in 1987. Do called the men to a meeting. He told them that a female member, Lvvody, had once worked as a nurse under a surgeon who'd performed orchiectomies – removal of the testicles. She reckoned she knew how to do it. Do wasn't ordering they be castrated, just pondering the possibility. Around this time, Swyody had entered a state of rivalry with another player, Srrody. 'His vehicle was Irish and a red head and he was quick as a fox in everything he did,' he writes. Srrody was a 'Johnny on the spot' always too eager to please Ti and Do. 'I had this thought that was sort of competitive with Srrody. I decided I would show Do how badly I wanted to be castrated.' When Do asked him if he had any reservations, he replied, 'My vehicle isn't looking forward to it, but I'm overriding my vehicle.'

But there was a problem. Srrody also wanted to be castrated. They decided on a coin toss. To Swyody's disappointment, Srrody won. Lvvody put a sign on the door of their makeshift surgery that read 'Mexico' so 'if there was any problem we could honestly say we went to Mexico to have the procedure done'. Srrody climbed on a table. Lvvody lifted his penis, shaved his scrotum and injected it with local anaesthetic. Then she picked up a scalpel, made an incision and opened his scrotum up. 'I got weak in the knees and almost passed out.' Swyody was helped back up by Do, who said, 'Well if this doesn't bond us, nothing will.' With the scrotum yawning, Lvvody reached in with her surgical scissors, made some snips and plucked out both testicles. But once her patient was stitched up, he began to swell. 'Srrody's sack was as big as a baseball.' Swyody took him to hospital, telling the doctors the patient was a monk who'd had the operation in Mexico. He healed perfectly. Too perfectly. Swyody became jealous. 'I was disappointed that I didn't have the procedure.'

Over the coming months, Swyody's sexual urges became more

explosive than ever. 'I felt like I was plugged into a socket,' he writes. 'I didn't even touch myself and I had an orgasm and then another minutes later.' Eventually, he gave up, and found himself with a masturbation habit. 'I didn't even have the desire to change. It was like I was now a different person.' In September 1994, after nineteen years of loyal play, Swyody exited the cult that was now calling itself Heaven's Gate. After his departure, Do arranged for seven more men, including himself, to be castrated, this time by real surgeons in real Mexico.

The month Swyody left, Do gathered the group in a warehouse for a meeting. Back in 1985, their leader Ti had died of cancer. This was a severe challenge to the dream they'd woven for their followers to live and play in: Ti and Do were supposed to personally and physically escort their followers onto the UFOs that would take them to the Next Level. Ti's death led Do to revise the story. He'd decided it *was* actually possible to ascend to the level above human having exited your body. They could graduate when dead. And so he had something to ask them. 'What if we had to exit our vehicles by our own choice? Do we have a problem with that?'

Only one or two did. In March 1997, thirty-nine remaining members including Do committed suicide by swallowing barbiturates and vodka sweetened with 'pudding', then tying bags over their heads. They killed themselves in three waves, each cadre following the agreed procedure precisely, dressed identically in grey shirts, dark tracksuit trousers and black-and-white Nike Decades. On their shoulders, they wore patches that said 'Heaven's Gate Away Team'. The mass suicides became international news. Journalists descended upon the area, trying to piece together their final days. The week prior to their departure to the Next Level, it was discovered they'd treated themselves to a last supper at Marie Callender's restaurant in Carlsbad. A bewildered waiter told reporters: 'They all ordered the exact same thing.'

The conventional account of human life cannot explain Heaven's Gate. When called upon to do so, we reach for the moral cartoon. Cult members are 'brainwashed', trapped under the control of evil masterminds who are in it only for sex or money. There's no doubt cults do resort to aggressive means when members insult their sacred beliefs by not conforming sufficiently or seeking to leave, and that some leaders are motivated partly by crotch and wallet. But no cult could survive if it didn't offer players something critical. The members of Heaven's Gate weren't there because their brains had been washed; their brains were doing what brains naturally want to do.

We seek rules and symbols by which to play a status game. When we find one that's suitable, and that feels right, we're vulnerable to absorbing its story, no matter how berserk. This is true of the Satan-hunters, the anti-vax mothers, the yam growers of Pohnpei, ISIS, the online mobbers and religious adherents world over. One Heaven's Gate veteran of thirteen years told researchers, 'We were protected. We didn't like the rules of the world, so we created our own. It was a utopia.' Brains want to know, *who do I have to be to earn connection and status*? Ti and Do wove a fantastic dream that offered precise instructions, telling them exactly who to change into. And so that's what they did.

There was little need for external cousins to police conformity: the cousins were inside them. In his memoir, Swyody resorts to all caps to make this point: 'I WANTED TO BE IN TI AND DO'S PROGRAM AND WANTED TO ABIDE BY ALL THEIR RULES. [Not conforming] would be tantamount to wanting to be a NASA astronaut but deciding this or that procedure didn't need to be adhered to.' Players were so enthusiastic they'd call confessional 'slippage meetings' themselves. One wrote, 'We used to joke in the class that we were the cult of cults. We weren't here to be programmed or brainwashed. We were here to beg to be brainwashed.' The thirty-nine killed themselves by choice. Sociologists Dr Robert Balch and Professor David Taylor write that their deaths 'resulted from a deliberate decision that was neither prompted by an external threat nor implemented through coercion. Members went to their deaths willingly, even enthusiastically, because suicide made sense to them in the context of [their] belief system.' This wasn't death, it was victory; a glorious claiming of the status they'd earned of the level above human.

Two months after their deaths, a former member caught them up. After leaving the group, Gbbody had been regretful over missing their departure to the Next Level so he killed himself. Back in 1995, shortly after he'd quit, he'd written tenderly of his time with Heaven's Gate: 'more than anything else they were my family. I loved them dearly. We were a tight group.'

22

Status Generating Machines

SUCCESSFUL GROUPS ARE status generating machines. They thrive when they make status, both for their players and for the game itself. This is true in times of war and peace and in modes of tightness or looseness; it's true in political games, in cults, in gangs, in goldrush movements, in corporations, in religions, in sports teams, in inquisitions, in mobs, in any game you might imagine. As we've learned, people *need* status: they look to their games to get it. A statusful woman or man who's leading a major game can certainly seem all-powerful when they're being cheered by hysterical crowds under blinding spotlights, gossiped about in world media and deferred to by platoons of acolytes. But the vision is deceptive: it's the subordinates who are ultimately in charge.

Leaders rent their thrones from these subordinates. If their formal position at the heights is to be assured, and they're to remain comfortable behind their giant desk, they must earn true status in the minds of their players. This means succeeding in the grind of making status for the group, and distributing it down through the hierarchy in ways that generally adhere to its rules. It might come in the form of titles or money or medals or secret knowledge or a ladder to heaven or the Level Above Human, or just simple appreciation. Even dictators have players to please, not least their military elites who ought to be rewarded if their reign of dominance is to continue. No game – not even a cult – can survive when every player but one feels hopeless and useless.

The strategist of legend Niccolò Machiavelli knew this well. A successful prince, he counselled, should, 'show his esteem for talent, actively encouraging the able men and honouring those who excel in their profession'. Naturally this munificence should extend to any player who belonged to his elite. A prince 'must be considerate towards him, must pay him honour, enrich him, put him in his debt, share with him both honours and responsibilities. Thus [he] will see how dependent he is on the prince.' More sneakily, Machiavelli advised leaders to encourage the belief that such prizes can only be assured under their charge: 'a wise prince must devise ways by which his citizens are always and in all circumstances dependent on him and on his authority; and then they will always be faithful to him'.

Centuries later, some of Machiavelli's notions have been found to be true. One analysis concluded successful organisations 'help keep their most talented employees from leaving by providing those individuals with high status'. When rewarded with status, workers identify more with their group, are more committed to it and come to view it more positively. Sociologist Professor Cecilia Ridgeway writes that there's 'overwhelming evidence' status hierarchies operate in this way, by awarding esteem and influence 'in exchange for a recipient's perceived value for the group effort'. We reward players who help our games win. We raise them in rank. If they prove themselves sufficiently useful, we might even allow them to lead us for a while.

Successful leaders tell their players the same irresistible story: we deserve more status and, under my direction, we'll get it. The forty-fifth President of the United States, Donald Trump, told this story, by promising to 'Make America Great Again'; so did his predecessor

Barack Obama by seeking to embody 'Hope'. Whilst the terrorist group ISIS used the dread machine of social media to terrify their enemies, they wove for themselves an altogether different fantasy. One analysis of their glossy magazine *Dabiq* found only 5 per cent of its imagery featured violence; far more prevalent was that depicting their glorious future in an 'idealistic caliphate'.

But stories of happy endings can be more seductive still when they're menaced up the back end by the threat of rivals. When games feel their status is being endangered by foes, their players are more likely to join the battle in support of it and endorse leaders that show zeal for the fight. Researchers find rivalrous anger, when combined with optimistic enthusiasm for the win, can be especially potent in motivating players: in studies, when people read a political message that makes them feel highly angry or enthusiastic, 'they want to jump into the ring', writes political psychologist Dr Lilliana Mason. 'They want to get involved.' Threats from rival games help motivate by increasing the poisonous narrative of prejudice. 'Without a threat to a social group, members are less likely to derogate outgroups, and they have less of a motivation to improve the status of the group.'

Loathe him or loathe him, Adolf Hitler was, for a time, one of the most successful leaders in modern history. As historian Professor Ian Kershaw writes, 'few, if any, twentieth-century political leaders have enjoyed greater popularity among their own people than Hitler in the decade or so following his assumption of power'. Since the end of the Second World War, many have puzzled at how the forces of irrationality and evil could have risen with such ferocity in a nation as advanced as Germany. Once again, it conflicts with our fundamental ideas about human nature. How could such a cultured and brilliant people have voted a violent anti-Semite to be their leader? And then cheered him hysterically, in squares crammed with thousands, as if he were a god? But, viewed from the perspective of the status game, the rise of the Nazis becomes explicable.

Already, our strange travels have brought us into the company of three mass-killers: Elliot Rodger, Ed Kemper and Ted Kaczynski. All were grandiose, secure in their entitlement to being treated as high-status individuals, but who nevertheless suffered chronic and serious experiences of humiliation. Humiliation, as we've learned, is the ultimate psychological de-grading: the 'nuclear bomb of the emotions' that can cause the 'annihilation of the self' and lead to major depressions, suicidal states, psychosis, extreme rage and severe anxiety. It's also thought to be a propulsive force for honour killers who similarly seek to restore their lost status with violence. And this is just what we find in pre-war Germany: the humiliation of the grand, but on the level of the nation.

Before the First World War, Germany had been the wealthiest and most highly developed society in Europe. Here was a nation in which 'capitalist enterprise had reached an unprecedented scale and degree of organization', writes historian Professor Richard Evans. Germany produced two-thirds of all the steel in continental Europe, half its coal and 20 per cent more electricity than Italy, France and Britain combined. Many of its major industries – chemicals, pharmaceuticals, electricity – were world leaders, its corporations, including Siemens, AEG, BASF, Hoechst, Krupps and Thyssen enjoying stellar reputations for quality. Even their farmers were brilliantly successful: Germany grew a third of the planet's potatoes. Living standards had been soaring since the century's start. As the war began, there'd been a widespread assumption of quick victory for the superior Germans, a view encouraged by fantastic victories on the Eastern Front and the swift taking of Poland. Even when Germany suddenly and shockingly declared defeat, there'd been an expectation that the terms of peace, in the Treaty of Versailles, would be fairly measured.

They weren't. 'No one was prepared for the peace terms to which Germany was forced to agree,' writes Evans. It was compelled to

accept 'sole guilt' for the conflict and responsibility for its consequences. This meant: surrendering vast tracts of land in Europe;
renouncing their colonies elsewhere; handing over enormous piles
of military equipment, including all their submarines; destroying
six million rifles, over fifteen thousand aeroplanes and more than
one hundred and thirty thousand machine guns; adhering to severe
restrictions on future military activity, including their possessing only
six battleships and no air force at all; paying the modern equivalent
of nearly three hundred billion pounds in cash reparations, plus
copious booty including twenty-four million tonnes of coal. A ruinous
economic blockade of Germany was to continue. 'These provisions
were almost universally felt in Germany as an unjustified national
humiliation.'

But there was more. As well as covering the costs of everyone
else's war, the Germans had to pay for their own. The government
had been expecting reparations and wealth from newly annexed
industrial zones to flow inwards, rather than outwards, and had been
printing and spending cash accordingly. Its defeat helped trigger a
state of hyperinflation so nightmarish it bordered on the comic. Prices
rose with such rapidity shopkeepers had to write them on black-
boards: one newspaper reported that a gramophone costing five
million marks at 10 a.m. cost twelve million five hours later. A coffee
at a cafe might cost five thousand marks when you ordered it and
eight thousand when you'd finished. In August 1922, one US dollar
cost around 1,000 marks; by December 1923 that same dollar cost
4,200,000,000,000 marks. Workers were collecting wages in wheel-
barrows. These humiliations triggered yet further humiliations: when
Germany fell behind on its reparations of gold and coal, the French
and Belgians occupied their main industrial area, the Ruhr, to seize
what they were owed.

How could all this have happened? 'The sense of outrage and
disbelief that swept through the German upper and middle classes

like a shock wave was almost universal,' writes Evans. 'Germany had been brutally expelled from the ranks of the Great Powers and covered in what they considered to be undeserved shame.' Germany was superior, and Germans knew it. They looked at the ruined hierarchy and wove around it a self-serving story that said their defeat was engineered by powerful and sinister forces. Military leaders, among many others, began claiming they'd been the victim of a 'secret, planned, demagogic campaign' by deviants. It was a time of gossip, accusation and moral outrage. The national culture had tightened up for the First World War and, in its peril and shame, it never loosened. Germany 'remained on a continued war footing; at war with itself, and at war with the rest of the world, as the shock of the Treaty of Versailles united virtually every part of the political spectrum in a grim determination to overthrow its central provisions, restore the lost territories, end the payment of reparations and re-establish Germany as the dominant power in Central Europe once more.'

After hyperinflation was brought under control, the Great Depression struck; by 1932 it was reported around thirteen million people were in out of work families. Disillusionment with the capitalist system was now driving people in ever greater numbers to the Communists who, since the revolution in Russia, were becoming an alarming and genuine threat, not least to the industrialists and middle classes who'd seen their equivalents in the East robbed and tortured, murdered and disappeared. This was an era in which antisemitism was relatively common throughout Europe. In their hunt for deviants, many Germans accepted a convenient illusion which said the Jews were to blame for the depression *and* the Communist peril *and* the unjust loss of the First World War *and* all its attendant humiliations.

There were, at that time, around 600,000 practising Jews in the German Empire. Generally speaking, they were a high-status group, upwardly mobile, successful economically and culturally, with prominent families in finance and retail and prestigious Jewish names throughout the elite games of the arts, medicine, law, science and journalism. Stewing with powerful resentments, and the story that Germany was the victim of a 'Jewish-Bolshevik conspiracy', were new scientific ideas about heredity: theories about how unwanted traits might be bred out of the national gene pool for the sake of Germany's elevation. The nation had won major status in revealing the causes of diseases including cholera and tuberculosis, which triggered a surge in interest in matters of hygiene. These notions combined to form a noxious preoccupation with Germany's 'racial hygiene' – and not just in players of the extreme right.

But whilst plenty of Germans blamed the Jews for their humiliation, relatively few endorsed brutal actions against them. They were much more concerned with their glorious journey towards national order, unity and restored status. For Evans, 'among ordinary Party activists in the 1920s and early 1930s, the most important aspect of Nazi ideology was its emphasis on social solidarity – the concept of the organic racial community of all Germans – followed at some distance by extreme nationalism and the cult of Hitler. Antisemitism, by contrast, was of significance only for a minority, and for a good proportion of these it was only incidental.' Aware of this, Hitler made a public step away from antisemitism. Prior to 1922 he'd been ranting about the Jews persistently; afterwards, and throughout most of the 1930s, he raised the 'Jewish Question' relatively rarely in his speeches. Incidents of antisemitic violence were viewed, by the many, as unfortunate but understandable flare-ups of overenthusiasm by a violent fringe.

Far more effective than racial hatred was the promise of future status. Hitler's party positioned itself as young and forward-thinking and in unique possession of the strength, organisation and zeal necessary to restore Germany's rightful place. He wove a fantastic dream that millions of intended voters found irresistible: they were members of an elite Aryan master race, 'the Prometheus of mankind, out of whose bright forehead springs the divine spark of genius at all times'. The story he told of the status game was that race, not class, was what mattered: 'there are no such things as classes: they cannot be. Class means caste and caste means race.' The Germans, he said, had been the victims of 'the greatest villainy of the century'; when he heard of their defeat in the war, 'everything went black before my eyes' and he wept. But this period of humiliation would end when they came together as one people. Under his leadership they'd rise to ever greater heights in the form of a glorious thousand-year Aryan kingdom: the Third Reich.

'Finally a practical proposal for the renewal of the people!' said one 18-year-old supporter in 1929. 'Destroy the parties! Do away with classes! True national community! These were goals to which I could commit myself, without reservation.' On 5 March 1933, Hitler's party won the election, albeit with less than 50 per cent of the vote. The Nazis quickly began imposing the rules and symbols of their game onto the nation at large. Propaganda minister Joseph Goebbels declared Germany had 'to think as one, to react as one, and to place itself in the service of the government with all its heart'. On 21 March the Malicious Practices Act was introduced. It compelled 'every nationally minded' person to report to the authorities anyone 'responsible [for] any insulting of the Reich government or any degradation of the national revolution'.

Just three weeks after the election, Goebbels informed radio broadcasters that nonconformists would be 'purged' from their stations: they were to cleanse their staff of undesirables themselves or have it done for them. The removal of ideological enemies and Jews from positions of status continued: incorrect-thinking university professors, artists, writers, journalists and scientists, including twenty past or yet-to-be Nobel laureates, Albert Einstein and Erwin

Schrödinger among them, were dismissed. The game was tightening to a Heaven's Gate level of extremity: players were to earn Nazi status or no status at all. Cousins and warriors ran rampant. Just as in the tight days of the Spanish Inquisition, a wave of denunciation began, often triggered by personal grudges, which created an 'atmosphere of intimidation and vigilance against a careless remark which prying ears might seize upon'. The day after the election, the Communist Party was formally banned. By the end of the year, members numbering at least in the tens of thousands had been imprisoned or killed, a 'massive, brutal and murderous assault' predicated on the belief they'd been mounting a revolution. Soon, all other political parties were banned. A decree made the 'Heil Hitler' salute compulsory for state employees and added, 'anyone not wishing to come under suspicion of behaving in a consciously negative fashion will therefore render the Hitler Greeting'.

But the fact remained that millions of Germans – over half the nation – had not voted for Hitler or his party. As ever in times of tyranny, citizens were divided between true believers, false believers (a then-teenager reported, if a teacher 'wanted to be promoted he had to show what a fine Nazi he was, whether he really believed what he was saying or not'), the disinterested and the rebels. The keen brains at the heart of the Nazi regime knew dominance strategies alone wouldn't seduce the strays. In his first address to the media after taking office, propaganda chief Goebbels told journalists: 'There are two ways to make a revolution. You can blast your enemy with machine guns until he acknowledges the superiority of those holding the machine guns. That is one way. Or you can transform the nation through a revolution of the spirit, and instead of destroying your enemy, win him over.' And so the Nazis played both strategies.

Spreading a game throughout society means controlling the smaller games that make it up: the bureaucracies, communities, media hubs and clubs, everywhere people play by rules to make status. The universities were already theirs, the 'vast majority of professors' being 'strongly nationalist' and antisemitic. Respected university staff who didn't conform were replaced by 'often mediocre figures whose only claim to their new position was that they were Nazis and enjoyed the support of the Nazi students' organization', writes Evans. They were teaching students who were 'an elite to which racism, antisemitism and ideas of German superiority were almost second nature'. These ambitious warriors 'organized campaigns against unwanted professors in the local newspapers, staged mass disruptions of their lectures and led detachments of stormtroopers in house-searches and raids'. In May 1933, they held a coordinated 'act against the un-German spirit' across numerous universities, removing books from libraries they deemed politically incorrect and burning them in piles.

But the universities weren't enough: the rules and symbols of the Nazis had to colonise every game possible, replacing the old criteria for claiming status with the new. By the end of 1933, the Hitler Youth accommodated over two million adolescents. By 1935 membership had almost doubled and in 1939 it was required legally for children over 10. The Nazis staffed their enormous social welfare administration with professionals who believed in concepts of racial purity, beliefs which radiated through the powerful bureaucracies of medicine, law enforcement, and the prison system. Voluntary associations in every village, town and city went through a process of Nazification; the party itself established local games, with organisations at the regional, district and local levels 'staffed with loyal and energetic functionaries, many of them well educated and administratively competent'; a Nazi women's organisation was founded, as were special groups for civil servants, farmers and the war-wounded, 'and for many other constituencies, each addressing its particular, specifically targeted propaganda effort'. The party finessed their message to suit the values of every game that mattered: there was a Hitler for rural workers, a Hitler for thinkers, a Hitler for war veterans, a Hitler for businessmen, a Hitler for women. Writes historian and marketing researcher Professor Nicholas O'Shaughnessy, 'the Nazis offered something for everyone'. Just as during the goldrush of the Satanic Panic, these groups were status games, acting as accelerators for the rules and symbols of Nazi play.

For most Germans, the Nazi game became the only one that could offer significant status. Within months of Hitler's appointment to the Chancellorship, party membership tripled to two and a half million – so many that a moratorium on joining had to be announced. By 1939 'at least one-half and most likely two-thirds of all Germans' belonged to some Nazi organisation. 'Membership was key to upward career and social mobility. With its dense network of organisations, the Nazi Party created a host of well-paid functionary and around two million prestigious volunteer positions.' Once individuals start to play and begin to enjoy a game's rewards, it becomes part of their identity. They come to rely on it, to defend it, to evangelise it. And so the game becomes self-supporting, self-reinforcing, as each individual player now requires it to be real and true in order for their status to be real and true. The tyrannical cousins roar forth in their behaviour. As the goldrush grows, the game attracts new players, drawn to its increasingly splendid rewards; as it becomes more powerful, more and greater status is made available; it becomes larger and more powerful still.

There's a critical warning in all this: tyrants often start by telling you what you already believe. When they arrive, they weave their irresistible self-serving dream, promising that you deserve more status, just as you'd always suspected, and pointing accusingly at those you'd already figured to be your enemies – child abusers, *conversos*, big business, Communists, Jews. They make accusation and gossip; you become angry, enthusiastic and morally outraged. You begin to play. Once they've got you, they tighten up. Their beliefs become more extreme, more specific and are policed more severely; second-self tactics of dominance are widely deployed. The most tyrannical games – cults and fundamentalist political and religious movements – insist on complete conformity in thought and deed; their dream of reality colonising your neural territory entirely. They seek to become a player's sole source of status; no rival games are easily tolerated. On the scale of the nation, which requires other games to exist in forms such as universities, the media and state bureaucracies, all must become subservient: no matter where games take place, status is awarded for play that serves the tribe, whilst dreadful consequences await suspected deviants.

None of this would've succeeded if Hitler hadn't created status for his players. If it seems reprehensible to face the Nazi regime's apparent 'successes', it's because we tell a sacred story about its monstrousness: anything that sounds even dimly positive rings the alarms of taboo. But we must be brave. Monsters exist only in the imagination. The Nazi catastrophe can't be understood without acknowledgement of *why* the Germans came to worship their leader as a god and how they achieved the aims of Goebbels who stated, on their election in 1933, that they'd win over doubters by working on them 'until they have become addicted to us'.

The list of his regime's major perceived victories is long and dizzy (please feel free to skip to the end when you get the point): months after taking office, they authorised the construction of a brand new, ultra-modern form of road, the motorway, with Hitler personally signing off the design of bridges and service stations; by 1935, 125,000 men were working on them and by summer 1938, they'd built 3,500 kilometres; by the end of that year five billion marks had been spent on job-creation schemes; they gave out subsidies for house purchases, conversions and maintenance; spent substantial amounts in deprived areas; offered young engaged couples interest-free loans to help get them started (nearly a quarter of a million loans were issued in the first year alone); through their leisure organisation Strength Through Joy they bought and subsidised thousands of theatre tickets (accounting for more than half of all Berlin ticket sales in 1938); put on music concerts in factories; built theatres; organised exhibitions, operas and plays (in 1938, nearly seven and a half million went to its plays and six and a half million to its opera and operetta evenings); offered heavily discounted package holidays to locations such as Libya, Finland, Bulgaria and Istanbul, offering 75 per cent off rail tickets and 50 per cent off hotels (in 1937 alone, 1.7 million Germans went on a Strength Through Joy holiday whilst nearly seven million went on one of their weekend mini-breaks – accounting for as many as 11 per cent of overnight stays in all German hotels); they put on cruises (140,000 passengers in one year alone); their annual Winter Aid drive raised hundreds of millions of marks for the needy, providing them with food, clothing and fuel; Hitler hired Ferdinand Porsche to help create an affordable 'People's Car' (now known as the VW Beetle) whose design was a huge public success (although the war meant none were sold); foreign debt was stabilised; a wide range of advanced public health measures were introduced, including far-sighted restrictions on asbestos, radiation, pesticides and food dyes, and occupational health and safety standards that were 'decades ahead of other countries'; Nazi scientists were the first in the world to definitively link smoking with lung cancer and the party campaigned aggressively against the habit; when the party came to power a third of the population, 6.1 million people, were unemployed – by 1935 it had dropped to 2.2 million, by 1937 it was under a million, by 1939 full employment was claimed; between 1933 and 1939, the agricultural economy grew by 71 per cent; between 1932 and 1939 gross national product soared by 81 per cent.

Of course, life was very far from perfect. Some of these are official numbers and disguise the role of factors including luck, timing and statistical massage; we should also acknowledge their malevolence:

they were racially exclusionary and many jobs 'created' were forcibly vacated or made in preparation for war. Partly as a result of resources being redirected to the military, there remained shortages: in his diary, journalist William Shirer writes of clothes being made out of wood pulp and 'long lines of sullen people before the food shops'. It's also important not to over-claim for the role of status: the relief felt by the impoverished when they were provided for isn't status; the pleasure of cheap holidays isn't status; the convenience and thrill of motorways isn't status; respite from the anxiety of unemployment and the Communist menace isn't status. But neither is status absent from these occurrences: the sense that life for each individual affected, and the nation itself, was essentially on the rise and that honour was being restored; that Germans and Germany could once again hold their heads high in the knowledge that their journey towards the promised land was in motion.

Our quarry is yet more evident in Hitler's victories on that journey. For Kershaw, 'the overwhelming majority of the population clearly wanted "national success" – the restoration of Germany's power and glory in Europe'. The scenes we tend to associate with Hitler-madness frequently took place when he'd somehow heal the humiliations of the detested Treaty of Versailles: his 1936 re-taking of the Rhineland, without serious resistance from the Allies, sent admiration 'soaring to a new pinnacle', and led to scenes of 'frenzied acclaim', with one contemporary noting, 'the spirit of Versailles is hated by all Germans. Hitler has now torn up this cursed treaty and thrown it at the feet of the French'; the similarly easy taking of Austria in 1938 brought his popularity to 'unprecedented heights' with hundreds of thousands of Germans swarming the streets of its cities in riotous ecstasy, and one contemporary noting even doubters were now admitting, 'Hitler is a great and clever statesman who will raise up Germany from the defeat of 1918 to greatness and standing again.' Even when he took Germany into war, against the popular will, he achieved a series of rapid and stunning successes, including the taking of its hated France, their capitulation, writes Kershaw, 'symbolically wiping out the humiliation of the German capitulation in the same spot in 1918'.

Partly through effective propaganda, Hitler himself became highly symbolic of the resurgent Germany: by the logic of the status game, he became sacred, the literal equivalent of a god, a figure that symbolised all that his players valued and who, in effect, *was* their status. One contemporary observer, Otto Dietrich, wrote: 'We see in . . . him the symbol of the indestructible life-force of the German nation, which has taken living shape in Adolf Hitler.' Another, Bavarian minister Hans Schemm: 'In the personality of Hitler, a million-fold longing of the German people has become a reality.' As the propaganda slogan said, 'Germany is Hitler, and Hitler is Germany'.

Despite all this, it remained true that Hitler was merely renting his throne from the people: acclaim peaked and troughed with the national highs and lows he oversaw. But the power of this game we play, and the madness of the dreams we weave of it, has rarely been more apparent than in his periods of success. In hundreds of towns and villages, 'Hitler-Oaks' and 'Hitler-Lindens' were planted; squares were renamed 'Adolf-Hitler Platz'; female babies were named Hitlerine, Adolfine, Hitlerike and Hilerine; flags and banners were hung; shop windows displayed portraits and busts of Hitler adorned with flowers; beautiful weather became known as 'Hitler weather'; thousands of letters, gifts and poems were sent on his birthday: 'My fervently adored Führer! *You* have a birthday and *we* know only two ardent wishes: may everything in our Fatherland be now and in future just as *you* want it to be, and may God provide that you be preserved for us for ever'; patients with tuberculosis gazed at Hitler's image for hours to 'gain strength'; a belief spread that the walls of bombed houses holding Hitler's portrait always remained standing; swastika sausages were sold; schoolgirls got swastika manicures; a butcher sculpted Hitler in lard; young women 'vowed to Heil Hitler and give the Nazi salute at the point of orgasm'. Hundreds of thousands, 'perhaps even millions' marched through the streets in parades. Journalist William Shirer, was 'caught in a mob of ten thousand hysterics who jammed the moat in front of Hitler's hotel, shouting: "We want our Führer." I was a little shocked at the faces, especially those of the women, when Hitler finally appeared on the balcony for a moment. They reminded me of the crazed expressions I saw once in the back country of Louisiana on the faces of some Holy Rollers who were about to hit the trail. They looked up at him as if he were a Messiah, their faces transformed into something positively inhuman.'

Was it a religion? Was it a cult? It was both and it was neither: it was a tyrannically tight status game, and it was working.

23

Annihilation Part Two

WHEN A GAME becomes tight, so does the story it tells of the world. It looks at the hierarchy – at where it sits versus its rivals – and conjures a simplistic, self-serving, moralistic tale that explains how that hierarchy came to be. This story is always the same: we're the virtuous players, deserving of more, and those who block our path are evil. The story is seductive: it's what players want to believe. It becomes a source of status and of hope for more status, and of resentment – an almighty resentment, the rage of the gods – that's aimed at the enemy. It is a sacred story. Everyone must believe it in every detail. As the cousins run rampant, threatening and enforcing, we can be swept into it, a leaf in the torrent. The narrative becomes more extreme and more deranged. But we keep believing. *It feels so real.* We're dreamers, and the dreams we dream are those of our games. We inhabit them. We enact them. And when dreams turn dark we become their nightmares.

And so our journey into the status game arrives at hell. At an earlier stop, we encountered the disordered interior worlds of individual killers and there discovered powerful currents of grandiosity and humiliation. We found these same currents in the collective dreams of one of history's most lethal games. The Nazis were Elliot Rodger,

Ed Kemper and Ted Kaczynski on the level of a culture. They told a self-serving story that explained their catastrophic lack of status and justified its restoration in murderous attack. But it's not just Germany that's been possessed in this way. Nations the world over become dangerous when humiliated. One study of ninety-four wars since 1648 found 67 per cent were motivated by matters of national standing or revenge, with the next greatest factor – security – coming in at a distant 18 per cent. Anthropologists Professors Alan Page Fiske and Tage Shakti Rai find that frequently, 'decision-makers and public opinion are motivated to declare war to maintain or raise the rank of their nation vis-a-vis other nations, particularly when they feel that they have been unjustly pushed down to a low rank among other nations'. The warring party will tend to attack in a dream of toxic morality, convinced of its virtuous intent: 'the more a nation feels humiliated by a moral violation against it, and the more the nation experiences the act as morally outrageous, the more it seeks vengeance'.

Grandiosity and humiliation powered the dreams of the young Red Guard warriors who fought the Cultural Revolution in China, during which between 500,000 and two million people were killed. Leader Mao Tse Tung was a notorious narcissist, believing he'd be 'the man who leads planet Earth into Communism'. But, following a disastrous 1959–1960 famine there emerged signs of rebellion against him. Mao's party told a story that said his nation's glorious rise was being undermined by secret capitalists who were plotting to create a 'dictatorship of the bourgeoisie'. The masses were urged to root out these 'monsters and ghosts' who were the 'representatives of the bourgeoisie who have sneaked into the party' and 'clear away the evil habits of the old society'. Students began denouncing their teachers on 'big character posters' – like tweets, but painted on paper and hung in public. Former Red Guard Dai Hsaio-Ai recalled being surprised when one of his favourite tutors was denounced. 'I was unwilling to criticise or to struggle against her, but my classmates accused me of being sentimental and warned me that I was becoming like her. They even told me I was heading for trouble. I gradually realised that they were right. The Party could not be wrong and it was my duty to join the struggle. I did so and eventually with enthusiasm.'

Suspects were forced to undergo 'struggle sessions' at which Red Guards would strafe them with accusation, sometimes for days and weeks, insisting they confess. These sessions were 'always very intense', Dai has said. They were butcheries of humiliation, their purpose to strip status and the ability to claim it from the bones of their elders. 'We forced the teachers to wear caps and collars that stated things like "I am a monster." Each class confronted and reviled them in turn, with slogans, accusations, and injunctions to reform their ways. We made them clean out the toilets, smeared them with black paint and organised "control monster teams" to see that it was done properly . . . It took nearly a week of constant struggle to make [a teacher] admit he had said "Mao was wrong" in conversation . . . After about two weeks, we were afraid that the literature teacher would kill herself. We kept her under constant surveillance and even wrote a poster and attached it to the mosquito net over her bed reminding her that she was being watched and could not succeed in committing suicide.' Dai's biographers note he 'admitted to enjoying this sheer cruel fun of humiliating [the] power holders, particularly the principal. On one occasion, for example, he devoted an entire day to the co-operative manufacture of an enormous cardboard replica of a cow's head, intended as symbolic of an appropriate crown for Principal Chen.' The teachers submitted to their mobbing, writing on big character posters, 'We Welcome Criticism and Repudiation from Our Fellow Students.'

When the revolution spilled into the streets, Red Guards searched house after house looking for 'old things' that, in their vindictive dream of reality, symbolised a secret commitment to the pre-Communist game: scrolls, jewellery, books, tight-fitting jeans, pointed shoes, quilts made in Hong Kong. 'Some of us would tear down the walls and look behind the plaster while others seized shovels and picks and tore up the cellars looking for hidden items,' said Dai. 'I even recall seeing two or three people in my group squeezing a tube of toothpaste for hidden jewellery.' While they searched, the occupants were forced to wait outside and confess counter-revolutionary crimes. 'If the women had long hair, we cut it. Sometimes we would shave half of the hair on a man's head and defy him to shave the rest of it. Our object was to humiliate these people as much as we could . . . I thought what we were doing was important; therefore, I enjoyed myself fully. It was a great deal of fun.'

He found it fun. What sense can the standard account of human nature make of this? None, so it reaches for the cartoon: Dai was evil, and that was all. But Dai wasn't a devil in a story, he was an ordinary human with an ordinary brain, and he was playing a status game just as he was designed to. Status depended on conforming not with mere belief, but active belief. Having been warned away from his doubts, he allowed himself to be washed into the nightmare perception of his game: *I gradually realised that they were right. The Party could not be wrong and it was my duty to join the struggle. I did so and eventually with enthusiasm*. He believed what he was doing was important. This revolution he'd joined was a status goldrush: its rewards were immense. Of course it was fun. For willing players on the right side of the gun, tyranny always is.

Humiliation can also be found at the root of many acts of terrorism. In his first public statement following 9/11 Osama bin Laden said, 'What America is tasting now is only a copy of what we have tasted. Our Islamic nation has been tasting the same for more than eighty years of humiliation and disgrace.' Researchers find a primary motivation for suicide bombers is 'the shame and humiliation induced by foreign troops in their country'. Dr Eyad El-Sarraj, psychiatrist and founder of the Palestinian Independent Commission for Citizens' Rights, writes that Palestinian suicide bombers are motivated by 'a long history of humiliation and a desire for revenge'. Such emotions are thought to be especially acute in Middle Eastern cultures, in which honour is of greatly heightened importance, a mindset that recalls our grandiose American mass-killers who also sought to restore their outrageous de-grading with violence. They play a game that – like the Heaven's Gate cult – holds such seductive power it lures players willingly to death. An academic interviewing a Muslim extremist in Indonesia had the following exchange:

'What if a rich relative were to give a lot of money to the cause in return for you cancelling or just postponing a martyrdom action?'

'Is that a joke? I would throw the money in his face.'

'Why?'

'Because only in fighting and dying for a cause is there nobility in life.'

Terrorists believe in their moral virtue, and so do racist colonialists. The imperialists of the British Empire told a self-serving story that said they were leading lower forms of life on a journey towards the promised land of civilisation. Poet Rudyard Kipling captured this sentiment in 'The White Man's Burden': 'Take up the White Man's burden / And reap his old reward / The blame of those ye better / The hate of those ye guard / The cry of hosts ye humour / (Ah, slowly!) toward the light.' The white settlers of the United States believed they, too, were on a civilising mission. For the twenty-sixth president, Theodore Roosevelt, 'the settler and pioneer have at bottom had justice on their side; this great continent could not have been kept as nothing but a game preserve for squalid savages'.

Humiliated grandiosity can trigger murder on an enormous scale because perpetrators inhabit a heroic story that says they're categorically superior to their victims – effectively a different species of being. It's typical for targets to be described in terms of low-status creatures: to the Communists, the middle classes were 'leeches'; to the Nazis, the Jews were 'lice'; to the French in Algeria, the Muslims were 'rats'; to the Boers, the Africans were 'baboons'. Any attempt at defence or retaliation implies their dream is an illusion and their criteria for claiming status is therefore false. This is disturbing to them. It often triggers a response of overwhelmingly disproportionate dominance. So morally outraged are they by insubordination from their subhuman targets, they strike back on the principle of two eyes for an eye – or two hundred eyes, or two thousand, or however many they consider morally equivalent to their precious one. When Algerians killed 103 French people following a riot, their colonialist masters sent aeroplanes to destroy forty-four villages, a cruiser to bombard coastal towns and commandos to slaughter on land: the French admit to 1,500 deaths, the Algerians claim 50,000. It's for reasons like these that psychologist Dr Evelin Lindner has concluded that, 'The most potent weapon of mass destruction' is 'the humiliated mind'.

Sociologist Professor Bradley Campbell has undertaken an extensive study of our most bestial mode of play. He finds genocides can happen when a high-status group, 'experiences a decline in or threat to its status' or a low-status group 'rises or attempts to rise in status'. It's the reduction in rank between them that helps generate much of the horrible madness. Toxic morality is deeply implicated in these episodes: 'genocide is highly moralistic'. Genocides are dominance-virtue games, carried out in the name of justice and fairness and the restoration of the correct order. They're not about the mere killing or 'cleansing' of foes, they're about healing the perpetrators' wounded grandiosity with grotesque, therapeutic performances of dominance and humiliation.

They're often notable for the killers' 'outright zeal in humiliating' their victims: during the Armenian genocide, Turkish *gendarmes* played a game of tossing people from horses onto swords sticking upwards from the ground; during the Gujarat genocide, Hindus pulled the beards of Muslims, defecated on the Koran, paraded them naked and with their fingers cut off, forced them to shout 'Praise Lord Ram' and played cricket with their decapitated heads; during the Rwandan genocide, the high-status Tutsi were symbolically 'cut down to size' by having their Achilles tendons severed, forcing them to crawl before being killed. Hutu rapists told their victims: 'You Tutsi women think you are too good for us'; 'You Tutsi girls are too proud'; 'Remember the past months when you were proud of your-selves and didn't look at us because you felt we were lower than you? Now that will never happen again.'

All this was true of the Holocaust, and the period leading up to it. The large-scale mass-killing of the Jews began after the war started going wrong for Hitler – his nation and its grandiose dream now failing. For survivor Marian Turski, the worst thing about Auschwitz wasn't the cold, the hunger or the beatings but 'the humiliation. Just because you were Jewish, you were treated not like a human being, you were treated like a louse, a bed bug, like a cockroach.' Whilst the Nazis 'cleansed' all manner of deviants from their game, including Communists, gypsies, homosexuals and the disabled, it was the envied and resented Jews they sought most conspicuously to treat this way. It happened again and again: Nazis publicly cut their hair, shaved their beards, paraded them with their trousers cut off and with signs around their necks, made them drink dangerous quantities of castor oil, ordered them to carry out pointless tasks such as carrying mattresses back and forth, endlessly building and rebuilding walls and squatting with heavy logs.

Just as for the cultural revolutionaries in China, forcing their targets to clean was a favourite activity for the Nazis. In Vienna, journalist William Shirer witnessed: 'gangs of Jews, with jeering storm troopers standing over them, on their hands and knees scrub-bing the Schuschnigg [an anti-Nazi politician] signs off the sidewalks.

Many Jews killing themselves. All sorts of reports of Nazi sadism, and from the Austrians it surprises me. Jewish men *and* women made to clean latrines. Hundreds of them just picked at random off the streets to clean the toilets of the Nazi boys.' In occupied Eastern Europe, a singing, laughing, accordion-playing crowd watched a group of Jews being made to clean horse manure off a garage floor, being beaten nearly to death with rifles and crowbars and then having high-pressure hoses forced into their mouths until their stomachs burst; when all were killed, a second group of Jews were instructed to clean away the blood and bodies. In another suburb, a prominent rabbi was discovered, 'bent over his blood-soaked books while his severed head looked on from the other room'.

None of these are acts of convenience, of the simple ridding of enemies for material gain. There's a message in these nightmares. They tell us something real about who we are and how we play.

24

The Road Out of Hell

THE COUSIN-STALKED GAMES we made throughout our history were nothing if not stubborn. Virtue-dominance play largely defined the tenor of existence for thousands of years. We'd be born into a kin-based network of cousins, uncles, aunts, in-laws and connected families, united by distinctive ways of living and working that stretched back into the deep past and added up to a group identity. Getting along and getting ahead meant conforming to these rules and symbols, policing them when others erred, deferring to superiors, meeting obligations, building a reputation for loyalty and duty and for offering value to the game's overall success. Their incredible persistence is partly due to the fact that these virtue games were prone to self-replicate. For centuries, marriage took place mostly within networks of kin. In the fourteenth century the French Knight of La Tour-Landry advised maidens to always 'marry into their own estate'. Still today, one in ten global marriages are between relatives including cousins.

But virtue and dominance aren't the only way humans evolved to make status. We can also use strategies of success. In the tribes in which we evolved, it was possible to earn rank by being useful to others with displays of competence: the best hunter, the best sorcerer, the best finder of honey. The modern world is heavily flavoured by the success games of scientists, technologists, researchers, corporations and creatives. Their status is won not by showing and enforcing moral correctness, but by becoming smarter, wealthier and more innovative and efficient.

Modernity was made in the West. There are many answers to the question of why this might be and none of them, it should hardly be necessary to note, involve there being anything inherently superior about those born on this chunk of the planet. The reasons are complex. Partly it has to do with lucky geography: climactic conditions that benefitted early crop farmers and keepers of livestock. Wheat, barley, sheep and cattle accelerated the process of settling down, accumulating wealth and dividing labour into caste-based specialisms. Elsewhere, researchers hunting the roots of Western individualism look to Ancient Greece. They, too, note its geography: it was a pointillist civilisation formed of around one thousand city states, dotted about many coasts and craggy islands in which large-scale farming was mostly impossible. This compelled people to get by, not as obedient members of agrarian communities, but as entrepreneurs: fishermen, makers of pottery, tanners of hides. The Ancient Greeks were self-starters who'd be regularly exposed to traders with new perspectives from other communities, even distant continents. This encouraged success-inflected games of individual ability and debate. From these games emerged an ideal of self, based on the all-powerful individual, that remains characteristic of Western culture.

But such accounts are only part of the answer. Another factor can be found by buckling up for an intense ride through the history of the status games of monotheism and money. Across the world, wealth and the great religions constituted major threats to the dominant powers of King, Queen and Emperor. The rise of holy leaders and rich traders saw new elites emerge, leading rival games. But it was in the West that success games first managed to overpower the old virtue games, and come to flower over a culture.

This happened not as a result of strategy or guile, but of chance and unintended consequence. It's a process that demonstrates how powerful the games we play for status can be in defining self, culture and history. Individuals want to know: *who do I have to be to get along and get ahead?* Those born in an environment of dominance, virtue and obedience to caste and kin will become those people and play those games. They'll live the dream they've been woven. But at the start of the modern era, initially in the West, we began looking outside our kin groups for connection and status. We became interested in novel, useful ideas from foreign clans and continents. We began generating major status by studying, innovating and making correct predictions about reality; rewarding each other for discovering truth and making use of it. These success games became a goldrush that spread across Western Europe, the USA and then the rest of the world. They changed everything. They were our road out of hell.

And they might never have come about if it wasn't for the Catholic Church's weird preoccupation with incest. Over a period of more than a thousand years, starting in AD 305, the Church instituted a series of rule changes that combined to disable the old inward-looking virtue games, based on kin and extended family, and compel people to play in new ways. It banned: polygamous marriage; marriage to blood relatives including up to sixth cousins; marriage to in-laws, including that of uncles to nieces and men to stepmothers and step-daughters. It also suppressed forced marriages, encouraged newlyweds to set up their own households away from the extended family and promoted individual inheritance by will and testament, rather than the automatic handing-down of assets to the clan. It would take many centuries, but by the accident of its unholy obsession, it was to change the game forever.

These rule alterations and their historical effects were discovered by Joseph Henrich, a Professor of Human Evolutionary Biology. He and his colleagues have produced an impressive constellation of evidence in support of them. Henrich argues these changes 'systematically broke down the clans and kindreds of Europe into monogamous nuclear families'. People were forced to seek status outside their kin networks and play with strangers. Learning to 'navigate a world with few inherited ties' meant developing a novel psychology, and so the coding of their game-playing machines was rewritten. They made games for themselves in which 'success and respect' depended on 'honing one's own special attributes; attracting friends, mates, and business partners with these attributes and then sustaining relationships with them'. Crucially, Henrich's research shows the Catholics' new rules were causative in changing who we were: the longer a population lived by them, the looser their kinship groups and the more they became outward-looking, nonconformist, trusting of outsiders, self-focussed and individualistic.

This mass psychological recoding was only possible in the first place because the major religions had insinuated their dream of the game into the minds of millions. The spread of the two most successful faiths, first Christianity and then Islam, is partly thanks to a tweak in their theology: unlike pagan and animist traditions, with their teeming pantheons of gods, they were monotheistic. Their god wasn't a god, he was God. The One and Only. His moral rules were universal, applicable to all. Accepting the truth of other gods and breaking His rules was now a heresy, a significant rejection of the monotheist's criteria for claiming status. This incentivised believers to convert those around them and conquer their neural territory. Studies suggest religious belief doesn't fall upon populations as charismatic holy men ride into towns on pony-back and convert them en masse. Rather, it spreads through personal connections, as friends and family members convince those close to them to join.

And it works: research on the effects of religious conversion finds the 'psychological and emotional condition of most converts improves' after joining.

The dream the monotheists wove atop the game of life called for absolute faith. God couldn't be worshipped by sacrifice, like pagan gods, but by 'proper belief', writes New Testament researcher Professor Bart Ehrman. 'Anyone who didn't believe the right things would be considered a transgressor before God.' Punishments for incorrect belief were as severe as an imagination could allow: an endless degrading in the torments of hell. Its tortures, often based around the body being 'eternally burned, without being consumed' were threatened in sermons such as this, from Saint Leonard: 'Fire, fire: such is the reward for your perversity, you stubborn sinners. Fire, fire, the fire of hell. Fire in your eyes, fire in your mouth, fire in your bowels, fire in your throat, fire in your nostrils, fire within, fire without, fire below, fire above, fire all about. Ah, wretches, you will be like burning embers in the middle of this fire.' Unbelief could also mean dropping in status in the here and now, with sometimes all-too-real consequences: if the faithless didn't suffer outright perse-cution, they were often denied legal and social privileges and, in some Muslim communities, paid higher taxes. The reward for playing was connection and status in this life, and infinite paradise in the next. 'Religion had never promoted such an idea before,' writes Ehrman. 'Christians created a need for salvation that no one knew they had. They then argued that they alone could meet the need. And they succeeded massively.'

By the medieval era, the Catholic Church had become the most powerful institution on earth; its leader the most powerful human alive. The pope and his bishops and priests, at the top of the game, were divinely appointed, part of an 'apostolic succession' leading back directly to the apostles of Christ. To insult a priest was a crime against God. The Church became rich, the largest landowner in

Europe, owning 44 per cent of France and half of Germany. Inevitably, its professional class became status drunk, surrounding themselves with treasures, wearing large hats, insisting on absolute deference in their presence – knees bent, hats doffed – and to be addressed by titles such as Your Holiness, Your Excellency and Your Grace. Much of its wealth came from a crafty alteration to one of the game's rules. It might've been true that Jesus once said it was 'easier for a camel to go through the eye of a needle than for a rich man to enter the kingdom of God', but a cheat was added: the wealthy could enjoy their riches in life then donate it to the Church just prior to death – after all, if you'd been relieved of your wealth even one second before your heart stopped, strictly speaking, when you reached heaven's gates you were poor.

Academics argue about the extent to which ordinary medieval people bought the dream of Christianity. Some inevitably doubted and many played a double game, still honouring the old polytheistic traditions (many of which were regurgitated by Christianity, with its buffet of saints and its hopscotching of pagan feast days). But hope in heaven and dread of hell certainly seem real and widespread: the wealthy gave so much to the Church, to buy themselves a better afterlife, secular leaders enacted laws to limit their spending.

Catholicism was a virtue-dominance game in which players required God's mercy to drag themselves off the bottom: 'What is a man by himself, without grace? A being more evil than the demon,' wrote Saint Catherine of Genoa. Life was a game for status that was mostly won in the eternity; where you ended up was a matter of how well you played. The rules were slightly complicated. God, being ever-loving, granted mercy to all believers, but players had to demonstrate their acceptance of his generous offer by performing good works on earth. 'The tricky thing', writes historian Professor Peter Marshall, 'was knowing whether one had done enough to count as an unqualified "yes" to God's invitation.' For many terrified people, this question became an obsession. By the late medieval, it's argued, a 'widespread and morbid' sense of 'salvation anxiety' had taken hold of much of the Christian world.

In salvation anxiety, the Church smelled opportunity. The Pope claimed the ability to guarantee someone's place in heaven, by drawing from the 'surplus' good deeds of the saints as currency. He began issuing letters, called indulgences, that would forgive sins and ease a person's passage in the afterlife. First intended as bribes to persuade men to join the Crusades against the Church's Muslim rivals, they soon became a way of gathering revenue, not least for the building of conspicuous status symbols such as churches and cathedrals. A market for indulgences grew, in which forgiveness for sins including cousin marriage could be bought. They even sold forgiveness for future sins. One spectacular section of Rouen Cathedral is known as 'The Butter Tower', its construction financed by indulgences permitting the eating of butter during Lent.

But there was a problem. Centuries earlier, the same Church had begun rewiring the brains of its players. Its obsession with incest had led to a series of rule changes that had been breaking apart the old ways of living based around caste and extended family. No longer was it possible for many Christians to survive wholly by turning inwards. They lived increasingly in their own homes, in nuclear families with two to four children. Some worked the land for a Lord of the Manor; others moved into towns and cities. Further encouraged out of the countryside by wars and plagues, they found themselves populating streets, markets and squares, mingling with strangers with whom they'd have to sustain fruitful, trusting, professional relationships.

The business of getting along and getting ahead had been changing. Universities had been founded, with more than fifty established by 1500, producing lawyers, writers, mathematicians, logicians and astronomers. Craftsmen, now freer to choose an occupation based on individual preference rather than accident of birth, formed professional guilds. Guilds were success games. They sprang up around all manner of trades, including blacksmiths, brewers, weavers, glassmakers, dyers, shoemakers, locksmiths, bakers and skinners. Each had their own set of rules and symbols by which they awarded success-based status, with members granted the title 'master craftsman'. Ambitious young players apprenticed themselves to a master, learned a trade, joined the game, before moving on to another master to learn more. As expertise developed, demand for quality goods increased. A 'work ethic' came into being, in which toil itself became prestigious. 'This shift can be understood as the beginning of a work-centred society', writes historian Professor Andrea Komlosy, 'in which the diverse activities of all of its members are increasingly obliged to take on the traits of active production and strenuous exertion.'

We were getting our status from new kinds of games. Slowly, and in fits and starts, our focus had been juddering from duty to the clan towards individual competence and success. This changed our psychology, rewriting the cultural coding of our game-playing brains, turning us into new sorts of humans. We were more independent, more self-focussed, more outward-looking, more interested in personal excellence, less conformist and less in awe of tradition, ancestry, duty and authority. In short, we were no longer the kind of people prepared to be bullied, threatened, bribed and insulted by a corrupt and status-drunk Church. By the sixteenth century the Catholic Church, and the psychological nature of its players, had grown apart. Something would have to give.

It gave in October 1517. The Pope had been selling indulgences to raise funds for the building of yet another gaudy status symbol, St Peter's Basilica in Rome. Sales in Germany were headed up by a pushy friar, Tetzel the Persuader, whose pitch went: 'as soon as the coin in the coffer rings, a soul from purgatory to heaven springs'. His arrival infuriated a professor of moral theology at the University of Wittenberg, Martin Luther, who wondered, 'Why does not the Pope, whose wealth is today greater than the riches of the richest, build just this one church of St Peter with his own money, rather than with the money of poor believers?' Luther noted his protests in a document called the Ninety-five Theses, mailed it to the Archbishop and nailed it to the doors of the city's churches. If the psychology of the European masses hadn't been changing over the centuries, they'd likely have ignored this small, local rebellion. Instead, Luther sparked a revolution.

His movement won the approval and support of the elites: local rulers such as kings, princes and dukes. He also took advantage of the latest technology. With the help of the printing press, Luther's writings spread far and fast: between 1517 and 1520, more than three hundred thousand copies of his books, pamphlets and broadsides were distributed. He and other thinkers, most famously John Calvin, disagreed on much, but eventually a new form of Christian game, for 'Protestants', came into being. It had a revised set of rules and symbols, one fit for the success-focussed player of town, university, guild and marketplace.

For Protestants, life was no longer a gruelling test for heaven or hell. God already knew where you were ending up. Believers were to look for clues of 'assurance' to see if they were saved or damned: signs of 'elect status' could be found in their own personal behaviour such as virtuous and sober living, but also in the accrual of wealth and rank on earth. Believers were said to have a personal 'calling'. God had endowed them with special talents that they should seek to maximise by choosing the right occupation or vocation, then working hard in it. Those acting with toil and self-discipline in a freely chosen game were allowing God's gift to flourish. Playing for personal success became holy, an act of worship. With a few hundred years of hindsight, we can see these cultural innovations for what they are: a long step towards modernity.

But the changes didn't stop there. No longer was a Christian's relationship with God to be mediated by an elite caste of clergy: 'we are all equally priests', wrote Luther. Players would learn to read Bibles themselves, translated from the Latin. A sacred virtue was made of education: reading wasn't merely encouraged, it was a foundational rule of the game, necessary for developing individual moral behaviour and building a personal relationship with God. This single rule change seems to have helped encourage a further massive alteration to our psychology. And once again, research suggests the change was causative. Analysis by Henrich finds literacy rates grew 'fastest in countries where Protestantism was most deeply established'. For centuries after Luther's death, more Protestants in any country meant higher rates of literacy.

The Protestants' remixed religion spread rapidly throughout Western Europe, through populations of relatively self-focussed players, drained by salvation anxiety and no longer prepared to be conned and insulted by their elites. The popular fury of the time is evident in anticlerical propaganda that depicted monks as wolves, friars as demons and the Pope as a dragon. In one Cambridgeshire village, in the 1520s, a man encountering a priest with a freshly shaven head 'took up a cow's dung with his spade and clapped it upon his crown, adding with these words: 'You, said he, all the sort of you will, ere it be long, be glad to hide your shaven pates rather than that they should be seen.' The Church had split. Catholics and Protestants went to war; in some places they're still fighting.

But virtue games were still in charge. As radical as the Protestant game seems, for these deeply religious people 'success' wasn't categorically separate from 'virtue' but an extension of it. They were awarding status for shows of competence but still in the context of, and heavily mediated by, a powerful Christian virtue game. Ultimately, whether it was priests, bishops and popes in charge, or princes, dukes and kings, these were still games of obedience and duty. If the new-style success-oriented players were to ever over-whelm the entrenched authorities, they'd need to form powerful elites of their own. They'd do so by becoming rich.

For centuries leading up to Luther's revolution, wealth had given players from non-holy and non-royal castes a route to high social rank. These new elites thrived on the profits of status-striving. In the middle centuries of the last millennium, trading routes into Asia, Africa, Indonesia and the Americas made fashionable the use of luxury high-value goods such as spices, silks, sugar, opium, cannabis, velvet, ebony, ivory, sandalwood, tulips, coconuts, colourful dyes, bananas, papayas, rhubarb, potatoes, pineapples, sex toys and perfumes of musk and civet. Slaves were also traded. Meanwhile, Europe exported the goods made by skilled craftsmen such as textiles, timber, glassware and paper. The merchants who ran these operations became wealthy, often fabulously so. Some merchant families began funding expeditions by offering credit to adventurers in return for repayment with interest. These 'merchant bankers' also became wealthy, even more fabulously so. There was social mobility: ambitious entrepreneurs without significant financial resources could start their careers travelling with cargo on such expeditions, earn capital, then move up the trading game. Eventually trading companies recruited their own private armies and founded colonies in distant continents.

Riches generated by trade; the rise of middle-class artisans and craftsmen; the Black Death leaving resources to be spread around fewer people; games being played for competence and success: it all added up to more money washing down through the game. This new wealth was threatening to the old powers. Winners of success games began enjoying the same status symbols as the winners of virtue games. This outraged the old elites. Special rules, called sumptuary laws, were instituted that sought to control how members of each social rank could express themselves with status goods and behaviour. They dictated what they could wear, eat, how they could organise their funerals and weddings, what carriages they could own and how they could be upholstered. In England, in 1363, legislation was introduced to curb 'the Outragious and Excessive Apparel of divers People, against their Estate and Degree, to the great Destruction and Impoverishment of all the Land'. It defined what those of different ranks, from carters, oxherds and ploughmen all the way up to knights, could spend on clothing. Other legislation forbade the 'outrageous consumption of meats and fine dishes' by some and ordered that 'no knight under the estate of a lord, esquire or gentleman, nor any other person, shall wear any shoes or boots having spikes or points which exceed the length of two inches, under the forfeiture of forty pence'. In 1574, one Londoner was imprisoned for the crime of wearing 'a pair of hose lined with taffety, and a shirt edged with silver contrary to the ordinances'. It wasn't only in the West that the rise of the wealthy, and their symbols of status, were creating anxieties for the old elites. One Chinese writer in 1591 complained that 'a family without as much as an old broom go about in carriages . . . and dress themselves up in the hats and clothing of the rich and eminent'.

Among the world's wealthiest regions were the trading cities in present-day Italy: Genoa, Florence and Venice. These were not the societies of sharply divided inequality that were seen in earlier eras, in which elites played in an exalted distance far above the gruelling toil of the masses. Their success games generated a healthy middle class, including artisans and shopkeepers; inequality is thought to have been roughly comparable with modern day USA. With this relatively equal society came a new kind of culture in which elite players, finding it harder to distinguish themselves, had to continually find fresh ways to signal their status. They used expressions of taste and beauty, in gardens, squares, houses, sculpture, furnishings and personal appearance. This fed a market for yet more success games – for painters, sculptors, architects, potters and makers of hair extensions and false teeth. One poet of the time, Giovanni Pontano, even wrote a treatise on the virtue of spending money in pursuit of private enjoyment.

This modern aspiration for luxury and elegance can be seen most clearly in Italian status play around food. In other parts of Europe, habits of dining remained basic. One 1530 book of etiquette, by Erasmus of Rotterdam, describes diners sitting down to a goblet and helping themselves to communal meat using the knife they carried with them daily. Plates were relatively rare and tended to be made of pewter; more often you'd eat off a thick piece of bread. Everyone, even kings and queens, ate with their hands. Erasmus discouraged the holding in of flatulence, for reasons of health, and similarly advised you vomit if you needed to: 'for it is not vomiting but holding the vomit in your throat that is foul'.

It wasn't like this in Italy. The nobility and middle classes of its rich trading cities were eating off porcelain plates using forks, knives and spoons. In 1475 one Florence banker ordered a set of four hundred glass beakers; a single banquet in 1565 made use of 150 plates and fifty bowls 'all of porcelain'. Wealthy merchant and noble families collected services made up of hundreds of individual pieces. Historian Professor Richard Goldthwaite writes, 'the preparation of food, along with manners, entered into the game of competition for status in a society increasingly conscious of hierarchy'. Foreign visitors could find Italian food culture lavish and preposterous. French intellectual Montaigne thought it remarkable that diners were issued napkins and their own set of silverware. One Italian chef he encountered 'gave me a discourse on this science of supping with a grave and magisterial countenance, as if he were speaking of some grand point of theology . . . he unravelled the differences in appetite for me . . . after that, he embarked on the order of the courses, full of important and fine considerations . . . and all this bloated with grand and magnificent words, such as one might use in describing the government of an empire.'

But as powerful as the success games of the artisans and traders were, their cultures were still ruled by the virtue games of religion and nobility. They remained essentially backwards-facing: whether it was the Bible or the ancient classics that Italy's elite saw as an aid to moral improvement and employment potentialities, the belief held that solving problems in the present meant consulting the wisdom of the past.

But then, in the West, that began to change. Many centuries earlier, the Christian elites had started rewiring its players to become more open and less in awe of their own groups. This gave Westerners an increased openness to novel ideas. Whilst the inward-looking East adopted relatively few Western technologies and notions, the West was voracious in appropriating theirs – as the Italian love of eating off 'china' indicates. It wasn't only their beautiful, delicious and intoxicating goods we imbibed, it was their genius, including the Hindu-Arabic numeral system of zero to nine and its calculation and accountancy applications: decimal points, addition, subtraction, multiplication, division, principles of interest and bills of exchange.

This openness to novel ideas became a status-making pursuit. At first in Italy in the 1500s, and then across Western Europe, there spread a fashion for possessing 'useful knowledge'. In the beginning, this manifested as 'an upper class fascination with learning and the arts, combining the features of the scholar and gentleman into a serious if perhaps somewhat amateurish intellectual', writes economic historian Professor Joel Mokyr. These gentleman thinkers, known as 'virtuosi', wrote books on subjects as disparate as forestry, mathematics and sumptuary laws. Their success-play was founded on a love of knowledge for its own sake. The virtuosi, 'turned curiosity, once regarded as a vice, into a virtue'. Showing knowledge had become a status symbol: 'the courtier had become a scholar, and culture for social ornament passed into learning for fame and admiration'.

As the dreams of the virtuosi spread downwards from the nobility towards a broader expanse of intellectuals, a significant status game formed around new and useful knowledge. Named by the Venetian statesman and thinker Francesco Barbaro as the *Respublica Literaria*, or Republic of Letters, this game was made possible by the postal system that had been established across much of Western Europe. Men and women of excellence were now able to communicate their ideas in pamphlets, periodicals, books and personal correspondence. Their expertise ranged across disciplines including medicine, science, philosophy, theology, astronomy and philology. They created an international success game in which major status was awarded for dazzling displays of competence.

Merely mastering the knowledge of the past was of little value in this game. Earning status was about the new: progress, innovation, insight and originality. The financial rewards could be significant: the best players earned patronage by dukes, princes and kings, who'd boast of having the finest minds in their employ, and make profitable use of their expertise in their state-building; merchants similarly recruited mathematicians and engineers to help give them an edge. But money wasn't the driving force of the Republic of Letters. As Mokyr writes, 'reputation based on peer evaluation was what counted . . . to be recognised by one's peers as a master is enormously desirable and this was the driving motive behind most scholarly effort in early modern Europe'. Players could win major status by becoming international superstars, their fame spanning the continent, and have their discoveries – laws, methods, processes, astral bodies, parts of the brain and body – named after them.

The rules by which the Republic's game was played reads like a manifesto for the future of science and technology. Rather than jealously protecting their ideas, players would be open with them; knowledge was seen as a common good, but originators of new ideas could rightfully profit from them; intellectual debts would be acknowledged, the theft of ideas being disgraceful; letters should be responded to; new ideas could and should be contested; there were to be no boundaries of kin, clan, nation or religion. A 'scientific method' for the testing of theories was developed that, wrote one scholar, 'teaches men humility and acquaints them with their own errors and so removes all overweening haughtiness of mind'. Strict standards would be applied to these experiments: there should be unbiased analysis of data; accurate records kept; they should be reproducible; results should be published.

The establishment of the Republic of Letters is a major event in human history. It earns its notch on the ruler of time alongside fire and campsites, gossip and reputation and rise of empires and conquering religions. It takes two electrical wires, jams them together and makes an explosion that blasts us into a new epoch. The first live wire was our *capacity for culture*. Humans had been able to conquer the planet partly because we exist in a web of stored information. Every individual born didn't have to learn everything for themselves afresh: knowledge was communicated by elders and passed down through the generations. But in the old kin-based virtue games, this knowledge often just bounced around the group. The ideas of other collectives were typically of little interest. Innovation never sat well in these virtue games, where worship of ancestry and the wisdom of the past dominated a player's thoughts. As problems were encountered and solved, innovation naturally took place, but not often for its own sake. In the era of virtue games, aside from relatively rare bursts here and there, progress was usually slow.

The second live wire was *status from success*. Human brains want to know, *Who do I need to become to win rank?* In Pohnpei, a success game evolved around the growing of enormous yams. The result was enormous yams. In the Republic of Letters, a success game evolved around our capacity for accumulating knowledge. The result was enormous accumulations of knowledge. We'd win by making correct observations and predictions about reality and storing what we'd learned in letters, pamphlets and books, allowing it to build and become even more useful, being adapted and improved by other players. The Republic's rules were such that findings were freely shared and judged by peers; winners were reliably celebrated, moving up in rank. It was a beautifully constructed success game. Its players couldn't know it, but the Republic of Letters was riding on ancient circuitry that had evolved to help co-operative hunter-gatherer tribes survive. By connecting our ability to accumulate knowledge to our desire for status, they'd discovered the future.

But the future wasn't ready for them yet. The Republic of Letters was tiny; a game played by a narrow elite of intellectuals and nobles. It wasn't nearly powerful enough to insinuate itself into the minds of millions and define a culture, as kingdoms, empires and the great faiths had done. The kin-based virtue games of royalty and religion jealously maintained their dominance; the empires struck back. In Italy the old elites eventually re-established their dominion over the new. In Venice, entrepreneurial merchants and bankers were shut out of The Great Council, its centre of political power. The Council was colonised by a hereditary aristocracy who then ate away at the traders' ability to create wealth, leading to the city's decline.

But there was one place in the world in which the old orders failed to restrain the new: Britain. Back in 1215, an elite caste of barons had forced King John to sign Magna Carta, a deal that challenged the throne's power in various ways, such as restraining its ability to raise taxes. They formed a council to ensure royal compliance. 1265 saw the first elected Parliament, which eventually came to consist not only of nobles, knights and aristocrats, but wealthy farmers and leaders of industry and commerce – winners of success games. Following the 'Glorious Revolution' of 1688 a 'bill of rights' was negotiated that established Parliament as the nation's ruling power. No longer did the crown have total control. Then came a slew of rules and institutions that benefited games of success. The Bank of England was founded. Credit was made available to the many. Legal innovations, such as secure property and patent rights and the principle that the law should be applied equally to all, made it safer for entrepreneurs to entrepreneur and their success games to form and flourish. Monopolies were abolished; the principle of free trade established; merchants were assisted and defended with the full force of the state. It was in this unique environment, write the economists Professor Daron Acemoglu and James A. Robinson, that innovators, 'were able to take up the economic opportunities generated by their ideas, were confident that their property rights would be respected, and had access to markets where their innovations could be profitably sold and used'.

Britain had many active members in the Republic of Letters, including architect Christopher Wren, philosopher Robert Boyle, economist William Petty and polymath Robert Hooke. Their nation increasingly took over from Italy as the place in which the future was being made: in 1675, it's thought not a single household in London owned porcelain dishes; by 1725, 35 per cent did. With power increasingly removed from the old virtue games of royalty and Church, Britain was a nation uniquely capable of taking the tiny knowledge-based success game of the Republic of Letters and spreading it to the masses. Not only could successful innovators win fame amongst their peers, Britain's institutions allowed them to earn major wealth and even national celebrity, their stores of status swelling spectacularly. Increasingly, it became a game open not only to an intellectual elite but to thousands of mechanics, entrepreneurs, engineers, tinkerers and artisans.

This 'Industrial Revolution' was a status goldrush. It came to define the country's mood and culture. Britons 'became innovators because they adopted an improving mentality', writes historian Dr Anton Howes. This mentality spread like a 'disease' that could infect 'anyone . . . rich and poor, city-dwellers and rustics, Anglicans and dissenters, Whigs and Tories, skilled engineers and complete amateurs'. A growing number 'published about innovation, lectured on it, exhibited it, and funded it'. They formed themselves into communities based around their interests and established societies devoted to spreading the mindset further. These organisations were generators not only of new and useful knowledge, but major status for successful innovators.

The revolution took off on an eruption of status games. Britain became, in the words of historian Professor Peter Clark, an 'associational world'. Players formed games around their specialisms. They met at clubs and conversation societies; they gathered at coffeehouses, of which, by 1700, there were around two thousand in London alone. They founded learned organisations dedicated to the accrual and spread of new and useful knowledge that, according to economist James Dowey, numbered less than fifty in 1750 and around one and a half thousand by 1850. One of these, The Society for the Encouragement of Arts, Manufactures and Commerce, began in a London coffeehouse and awarded thousands of cash prizes or medals to members who solved problems or produced ingenious inventions, including the inventors of the lifeboat; a safer pneumatic braking mechanism for cranes; and a mechanical method of cleaning chimneys that made possible laws banning the use of boys as young as four. That association still exists today, better known as the Royal Society of Arts.

These associations were success games, awarding status for displays of competence. Dowey finds the Royal Society spent more in its first two decades on medals for inventors than it did on cash premiums. Its awards, he argues, had a major societal impact via their effect on ambitious onlookers: as a 'nationally visible institution patronised by London's social, intellectual and commercial elites' its most important contribution to innovation 'was to promote and bestow prestige upon inventing in general'. These dynamics made status games such as the Royal Society foundries of innovation. As players strived for acclaim and respect, they themselves became generators of new and useful knowledge. Dowey's analyses reveal that more societies in a particular region led to more patents being awarded there; the same pattern was found in his analysis of exhibitors at London's 1851 Great Exhibition: more societies in any region predicted higher representation at the event, and more prizes. For every 746 society members, in any given region, its number of exhibits grew by 42 per cent, its prizes by 48 per cent. The relationship between learned societies and innovation during the Industrial Revolution, Dowey concludes, 'should be interpreted as causal'.

And so, out of this status goldrush, came accumulations of knowledge never before seen in human history. The atmosphere of the time was described in a speech by a mathematician, Dr Olinthus Gregory, delivered in 1826: 'Agriculture, manufactures, commerce, navigation, the arts and sciences, useful and ornamental, in a copious and inexhaustible variety, enhance the conveniences and embellishments of this otherwise happy spot. Cities thronged with inhabitants, warehouses filled with stores, markets and fairs with busy rustics; fields, villages, roads, seaports, all contributing to the riches and glory of our land . . . New societies for improvement . . . new machines to advance our arts and facilitate labour; waste lands enclosed, roads improved, bridges erected, canals cut, tunnels excavated, marshes drained and cultivated, docks formed, ports enlarged: these and a thousand kindred operations which present themselves spontaneously to the mind's eye, prove that we have not yet attained our zenith, and open an exquisite prospect of future stability and greatness.'

The Industrial Revolution soon spread to other parts of the world. When the fever for improvement caught the United States, it first rivalled and today easily surpasses Western Europe in its genius for innovation. Much of that nation's remaining prestige is earned by its Silicon Valley technology companies. The games those innovators play were invented by scholars of the Republic of Letters and given the power to transform the world by the revolutions and institutions of bygone Britain.

The thinkers of the Enlightenment who, in the seventeenth and eighteenth centuries, further transformed Western Europe and then the world with their ideas about reason, liberty, tolerance, and separation of Church and State, were also inheritors of the games that formed before them. One of the most famous, Scottish economist Adam Smith, is commonly known as the 'Father of Capitalism'. Perhaps more than anyone, the hyper-individualistic, self-interested money-obsessed world we live in today is linked to him and his theories of how free markets and competition generate prosperity. But Smith didn't believe greed for wealth was the ultimate driver of economies. He thought something else was going on, something deeper in the human psyche. 'Humanity does not desire to be great, but to be beloved,' he wrote in 1759. 'The rich man glories in his riches because he feels they naturally draw upon him the attention of the world . . . and he is fonder of his wealth on this account than for all the other advantages it procures him.' This need for attention and approval was, for Smith, a fundamental part of the human condition. We strive to better our lot because we seek to be 'observed, to be attended to, to be taken notice of'. It's the dream that says status symbols such as wealth will make us perfectly happy that inspires us to 'cultivate the ground, to build houses, to found cities and commonwealths, and to invent and improve all the sciences and arts, which ennoble and embellish human life; which have entirely changed the whole face of the globe'.

We're immeasurably better off for our modern strivings towards excellence. By the end of the nineteenth century, life expectancy and living standards were rising, extreme poverty and infant mortality were falling and the threat of famine and starvation that had forever haunted the masses was beginning to recede. Our relentless accumulations of useful knowledge brought astonishing innovations in technology, medicine and science. The road out of hell is mapped across the data of human health and thriving. For all of history prior to the Industrial Revolution, global life expectancy bounced around the age of 30. It's since soared to over 70 – and, in developed nations, over 80. Scientific advances have saved the lives of billions: water chlorination has saved 177 million; smallpox eradication 131 million; the measles vaccine 120 million; infectious disease controls have saved over a hundred million children since 1990; in 2021 multiple coronavirus vaccines began saving the entire world. We're also better fed than ever. In 1947, around half the planet's population was undernourished; that number now stands at 13 per cent in the developing nations and, in the developed, less than 5 per cent. We're also wealthier. In 1800, nearly 95 per cent of humans lived in extreme poverty. Between 1990 and 2018 alone that number fell from nearly 1.9 billion to about 650 million.

History is not made by individuals, but by individuals connected into groups. Those groups are status games. The data, and our history, are clear. If we truly want to help others and make the world a better place, we must play games of success.

25

The Neoliberal Self

AND SO OUR journey arrives at today. We are, in the twenty-first century, as we've always been: great apes hunting connection and status inside shared hallucinations. The contemporary Western self is a strange, anxious, hungry thing. It emerges out of a market economy that's heavily focussed on success. Whilst we'll never stop playing games of dominance and virtue, our societies emphasise individual competence and achievement. We win points for personal success throughout our lives, in the highly formalised and often precisely graded games of school, college and work. In the street, in the office and on social media we signal our accomplishments with appearance, possessions and lifestyles. We're self-obsessed, because this is the game we're raised to play.

As individualists we've always been relatively me-focussed. But the latter twentieth century saw us transform into a heightened mode of self-obsession. Following the depression and world wars, the economies of the USA and Britain became more rule-bound, virtuous and group-focussed: it was an era of increasing regulation over banking and business, high taxation (topping out at 90 per cent in America in the 1940s and 1950s), broad unionisation and 'big government' innovations such as the New Deal, the Social Security Act, the minimum wage and the welfare state. American and British players became concomitantly collective: the monkey-suited 'Corporation Man' of the 1950s suburbs gave birth to the even more collectively minded hippies, with their anti-materialistic values. As ever, the great game was inside us; its rules and symbols were written into our game-playing equipment; we dreamed its dream and lived its iteration of self.

But in the 1980s, the game changed again. During the previous decade, the economies of the West had started to fail. New ways of playing were sought. The leaders of the UK and USA, Margaret Thatcher and Ronald Reagan, decided to make the game significantly more competitive. In 1981, Thatcher told journalists, 'What's irritated me about the whole direction of politics in the last thirty years is that it's always been toward the collectivist society.' Thatcher and Reagan's governments commenced a series of brutal attacks on these older, more virtue-bound ways of playing. They rolled back the protections of the state, cut taxes, deregulated banking and business, privatised national assets, defanged the unions and reined in employee rights. In this new age, wherever possible, the markets, not the politicians, would be in charge. This 'neoliberal' game was freer, less rule-bound – and more individualistic. To win, our equipment would have to be re-coded yet again. To get along and get ahead, we'd have to become more competitive, more materialistic and more self-focussed.

And so we did. It's astonishing to think of who we were, as a people, in 1965 versus who we'd become by 1985. In just twenty years we'd gone from *fuck The Man* to *greed is good*. The deeper we moved into the neoliberal age, the more we were consumed by its dream. The transformation was rapid. One study of over three hundred million births found that, starting in 1983, Americans began giving their children uncommon and unusually spelled names. Parents, wrote co-author Professor Jean Twenge, wanted their kids to 'stand out and be a star'. As the 1980s rolled on, we made a culture of million-selling keep fit videos, cocaine yuppies and Whitney Houston's chart-topping hymn that taught us 'learning to love yourself' was 'the greatest love of all'. This narcissistic notion became a cultural value: a Gallup poll for *Newsweek* in 1992 found 89 per cent of respondents believing the 'most important' factor in 'motivating a person to work hard and success' was 'self-esteem' (the least important, they thought, was 'status in the eyes of others'). Neoliberalism's spirit rings out in a 1987 advert for a Gold MasterCard: 'All it takes is success.' Players in the game agreed: high-school children in the 1970s were half as likely as those in the 1990s to believe 'having lots of money' was 'very important'.

As neoliberal values became more entrenched in the new millennium, we became increasingly interested in fame. A 2006 survey of 2,500 UK children under the age of 10 found their 'very best thing in the world' was 'being a celebrity' (their second and third very best things in the world were 'good looks' and 'being rich'). In 2003, Sony launched the first phone with a front-facing camera. It was intended for use in business meetings. But that's not what we chose to do with this technology. By 2019, Google revealed users of Android devices alone were taking 93 million selfies every day.

As neoliberalism rose, the old games of connection and status that were once widely played among friends and neighbours in their communities decayed. Political scientist Professor Robert Putnam has charted their collapse. 'During the first two-thirds of the century, Americans took a more and more active role in the social and political life of their communities – in churches and union halls, in bowling alleys and clubrooms, around committee tables and card tables and dinner tables,' he writes. Such groups 'seemed to be on the threshold of a new era of expanded involvement'. But then, 'more or less simultaneously, we began to do all those things less often'.

When discussing his play *Death of a Salesman*, Arthur Miller described its tragic hero Willy Loman's worldview thusly: 'The law of success is that if you fail you're dead. And you're weighed on that scale the way God used to weigh people in the old days.' The neoliberal age saw us all becoming little Lomans. Today, more than at any previous time in history, we measure our status by professional success and its symbols. Our daily pursuits – even those in education and the arts – are increasingly directed at financial ends, their victories measured in wealth. Research suggests busyness itself has come to be considered a status symbol. In a series of studies, busy people were viewed as having 'more status because they were perceived as more competent and ambitious, as well as to be more scarce and in demand'.

The neoliberal dreamworld glisters with such symbols. Success cues might've started in ropes of teeth around a hunter's neck, but in twenty-first-century Westernised cultures, they're everywhere. Maddened by them, we sweat and spend and hurry to keep up. We strive to improve, to bend our personalities into a certain shape, to become a better, different person. But where does it come from, the contemporary ideal of self? We see this perfect human all around us, beaming with flawless teeth from advertising, film, television, media and the internet. Young, agreeable, visibly fit, self-starting, productive, popular, globally-minded, stylish, self-confident, extrovert, busy. Who is it, this person we feel so pressured to punch ourselves into becoming? It's the player best equipped to win status in the game we're in. It's the neoliberal hero, the fantasy of an economy. And when we don't measure up, we read these success symbols as signals of our failure. We're individualists: believing it's in our own power to win means believing that, when we don't, it's our fault and our fault alone. So we're a loser, then: that's who we are. We've been weighed on God's scale and found wanting.

Psychologists have a name for people with a heightened sensitivity to signals of failure: perfectionist. There are various forms of perfectionism: 'self-oriented perfectionists' have excessively high standards and often push themselves harder and harder in order to win; 'narcissistic perfectionists' already believe they're number one and experience anxiety when the world treats them as less; 'neurotic perfectionists' suffer low self-esteem and often believe with the next victory they'll finally feel good enough. But there's one species of perfectionism that's especially sensitive to the neoliberal game: 'social perfectionists' feel the pressure to win comes from the people with whom they play. They'll tend to agree with statements such as, 'People expect nothing less than perfection from me' and 'Success means that I must work harder to please others.' Social perfectionists are highly attuned to reputation and identity. They'll easily think they've let their peers down by being a bad employee, a bad activist, a bad woman. An especially hazardous quality of social perfectionism is that it's based on what we believe other people believe. It's in that black gap between imagination and reality that the demons come.

Living the neoliberal dream, with its zero-sum, formal games and its galaxy of signals of failure, seems to be making us more perfectionistic. Further powerful evidence that altering the rules of our status games changes who we are can be found in a study of more than forty thousand students across the USA, Britain and Canada. Led by psychologist Dr Thomas Curran, the researchers discovered all the forms of perfectionism they looked at had risen between 1989 and 2016. Social perfectionism had grown the most. The extent to which people felt they had to 'display perfection to secure approval' had soared by 32 per cent. They concluded, 'young people are perceiving that their social context is increasingly demanding, that others judge them more harshly, and that they are increasingly inclined to display perfection as a means of securing approval'. In speculating why, the authors pointed to neoliberalism. They noted the Western nations under study had 'become more individualistic, materialistic, and socially antagonistic over this period, with young people now facing more competitive environments, more unrealistic

expectations, and more anxious and controlling parents than generations before'. Both social perfectionism and materialistic goal-seeking
have been linked to a witchbag of psychological maladies, including
depression, anxiety, eating disorders and self-harm, rates of which
have been climbing in recent years, especially in the young.

There's an injurious mismatch between the design of our brains
and the vast and vastly unequal games that comprise neoliberal life.
Status is relative: the amount we feel we have depends on how much
we perceive others have. Much of our status play involves fighting
over formal, zero-sum prizes in gargantuan corporate reinventions
of tribe. Today, sixty-nine of the hundred largest economies on earth
are not nations but corporations. In the first quarter of 2021 alone,
technology company Apple made more money than the annual GDP
of 135 countries; its market valuation was higher than the GDP of
Italy, Brazil, Canada, South Korea and Russia. It's all too easy, in
these modern-colossal hierarchies, to feel as if we're failing, even as
we provide food, shelter and security for our families that's ample.
To live in the neoliberal dreamworld is to suffer some form of status
anxiety. It's standard. It's who we are and how we play.

And the game is getting harder. The neoliberal age has seen
rewards being distributed with increasing unfairness. Between 1978
and 2014, inflation-adjusted CEO pay in the USA increased by nearly
1,000 per cent; in a similar period, 1975 to 2017, inflation-adjusted
US GDP nearly tripled and worker productivity grew by around 60
per cent. And yet, while a subset of US workers did see some increases
in pay, real hourly wages for most Americans froze or fell. The
picture has been similar in the UK: the richest one per cent took 7
per cent of national income in 1970; by 2005 it was 16 per cent. And
yet the Office of National Statistics reports wages have 'been on a
broadly downwards trend' since the 1970s.

As the game has become dominated by vast corporations, the
quality of the status on offer to many has diminished. This was

brought home to me when I visited the Welsh town of Ammanford, once a proud mining community filled with independent, locally owned businesses. The mines closed in 1976 and then the big super-market came. 'The Tesco's killed off our local trade: the butchers, the greengrocers,' said my young interviewee, who described his generation getting, 'drawn into just going back and forth down between the shelves with no real end. You're not going to work for Tesco's for years and come out going, "I've really achieved something with my life!" You get nothing out of it.'

Over a million Britons are on 'zero hours' contracts that stack rights in the favour of the employer and offer no guarantee of work. Academic Professor Guy Standing argues the UK has seen the emergence of a new social class, the 'precariat': extremely low-paid, often immigrant workers who survive in a series of underpaid, short-term jobs. 'The precariat have lives dominated by insecurity, uncertainty, debt and humiliation,' he writes. 'They are denizens rather than citizens, losing cultural, civil, social, political and economic rights built up over generations.' Much of their existence is characterised by almost total deference and barely any influence, even over their own lives. Because profit-making companies fail to pay them enough to live, their wages are topped up by welfare credits. This arrangement neglects to consider the overwhelming importance of status. When we force hardworking people to accept handouts, we commit on them an injustice: we steal from them something they've earned.

Political battles between the left and right are often concerned with how success games create and share the wealth they produce. Is it better to allow creators maximal freedom to make as much cash as possible, and feed the economy? Or do we tighten control, increasing their virtue element via tax and regulation, forcing more fairness throughout the game? These are essential debates. Whilst it's clear capitalism has an almost magical capacity to raise living standards and life expectancy, it's no less clear that leaders of success games can be relentless and sociopathic in their desire to win.

Following the pressure of 2008's global financial crisis, psychologists surveying college students found evidence of a tightening. As the perception spread that the neoliberal game was broken, and its expected rewards were no longer paying out, markers for individualism and narcissism among the students declined. The same period saw the emergence of what looks like a Social Media Self. Cadres of people who'd been partly socialised online, using the rules and symbols of websites such as Twitter, Tumblr and Reddit, brought these platforms' harsh, virtue-bound and identity-fluid modes of play into the offline world. Rebellious and furious, their games have now become something of a status goldrush for young and privileged players. The coming years might see them undergo a significant expansion. Many of the battles they fight centre on the failures of neoliberalism, and the fact that we still struggle to offer equal opportunities to play across categories of race and gender.

26

Fairness, Unfairness

IN THESE EARLY decades of the twenty-first century, we're still riding the blast of cultural innovations triggered in the sixteenth. For players in the Republic of Letters, what mattered wasn't your country of birth but the quality of your ideas. This is how the success games that underpin modernity want to be played: acclaim is earned by what you do, not who you are. As the Industrial Revolution spread, and these games won increasing influence over culture, the worth and wellbeing of the individual player took on a more central importance. In Britain, 1859 saw the publication of *Self-Help* by Samuel Smiles, the first book of its kind. Filled with inspiring case studies, it argued even players at the bottom of the game could move up with hard work and perseverance. Smiles began with a quote from philosopher John Stuart Mill: 'The worth of a State, in the long run, is the worth of the individuals composing it.' It was an instant bestseller.

Where once we belonged to our tribe, we began to belong to ourselves. Every human was precious; individuals had rights. The rule that grew out of this – that the great game should be played without boundaries of class, race, gender or sexuality – is radical and new. Its struggles still possess the everyday lives of millions, their tales of injustice often dominating the modern gossip networks of traditional and social media. In the anxious fury of all this, it's easy to lose sight of the extent to which our basic ideas of fairness have been revised. The Enlightenment thinker David Hume was a critic of slavery, but nevertheless wrote in 1754 that he was 'apt to suspect the Negroes and in general all other species of men (for there are four or five different kinds) to be naturally inferior to the whites'. In 1879, the pioneering and influential social psychologist Gustave Le Bon wrote, 'there are a large number of women whose brains are closer in size to those of gorillas than to the most developed male brain . . . Without doubt there exist some distinguished women, very superior to the average man, but they are as exceptional as the birth of any monstrosity, as, for example, of a gorilla with two heads.'

Today these views are more than outrageous, they're taboo. Even extremists who cling to them understand that publicly voicing these beliefs in the West is to contravene sacred rules and so to risk prosecution, expulsion from employment, public shaming and perhaps physical attack. But, only recently, deeply prejudicial concepts like these were mainstream and accepted by many of the world's smartest thinkers. When seeking to explain the game of life, the brain tells a simplistic and often self-serving story about why things are the way they are. Intellectuals such as Hume and Le Bon experienced a reality in which there was a reliable ranking of gender and race. They wove a status-making dream around that hierarchy that told of white male superiority. They couldn't know, as we know now, that Western European culture was not a product of innate superiority or even deliberate planning, but luck, accident and unintended consequence; they hadn't yet realised the global oppression of women was not an inevitable pattern of nature but an epic historical injustice.

But the rule tweaks that created Western success game culture were soon to transform our conception of each other and what we considered fair play. Towards the end of the eighteenth century, discussion of 'human rights' became more common in the West, with published use of the word 'rights' quadrupling between the 1780s and 1790s. The same period saw a series of legal reforms that speak to a rising belief in the value of the individual. Torture increasingly fell out of fashion, with European nations including Prussia, Sweden, Bohemia and France abolishing it between 1754 and 1788, the American physician Benjamin Rush arguing in 1787 that even criminals, 'possess souls and bodies composed of the same materials as those of our friends'. Public executions in the UK had once drawn huge and raucous crowds, with contemporary reports at London hangings telling of the 'most amazing scenes of drunkenness and debauchery' and a 'remorseless multitude . . . shouting, laughing, throwing snowballs at each other'. In 1868 Parliament abolished them. It wasn't even eighty years earlier that they'd banned burning women at the stake.

For historian Professor Lynn Hunt, such shifts were inspired by profound changes in how we viewed the individual player: 'Since pain and the body itself now belonged only to the individual, rather than the community, the individual could no longer be sacrificed to the good of the community, or to a higher religious purpose.' Cruel practices such as torture and public execution began to end because 'the traditional framework of pain and personhood fell apart, to be replaced, bit by bit, by a new framework in which individuals owned their bodies, had rights to their separateness and to bodily inviolability, and recognised in other people the same passions, sentiments and sympathies as themselves'.

The principle of equal rights spread to religious and racial minorities and women. Slavery, which has existed across the world since the first civilisations, finally began to end: Denmark banned participation in the slave trade in 1804, Britain voted to end participation in 1807, abolishing it in most colonies in 1834. In the USA, Congress passed the thirteenth amendment, abolishing slavery, on 6 December 1865. In 1918, the UK's Representation of the People Act extended the vote to unpropertied men and some propertied women. It passed by a majority of 385 to 55. Women won equal voting rights ten years later. In the US, full suffrage was won in 1920 (it took the Swiss until 1971). Capital punishment, which is thought to have once been a human universal, was increasingly outlawed. In the seventeenth century, residents of New Haven in America could be put to death for masturbating; until 1834 Britain was still gibbeting the corpses of murderers. By 2020, over half the world's nations had formally abolished it. Most recently, the principle of equality has been extended to sexual minorities. At the time of writing, same-sex marriage has been legalised in twenty-eight nations, almost all of them Western in culture.

But this process is still in play. The focus on competence over caste-identities such as race, gender and sexuality is a recent development. Billions of people still play these games, drawing significant amounts of status from the colour of their skin, their country of birth or whether they have XX or XY chromosomes. This is virtue play. It's inward-looking and concerned with defence of our kin: honour, duty and moral arguments usually take precedence over skill, talent or knowledge. Unfortunately, the human brain isn't literally a computer. We can't program everyone with a wholly new operating system, instructing them to accept players of any gender, race and sexual identity without prejudice. As we've learned, we still operate basic coding that, when seeking others with which to play games, uses 'self-similarity' as a cue. We're drawn to our own.

The research literature on racial injustice groans with shame. One major investigation of more than 200,000 job applications in nine Western nations examined how racial identity influenced the likelihood of any applicant receiving a callback. It found evidence of 'pervasive hiring discrimination against all non-white groups' in every country, with France and Sweden showing the gravest problems: in those nations, members of minority groups would have to send between 70 and 94 per cent more applications than whites to receive the same number of callbacks. Britain was third on the list, at 55 per cent.

But there were some encouraging glimmers. Despite its well-known problems with race, the USA was third from bottom. The researchers thought this was because major US companies have to report the racial make-up of each rank of their business to the Equal Employment Opportunity Commission, a mode of monitoring that doesn't happen in the European nations. Even more encouraging news came from Germany, a nation whose reputation for racism was once pre-eminent. Of the nine nations studied, they were the most equitable. Sociologist Professor Lincoln Quillian argued one reason for its 'low discrimination' is that a variety of supporting documents, such as apprenticeship reports, have to be submitted with job applications. 'Having a lot of information at first application reduces the tendency to view minority applicants as less good or unqualified,' he has said. The more an employer knows about a candidate's competence, the weaker their prejudice seems to become.

Other studies support this. In one, the initial racial biases of group members were overcome by experimenters introducing 'additional legitimate and unambiguous status information that is directly relevant to the group task and that advantages the actor over the others present'. A similar effect was found in a study in which white players who'd been sorted into a team with black players expressed a bias in favour of their team that 'outweighed their initial racial bias'. Such research offers hope. Humans aren't programmed to be racist but to be biased towards their groups. If we plug our desire for status too strongly into our racial identity, we'll end up playing racial games. But we don't have to do this. Humans want to win. They want their games to win. If their need for status is plugged into a success game, they're often more interested in a player's competence than the colour of their skin.

Future generations will also continue the struggle for gender equality. Sexist assumptions remain widespread. One survey across the G7 nations of Canada, France, Germany, Italy, Japan, the UK and the USA found around 80 per cent of respondents believing men and women were equally suited to leadership in media, science, medicine, law, politics and finance. In sports, technology, aerospace and engineering, it was between 65 and 75 per cent. For defence and police, fashion and beauty and childcare, only about half thought there was no gender difference in leadership ability. Presumably, many respondents noted higher male presence in engineering, say, and higher female presence in childcare, and concluded one gender was *better* at these occupations. This is proving a frustratingly stubborn lesson to learn: underestimating a player on the basis of their gender is not only ignorant, it's a terrible strategy for success.

The truth, of course, is that men and women are equally suited to leadership in all these professions. But the reasons some become more populated by one gender or another are in dispute. Many researchers suspect generalised variations between the sexes is part of the answer. Almost nobody believes, these days, that male and female psychology is *categorically* dissimilar: we're not from Mars and Venus; furthermore, it's now understood men and women are far more alike than different. But studies suggest the sexes do, on average, show differences in personality, interest and vocational preference that affect their distribution in the games of life. One study, taking in 200,000 respondents across 53 countries, found women differed significantly in some personality traits and found a 'large and consistent sex difference' in preference for occupation. A commonly noted finding says men tend to be more interested in working with 'things' whilst women tend to be more interested in working with people. An analysis of more than half a million individuals found a 'large effect size' on this dimension that was 'remarkably consistent across age and over time'. According to psychologist Professor Steven Pinker, 'there's an enormous average difference between women and men in this dimension'.

Such variations can't help but reflect in the gender-balance of our games. But there are two crucially important things to note about them. Firstly, these are average statistics across large groups of people. They say nothing about any individual woman or man. Secondly, preference is not ability. As the leadership survey suggests, a common sexist interpretation has it that men are *better* at some things and women are *better* at others. This is not correct. Rather, it is about the weight of numbers. If you were to gather one hundred men and women and ask those who were interested in tractors to step forwards, more men than women might take that step. The real-world ramification would be more men working in a tractor factory and more male leaders in that industry. What it *wouldn't* mean is that women working at the tractor factory would be any better or worse at their jobs than men.

Feminist scholars often deny the validity of these kinds of findings. They sniff in them an all-too-convenient excuse for maintaining the status quo. They also debate their cause. Is it purely cultural coding? That is, are women raised in sexist environments and programmed to believe they're not supposed to be interested in tractors? Or is this coding sufficiently ancient that it's written into the hardware of our DNA? Are women more interested in games relating to people, partly because of division of labour going back millions of years and the biological fact of motherhood? Needless to say, such arguments are controversial. Because they connect directly to matters of status, they're fraught and can be dangerous to have. They incite the cousins by threatening a sacred story, believed by some, that says gender inequity can only ever be caused by male evil. But there are reasonable and well-meaning experts in both camps, each with considered sets of evidence. Neither side doubts gender inequality is real and significant or that sexist assumptions are a problem. If it turns out the causes are partly genetic, the fight will be on to somehow arrange society and economy such that millions of women are no longer unfairly penalised for expressing who they are.

Gender and race aren't the only injustices built into the games we play today. Five hundred generations after the dawn of agriculture, we're still born into a social caste that helps direct our position in the hierarchy and future profession. Class is stubborn because, as Professor Kusserow found in her study of parenting in Manhattan's Upper East Side, children raised in these games have elite rules and symbols written into their brains from birth. Social class isn't simply about wealth and ancestry, it's about taste in the arts, food, sports, holidays and clothing. It's in a person's accent and the words they use. Nancy Mitford, the aristocratic daughter of the 2nd Baron Redesdale, caused a minor sensation in 1955 with her essay exploring the 'Upper Class English Usage' of language. Mitford listed 'U' ('upper class') versus 'non-U' words: 'Sweet: non-U for U pudding'; 'Toilet paper: non-U for U lavatory paper'; 'U-speakers eat luncheon in the middle of the day and dinner in the evening; Non-U-speakers (also U-children and U-dogs) have their dinner in the middle of the day'. Mitford also documented the U use of the scolding, judgy silence: 'silence is the only possible U-response to many embarrassing modern situations: the ejaculation of "cheers" before drinking, for example, or "it was so nice seeing you," after saying goodbye. In silence, too, one must endure the use of the Christian name by comparative strangers and the horror of being introduced by Christian and surname without any prefix.'

Today, the elite school at Eton provides a glossary as part of its 'New Boy Guide', so arriving scholars can learn an esoteric language no less bizarre than that spoken by the members of Heaven's Gate: 'Beak, a master, i.e. teacher'; 'Dry Bobs, cricketers'; 'Oppidan, any boy who is not a Colleger'; 'Porny School, a primary school in Eton High Street'; 'The Wall, the wall against which the wall game is played.' It's not uncommon for elite educational institutions to have their own esoteric language. Players refer to the terms they grew up with as 'an Eton notion' or 'an Oxford notion'. Old Etonians, writes Robert Verkaik, find 'subtle ways of identifying each other beyond the accent and tie. An Etonian greeting between two men who suspect they were educated at the same place is: "Did you go to school?"'

These special languages bestow 'an instant sense of belonging on a select community' that serve, in Verkaik's view, to separate the scholars from the townsfolk with whom they share the streets. This might sound reprehensible, but all status games behave this way. Knowing the meaning of 'oppidan' and 'dry bobs' and to use the 'lavatory' not the 'toilet' is to know that comparing India to Mars is racist and colonialist and that you should never glance at another man's yam pit. These imaginary agreements we make with our co-players are the shared territory in which we play. They allow us to feel comfortable in each other's presence, and valuable too, awarding each other status for knowing our rules and symbols and following them. They're magic words that identify kin.

In an address at King's College Chapel, Cambridge, the writer Alan Bennett said, 'Private education is not fair. Those who provide it know it. Those who pay for it know it. Those who have to sacrifice in order to purchase it know it. And those who receive it know it, or should.' Britain's most prestigious games, in law, government, the media and the arts, are famously over-represented by such players. Around 7 per cent of Britons have been privately educated, yet they make up over 70 per cent of the nation's barristers and 60 per cent of its Oscar winners. Less than one per cent of the population attended Oxford or Cambridge, yet their graduates have produced the majority of the nation's prime ministers. A 2019 study found 71 per cent of senior judges, 57 per cent of cabinet ministers and 44 per cent of newspaper columnists went to Oxford or Cambridge. In the 2010–2015 parliament, the Prime Minister and the Leader of the Opposition had both taken exactly the same degree: Philosophy, Politics and Economics at Oxford (as had the Shadow Chancellor, the Foreign Secretary and the Chief Secretary to the Treasury).

A major cause of this unfairness is the 'old boy network' that allows direct access into elite games. Eton maintains a database of former pupils that can be accessed for contacts, for life. Other forms of injustice are more subtle. When these old boys and girls meet in boardrooms and members clubs, they'll speak the same status game language – and not just in the form of magic words. Their virtual reality machines having been forged in the same factory, they can identify one another near instantly by the detection of numberless cultural clues, many of them subconscious. They feel automatically reassured by their presence, being a source of one another's status, a living affirmation of the truth of their dreams. The powerful connection felt by those educated at Eton and similar elite schools can unjustly prevent ambitious, deserving players from breaking in. Otherwise exceptional people can feel disorientated and excluded, as their own subconscious language of status fails to connect.

This sense of alienation was recorded in a survey led by sociologist Professor Mike Savage. One interviewee, Louise, was raised on a south London council estate and couldn't read or write at age 14. And yet, as an adult, she sat on the boards of several major beauty brands, earning over a quarter of a million pounds a year. Louise played daily with people raised in elite families. She said these people respected her background and journey. And yet she reported a 'strong sense of isolation' that felt rooted in a 'culture of informal chatting in the workplace, where talking about the arts, sharing anecdotes about holidays or discussing children's schooling can be an important way of oiling the wheels of business relationships or building rapport with senior colleagues'. Louise told the researchers, 'I don't really participate, you know, I'm very distant.'

Similar experiences of alienation can be felt by those moving sideways between games at the cultural level: often immigrants raised with one set of rules and symbols only to live an adult life immersed in others. Savage's team interviewed Gita, whose parents had come from Uganda to London's East End where they ran a newsagent. Gita went to university then became a successful graphic designer. The researchers describe her negotiating 'an exhausting balancing act between the cultural values of her working-class, ethnic and middle-class occupational identities'. Gita told them, 'I've always thought I've never really belonged, but then I always thought it was just me, y'know? Because I felt I didn't believe totally in the Indian culture, but I didn't belong in my English friends' lives because they were a lot more free. So I've always drifted, dipped in and out of different cultures, always been quite a detached person wherever I go.'

That distance, that detachment, that alienation: Louise and Gita might well suspect it could hold them back in their status play. Success can just be easier for those raised in an elite class or even a nation's most populous culture. This doesn't mean those they encountered were operating with malice. They were simply playing by the rules and symbols that had been built into their brains, being human in the only way they knew. But it's equally true these players entered the games of life with a head-start – with privilege.

Privilege is an explosive notion. As we've learned, humans are designed to be maddened by others they experience as prancing about above them, their status unfair and on display. Resentment pricks us into desiring to pull them down, whether by social distancing, mockery, humiliation, ostracization or execution. Such resentments have helped power some of the most lethal events in human history. The Nazis and the Communists aimed their hatred at groups they perceived as having status that was unearned. They told a story in which groups had grabbed wealth, influence and power that wasn't their due, and that wrenching them from their privileged heights by hunting and murdering them was fair play.

The danger is in the dream. Those above us might've climbed up there through sweat and ability; they might've schemed and dominated. Most likely, they'll have used all available strategies. Whatever the truth, we're vulnerable to believing simplistic brain-spun tales that say they've simply cheated and their visible thriving is cheating us. How their thriving happens to manifest depends on the game we're playing: they might enjoy greater wealth than us; their games might be more venerated by society; their sacred beliefs might be more influential and win frequently over ours. But however we're measuring status, the feeling that our own stores of the great prize are being nibbled away by these swaggering rats can easily come to obsess us. The warriors who stand up and tell such stories can earn significant rank themselves, helping foment status goldrush movements by blaming: *bloody immigrants, bloody whites, bloody men, bloody women, bloody millennials, bloody boomers . . .*

Wherever you hear such sentiments, you're being sold a simplistic story about a Gordian reality. Consider race. It's true that there's white privilege. But it's also true the most successful UK ethnic groups by income aren't white, but Chinese and Indian. The Chinese earn fully 30 per cent more than their Caucasian counterparts. 69 per cent of Chinese-background state school pupils in the UK win passage to university, as do 50 per cent of Asian and 44 per cent of black students. At the bottom? White kids, at 30 per cent. Similarly, in the USA, the most successful demographic by income aren't whites, but Asian Americans. None of which is to argue racism isn't real, serious and deserving of urgent attention. It's simply to observe the world is often more confusing than the warriors allow.

There are any number of ways to have privilege in the game of life. You can be: smart; attractive; mentally healthy; talented; able-bodied; male in a male-dominated game; female in a female-dominated game; under the age of 30; privately schooled; university educated; not born into poverty; professionally connected; have the right kind of accent; live in the right part of the country; have successful, kind or connected parents; live in a Westernised culture with its freedoms, opportunities and concern with equality and human rights, and so on. The truth about privilege is that it's a combination of all these factors and more: it's complex, dynamic and unique to who we are and what games we're trying to play.

A major form of privilege is genetic. It takes a certain kind of personality to thrive and much of our temperament, grit, intelligence, sociability and relative desire for status is hereditary, born into us – and then bred into us further, if we're lucky enough to have that kind of parenting. Many of the elite are simply gifted, the gift they receive from the gods that of sliding from the right womb.

If the promised land comes and the old barriers of class, gender and race are removed, we'd find ourselves ruled principally by a genetic elite, privileged winners of the lottery of birth. These enviable few would live and work and play together, becoming a source of one another's status. They'd come to speak in a certain manner, dress in a certain manner, enjoy certain pastimes, adopting their own distinctive rules and symbols. They'd fix their games in conscious and unconscious ways, creating even more privilege for themselves and their children. And we'd admire them and mimic them and resent them, just as we do today. The problem with elites is they're an unsolvable problem; an inevitability of the game we're programmed to play. They'll always be there and they'll never not make us feel small.

27

When Dreams Collide

THERE'S A WAR raging across the neoliberal territories. It's being fought by rival coalitions who each inhabit a different dream of reality. Both believe the game of life to be fixed. One side perceives it to be unfairly dominated by white people, especially white men, especially straight white men. The other side thinks it's unfairly dominated by highly educated elites. In recent years, they've been making major incursions into the hierarchies of society. One side has won a series of impressive victories, colonising the games of culture, education and commerce. The other has won major victories in the political game, most notably in 2016, in the election of Donald Trump to the US Presidency and the vote for the UK to leave the European Union. Their battle marks what could be the beginning of the end of the neoliberal era as we know it.

These armies are known by a variety of insulting, unwieldy or inaccurate names: the wokes, SJWs or Progressive Activists on one side; on the other, the alt-right, white supremacists or National Populists. For the sake of brevity and fairness, we'll call them the New Left and the New Right. Both play virtue games. They seek moral status from their co-players by battling for their sacred symbols, including beliefs. They play tight and use dominance strategies, attacking online and in the streets, in violent protests, in the vandalization of the sacred symbols of their opponents and in shows of intimidation and force by groups such as Antifa on the left and The Proud Boys on the right. Each group is swept up by their own simplistic, self-serving story: they're moral heroes, punching upwards at the evil forces of injustice. This is a war of the fringes. Most of the population don't precisely share their perception of the game and how it operates. The trouble is, the New Left and New Right tend to see everyone who's not for them as the enemy. And so the political centre, where the majority live, finds itself under attack from both sides, leaving many feeling alienated, baffled, angry and afraid as the world churns around them.

The argument that follows is admittedly more speculative than any I've presented so far. But viewed from the perspective of the status game, the hidden forces that power the culture war at least begin to suggest themselves. We've already learned that, throughout history, societies have come under stress when the expected rewards of their games have failed to pay out. This has been the case for many on the New Left. Analysis from the UK reveals them to be the youngest of seven national demographic groups and over-represented by millennials and Gen Zs. This is a cohort who've felt their relative status pitch into a decline: they're more qualified than the baby boomers and yet 20 per cent less wealthy than they were at the same age; the average millennial's worth in 2016 was 41 per cent less than those of a similar age in 1989. They're also finding it harder to buy property and are heavily burdened with student debt, graduating with an average personal deficit of $32,700 in the USA and £40,000 in England.

A further historical precursor to societal collapse is thought to be 'elite-overproduction' – which, as we've learned, is when too many elite players are produced and have to fight over too few high-status positions. Something like this appears to be happening to many in the New Left. They're the elite caste of the seven national groups, coming from the wealthiest households and being the most highly educated. More on the New Left possess graduate degrees and higher degrees, such as PhDs or MScs, than any other. In 2019, 31 per cent of UK graduates were working in positions for which they were overqualified. In 1992 that figure was 22 per cent. A 2020 survey of 215,000 recent graduates found they were more anxious than the general population. In the USA, where an extraordinary 13 per cent of adults have a PhD, MSc or professional degree (a number that's doubled since 2000), 34 per cent of college graduates are underemployed, and 41 per cent of recent graduates. Whilst new roles are being created in expanding industries such as IT, other games are being disproportionately hit. In both nations, graduates in the arts, humanities and media are among the most underemployed of all.

This decline in relative status for young, internet socialised, highly educated players is turning into a growing rejection of the game. In just three years, between 2015 and 2018, support for capitalism among young Americans fell from 39 per cent to 30 per cent; a 2019 poll found 36 per cent of millennials saying they approve of Communism. Sociologist Professor Thomas Cushman writes, 'anti-capitalism has become, in some ways, a central pillar of the secular religion of the intellectuals, the habitus of modern critical intellectuals as a status group'. In 2020, satisfaction with democracy among millennials fell below 50 per cent for the first time. That study's first author, Dr Roberto Foa, said 'higher debt burdens, lower odds of owning a home, greater challenges in starting a family, and reliance upon inherited wealth rather than hard work and talent to succeed are all contributors to youth discontent'.

In the other corner, the New Right. This category doesn't include *all* Trump and Brexit voters, who number in the tens of millions and include ethnic minorities. Our focus is on the white base, the working and lower-middle classes without college degrees, whose relative status has been in decline in the neoliberal era. Between 1979 and 2005, the average real hourly wage for white working-class Americans without a high-school diploma declined by 18 per cent. Political scientist Professor Katherine Cramer describes the perception they're working as hard as their parents, yet are being rewarded with a poorer quality of life. 'They feel like they're doing what they were told they needed to do to get ahead. And somehow it's not enough.' Similar attitudes have been found amongst white working-class Tea Party supporters in Louisiana. Sociologist Professor Cecilia Ridgeway writes of research suggesting they 'grew up seeing themselves at the respected centre of America with the status of hardworking, traditional, middle Americans' but now feel undermined socially and economically and 'treated with contempt by coastal Americans and urban elites who looked down on them as ignorant, prejudiced hicks and who gave special privileges to other social groups who, they felt, hadn't worked as hard as they had'. These resentments easily curdle into racism: these 'other social groups' who they see as benefitting from 'special privileges' include African Americans.

The story told by this cohort of whites says that highly educated elites hold all the power and insult and de-grade them as 'trailer-trash' and 'deplorables', whilst unfairly boosting the rank of minorities. Their equivalents in the UK tell the same tale. There, these minorities are more likely to be immigrants. In both nations, educated elites have spent decades promoting the neoliberal project of globalisation, which seeks to turn as much of the world as possible into an open market around which goods, services and labour can freely flow. The white working-class communities of Britain have been significantly impacted by incoming populations of black, eastern European and Muslim workers. The economic transformation wrought by this neoliberalist plan has 'fuelled a strong sense of relative deprivation – a belief among certain groups that they are losing out relative to others', write Professors of Politics Roger Eatwell and Matthew Goodwin, authors of an extensive analysis of the rise of National Populism. 'This means they are very fearful about the future and what lies ahead for themselves and their children. This profound sense of loss is intimately entwined with the way in which people think through issues like immigration and identity. Today there are millions of voters who are convinced that the past was better than the present and that the present, however bleak, is still better than the future.'

The political positions of the New Right are held in abhorrence by many across the left, and some on the centre-right. They're pro-nation state, anti-globalisation, anti-immigration, anti-'hyper ethnic change'. They back politicians who 'prioritize the culture and interests of the nation, and promise to give voice to a people who feel that they have been neglected, even held in contempt, by distant and often corrupt elites', write Eatwell and Goodwin. This perception of relative deprivation – of the game failing for their group – is 'absolutely central' to the movement. Neoliberalism and globalisation have 'impacted strongly on people's perceived levels of respect, recognition and status relative to others in society'. In recent years white male workers with few qualifications who have found themselves 'ill equipped to navigate the economic storms have become especially likely to feel as though their status in society has declined relative to others and they are no longer fully recognised and valued members of wider society. These are people who have borne the full force of the economic winds – the decline of secure, permanent and well-paid jobs, and a knowledge economy that puts a premium on the college degrees they do not have.' These were the concerns that 2016's Brexit and Trump campaigns so successfully connected with. They're on the rise, too, across Europe, embodied in figures such as Marine Le Pen in France, Matteo Salvini in Italy and Viktor Orbán in Hungary.

The clashing dreams of the New Right and New Left are neatly illustrated in a sequence of tweets by a US journalist, Rani Molla. Linking to a report on the plight of poor white workers in a rural chicken processing plant earning as little as thirteen dollars an hour, she commented: 'oh shut the fuck up . . . alt title: "How does it feel to have every advantage and still be a whiny asshole?"' Molla has written for the *Wall Street Journal*, Bloomberg and Vox and has degrees from Oberlin College and the Columbia Journalism School, both elite institutions. Molla and the New Left see the game as fixed one way: biological categories such as whiteness supply players with 'every advantage'. But their opposites see the game as fixed in another way: Molla's elite education has given her and those like her 'every advantage'. When the New Right look upwards, 'they often see people who have had a completely different upbringing, lead fundamentally different lives and hold very different values', write Eatwell and Goodwin. 'Education lies at the heart of this divide.' Most of the 41 per cent of white millennials who voted for Trump in 2016 didn't have college degrees. In all, white non-college voters comprised around three-fifths of Trump's support in 2016; 74 per cent of people with no qualifications supported Brexit, the educational divide being greater than that of social class, income or age.

College attendees are more likely to have a 'culturally liberal mindset' than those who don't. This mindset includes a set of beliefs around nation and immigration which are core issues for both New Left and Right. In the UK, the highly educated New Left have been found to be less proud of being British than any other demographic and strongly believe immigration has a positive impact on the UK, with 85 per cent agreeing compared to 43 per cent nationally. Their rivals play nationalist games. Languages, shops, foods and religions that aren't white and Christian that replace their own are experienced as symbols of defeat. The New Right feel alienated from the game that's being played around them and can only see the likelihood of new humiliating de-gradings in the future.

They're maddened, too, by symbols in the wider culture that their enemies are winning. Their victories are conspicuous in many elite games that make up society. They're in our corporations: in Starbucks, who sold iced shortbread cookies promoting controversial trans rights charity Mermaids; in the razor company Gillette who ran an ad depicting men (almost all white) as bullies, sexists and sexual harassers, announcing, 'it's been going on far too long'; in the US streaming company Hulu, who tweeted: 'If you're dressing up for #Huluween this year, this is your reminder to wear a costume that is culturally appropriate and respectful to others.' Their rise can also be seen in the leading positions New Left players hold inside an array of elite games: the Chief Librarian of the British Library Liz Jolly, who said 'racism is the creation of white people'; Edinburgh Comedy Awards director Nica Burns, who said she was 'looking forward to comedy's future in the woke world'; the American Psychological Association, who approvingly press-released member Dr Theopia Jackson saying: 'every institution in America is born from the blood of white supremacist ideology and capitalism – and that's the disease'; in the *New York Times* electing to its editorial board Sarah Jeong, a journalist with a history of racist tweets, including: 'oh man it's kind of sick how much joy I get out of being cruel to old white men'; 'White people have stopped breeding. you'll all go extinct soon. that was my plan all along'; 'White men are bullshit'; 'Dumbass fucking white people marking up the internet with their opinions like dogs pissing on fire hydrants'; '#cancelwhite-people'.

The New Left have also been brilliantly successful in institution-alising their game and its dream of reality through the rapidly expanding Diversity, Equity and Inclusion industry. Many universi-ties contain large DEI bureaucracies, often with extensive teams of evangelising staff who oversee multimillion-dollar budgets. The University of Michigan's DEI mission has an annual employee bill of over $11 million, and has nearly one hundred full-time staffers, twenty-five of whom earn over $100,000 a year. Yale has more than one hundred and fifty staff and student representatives serving DEI aims. One study of 669 US universities found nearly a third put its faculty through mandated DEI training.

And it's not just the universities. In 2019, the *New York Times* reported the DEI industry to be 'booming, creating new career paths and roles'. One US job agency reported ads for such postings had risen 18 per cent between 2017 and 2018; between 2018 and 2019 it jumped a further 25 per cent. A survey of 234 companies in the S&P 500 found 63 per cent had appointed or promoted DEI professionals in the past three years. Universities, including Yale, Cornell and Georgetown, have begun offering relevant certificate programmes. DEI conferences are charging up to $2,400 just for registration; Google spent $114 million on DEI programmes in 2014 and a further $150 million in 2015. It's estimated that US companies spend eight billion dollars every year on DEI training. Where does all that money go? According to leaked documents, between 2006 and 2020, one consultant alone billed US federal agencies, including the Justice Department and the Office of the Attorney General, over five million dollars for diversity trainings; in 2011 he charged NASA half a million dollars for his 'power and privilege sexual-orientation workshops'.

Elsewhere, it's reported the charity Time's Up, created in the aftermath of the #MeToo movement, raised $3.6m in its first year, spent $1.4m on salaries – including $342,000 for the CEO, $295,000 for the Chief Marketing Officer and $255,000 for the treasurer – yet contributed just $312,000 to the fund set up to help victims of sexual abuse. All this suggests the New Left has become a powerful goldrush movement, awarding prizes of major status and its symbols, including wealth, to those who play sufficiently well. Untold thousands of livelihoods now depend on active belief in its tenets and countless individuals make major status for themselves in the games of journalism, publishing, politics and social media by warring for them. Its success has been boosted by its appropriation of a trick pioneered by the monotheists. The Christians conjured hell, which generated salvation anxiety, then presented their game as the only way to escape it. Similarly, New Left activists threaten hell by radically rewriting the terms by which accusations of bigotry can be made, lowering the bar such that mere whiteness or masculinity are signs of guilt. Having generated salvation anxiety, they present their movement as the sole available remedy. Hell's threat can only be escaped with conspicuous, zealous and highly correct play.

Tight virtue games weave hostile dreams. They live inside imagined territories that are blasted by the winds of toxic morality. Their players believe themselves to be heroes battling grotesque forces of injustice. These cartoons of reality become dangerous by casting their enemies into the role of one-dimensional baddie. Whilst the civilising mission of the New Left demonises white people (especially white men etc.), the New Right demonise ethnic minorities they see as being gifted unfair rank by the educated elites. Justin Gest, Associate Professor of Policy and Government, found this in two white working-class neighbourhoods, Youngstown in Ohio and Dagenham in east London. In both places, the white working class felt outnumbered by minority groups, excluded from the political process and subject to racial prejudice. 'Many white working-class individuals view the struggle for equal treatment as a personal loss of status – a campaign to demote white people, rather than to promote others.'

Over the last century, Youngstown has declined from its self-proclaimed position of 'steel capital of the world' to producing an average income of just $14,996. 'It's the American Nightmare,' one man told Gest. 'The way I see it, you don't have a fucking shot.' When Gest asked members of the white working class who looked out for their interests, typical answers included, 'nobody', 'you and me' and most commonly 'I look out for myself.' Racial resentments were common, often resolving around the story that African Americans were both looked after and worried over in ways that they weren't. A mother of two told Gest, 'Everyone acts like the white people are well off. You're white, so you must be rich. We work two jobs and struggle to get our kids through school. But you're white, you can afford it. You don't need help, no minority loan, no government discount.' She pointed to a house next door. 'There are gang members in that home . . . they are running down our neighbourhoods. That's why we are getting the hell out . . . You do not touch, talk to, or threaten a black child. They can say or do whatever they want to a white child though.' Another complained, in apparently coded language, about people 'driving around in new cars and I can't even afford a vehicle. The government pays their rent and utilities, and so they spend the cash on gold chains and a Cadillac, when I can barely afford a Cavalier.'

Such codes weren't in evidence in Dagenham. Once a mostly white British community, today nearly half its population are of African, Afro-Caribbean, South Asian and Eastern European origin. Work used to centre around a Ford car production plant that ceased operations in 2002. Gest visited the home of 59-year-old Nancy Pemberton who flew five Union Jacks in her garden, including one from a twelve-foot pole, and had flowers planted so they bloomed into the flag. 'It was a community back then,' she told Gest. 'It was predominantly English. There was an Asian girl. And there was one black boy whose mother was a big, fat lesbian who didn't live the quietest of lives. But we always got on and the English were the majority.' Pemberton believed the EU had been 'promoting' migration to England. 'It's the best place for benefits. And we've already got enough of our own who are too lazy to get off their arses. I got off the train in Barking one night and there were dozens of Romanian women with children, and it's clear they had been on the nick. Vile people,

Romanians. Then you walk outside, and it's so loud with all the halal shops and rubbish in the streets. We look like a suburb of Nairobi.'

Racist views weren't limited to the elderly. A 22-year-old woman told Gest, 'If there's a job interview and an immigrant doesn't get it, they'll say the employer is racist. I feel like they're taking our jobs, homes, and everything that the government is trying to do for English people, they're getting it first.' An 18-year-old man said that Asians 'walk around like they're higher than us, when we were the ones who welcomed them into our country. Everyone is really annoyed with it. I feel like I'm on the outside looking inside to the immigrants.'

Also common was the 'I'm not racist, but . . .' conversational tic. For Gest, this wasn't a sincere request to be considered not bigoted, but an appeal to be heard: the word racist is 'a mute button pressed on someone while they are still crying out about a sense of loss'. Across forty interviews, Gest heard the 'I'm not racist, but . . .' appeal an extraordinary thirty-two times. Here's a small selection: 'I'm not racist, but this used to be a nice community of English people, before all the Albanians and Africans came over'; 'I'm not a racist. I fucking love goat's curry, pardon my language. But the principle of English families not coming first is just not right'; 'I'm not racist at all . . . but the Polish have been taking all of the work and running prostitution and drug rings'; 'I'm not racist but this country's covered by blacks and Bosnians.'

The white working-class residents of Dagenham live inside this toxic dream because they play games with the symbols of race and nationhood. The projects of neoliberalism and globalisation have de-ranked their games and covered their physical and neural territories with symbols of defeat. It doesn't matter to them that immigration is a win for the British economy; neither do they have a visceral experience of the automation and outsourcing that's also been responsible for their decline. All they see is their decline. 'I am proud to be English and I love England but I hate seeing it disappear and our language being lost among all these other tongues,' Nancy Pemberton wrote in a letter to a politician. 'I hate seeing our way of life eroding and all our values being ignored. I hate all our little bits of green being built on to house even more immigrants, who are a drain on our society, certainly of no benefit to us.' In 2007, a survey asked residents of Dagenham and Barking what could be done to improve their communities. The most common answer: 'make it like it used to be fifty years ago'.

The dreams we weave in our sleep are a combination of truth and madness. Our night-time visions are not completely fantastic: we are who we are and meet people we know in places we recognise, but these simulations of reality are intercut with delusion. The dreams we weave around life and its hierarchies are often little different. The New Left says the game is wholly sexist and white supremacist. It sees the bigotry of its foes. The New Right says the educated elites have stopped caring about them entirely. It sees their contempt for the white and in pain and their veneration of minorities. These are errors of exaggeration: not all white people are bigots just as not all the educated elites are prejudiced against the white working class. But they also mislead by omission. They fail to see that, in each clashing dream, there's both hatred and truth.

28

The Parable of the Communists

WHAT IF IT was possible to live without status? To create a society in which the requirement for getting ahead was eradicated, and getting along was all that mattered? The misery and injustice the status game creates, the envy and the fury and the sheer bloody exhaustion of it – all gone. Imagine! It would be a utopia, the coming of a true paradise on earth, the final, beautiful chapter in the story of human progress. But how would you go about it? Where would you start? Well, what creates these divisions between us in the first place? What makes inequality? Wealth. Private ownership – of property, of goods, of land, of businesses and industries, *of everything*. So that's where we'll start. No more private ownership. Everything must be shared. We'll live and work communally. If we all strive on behalf of one another, instead of ourselves, we'll create an incredible bounty that can be given out according to need rather than greed. We'll call it 'Communism'.

This notion is thought to have its roots in Ancient Greece: as the first place in which private land was commodified, it was also the first to see the inequalities such a system could bring. Plato argued for an ideal state in which everything, including wives and children, were shared, and 'the private and individual is altogether banished from life, and things which are by nature private, such as eyes and ears and hands, have become common'. The word itself was invented in 1840s Paris and spoke to an ideal of perfect Platonic equality, in which the individual effectively vanished from social reality and private property was outlawed. It also referred to a proposed programme and a hoped-for regime that would make this dream-world of pure connection come true.

It was in this period, following the eruption of the Industrial Revolution, that harsh inequalities between the classes were becoming increasingly apparent. Previously, 80 to 90 per cent of the world's economy had been based on agriculture. But now a new class – industrialists, capitalists, the 'bourgeoisie' – were becoming conspicuously wealthy, often on the back of herds of mistreated and humiliated workers. Anger began to swell, not only in pockets of the working class, but among intellectuals who resented the rise in status of these nouveaux riches. Among these thinkers were Karl Marx and Friedrich Engels who wrote, in 1848's Communist Manifesto: 'the theory of the Communists may be summed up in a single sentence: Abolition of private property.'

Under Communism, they believed, the division of labour that marked the birth of tens of thousands of years of inequality, would end. Humans wouldn't be devoted to a single game of competence at which they'd specialise: instead they'd dance about from one task to another. In a Communist world, wrote Marx, 'society regulates the general production and thus makes it possible for me to do one thing today and another tomorrow, to hunt in the morning, fish in the afternoon, rear cattle in the evening, criticise after dinner . . . without ever becoming hunter, fisherman, herdsman or critic'.

The dream woven by the Communists told of a rebirth of the human animal. Capitalist systems had forced people away from their natural state of cooperation and into one of competition, a harsh world where love and sharing had been monsterised into one of cost, benefit and trade in which a human being was of value only to the extent they could help another get ahead. This pursuit of status, that had been conjured by the greedy, capitalist 'bourgeoisie', had poisoned our very perceptions. 'A house may be large or small; as long as the surrounding houses are equally small it satisfies all social demands for a dwelling,' wrote Marx. 'But let a palace arise beside the little house, and it shrinks from a little house to a hut.' Even if that little house grows and grows, 'if the neighbouring palace grows to an equal or even greater extent, the occupant of the relatively small house will feel more and more uncomfortable, dissatisfied and cramped within its four walls'.

This bourgeois elite, the story said, were only able to fund their palaces and maintain their place at the top by private ownership of industry. They abused the power it gave them in order to exploit everyone else. It was ownership that created social classes, ownership that led to the 'pauperization' of the poor and ownership that 'grows the mass of misery, oppression, slavery, degradation, exploitation'. If a paradise of equality was to be achieved, their ownership of the means of production would have to end. And this would happen. Of that there was no doubt. Because the system was untenable: the capitalist bourgeoisie would eat each other, diminishing in number as a result of sheer competition, whilst the angry and exploited propertyless workers, or 'proletarians', would keep increasing. Revolution, all across the industrial world, was inevitable. 'Let the ruling classes tremble at a Communist revolution,' they wrote. 'The proletarians have nothing to lose but their chains. They have a world to win.'

And, when they did, our species would arrive at a promised land, reborn into a level of transcendental status akin to that imagined by the Nazis and the Heaven's Gate cultists. 'The human species, the sluggish Homo sapiens, will once again enter the state of radical reconstruction,' wrote revolutionary and theorist Leon Trotsky. Man will become 'a higher sociobiological type, a superman, if you will . . . incomparably stronger, wiser, more subtle. His body will become more harmonious, his movements more rhythmic, his voice more melodious . . . The average human type will rise to the heights of an Aristotle, Goethe, Marx. And beyond this ridge, other peaks will emerge.'

The person most credited with attempting to realize this dream is Vladimir Ilyich Ulyanov, better known as Lenin. His hatred for the bourgeoisie was blinding, violent and total; many contemporary historians see its genesis in the humiliation his own upper-middle class family suffered after his brother, Sasha, was executed for a 'laughably amateur' but nearly successful assassination plot. Lenin's parents had been socially ambitious and remarkably successful in gaining status. Born to a tailor in 1870, his father had risen to the rank of a member of the nobility and won the prestigious award of the Order of Saint Vladimir, 3rd Class. But the family's arrival in these rarefied planes wasn't as sure as it should've been. Writes historian Professor Robert Service, 'the mass of Simbirsk province's noblemen had enjoyed this status for several generations'. As a newcomer, Lenin's father was often treated by the city's elites with snobbish disdain.

Following Sasha's arrest and execution, the proud family were tossed back to the 'margins of society'. Dignitaries who'd once been guests stopped visiting; old friends never called; strangers stared at them in the streets. 'Respectable Simbirsk – its doctors, teachers, administrators and army officers – indicated its abhorrence' for them. Every member of the family was held responsible for the crime, including the children, and faced 'unending social ostracism'. Their shunning was so intense they had to move away. Writes historian Professor Victor Sebestyen, 'This triggered the vitriolic, sometimes uncontrollable, loathing for liberals and "middle-class do-gooders" that [Lenin] would henceforth show until his dying day. "The bourgeois . . . they will always be traitors and cowards," he declared with monotonous frequency from now onwards. Politics is personal – and this was personal.' He became 'radicalised almost overnight'. One of Lenin's collaborators would later write his principal characteristic was not concern for the poor, but hatred.

His was a hatred that would change the world. Lenin's October Revolution of 1917 saw the dawn of over seven decades of Communist rule in Russia; by the 1970s the dream would reign over more than a third of the global population. But, at least at first, his 'Bolshevik' party wasn't popular: even at their most successful, they won under a quarter of the vote. After seizing power violently in a coup d'état, the Bolsheviks found themselves not only lacking majority support in the nation, but were surrounded by rival factions of socialists and anarchists. Here was a grandiose man driven by the wounds of humiliation; he was leading a high-status group conspicuous for its use of intense dominance-virtue play that was paranoiacally insecure about its position, and surrounded by high-status foes both real and imagined. By the logic of the status game, this was a situation immaculately designed to generate hell.

Before the new classless utopia could emerge, Marx argued there would be a necessary but temporary transitional state in which dominance would be used to rearrange society and wrest ownership from the claws of the capitalists. This would be the 'dictatorship of the proletariat'. And so Lenin authorised his leaders to begin 'the looting of the looters': the taking of cash, goods and property from the bourgeoisie, who were humiliated by being forced to carry out menial public works such as snow clearing and street cleaning. As one leading revolutionary put it: 'for centuries our fathers and grandfathers have been cleaning up the dirt and filth of the ruling classes, but now we will make them clean up our dirt'. They were classed as 'former people' and 'struggled to survive', writes historian Professor

Orlando Figes. 'They were forced to sell their last possessions just to feed themselves. Baroness Meyendorff sold a diamond brooch for 5000 roubles – enough to buy a bag of flour.'

Communist domination of the nation's neural territory had to be total, its criteria for claiming status the only ones available. Lenin banned other political parties and the formation of subgroups within his own. All possible threats were deemed 'class enemies' and terror-ised. These included the Christians, a formidably high-status group in Russia: thousands of priests and nuns were 'killed, some crucified, castrated, buried alive or thrown into cauldrons of boiling tar'. In 1918, after an attempt on Lenin's life, his game tightened yet further. The press demanded revenge on the bourgeoisie; thousands were arrested, many were tortured, some by having their hands boiled until a glove of skin could be peeled off.

After announcing state ownership of all the nation's grain, armed forces stormed the countryside to claim it. When not enough was found, Lenin dreamed into being a flock of scheming witches: rela-tively wealthy and successful peasants – *kulaks* – who he accused of being capitalists and hoarding their grain. 'The *kulaks* are the rabid foes of the Soviet government,' he wrote. 'These bloodsuckers have grown rich on the hunger of the people. These spiders have grown fat out of the workers. These leeches have sucked the blood of the working people and grown richer as the workers in the cities have starved. Ruthless war on the *kulaks*! Death to all of them.' His psychopathic ruthlessness is apparent in this 1918 telegram:

Comrades!

The *kulak* uprising in your five districts must be crushed without pity. The interests of the entire revolution demands this, for we are now facing everywhere the final decisive battle with the *kulaks*. We need to set an example.

1. You need to hang (hang without fail, so that the people see) no fewer than 100 of the notorious *kulaks*, the rich and the bloodsuckers.
2. Publish their names.
3. Take all their grain from them.
4. Identify hostages . . .

Do this so that for hundreds of miles around the people can see, tremble, know and cry: they are killing and will go on killing the bloodsucking *kulaks*.

Telegraph us concerning receipt and implementation.

Yours, Lenin.

P.S. Find tougher people.

As for the new classless utopia, that was still on the way. The Communists 'favored policies that strongly discriminated against "former people," members of the old privileged classes, and in favor of workers, the new "dictator class",' writes historian Professor Sheila Fitzpatrick. One way this new status hierarchy began to emerge manifested in food rations. Red Army soldiers and bureaucrats were at the top and ate the most; then came workers and then, finally, the hated bourgeoisie who were given, in the words of one senior revolutionary, 'just enough bread so as not to forget the smell of it'. The surest way of rising in this new Communist game, the people realised, was to join the party or work for it. By 1920, 5.4 million were directly employed by the government. 'There were twice as many officials as there were workers in Soviet Russia and these officials were the main social base of the new regime,' writes Figes. 'This was not a Dictatorship of the Proletariat but a Dictatorship of the Bureaucracy.'

As players play, they come to believe. Millions plugged their own personal status into the game of the Communists, absorbed the dream and became loyal and true. Their leaders told an irresistible story in which the USSR would rise from being considered a backward society, far behind the West, to being the most advanced in the world. Writes Professor of Political Science, Leslie Holmes, 'There can be little doubt that, as of the mid-1920s, many Soviet citizens were enthusiastic about the future of their country.'

The game was spreading outside the USSR too. A fascinating insight into the mindset of the convert can be found in an essay by author Arthur Koestler, who joined the Communist Party in Germany in 1931. After the economic crash decimated the middle classes, Koestler witnessed them fleeing to the far left and far right. In the Communist Manifesto he read Marx's prediction that 'entire sections of the ruling classes' would supply the movement with 'fresh elements of enlightenment and progress'. He liked the sound of that: 'That "fresh element of enlightenment," I discovered to my delight, was I.'

Once he'd joined, the rules and symbols began being written into Koestler's game-playing equipment. Just as we've encountered in the worlds of the Eton schoolboys and Heaven's Gate, membership was symbolised in esoteric language. After being handed his party card, he was told he should, from then on, say 'thou' instead of 'you'. He discovered that 'spontaneous' wasn't used, due to its association with Leon Trotsky, who'd by then become a class enemy. Likewise, there was no such thing as a 'lesser evil', which was a 'philosophical, strategical and tactical fallacy; a Trotskyite, diversionist, liquidatorial and counter-revolutionary conception'. Words and phrases in favour included 'the toiling masses', 'sectarian', 'herostratic' and 'concrete' (as in, 'You must put your question into a more concrete form, Comrade'). During the Nazi clampdown, one woman known to Koestler betrayed her membership of the party by her use of the word 'concrete'. 'The Gestapo Commissar had listened to her with boredom, half-convinced that his underlings had blundered in arresting her – until she used the fatal word for the second time.'

As the game increasingly colonised Koestler's neural territory, and his *copy, flatter, conform* circuitry switched on, he found his artistic and musical tastes became that of his elites: Lenin had read Balzac, so now Balzac was 'the greatest of all times'; any painting without a smoking factory chimney or a tractor in it was dismissed as 'escapist'. Truth itself became swallowed by the dream. Any questioning of the party line was seen as sabotage; during meetings they'd acclaim one another for taking turns to repeat correct beliefs. The value of free speech was seen as deviant. 'One of the slogans of the German Party said: "The front-line is no place for discussions." Another said: "Wherever a Communist happens to be, he is always in the front-line."'

Just as in the Heaven's Gate cult, where people were instructed to hold a 'blank card' up to incorrect thoughts, Koestler learned to think correctly. In his early days, when he questioned the party's analysis as being contrary to the obvious truth, it was explained that he was still suffering from a 'mechanistic outlook'. Instead, he had to think 'dialectically' and interpret the world through the eyes of the party. 'Gradually I learned to distrust my mechanistic preoccupation with facts and to regard the world around me in the light of dialectic interpretation. It was a satisfactory and indeed blissful state; once you had assimilated the technique you were no longer disturbed by facts; they automatically took on the proper colour and fell into their proper place.' Like the cult members, Koestler found himself willingly lost in the dream of his game. 'We craved to become single and simple-minded.' As the game gripped in, and he strove for status within it, this highly intelligent man's grip on reality loosened more and more: 'Faith is a wondrous thing; it is not only capable of moving mountains, but also of making you believe that a herring is a race horse.'

Back in the USSR, the perfect classless utopia was still taking its time. In 1921, to give the economy a shove, Lenin introduced a 'New Economic Policy' (NEP) that would take cues from capitalism: for example, some small businesses would be permitted; the taking of grain from peasants would be replaced with taxation. The economy grew rapidly. But the NEP was never popular amongst the righteous, who called it a 'new exploitation of the proletariat'.

Lenin's health began to fail; he died in 1924. His successor Stalin replaced the NEP with a programme of rapid industrialisation and the forced collectivisation of farms. Armed squads were sent into the countryside to reorganise the practice of agriculture. They were also to fetch grain to feed the nation and fund the building of the glorious future in which they'd surpass their rivals in the West. 'We are advancing full steam ahead along the path of industrialization – to socialism, leaving behind the age-old "Russian" backwardness,' he wrote. 'We are becoming a country of metal, a country of automobiles, a country of tractors. And when we have put the USSR on an automobile, and the peasant on a tractor, let the worthy capitalists, who boast so much of their "civilization", try to overtake us! We shall see which countries may then be classified as backward and which as advanced.'

With this new assault on the countryside, the witch-hunt directed at the most competent peasants, who'd once produced nearly three-quarters of the nation's commercial grain, began once more. Stalin sought the 'liquidation of the *kulaks* as a class'. In the first two months of 1930 alone, about sixty million peasants were forced into collective farms. Two years later, around 1.4 million were sent to 'special settlements' in the frozen north. Records show one single train leaving the small regional station of Yantsenovo for Siberia was sixty-one cars in length and carried around 3,500 *kulaks*. Such journeys had a mortality rate of around 15 per cent. One witness recalled becoming 'used to seeing corpses there in the morning; a wagon would pull up and the hospital stable-hand, Abram, would pile in the bodies. Not all died; many wandered through the dusty mean little streets, dragging bloodless blue legs, swollen from dropsy, feeling out each passerby with doglike begging eyes . . . they got nothing.'

In 1933 around five thousand *kulaks* and 'déclassé elements' were dumped on an island in the Ob River with only a few bags of mouldering flour to eat. Some attempted to swim to shore and drowned in icy water; others turned on each other and were killed for a pair of shoes or a hunk of bread. Some of the people were eaten. On one day alone five bodies were discovered from which, 'the liver, the heart, the lungs and the fleshy parts of the bodies (breasts, calves) had been cut off', according to an official report. A witness remembered a 'pretty girl' a young guard named Kostia Venikov had been courting. 'He protected her. One day he had to be taken away for a while, and he told one of his comrades, "Take care of her" . . . People caught the girl, tied her to a poplar tree, cut off her breasts, her muscles, everything they could eat . . . When Kostia came back, she was still alive. He tried to save her but she had lost too much blood. She died. The boy was out of luck.' Across the Soviet prison system, cannibalism was common enough that a name was coined for those doomed to be eaten: cows. Stalin's interpreter and subsequent gulag inmate Jacques Rossi writes, 'the "cow" is a novice whom the convicts ask to join them in attempting to escape. In general, the novice is flattered to find himself associating with famous criminals. However, he does not know that if they run short of food, he will be killed, and his blood eaten.'

For those responsible for the 'dekulakisation' of the USSR, status was awarded for actively suppressing natural human sympathy. 'Throw your bourgeois humanitarianism out of the window and act like Bolsheviks worthy of Comrade Stalin,' they were instructed. 'The last decayed remnant of capitalist farming must be wiped out at any cost!' One, Lev Kopelev, scolded himself when he became upset by the sounds of screaming children, and told himself a heroic story in which it was immoral to 'give in to debilitating pity. We were realizing historical necessity. We were performing our revolutionary duty. We were obtaining grain for the socialist fatherland.' Another reassured herself, 'they are not human beings, they are *kulaks*'.

Many *kulaks* starved. A decree in 1932 ordered ten years' hard labour or the death penalty for 'any theft or damage of socialist property', which included taking a few stalks of grain for food; peasants began eating grass and tree bark. As mountains of their grain, milk, dairy, eggs and meat were shipped out of the countryside and sold internationally to fund Stalin's industrialisation programme, around six million peasants starved to death. The destruction of the *kulaks* was a 'catastrophe for the Soviet economy', writes Figes. 'It deprived the collective farms of the best and hardest-working peasants, because these are what the "*kulaks*" actually were, ultimately leading to the terminal decline of the Soviet agricultural sector.' At the start of the 1930s goods began disappearing from shops in the towns and cities; severe shortages of foods, clothes and other essentials began. By 1933, according to economist Professor Alec Nove, the USSR had suffered 'the most precipitous peacetime decline in living standards known in recorded history'.

Then, in 1936, the harvest failed.

Someone must be to blame for the revolution's problems. It obviously couldn't be the Communists. Who was it then? Hostile forces plotting against the revolution: deviants, secret capitalists, *witches*. The problem was finding them. This was an extremely tight game that had, by now, been being played for nearly two decades: conformity was the defining mode of life. The party didn't accept the concept of the private life. 'Everything people did in private was 'political',' writes Figes, and as such 'was subject to the censure of the collective'. A pro-Communist writer, visiting the USSR from France in 1936, commented on the 'extraordinary uniformity' in dress in the people he encountered, adding 'no doubt it would be equally apparent in their minds . . . the individual is sunk in the mass and so little particularized that one feels as though in speaking of people here one ought to use a collective singular and say not, "here are men" but "here is some man"'.

But if everybody was *saying* they believed the Communist dream, how could we find out who the deviants were? How could Stalin know which of his elite were truly loyal and which were playing a different game in the secret worlds inside their heads? Although he was at the absolute pinnacle in the *formal* Communist game, Stalin had no way of knowing where he stood in the *true* game that was playing in the minds of those around him. 'The purges began here', writes Figes, 'in the Bolsheviks' need to unmask potential enemies.'

And so began what remains arguably the most notorious case of status paranoia in history: the Great Terror. Good Communists had to be in a state of constant vigilance for the dangerous deviants with dangerous deviant thoughts who moved among them and were disguised as good Communists. It was announced that 'open and secret violators' of the party who 'cast doubt on and discredit its decisions and plans' would be expelled: over half a million party members were. For many, being accused and ejected from the game to which they'd devoted their lives was agonisingly alienating. One complained he was now 'isolated from everybody, an enemy of the people, in an inhuman position, completely isolated from everything that constitutes the essence of life'. Another asked, 'Can everything be collapsing this way? Is it possible that I could have become the enemy of the party which has formed me? No, it is a mistake.'

The elites and former elites came under heavy suspicion: members of the pre-revolutionary intelligentsia were smeared as 'bourgeois specialists'. Also attacked were priests, *kulaks* and the so-called 'Nepmen' – the entrepreneurs who'd run those small businesses during Lenin's NEP. Many who were suspected of incorrect thought were interrogated about their beliefs at purge meetings. '"Going through the Purge" meant confessing your sins endlessly, especially membership of oppositions and bad social origin,' writes Fitzpatrick, 'but there was no provision in the ritual for being relieved of the burden. You "recognized your errors", you apologized and, if lucky, you were sent away with a warning. But the errors were still there the next time.' Show trials were held, their always-guilty victims sacked, shot or exiled to the gulags. One victim raged, 'the shameful example of my fall shows that the slightest rift with the Party, the slightest insincerity towards the Party, the slightest hesitation with regard to the leadership, with regard to the Central Committee, is enough to land you in the camp of counterrevolution'.

Just as we've seen in periods of extreme tightness under the Nazis and the Spanish Inquisition, a wave of denunciations began. There were millions of informants: friends, colleagues and family members, some motivated by fear, others grudge and resentment and personal ambition and others by true belief. People denounced celebrities they read about in newspapers; workers denounced their managers; the wife of a biologist denounced her husband's academic rival as 'a vulgarian who pulls the wool over people's eyes, a pitiful scientific pigmy, a plagiarist and compiler'; historians have uncovered 'many letters from leading actors, actresses, and opera singers denouncing the theater directors who had insulted them and failed to give them appropriate roles'.

One poet was denounced for not signing a group request for the execution of two elder revolutionaries; a writer was denounced for being the drinking companion of someone else who'd been denounced. University students were denounced for having *kulak* fathers or being 'brought up by a merchant'. When a photographer complained that photographic paper was better before the revolution, he was denounced by his apprentice and executed. Some ambitious warriors became 'super-denouncers', writes Fitzpatrick, 'virtually professional public denouncers'. One later described how he and a partner would go to meetings with 'readymade lists of persons whom we intended to accuse of being enemies . . . when we appeared it not only caused embarrassment at the meeting, but frightened party members would quietly run out of the building'. When true-believing Communists were arrested, still lost in the dream of the party's total infallibility, they were baffled. One wrote: 'the fact that I am here must mean that I have committed some wrong – what I do not know.'

During the Great Terror, the police were issued quotas for what percentage of their district was to be shot or sent to the camps. On 2 June 1937, it was ordered that 35,000 were to be 'repressed' in one district, 5,000 of whom were to be shot. Between 1937 and 1938, 165,200 priests were arrested, 106,800 of whom were shot. In the same period, an average of one and a half thousand people were executed daily. One and a half million ordinary Russians were arrested by the secret police, nearly seven hundred thousand were executed for 'counter-revolutionary activities'. All of Stalin's close political rivals were wiped out, including almost the entire generational elite of the Lenin era.

Stalin might have destroyed national agriculture and ended the lives of millions via purge, liquidation and famine, but he'd also been busy forcing modernisation onto the USSR. He'd ordered the construction of new cities, factories and plants: many workers toiled, in service of the future, seven days a week. By the fact of its massive and lethal focus on successful players, the Great Terror created new vacancies, which meant new opportunities for millions. There began an intense programme of 'proletarianizing' the intelligentsia: those who entered this new game 'achieved extraordinarily rapid promotion during the Great Purges'. They became a new elite populating the games of industry, arts and politics. The Soviet bureaucracy became filled with inexperienced former low-status players, many of whom were semi-literate. 'All over the Soviet Union, at every level, people were changing their social status,' writes Fitzpatrick, 'peasants moving to town and becoming industrial workers, workers moving into technical jobs or becoming party officials, former school teachers becoming university professors.'

Stalin was creating status games for people, generating aspiration and ambition and meaning. These new upwardly mobile classes were encouraged further by Stalin's stunning turning away from the founding dream of perfect equality. Rather than there being no social classes, he declared there were actually three: workers, peasants and intelligentsia. Old symbols of hierarchy, including degrees and honorary titles, were brought out of abolishment just as new titles such as 'The Hero of the Soviet Union' and 'The Distinguished Master of Sport' were introduced. In the military, titles, ranks and status signifiers such as epaulettes had been abolished: now they were back. The 'egalitarianism' that said workers should be paid the same no matter their level of competence was an 'ultra-left' idea. He derided it as 'equality mongering'. He defended the notion of citizens owning their own cattle: 'a person is a person', he said. 'He wants to own something for himself.' There was 'nothing wrong in this'.

There'd once been a 'Party Maximum' wage cap, even for those at the top. Not anymore. Stalin 'vigorously demanded that individual skills and efforts be rewarded with higher wages and other material rewards', writes sociologist Professor Jukka Gronow. 'In his opinion, it had now become necessary to encourage workers to get personally interested in the results of their own work.' Hundreds of thousands of players became more prosperous. But what use was money when there were so few status symbolising goods to spend it on? 'The authorities clearly understood, new and higher quality material goods, along with the shops to sell them, were crucial.'

In 1936, following a personal intervention by Stalin, the Soviet champagne industry was born. A director of champagne production was paid two thousand roubles per month, more than ten times that of an industrial worker. Beers, wines and liqueurs also began to be produced, as were ketchups, perfumes, sweets, ice creams and chocolates: in 1934 1,400 tonnes of cocoa beans were imported; by 1937 it had increased to 11,100 tonnes. Christmas trees, which had been banned, were brought back as 'New Year's trees': in 1938, 210,000 were sold in Leningrad alone. One city grocery shop boasted selling fifty kinds of bread, two hundred varieties of sweets and chocolates and thirty-eight types of sausage, 'including twenty new types that have not been sold anywhere before'.

There was an increased focus on quality and innovation, often driven by agonised comparison with their rivals in the West. Reports sent back from the capitalist territories detailed the methods by which the Americans made five thousand hamburgers an hour and the Germans used disposable tableware: 'in Germany ice cream is sold in paper cups. In the same shops it is possible to eat sausages on paper plates. We have to organize immediately within the system of Trade Ministry special shops in which everything is sold on paper plates and in paper cups.' Soviet innovations included a folding umbrella and thermos plates (which turned out not to be a commercial success). Restaurants were opened, one strata of which were permitted to raise prices by 30 per cent to improve quality and service. Some, proud of their success, began promoting themselves as superior. This led to a potentially deadly dissonance: these ambitious players of success games were denounced as a 'group of fascist bandits' and accused, writes Gronow, of 'vigorously promoting a policy geared toward the establishment of quality restaurants'.

Throughout the 1930s, there came into being a complex hierarchy of status. Stalin might have admitted there were now three classes, but sociologists found at least ten: the ruling elite; superior intelligentsia; general intelligentsia; working-class aristocracy; white collar; well-to-do peasants; average workers; average peasants; disadvantaged workers; forced labour. His regime 'introduced systematic discrimination on the basis of class in all sorts of contexts important for everyday life: education, justice, housing, rations, and so on', writes Fitzpatrick. 'Even the right to vote was reserved for those who came from the "toiling" classes. A young worker had privileged access to higher education, Communist Party membership, and a host of other benefits, while the son of a noble or a priest suffered corresponding disadvantages and restrictions.' A person's social class was even listed on their passport.

Party membership was made on a discriminatory basis: the admissions procedure included letters of reference and investigations of social background; those from working families were privileged. College admissions were similarly policed. In the arts, prestigious awards were often reserved for those of minority backgrounds: 'They give medals to Armenians, Georgians, Ukrainians – everyone except Russians,' complained one artist. Engineers and the new, approved, politically correct intelligentsia also received special privileges. Industrial workers comprised about 40 per cent of the workforce but received around 75 per cent of the food. Even work canteens were stratified this way: 'the most important workers of the most important factories ate the best food at lower prices', writes Gronow. Workplace canteens were often themselves divided into at least three sections based on status. 'This principle of hierarchy – rewards in relation to the imagined input based on the position or the type of work in question – permeated all fields of society.' Stalin bought 'the loyalty of the new middle class with "trinkets" but also with real privileges . . . thereby allowing for widening status differences'.

The new elites gained access to special apartments and had the best goods automatically reserved for them. Their children were sent to exclusive summer camps. They received holidays, chauffeur-driven cars and money. It became 'normal' for them to have live-in servants. Many of these servants were provided with no bed and forced to sleep in the kitchen, under a table or on chairs. 'They are even worse than the "ladies" of earlier times, these wives of engineers, doctors and "responsible" cadres,' said one brave complainant. They managed to calm the dissonance of their elevated lifestyles partly via the dodge that, under Communism, they didn't actually own any of these amenities. They belonged to the state. Privilege, for them, was about access instead of ownership – and abolishing ownership was the whole point of this, right? As for the state itself, it argued their privilege was temporary: soon all of the USSR would live like this. They were not a privileged elite, went the thinking, they were a *vanguard*.

The elite in the Communist Party, including administrators and higher army and government officials, became known as the *nomen-klatura*. In 1933, at the height of the famine during which *kulaks* were eating grass, tree bark and each other, luxury trains were taking its members on holidays to health spas in the south. One official document notes a single month's tally in just one of their restaurant cars: 200 kg butter; 150 kg Swiss Cheese; 500 kg sausages; 500 kg chicken; 550 kg of different kinds of meat; 300 kg fish (plus 350 kg canned fish and 100 kg herring); 100 kg caviar; 300 kg sugar; 160 kg chocolate and sweets; 100 boxes of fruit; 60,000 cigarettes. One member wrote: 'The *nomenklatura* is on another planet. It's Mars. It's not simply a matter of good cars or apartments. It's the continuous satisfaction of your own whims, the way an army of boot-lickers allows you to work painlessly for hours. All the little apparatchiks are ready to do everything for you. Your every wish is fulfilled. You can go to the theater on a whim, you can fly to Japan from your hunting lodge. It's a life in which everything flows easily . . . You are like a king: just point your finger and it is done.' By the time the Soviet Union collapsed, the *nomenklatura* and their families numbered around three million, about 1.5 per cent of the population. This, observes historian Professor Richard Pipes, is 'approximately the same proportion of nobles under tsarism in the eighteenth century. And the favors it enjoyed resembled those of the magnates of that age.'

What had gone wrong? Communism was supposed to bring about a 'kingdom of equality'. It wasn't that the Soviet Union had been merely unlucky in having Lenin and Stalin lead it, or that their class-ridden tyranny was somehow peculiar to their cultural character: hierarchies and horrors emerged also in Cambodia and China. In fact, the error the Communists made can be traced back to the arguments of Plato. More than two thousand years before the revolution, the Ancient Greek who'd first dreamed the Communist dream had been corrected by his student, Aristotle, who'd pointed out it wasn't actually wealth or private ownership that created the human yearning to get ahead. That yearning was a part of our nature: 'it is not possession but the desires of mankind which require to be equalized'.

The parable of the Communists reveals the impossibility of ridding human existence of the game. The drive to get ahead will always assert itself. It's in us. It's who we are. The first decades of the Soviet Union find the status game in all its details: its irrepressibility; its capacity to raise violence; the grandiosity it inspires in winning players and leaders; the inevitability of elites; the flaw that makes people believe they're always deserving of more status; the use of humiliation as the ultimate weapon; the horror of the cousins and their genius for tyranny; the ideological war games that rage across neural territories; our vulnerability to believing almost any dream of reality if our status depends on it; the capacity for that dream to pervert our perception of reality; the danger of active belief; esoteric language; zealous leaders who cast visions of heavenly status in future promised lands and target enemies to its rising; the anger and enthusiasm they inspire; the cycle of gossip, outrage, consensus and harsh punishment; the paranoia that can afflict leaders and the terrors it brings; the grim magic of toxic morality and its conjuring trick of making evil seem virtuous; the necessity of games to generate status if they're to endure; the world-changing power of the status goldrush.

The story idealists sometimes tell of humanity says we're natural seekers of equality. This isn't true. Utopians talk of injustice whilst building new hierarchies and placing themselves at the top. Such behaviour is in our nature. The urge for rank is ineradicable. It's a secret goal of our lives, to win status for ourselves and our game – and gain as much of it over *you* and *you* and *you* as we can. It's how we make meaning. It's how we make identity. It's the worst of us, it's the best of us and it's the inescapable truth of us: for humans, equality will always be the impossible dream.

29

Seven Rules of the Status Game

THE PLEASURE OF status is our prize for playing by the rules of human life. Nature has to bribe us to endure the acts necessary for our survival and reproduction, in all their horror-show weirdness. To persuade us to push a penis in and out of a vagina, it invented orgasm. To persuade us to sacrifice our wellbeing for a screaming, shit-smeared infant, it made love. To persuade us to force mashed-up foreign objects down our throats, it evolved taste and appetite. To persuade us to engage in groupish, co-operative living, it conjured the obsessive joys of connection and acclaim. Follow the rules, and follow them well, and you can expect to feel great.

But, as we've discovered, the game of life contains hidden rules and traps. Many of the problems of social existence are generated in the disconnect between reality and the illusion, as the brain tricks us into believing the myths and prejudices of our groups, and convinces us that we're not players of games but moral heroes in stories. This makes our species liable to becoming hubristic, aggressive and deluded. As we play for ever-greater status, for ourselves and our games, we weave a self-serving and highly motivating dream that writhes with saints and demons and irrational beliefs. This dream is presented to us as reality. It's entirely convincing, in all its colour, noise and pristine focus. We see evidence everywhere that it's true. It has the power to seduce us into the most depraved acts of hatred and barbarity. But it can also lead us into modes of play that truly make a better world.

If the dream is so persuasive, how do we know we're playing the right games? And when we're playing them, how can we win what we need? To help improve our lives, and protect ourselves from peril, we can remember seven rules.

I

Practise Warmth, Sincerity and Competence

Ever since the days of the hunter-gatherer tribe, prestige has been freely awarded by our co-players. The ways in which we present to people socially can have a huge effect on how much they'll grant us. Psychologists studying optimal self-presentation discuss a set of closely related ideas. Professor Susan Fiske argues that, when encountering others, people ask of them two fundamental questions: 'What are their intentions?' and 'What's their capacity to pursue them?' If we want to supply the right answers, and so be received positively, Fiske finds we should behave in ways that imply warmth and competence. More recently it's been argued a third component should be added. For Professor Jennifer Ray, morality is 'not only a critical and separable dimension . . . it may even be the primary dimension'. Elsewhere, 'perceived sincerity' has been found to be essential to successful 'impression management'.

Taking these arguments from a status game perspective, I believe we can usefully settle on three dimensions for successful play: warmth, sincerity and competence. This constitutes a kind of blessed triumvirate of human behaviour and, whilst undoubtedly being easier said than done, it at least offers an ideal to aim at. As we've learned, there are three major routes to status in human games: we can grab it in acts of dominance or we can earn prestige by proving ourselves useful to our group, with acts that signal virtue or success. When we're warm, we imply we're not going to use dominance; when sincere, that we're going to play fairly; when competent, that we're going to be valuable to the game itself, both in its own battles for status, and to individual players who might learn from us.

For leaders, this *warmth, sincerity, competence* rule is slightly different. Whilst warmth can certainly be advisable, especially when dealing with pampered elites, it's perhaps more critical to show zeal on behalf of the game. Throughout history, leaders have succeeded by telling a story that says their group is deserving of more status, which, under their direction, they'll win. But it remains important this evangelical passion doesn't morph into arrogance. No one likes a big shot.

II
Make Small Moments of Prestige

We find it all too easy to make small moments of dominance. During our investigation, we focussed on dominance play in some of its strongest manifestations. Caren Turner, the online mobbers, mass-murderers and the tyrannical cousins of history all attempted to attain elevated status by force. Like them, we're vulnerable to slipping into these second-self states and, in overwhelming moments, making mistakes we might even regret for life. But just as consequential are the accumulations of damage we can cause with subtle moments of dominance. The glowers, the sighs, the wails of complaint: such twitches of animalism might help us achieve some immediate goal, but they'll lead to our being de-ranked in the minds of others.

Often, these incidents of pointless tension are the result of our game-playing circuitry never switching off. We're routinely pitched into senseless competitions at the hyper-local level. When we're in airport security queues or on the phone to call centres, we can remind ourselves the person we're dealing with might be obstructive or rude, but we don't have to take it as a challenge to our rank. We can consciously override any urge to push back in dominance and provide, instead, a prestigious response, by offering respect and acclaim for their efforts. We might not get what we want (although our chances could improve) but at least everyone will leave feeling better about who we are as a person – including ourselves. In this way, accumulations of dominance become accumulations of prestige, leading to potentially dramatic improvements in reputation over time, and all the rewards that can bring.

It's easy to forget we have status to give, that it costs nothing and it never runs out. Creating small moments of prestige means always seeking opportunities to use it. Allowing others to feel statusful makes it more likely they'll accept our influence. Whether we're asking a favour or issuing a task to a subordinate, it's advisable to resist even subtle markers of dominance, allowing them to reach the 'correct' decision without putting them under pressure. If they sense they've had no choice in the matter, they're robbed of the gift of feeling good about their action. How to go about this depends on the rules of your culture, and change especially as we move from West to East. But, researchers find, in individualist societies, 'evoking freedom' can have significant power to persuade. In one study, telling a stranger they were 'free to accept or refuse' a request for money for bus fare increased compliance from 16 to 40 per cent. I suspect this is largely down to status: if someone feels coerced into doing the 'right' thing, even if gently, they've only agreed out of dominance. This means the status isn't theirs to enjoy, it's with the player to whom they've deferred. But if they believe they've decided freely, they're not weak but virtuous and so able to rightfully enjoy their generosity's reward.

III
Play a Hierarchy of Games

One of the greatest dangers in this game of life is tyranny. Resisting it means understanding that tyranny is fun. It tempts us in with the lure of major status. Especially in the modern era, when wars tend to rage over psychological rather than physical territory, tyrants don't succeed by telling people they're wrong. Instead, they start by saying what we already believe. Their arguments make moral sense. Who could be against the end of the cruel exploitation of the Russian masses? Who could be against the restoration of the German economy and national pride, and the ridding of the Communist menace? Who could be against fighting child abuse? The Communists, Nazis and Satan-hunters each offered a game that felt virtuous and hopeful. Their leaders told their players a story that they wanted to hear – they were right, they were moral heroes and they were on a glorious path to a promised land of elevated status. Their players came to experience the dream they'd been sold as true: they believed, fully and sincerely, they were on the side of the good.

Given the game's ability to mould our perception of reality, how can we know if we've been seduced? It's possible to sense what kind of game we're in by observing the ways in which status is typically awarded. Tyrannies are virtue-dominance games. Much of their daily play and conversation will focus on matters of obedience, belief and enemies. Is the game you're playing coercing people, both inside and outside it, into conforming to its rules and symbols? Does it attempt to silence its ideological foes? Does it tell a simplistic story that explains the hierarchy, deifying their group whilst demonising a common enemy? Are those around you obsessed with their sacred beliefs? Do they talk about them continually and with greedy pleasure, drawing significant status from belief and active belief? Does it seek to damage and destroy lives, often with glee? Is this aggression made to feel virtuous? That's probably a tyranny. This might sound melodramatic, but we all contain the capacity for this dreadful mode of play: those cousins are built into our coding. If we're serious about 'never again' we must accept that tyranny isn't a 'left' thing or a 'right' thing, it's a human thing. It doesn't arrive goose-stepping down streets in terrifying ranks, it seduces us with stories.

Perhaps the best mode of protection is to play many games. People who appear brainwashed have invested too much of their identity into a single game. They rely on it wholly for their connection and status, the maintenance of which requires them to be filled up with its dream of reality, no matter how delusional. Not only does this put them at risk of committing harm to others, they risk catastrophic collapse themselves. If the game fails, or they become expelled, their identity – their very self – can disintegrate. No such risk can befall the player with a diversity of identities who plays diverse games. Indeed, doing so seems to be profoundly good for us. Psychologists find those with 'complex,' multiple self-identities tend to be happier, healthier and have more stable emotional lives.

But it's important, too, that every game isn't played with equal focus. If we're going to earn the prestige we desire, we must strive to become truly valuable to our co-players. This takes time. It requires an amount of dogged attention to one pursuit over others. Life, then, should be organised as a hierarchy of games, with that at the top drawing the most effort and generating maximal meaning.

IV

Reduce Your Moral Sphere

Some forms of status are easier to win than others. For those of us who aren't pretty, virtue is probably the easiest to find of all. It's as simple as judging people: because status is relative, their de-grading raises us up, if only in our minds. Smartphones and social media have placed global virtue games inside our pockets. Winning this form of status is now more convenient than ever. But it costs, not least in the misery it can cause others, especially when it's blended with dominance. Many of us could benefit from consciously reducing our moral sphere. How much time do you devote to the judging of other people? How much cheap and tainted status do you grab for yourself by doing so? Reducing our moral sphere means casting our eyes inwards, concerning ourselves mostly with our own behaviour instead of that of others. It means ceasing the casual condemnation of distant players living different dreams which we refuse to understand and are all too easy to belittle and hate.

V
Foster a Trade-Off Mindset

Morality poisons empathy. Because the dreamworlds we live in seem real and true, we believe the moral convictions that comprise them are also real and true, as if they're objects that can be dug out of the ground and observed by all, just as long as we make the right arguments. But moral 'facts' exist only in minds. Our insistence on their materiality blinds us to the perspectives of others: if our moral reality *is* reality then theirs must be a lie. So they're liars, then. Evil.

This mode of thinking trips us into arguing over questions with no answer. Asking whether immigration or neoliberalism or religion are 'good' or 'bad' is nonsensical. It's pure status play. Which moral class we assign them depends on which game we happen to be playing. The truth of such complex phenomena is usually that they're trade-offs: they have an array of positive and negative effects that impact different status games in different ways.

Rather than fighting to make our moral truths classed as materially real and deferred to absolutely, we should foster a trade-off mindset. This means viewing the world not in terms of winners and losers but of groups negotiating trade-offs. It means reaching past the self-serving fantasy of moral heroes and villains and seeing the ways different outcomes might injure our foes, whose pain is just as painful as ours. And it means empathising; sincerely attempting to understand the games played by our enemies and acknowledging their criteria for making status, even if we can never persuade ourselves of their validity.

Most of the time, in even intensely bitter conflicts, each side tells a story that holds part of the truth. We found this in the clashing narratives of the New Left and New Right. Both wove a dream that was simultaneously true and false: the nuanced reality is we need to ensure minorities have every opportunity to thrive, just as we need to understand that the alienation felt by the white and in-need exists, and hurts them. We must fight the bigotry of which both sides are guilty. Immigration isn't 'good' or 'bad', it's a deal that impacts different sets of people in different ways. The route forward is more likely to be found if we muster the wisdom to see through the moral cartoon and understand the world not as populated by dragons and dragon slayers, but by players negotiating trade-offs.

VI
Be Different

Life in the status game can be tough, not least in the hyper-individualist, neoliberal world in which we play today. Research suggests it's changing us: we're more sensitive to signals of failure in our environment and that makes us more perfectionistic. The standards by which we judge ourselves as being worthy are often so high, we settle for nothing less than perfect. But there is another way. Psychologists argue that it's possible to earn success-based status by engaging in 'minor acts of nonconformity that do not violate the group's basic standards for behaviour but attract attention'. Doing your own thing takes imagination and courage, but as long as you're being useful, and not breaking sacred rules, you have the potential to rise. Originality also makes it more difficult for rivals to catch you. This should be a relief to those of us who obsess, damagingly, over our failure to be perfect. Often, a better strategy lies in trying to be different.

VII
Never Forget You're Dreaming

A status game is a conspiracy we join to make ourselves feel important. Once our basic survival needs have been met, and we're connected with others, what's left is the contest. And for what? It's not as if we can go to some bunker in the desert, unlock a steel box and find our status inside it. We can't take our status to bed and give it a kiss. We concoct it, as if by magic, out of those endless symbols: deference, influence, money, flattery, eye contact, clothing, jewellery, professional titles, measures of orange juice, left or right on the plane. We invest the years of our lives into projects that become of all-devouring importance. Up and down and up and down and up and down we go. As we live, we soar and fall, our victories ecstatic, our losses so grave we can be driven to suicide, the bitterness of death seeming sweeter than failure.

Whilst we can never separate ourselves from the game, wisdom can be gained from simply knowing that it's there. In the years it's taken me to undertake this research, I've found its knowledge to be a comfort. This has come in a variety of contexts. For instance, I write to you in my forty-fifth year. Not too long ago, I'd sometimes feel self-conscious about my age and its various signs. I now realise these signs are symbols in a game I'm no longer required to play. Competing with the young in games of youth is not just hopeless, it's dull. The trick is to find new and better games. There are different worlds to explore, in the second half of life, most more meaningful than those of the first.

I'm also more conscious of my thoughts, and their capacity to twist into self-serving stories. I catch myself ruminating hotly on events, automatically weaving a moral tale of heroes and villains around small humiliations and global headlines. There are always status battles at the core of these imaginings; they come when I feel threatened. By noticing this happening, I'm now better able to hinder the process, to step outside it and restore at least a modicum of rationality.

Just as I'm aware of my own vulnerability to being swept into perilous fantasies, I'm aware of the extraordinary power of groups to do so. In what's becoming an increasingly angry and divided era, in the West, my knowledge of the game has enabled me to observe with a greater sense of assurance as new, wild dreams have formed across the culture and bewitched the masses. I'm better able to defend my own perception in the understanding that, just because large crowds of smart people have begun believing that which seems crazy, it doesn't necessarily follow that they're right. The fact of their numbers doesn't increase their trustworthiness and neither does their power, platform or intellect. Elites and their games have gone wrong throughout human history; there's no reason they should stop in our lifetime.

Finally, I've learned to recognise when the pressures of the game become overwhelming. In this strange and restless dreamworld, we're continually offered new and shifting symbols of what it is to be a winner: thinner, larger, whiter, darker, smarter, happier, brave-and-sadder with *this* career triumph and *that* many likes. I remind myself that these symbols we chase are often no less ridiculous than giant yams and that none of us are competing with everyone in the world, no matter how much it can feel that way.

I believe we can all take consolation in the knowledge that nobody ever gets there, not the superstars, the presidents, the geniuses or the artists we gaze up at in envy and awe. That promised land is a mirage. In our lowest moments, we should remind ourselves of the truth of the dream: that life is not a story, but a game with no end. This means it isn't a final victory we should seek but simple, humble progress: the never-ending pleasure of moving in the right direction. Nobody wins the status game. They're not supposed to. The meaning of life is not to win, it's to play.

A NOTE ON MY METHOD

MOST OF THE ideas covered in this book are well documented in a wide range of books, academic papers and periodicals which were my principal source for research. Most of the general concepts in this book are relatively uncontroversial. In the few areas where I explored more controversial science, I sought expert counsel where those studies threatened to be too complex for a lay person to appropriately understand. I then recruited a team of academics with appropriate specialisms to read the manuscript. They offered notes and advice where I had erred. I offer my huge thanks to Dr Stuart Ritchie, Professor Sophie Scott and William Buckner of the Human Systems and Behavior Lab who all helped in this regard, and were brilliant and patient with my questions. Further fact-checking was carried out by Madeleine Feeny and Isaac Scher. I accept full responsibility for any remaining errors.

I do not declare myself to be free of the biases that afflict any writer, and I'm certainly not immune to making mistakes. If any errors of fact are noted, or if new findings supersede claims made in the text, I would be very grateful to receive notification via my website, willstorr.com, so that future editions of *The Status Game* can be corrected and updated.

Naturally, this book contains only a fraction of the relevant science. Other academics will, surely, disagree with those whom I quote in these pages. If any of it piques your interest, I urge you to dig deeper, where you will no doubt find science that is newer and in conflict with some of the work here.

All interviews are edited. Some quotes have had their tenses switched, for ease of reading. The interview with Ben Gunn in chapter 1 previously appeared, in a different form, in the *Observer Magazine*.

ACKNOWLEDGEMENTS

If this page was a status game, at the top would be my incredible agent Will Francis, who is wise, honest, patient and sharp – the perfect agent, in other words – and also my fantastic and seemingly inexhaustible editor Shoaib Rokadiya – thanks for never taking the easy way out. I'm hugely indebted to the brilliant brains that have looked over my work with critical, expert eyes: Stuart Ritchie, William Buckner, Sophie Scott, Christopher Boyce, Madeleine Feeny and Isaac Scher. Special thanks, too, to all at William Collins, and to Tom Killingbeck, Ben Gunn, Maranda Dynda, Anton Howes, Richard Easterlin, Tim Dixon, Rob Henderson, Sci-Hub, Andrew Hankinson, Tim Lott, Iain Lee, Adam Rutherford, Jesse Singal and Rolf Degen. And finally, thanks to my brilliant and beautiful wife Farrah for pretending to listen as I've banged on about status for the last four years, for allowing me to disappear to distant countries for weeks on end as I've researched and written the book, and for reading at least eleven pages of it – I love you.

NOTES AND SOURCES

PROLOGUE

As psychologist Professor Brian Boyd writes: *On the Origin of Stories*, Brian Boyd (Harvard University Press, 2010), p. 109.

CHAPTER 1

The MP Michael Gove, who'd been campaigning for his release, told *The Times*: 'A life spent at Her Majesty's Pleasure', Damian Whitworth, *The Times*, 8 December 2010.

One study of more than sixty thousand people: 'Is the Desire for Status a Fundamental Human Motive? A Review of the Empirical Literature', C. Anderson, J. A. D. Hildreth and L. Howland, *Psychological Bulletin*, 16 March 2015.

an extensive review of the scientific literature concluded: 'Is the Desire for Status a Fundamental Human Motive? A Review of the Empirical Literature', C. Anderson, J. A. D. Hildreth and L. Howland, *Psychological Bulletin*, 16 March 2015.

CHAPTER 2

Humans are a species of great ape: https://australian.museum/learn/science/human-evolution/humans-are-apes-great-apes.

living in settled communities for around five hundred generations: *Private Truths, Public Lies*, Timur Kuran (Harvard University Press, 1995), p. 40.

'social status is a universal cue to the control of resources' . . . analysed 186 premodern societies: *Evolutionary Psychology*, David Buss (Routledge, 2015), p. 11.

people with depression tend to belong to 'far fewer' groups: 'Social group memberships protect against future depression, alleviate depression symptoms and prevent depression relapse', T. Cruwys, G. A. Dingle, C. Haslam, et al., *Social Science and Medicine*, 2013, 98, 179–186.

Studies across time suggest the more a depressed person identifies with their group: 'Feeling connected again', T. Cruwys, G. A. Dingle, C. Haslam et al., *Journal of Affective Disorders*, 2014, 159, 139–146.

One survey of nearly seven thousand residents of Alameda County in California: *The Village Effect*, Susan Pinker (Penguin Random House, 2014), p. 25.

'defensive crouch . . . more critical': *Loneliness*, John T. Cacioppo and William Patrick (W. W. Norton & Company, 2008), p. 30.

Rejected people are more likely to issue punishments . . . donate money or help strangers: *Loneliness*, John T. Cacioppo and William Patrick (W. W. Norton & Company, 2008), p. 6.

participants were told they were taste-testing chocolate chip cookies: 'Social exclusion impairs self-regulation', R. F. Baumeister, C. N. DeWall, N. J. Ciarocco and J. M. Twenge, *Journal of Personality and Social Psychology*, 88 (2005): 589–604.

'creatures shaped by evolution to feel safe in company': *Loneliness*, John T. Cacioppo and William Patrick (W. W. Norton & Company, 2008), p. 61.

words of psychologist Professor Robert Hogan: *The Redemptive Self*, Dan P. McAdams (Oxford University Press, 2013), p. 29.

wealthy smoker just one rung below: *The Status Syndrome*, Michael Marmot (Bloomsbury, 2004). Kindle location 793.

Workers 'at the bottom of the office hierarchy': *The Status Syndrome*, Michael Marmot (Bloomsbury, 2004). Kindle location 681.

These remarkable and telling findings have been confirmed in men and in women: *The Status Syndrome*, Michael Marmot (Bloomsbury, 2004). Kindle location 757.

They've even been found in baboons: *The Status Syndrome*, Michael Marmot (Bloomsbury, 2004). Kindle location 1472.

Tentative clues as to how this might happen . . . According to a world leader in this field, Professor Steve Cole: Interview with author.

'perceiving oneself as having low rank compared to others': 'Social rank theory of depression: A systematic review of self-perceptions of social rank and their relationship with depressive symptoms and suicide risk', Karen Wetherall, Kathryn A. Robb, Rory C. O'Connor, *Journal of Affective Disorders*, 2019, 246, 300–319.

'mentally withdraw from the competition for higher status' . . . keeps us off 'high-status individuals' radars' . . . 'reduced opportunities imposed by low status' . . . self-subordination: 'The Emotional Underpinnings of Social Status', Conor Steckler and Jessica Tracy, *The Psychology of Social Status*, 2014, 347–362. Accessed at 10.1007/978-1-4939-0867-7_10.

suicide 'concentrates among those': *Suicide: The Social Causes of Self-Destruction*, Jason Manning (University of Virginia Press, 2020). Kindle location 728.

'the greater and faster the downward mobility': *Suicide: The Social Causes of Self-Destruction*, Jason Manning (University of Virginia Press, 2020). Kindle location 715.

'suicide is encouraged not just by falling, but by falling behind': *Suicide: The Social Causes of Self-Destruction*, Jason Manning (University of Virginia Press, 2020). Kindle location 937.

status is a resource: *Why We Fight*, Mike Martin (Hurst & Company, 2018). Kindle location 856.

CHAPTER 3

David Eagleman, 'What we call normal perception': *Incognito: The Secret Lives of the Brain*, David Eagleman (Canongate, 2011), p. 46.

'a chattering stream of electrical pulses': *Livewired: The Inside Story of the Ever-Changing Brain,* David Eagleman (Pantheon, 2020), p. 27.

Sounds, colours, tastes and smells exist only: For an in-depth discussion of the concepts described in this section, see *Making up the Mind*, Chris Frith (Blackwell Publishing, 2007).

Our eyes, for instance, are able to pick up less than one ten-trillionth: *Incognito: The Secret Lives of the Brain,* David Eagleman (Canongate, 2011), p. 77.

Gazzaniga calls it the 'interpreter module' . . . 'the storyline and the narrative': *Who's In Charge?* Michael Gazzaniga (Robinson, 2011), p. 105.

It 'generates explanations about our perceptions': *Who's In Charge?* Michael Gazzaniga (Robinson, 2011), p. 102.

'That "you" that you are so proud of': *Who's In Charge?* Michael Gazzaniga (Robinson, 2011), p. 108.

remixing our memories: Social psychologists Carol Tavris and Elliot Aronson believe we use 'confabulations of memory' to 'justify and explain our own lives'. *Mistakes Were Made (But Not By Me)* by Carol Tavis and Elliot Aronson (Pinter & Martin, 2007), p. 76.

I deal in depth with untrustworthy memories in chapter 10 of *The Heretics* (Picador, 2013).

more correct in our beliefs: *How We Know What Isn't So*, Thomas Gilovich (Simon & Schuster, 1991), p. 78.

Untrustworthy beliefs are the subject of *The Heretics* (Picador, 2013).

have more hopeful futures in store: *Mindwise*, Nicholas Epley (Penguin, 2014), p. 50.

psychologist Professor Thomas Gilovich, the evidence is 'clear': *How We Know What Isn't So*, Thomas Gilovich (Simon & Schuster, 1991), p. 78.

participants guessed what percentage of time they exhibited a range of virtuous behaviours: 'The Illusion of Moral Superiority', B. M. Tappin, R. T. McKay, *Social Psychological and Personality Science*, August 2017, 8(6): 623–631. https://doi.org/10.1177/1948550616673878. Epub 10 October 2016. PMID: 29081899; PMCID: PMC5641986.

consciousness is 'not at the centre of the action': *Incognito: The Secret Lives of the Brain*, David Eagleman (Canongate, 2011), p. 9.

'carved by natural selection': *Incognito: The Secret Lives of the Brain*, David Eagleman (Canongate, 2011), p 5.

Neuroscientist Professor Chris Frith writes that the brain 'represents': *Making up the Mind*, Chris Frith (Blackwell Publishing, 2007), p. 97.

discover 'the valuable things in the world': *Making up the Mind*, Chris Frith (Blackwell Publishing, 2007), p. 110.

the subconscious has a 'status detection system . . . relevant cues in the environment to assess status': *The Psychology of Social Status*, Joey T. Cheng, Jessica L. Tracy, Cameron Anderson (Springer, 2014), p. 121.

one study of office life included: *The Psychology of Social Status*, Joey T. Cheng, Jessica L. Tracy, Cameron Anderson (Springer, 2014), p. 167.

When all the vice presidents at a US corporation: 'Is the Desire for Status a Fundamental Human Motive? A Review of the Empirical Literature', C. Anderson, J. A. D. Hildreth and L. Howland, *Psychological Bulletin*, 16 March 2015.

People have been seen to become become preoccupied with 'trivial': 'Is the Desire for Status a Fundamental Human Motive? A Review of the Empirical Literature', C. Anderson, J. A. D. Hildreth and L. Howland, *Psychological Bulletin*, 16 March 2015.

One analysis found 'an increase in logo size': 'Social Hierarchy, Social Status and Status Consumption', David Dubois, Nailya Ordabayeva, 2015. 10.1017/CBO9781107706552.013.

These apparently trite symbols matter. In one test . . . people wearing 'rich' or 'poor' clothes: 'Economic status cues from clothes affect perceived competence from faces', D. Oh, E. Shafir, A. Todorov, *Nature Human Behaviour* 4, 287–293 (2020). https://doi.org/10.1038/s41562-019-0782-4.

in forty-three milliseconds: *Behave*, Robert Sapolsky (Vintage, 2017), p. 432.

eye contact we're receiving . . . 'with numerical precision': *Subliminal*, Leonard Mlodinow (Penguin, 2012), p. 120.

speak more often and more loudly: *The Psychology of Social Status*, Joey T. Cheng, Jessica L. Tracy, Cameron Anderson (Springer, 2014), p. 330.

(although some of these symbols may vary culturally): Fact-checking note, William Buckner.

When researchers took candid photos: C. Anderson, J. A. D. Hildreth and L. Howland, *Psychological Bulletin*, 16 March 2015.

When speaking, we emit a low-frequency hum: *Our Inner Ape*, Frans de Waal (Granta, 2005), p. 56.

three-quarters of arguments between children aged 18 and 30 months: *Possessed*, Bruce Hood (Penguin, 2019), pp. 53–54.

'Owning stuff is all to do with status amongst competitors': *The Domesticated Brain*, Bruce Hood (Pelican, 2014), p. 195.

'sensitive to inequality', writes the psychologist Professor Paul Bloom: *Just Babies*, Paul Bloom (Bodley Head, 2013), p. 80.

5-year-olds seek relative advantage . . . 'fairness and a desire for absolute gain': 'When Getting Something Good Is Bad: Even Three-Year-Olds React to Inequality', Vanessa LoBue, Tracy Nishida, Cynthia Chiong, Judy DeLoache, Jonathan Haidt, *Social Development*, 2011, 20, 154–170. 10.1111/j.1467-9507.2009.00560.

'Why people prefer unequal societies', Christina Starmans, Mark Sheskin, Paul Bloom, *Nature Human Behaviour*, 2017, 1, 0082. 10.1038/s41562-017-0082.

desire for power over others is not fundamental: 'Is the Desire for Status a Fundamental Human Motive? A Review of the Empirical Literature', C. Anderson, J. A. D. Hildreth, L. Howland, *Psychological Bulletin*, 16 March 2015..

'After acquiring a moderate amount of power': *Status*, Cecilia L. Ridgeway (Russell Sage Foundation, 2019), p. 59.

the desire for wealth is not fundamental: Even Wall Street bankers behave as if they care more about status than money. For most of the twentieth century, announcements of security offerings were made in prestigious financial newspapers such as the *Wall Street Journal*. The banks involved would be listed in a full-page advertisement, their precise placements denoting their relative status, with the upper left segment being top rank. Bankers would obsess about their placement and back out of deals if unsatisfied. In 1979 Morgan Stanley walked away from an offering with IBM, who they'd been servicing for twenty years, because they were displeased with their ranking in an advertisement, shrugging off a roughly one-million-dollar fee. If they wanted to make more money in the future, they calculated, they first had to look after their status. *Status Signals*, Joel M. Podolny (Princeton University Press, 2005). Kindle location 799.

This has been found many times . . . study using data from twelve thousand British adults: 'Is the Desire for Status a Fundamental Human Motive? A Review of the Empirical Literature', C. Anderson, J. A. D. Hildreth and L. Howland, *Psychological Bulletin*, 16 March 2015.

'Money and Happiness: Rank of Income, Not Income, Affects Life Satisfaction', C. J. Boyce, G. D. A. Brown, S. C. Moore, *Psychological Science*, 2010, 21 (4):471–475. https://doi.org/10.1177/0956797610362671.

happiness goes down if others living nearby: 'Neighbors as Negatives: Relative Earnings and Well-Being', Erzo F. P. Luttmer, *National Bureau of Economic*

Research Working Paper Series, No. 10667, August 2004. dhttps://doi. org/10.3386/w10667.

For neuroscientist Professor Sophie Scott, 'perception has no': Email to author.

Researchers find reward systems are activated most: 'Socially relative reward valuation in the primate brain', M. Isoda, *Current Opinion in Neurobiology*, 8 December 2020, 68:15–22. https://doi.org/10.1016/j.conb.2020.11.008. Epub ahead of print. PMID: 33307380.

Some data, using cross-country evidence, does appear to show rising national income correlating with rising national happiness: For the contra argument, see *Enlightenment Now!*, Steven Pinker (Penguin, 2018), p. 268.

according to happiness researcher Dr Christopher Boyce: Email to author.

academics at the University of Oxford's Wellbeing Research Centre: 'Different Versions of the Easterlin Paradox: New Evidence for European Countries', Casper Kaiser, Maarten Vendrik, *IZA Discussion Paper* No. 11994.

Between 1965 and 1990: *The Status Syndrome*, Michael Marmot (Bloomsbury, 2004). Kindle location 1505.

In 1948, the anthropologist Professor William Bascom: 'Ponapean Prestige Economy', William R. Bascom, *Southwestern Journal of Anthropology*, 1948, Vol. 4, No. 2, pp. 211–221. www.jstor.org/stable/3628712.

vehicle manufacturers succeeded in persuading the US public: *The Status Seekers*, Vance Packard (Pelican, 1966), pp. 273–276.

'has to do with the fact that human social life inherently' . . . 'share in the perception of these symbols': *Mixed Messages*, Robert Paul (University of Chicago Press, 2015), p. 299.

CHAPTER 4

'our perception of the world is a fantasy': *Making up the Mind*, Chris Frith (Blackwell Publishing, 2007), p. 111.

there are 'two separate channels': *Mixed Messages*, Robert Paul (University of Chicago Press, 2015), p. 49.

One survey of sixty premodern societies: 'Is It Good to Cooperate?: Testing the Theory of Morality-as-Cooperation in 60 Societies', Oliver Scott Curry, Daniel Austin Mullins, Harvey Whitehouse, *Current Anthropology*, 2019, 60:1, 47–69.

Anthropologist Professor Kate Fox has noted: *Watching the English*, Kate Fox (Hodder, 2005), pp. 88–106.

tending towards conceited self-views: 'In search of East Asian self-enhancement', S. J. Heine and T. Hamamura, *Personality and Social Psychology Review*, 2007, 11 (1) 4–27.

healthy habits: 'Distortions in Reports of Health Behaviours: The Time Span Effect and Illusory Superiority', Vera Hoorens, Peter Harris, *Psychology and Health*, 1998, 13 (3): 451–466.

immunity to bias: 'The bias blind spot: Perceptions of bias in self versus others', E. Pronin, D. Y. Lin, L. Ross, *Personality and Social Psychology Bulletin*, 2002, 28 (3): 369–381.

driving skills: 'The Grand Delusion', Graham Lawton, *New Scientist*, 14 May 2011.

96 per cent of Americans: *Personality Psychology*, Larsen, Buss and Wisjeimer (McGraw Hill, 2013), p. 473.

86 per cent of Australians: *The Lucifer Effect*, Philip Zimbardo (Rider, 2007). Kindle location 6880.

East Asian games tend to be more collective: For a detailed and fascinating analysis of this subject, see *The Geography of Thought*, Richard E. Nisbett (Nicholas Brealey, 2003).

immature and uncivilised . . . sociologist Professor David Yau Fai Ho has: 'The Concept and Dynamics of Face: Implications for Organizational Behavior in Asia', Joo Yup Kim and Sang Hoon Nam, *Organization Science*, 1998, 9:4, 522–534.

In 1486, Dame Juliana Berners: *The Polite World*, Joan Wildeblood and Peter Brinson (Oxford University Press, 1965), p. 21.

In 1558, Florentine etiquette writer Giovanni della Casa: *The Civilizing Process*, Norbert Elias (Wiley-Blackwell, 2000), p. 111.

The Chinese Book of Etiquette and Conduct for Women and Girls: https://www.gutenberg.org/files/35123/35123-h/35123-h.htm.

As 2-year olds, we have around one hundred trillion connections: *The Brain*, David Eagleman (Pantheon Books, 2015). Kindle location 85.

At this age, we are better than adults at recognising faces: *The Self Illusion*, Bruce Hood (Constable, 2011), p. 28.

Connections start being culled at a rate of up to one hundred thousand per second: *The Self Illusion*, Bruce Hood (Constable, 2011), p. 15.

'social mirror': *Moral Origins*, Christopher Boehm (Basic Books, 2012), p. 172.

practised specifically to 'reduce attachment to the personal self': 'An Exploration of Spiritual Superiority: The Paradox of Self- Enhancement', R. Vonk and Anouk Visser, *European Journal of Social Psychology*, 2020, 10.1002/ejsp.2721. Mindfulness and meditation "lead to narcissism and spiritual superiority": Rhys Blakely, *The Times*, 29 December 2020.

'incapable of following the rules of society', the sociologist Professor Teppei Sekimizi: 'Japan's modern-day hermits: The world of hikikomori', France 24 via YouTube, 18 January 2019.

strongly agreeing with questions such as: 'New Insights Into Hikikomori', Emma Young, *The British Psychological Research Digest*, 22 May 2019.

CHAPTER 5

attractive people are judged and treated more positively: 'Maxims or myths of beauty? A meta-analytic and theoretical review', J. H. Langlois, L. Kalakanis, A. J. Rubenstein, A. Larson, M. Hallam, M. Smoot, *Psychological Bulletin*, May 2000, 126 (3): 390–423. dhttps://doi.org/10.1037/0033-2909.126.3.390. PMID: 10825783.

two and a half million years ago . . . frighteningly aggressive prehumans: *The Goodness Paradox*, Richard Wrangham (Profile, 2019). Kindle location 1860.

Our bones were thicker: *The Goodness Paradox*, Richard Wrangham (Profile, 2019). Kindle location 1015–1028.

double the muscular strength of today: 'The Domestication of Humans', Robert G. Bednarik, *Anthropologie,* 2008, XLVI/1, 1–17.

'Reactive aggression would have dominated': *The Goodness Paradox*, Richard Wrangham (Profile, 2019). Kindle location 2627.

'massive faces'... 'at least the Mid-Pleistocene': *The Goodness Paradox*, Richard Wrangham (Profile, 2019). Kindle location 2640.

after we came down from the trees: *The Secret of our Success*, Joseph Henrich (Princeton University Press, 2016), pp. 304–307.

our use of campsites: *The Social Conquest of Earth*, Edward O. Wilson (Livewright, 2012), p. 42.

Hyper-violent males who attempted to dominate: *The Goodness Paradox*, Richard Wrangham (Profile, 2019). Kindle location 2627.

a novel breed of human . . . subtly different patterns of hormones: *The Domesticated Brain*, Bruce Hood (Pelican, 2014), p. 7.

'clearly defined status hierarchies': *Evolutionary Psychology*, David Buss (Routledge, 2015), p. 110.

hierarchies would've naturally divided: *The Social Conquest of Earth*, Edward O. Wilson (Livewright, 2012), p. 48.

as they competed for females: *Evolutionary Psychology*, David Buss (Routledge, 2015), p. 344.

men were often automatically granted higher status: *The Psychology of Social Status*, Joey T. Cheng, Jessica L. Tracy, Cameron Anderson (Springer, 2014), p. 180.

toolmaker, tracker: 'The Appeal of the Primal Leader: Human Evolution and Donald J. Trump', Dan P. McAdams, *Evolutionary Studies in Imaginative Culture*, 2017, 1 (2), 1–13. https://doi.org/10.26613/esic.1.2.45.
The Goodness Paradox, Richard Wrangham (Profile, 2019). Kindle location 2559.

In Panama, members of the Kuna tribe . . . among the Meriam: *The Psychology of Social Status*, Joey T. Cheng, Jessica L. Tracy, Cameron Anderson (Springer, 2014), p. 17.

'gain great social status': *Evolutionary Psychology*, David Buss (Routledge, 2015), p. 79.

'competitive altruism': *Evolutionary Psychology*, David Buss (Routledge, 2015), p. 280.

'a dramatic boost in prestige': *Evolutionary Psychology*, David Buss (Routledge, 2015), p. 353.

this is why we evolved speech – to gossip: *Grooming, Gossip, and the Evolution of Language*, Robin Dunbar (Harvard University Press, 1996).

Who we gossip with can itself be a status symbol: Fact-checking note, Sophie Scott.

one of gossip's critical purposes was to demonstrate the rules: 'Gossip as Cultural Learning', R. F. Baumeister, L. Zhang, K. D. Vohs, *Review of General Psychology*, 2004, 8 (2):111–121. https://doi.org/10.1037/1089-2680.8.2.111.

Gossip has been described as 'an activity that is attention seeking': 'Gossip in Organizations: Contexts, Consequences, and Controversies', Grant Michelson, Ad Iterson, Kathryn Waddington (2010), *Group & Organization Management* 35, 371–390. 10.1177/1059601109360389.

universal and essential to our gameplay: *Moral Tribes*, Joshua Greene (Atlantic Books, 2013), p. 45.

children start to gossip almost as soon as they can speak: 'Gossip as Cultural Learning', R. F. Baumeister, L. Zhang, K. D. Vohs, *Review of General Psychology*, 2004, 8 (2):111–121. https://doi.org/10.1037/1089-2680.8.2.111.

'meant facing reputational damage': *The Secret of our Success*, Joseph Henrich (Princeton University Press, 2016), p. 319.

a 40,000-year-old figurine of a lion-man: *Transcendence*, Gaia Vince (Allen Lane, 2019), p. 156.

In the Ukraine, the remains of four monumental structures: *Transcendence*, Gaia Vince (Allen Lane, 2019), p. 171.

a frequency of less than one per cent: *The Goodness Paradox*, Richard Wrangham (Profile, 2019). Kindle location 344.

'several hundred to a thousand times' more aggressive: *The Goodness Paradox*, Richard Wrangham (Profile, 2019). Kindle location 322.

'Without symbolic prestige': 'Prestige and the Ongoing Process of Culture Revision', Barkow J. (2014), *The Psychology of Social Status*, edited by J. Cheng, J. Tracy and C. Anderson (Springer, 2014). https://doi.org/10.1007/978-1-4939-0867-7_2.

such as that of the Lepcha in the Himalayas . . . modern nations such as Ghana . . . associated with 'drastically elevated' rates of suicide: *Suicide: The Social Causes of Self-Destruction*, Jason Manning (University of Virginia Press, 2020). Kindle location 880–898.

53 per cent of Americans saying they'd prefer instant death: 'Death Before Dishonor: Incurring Costs to Protect Moral Reputation', A. J. Vonasch, T. Reynolds, B. M. Winegard, R. F. Baumeister, *Social Psychological and Personality Science*, 2018, 9 (5) 604–613. https://doi.org/10.1177/1948550617720271.

CHAPTER 6

Whenever a person shows they're valuable to their game, by being conspicuously virtuous or successful, it's registered: For a detailed analysis of these effects, see *The Secret of our Success*, Joseph Henrich (Princeton University Press, 2016).

maintain a hunched, subservient posture: 'The Evolution of Prestige: Freely Conferred Status as a Mechanism for Enhancing the Benefits of Cultural Transmission', Joseph Henrich and Francisco Gil-White, *Evolution and Human Behavior*, 2000, 22, 165–196.

'fear grimaces' in apes and 'smiles' in humans: 'Smiles as Signals of Lower Status in Football Players and Fashion Models: Evidence That Smiles Are Associated with Lower Dominance and Lower Prestige', Timothy Ketelaar, Bryan L. Koenig, Daniel Gambacorta, Igor Dolgov, Daniel Hor, Jennifer Zarzosa, Cuauhtémoc Luna-Nevarez, Micki Klungle and Lee Wells, *Evolutionary Psychology* (July 2012).

universal human nature . . . monkeys also copy high-status associates: 'Prestige Affects Cultural Learning in Chimpanzees', V. Horner, D. Proctor, K. E. Bonnie, A. Whiten, F. B. M. de Waal, *PLoS ONE*, 2010, 5(5): e10625. https://doi.org/10.1371/journal.pone.0010625.

Studies comparing infant humans to chimpanzees: *The Secret of our Success*, Joseph Henrich (Princeton University Press, 2016), p. 109.

This is thought to be the basis of the concept of faith: *The Secret of our Success*, Joseph Henrich (Princeton University Press, 2016), p..97.

children in countries such as India overcome the pain: *The Secret of our Success*, Joseph Henrich (Princeton University Press, 2016), p. 110.

'by age one infants': *The Secret of our Success*, Joseph Henrich (Princeton University Press, 2016), p. 41.

the *self-similarity* cue: *The Secret of our Success*, Joseph Henrich (Princeton University Press, 2016), p. 44.

'skill cues': *The Secret of our Success*, Joseph Henrich (Princeton University Press, 2016), p. 38.

global luxury market is worth around $1.2 trillion: *Possessed*, Bruce Hood (Penguin, 2019), p. 96.

Members of the Amazonian Tsimane' tribe: 'Is the Desire for Status a Fundamental Human Motive? A Review of the Empirical Literature', C. Anderson, J. A. D. Hildreth and L. Howland, *Psychological Bulletin*, 16 March 2015.

we look for 'prestige cues': *The Secret of our Success*, Joseph Henrich (Princeton University Press, 2016), p. 42.

Academics call this 'The Paris Hilton Effect': *The Secret of our Success*, Joseph Henrich (Princeton University Press, 2016), p. 126.

English explorer Captain James Cook: *The Secret of our Success*, Joseph Henrich (Princeton University Press, 2016), p. 139. www.captaincooksociety.com/home/detail/scurvy-how-a-surgeon-a-mariner-and-a-gentleman-solved-the-greatest-medical-mystery-of-the-age-of-sail-bown-stephen-r-2003.

'The moment they see their superiors': 'Captain Cook and scurvy', Egon Hynek Kodicek and Frank George Young, *Notes and Records*, Royal Society London, 1969, 2443–63. https://doi.org/10.1098/rsnr.1969.0006.

'I don't know if I can adequately convey to you': *White Heat 25*, Marco Pierre White (Mitchell Beazley, 2015), p. 110.

'Marco only came to steal my recipes,' wrote Chef Pierre Koffmann: *White Heat 25*, Marco Pierre White (Mitchell Beazley, 2015), p. 9.

Ramsay, who White would describe as: https://www.youtube.com/watch?v=55B4nJxoUwQ.

fashion brand Burberry's signature check design was adopted: 'Signaling Status with Luxury Goods: The Role of Brand Prominence', Y. J. Han, J. C. Nunes and X. Drèze, *Journal of Marketing*, 2010, 74 (4), 15–30. https://doi:10.1509/jmkg.74.4.015.

African Americans tend to abandon: 'Who drives divergence? Identity signaling, outgroup dissimilarity, and the abandonment of cultural tastes', J. Berger, C. Heath, *Journal of Personality and Social Psychology*, September 2008, 95 (3) 593–607.

'men of birth and quality': *The Honour Code*, Kwame Anthony Appiah (W. W. Norton & Company, 2010). Kindle location 736.

Hundreds of thousands lost their lives . . . 'prefer to die by a bullet': *Status Anxiety*, Alain de Botton (Hamish Hamilton, 2004), p. 115.

David Hume complained it had 'shed much of the best blood in Christendom': *The Honour Code*, Kwame Anthony Appiah (W. W. Norton & Company, 2010). Kindle location 590.

It's argued that one reason it fell from fashion: *The Honour Code*, Kwame Anthony Appiah (W. W. Norton & Company, 2010), Part One: The Duel Dies.

'I remember that some linen-drapers' assistants': *The Honour Code*, Kwame Anthony Appiah (W. W. Norton & Company, 2010). Kindle location 746.

eating of shark fin soup has declined significantly in China: 'Even as China turns away from shark fin soup, the prestige dish is gaining popularity elsewhere in Asia', Simon Denyer, *Washington Post*, 15 February 2018.

'tend to be more prominent in group discussions': *The Psychology of Social*

Status, Joey T. Cheng, Jessica L. Tracy, Cameron Anderson (Springer, 2014), p. 182.

top-ranking members spoke fifteen times: *The Psychology of Social Status*, Joey T. Cheng, Jessica L. Tracy, Cameron Anderson (Springer, 2014), p. 49.

CHAPTER 7

Easter Sunday 2018: https://www.youtube.com/watch?v=Y5zx1xzzi7k.

Turner resigned . . . in a statement she regretted letting 'my emotions': 'Port Authority slams Caren Turner over ethics, after sorry-not-sorry apology', Ted Sherman, NJ.com, 30 January 2019.

'the human expectation that social status can be seized': 'The Appeal of the Primal Leader: Human Evolution and Donald J. Trump', Dan P. McAdams, *Evolutionary Studies in Imaginative Culture* 1, no. 2 (2017), 1–13.

'underpinned by distinct psychological processes': 'The Psychology of Social Status', Joey T. Cheng, Jessica L. Tracy, Cameron Anderson (Springer, 2014), p. 19.

We tend to hold ourselves differently: 'Two signals of social rank: Prestige and dominance are associated with distinct nonverbal displays', Z. Witkower, J. L. Tracy, J. T. Cheng, J. Henrich, *Journal of Personality and Social Psychology*, January 2020; 118 (1) 89–120.

Studies show even children younger than 2: 'Infants distinguish between leaders and bullies', Francesco Margoni, Renée Baillargeon, Luca Surian, *Proceedings of the National Academy of Sciences*, September 2018, 115 (38) E8835-E8843. https://doi.org/10.1073/pnas.1801677115.

have more influence: *The Secret of our Success*, Joseph Henrich (Princeton University Press, 2016), p. 122.

have greater reproductive success: *The Psychology of Social Status*, Joey T. Cheng, Jessica L. Tracy, Cameron Anderson (Springer, 2014), p. 12.

one of the 'most robust predictors': *The Psychology of Social Status*, Joey T. Cheng, Jessica L. Tracy, Cameron Anderson (Springer, 2014), p. 13.

less effective than the prestigious: *The Psychology of Social Status*, Joey T. Cheng, Jessica L. Tracy, Cameron Anderson (Springer, 2014), p. 9.

own interests before the group: *The Psychology of Social Status*, Joey T. Cheng, Jessica L. Tracy, Cameron Anderson (Springer, 2014), p. 11.

less likely to seek advice . . . 'ego defensive aggression': *The Psychology of Social Status*, Joey T. Cheng, Jessica L. Tracy, Cameron Anderson (Springer, 2014), p. 236.

overbearing, like to publicly credit themselves: *The Psychology of Social Status*, Joey T. Cheng, Jessica L. Tracy, Cameron Anderson (Springer, 2014), p. 124.

men and women have picked silhouettes: 'A Dual Model of Leadership and Hierarchy: Evolutionary Synthesis', Mark Van Vugt, Jennifer E. Smith, *Trends in Cognitive Sciences*, 2019, Volume 23, Issue 11, 952–967, ISSN 1364-6613.

entailing the 'induction of fear': *The Psychology of Social Status*, Joey T. Cheng, Jessica L. Tracy, Cameron Anderson (Springer, 2014), pp. 4–12.

'status/reputation concerns': 'Aggress to impress: hostility as an evolved context-dependent strategy', V. Griskevicius, J. M. Tybur, S. W. Gangestad, E. F. Perea, J. R. Shapiro, D. T. Kenrick, *Journal of Personality and Social Psychology*, 2009, May 1996 (5) 980–994. https://doi.org/10.1037/a0013907. PMID: 19379031.

around 90 per cent of global homicides being committed by males, and 70 per cent being their targets: *The Ape that Understood the Universe*, Steve Stewart-Williams (Cambridge University Press, 2018), p. 103.

unemployed, unmarried, poorly educated . . . 'status-driven': *Why We Fight*, Mike Martin (Hurst & Company, 2018). Kindle location 959.

'time after time': 'Shame, guilt, and violence', James Gilligan, *Social Research: An International Quarterly*, 2003, 70 (4) 1149–1180.

working-class 16-year-olds in Britain: *Virtuous Violence*, Alan Fiske and Tage Shakti Rai (Cambridge University Press, 2014), p. 72.

'girls and boys are equally aggressive': 'How Social Media Is Changing Social Networks, Group Dynamics, Democracies, & Gen Z', Jonathan Haidt: https://youtu.be/qhwTZi3Ld3Y.

'women derogate other women's promiscuity': 'Sex differences in victimization and consequences of cyber aggression: An evolutionary perspective', J. P. Wyckoff, D. M. Buss and A. B. Markman, *Evolutionary Behavioral Sciences*, 2019, 13 (3) 254–264.

'the more ambiguous': *Collision of Wills*, Roger V. Gould (University of Chicago Press, 2003), p. 69.

those who talk of principle mean, 'the other party': *Collision of Wills*, Roger V. Gould (University of Chicago Press, 2003), p. 52.

CHAPTER 8

'She got very angry,' he recounted later: *My Twisted World*, Elliot Rodger, accessed at: https://www.documentcloud.org/documents/1173808-elliot-rodger-manifesto.html.

Ted was a gifted scholar ... he applied to take part in an experiment: Unless otherwise noted, my account of this experiment is from *A Mind For Murder*, Alston Chase (W. W. Norton & Company, 2003), chapter 15.

specifically the 'effects of emotional and psychological trauma': *Every Last Tie*, David Kaczynski (Duke University Press, 2016), p. 11.

'Every week for three years ... He never told us': 'My Brother, the Unabomber', Michaela Haas, 25 February 2016, Medium.

'the worst experience of my life': *Every Last Tie*, David Kaczynski (Duke University Press, 2016), p. 12.

'extremely domineering' ... berate him in public ... molest his sister: *Serial Killers*, Peter Vronsky (Berkley, 2004), p. 258.

none of the smart, beautiful young women: *Mindhunter*, John Douglas (Random House, 2017), p. 111.

'I had this love-hate complex with my mother': *Sacrifice Unto Me*, Don West (Pyramid, 1974), p. 191.

she always wanted people to 'look up to her': *Serial Killers*, Peter Vronsky (Berkley, 2004), p. 264.

'the nuclear bomb of the emotions': 'Genocide, Humiliation, and Inferiority: An Interdisciplinary Perspective', Evelin Gerda Lindner, 2009, in *Genocides by the Oppressed: Subaltern Genocide in Theory and Practice*, edited by Nicholas A. Robins and Adam Jones, pp. 138–158.

cause major depressions ... 'including ones characteristic of post-traumatic stress disorder': 'Humiliation: Its Nature and Consequences', Walter J. Torres, Raymond M. Bergner, *Journal of the American Academy of Psychiatry and the Law Online*, June 2010, 38 (2) 195–204.

describes the experience of humiliation as an 'annihilation of the self': 'Humiliation: Its Nature and Consequences', Walter J. Torres, Raymond M. Bergner, *Journal of the American Academy of Psychiatry and the Law Online*, June 2010, 38 (2) 195–204.

'a psychological truth exemplified by the fact that one after another': 'Shame, Guilt, and Violence', J. Gilligan, *Social Research*, 2003, 70 (4), 1149–1180.

humiliation is an absolute purging of status: 'Humiliation: Its Nature and Consequences', Walter J. Torres, Raymond M. Bergner, *Journal of the American Academy of Psychiatry and the Law Online*, June 2010, 38 (2) 195–204.

the 'wish to ward off or eliminate': 'Shame, Guilt, and Violence', J. Gilligan, *Social Research*, 2003, 70 (4), 1149–1180.

Elliot Rodger was said to be on the autism spectrum: 'California killer's family struggled with money, court documents show', Alan Duke, CNN, 28 May 2014.

Ed Kemper had paranoid schizophrenia (although this remains contested): Kemper's defence of insanity rested on this claim, which was disputed at trial by Dr Joel Fort.

'showed indications of schizophrenia': 'My Brother, the Unabomber', Michaela Haas, 25 February 2016, Medium.

'I cut off her head and I humiliated her corpse': *Murder: No Apparent Motive*, HBO documentary, 1984.

'seemed appropriate as much as she'd': *Mindhunter*, John Douglas (Random House, 2017), p. 108.

'He was a man on a mission': *Mindhunter*, John Douglas (Random House, 2017), p. 391.

'someone not born a serial killer but manufactured as one': *Mindhunter*, John Douglas (Random House, 2017), p. 114.

Acute or chronic social rejection has been found: 'Teasing, rejection, and violence: Case studies of the school shootings', M. Leary, R. M. Kowalski, L. Smith and S. Phillips, *Aggressive Behavior*, 2003, 29 202–214.

Kemper had an IQ of 145: *Serial Killers*, Peter Vronsky (Berkley, 2004), p. 259.

during a long drive with police officers: Kemper on Kemper, 2018 documentary.

It's even been suggested his confessions: 'Kemper and Me', Katherine Ramsland, *Psychology Today*, 17 March 2018.

'even the slightest disagreement': *Humiliation*, Marit Svindseth and Paul Crawford (Emerald, 2019). Kindle location 822.

From an early age Robert Hanssen: My account of the Hanssen incident comes from *Spy*, David Wise (Random House, 2013).

Humiliation is also a principal cause of honour killings: *Behave*, Robert Sapolsky (Vintage, 2017), p. 288.

usually with behaviours related to sexuality or being 'too Western': 'When Women Commit Honor Killings', Phyllis Chesler, *Middle East Quarterly*, Fall edition.

One albeit small study of thirty-one killings: 'When Women Commit Honor Killings', Phyllis Chesler, *Middle East Quarterly*, Fall edition.

viewed in their communities 'as heroes': 'Honor Killing Is Not Just A Muslim Problem', Phyllis Chesler, *Tablet*, 16 April 2018.

UN estimate of around five thousand such deaths a year is conservative: Advocacy groups go as high as 20,000.
Behave, Robert Sapolsky (Vintage, 2017), p. 290.

59 per cent of men and 45 per cent of women: *Evolutionary Psychology*, David Buss (Routledge, 2015), p. 310.

'Please listen to me': 'Elliot Rodger's Violent Video Games Like World Of Warcraft To Blame For The Santa Barbara Shooting, Says Glenn Beck', Patrick Frye, *The Inquisitr*, 30 May 2014.

Vice pointed to 'the addictive cycle of gaming': 'A Day at the First Video Game Rehab Clinic in the US', Jagger Gravning, 18 June 2014.

CHAPTER 9

in team tugs of war . . . runners and cyclists: *The Self Illusion*, Bruce Hood (Constable, 2011), pp. 135–136.

Studies find . . . all the time: Lautner, S. C., Patterson, M. S., Spadine, M. N., Boswell, T. G. and Heinrich, K. M. (2021), 'Exploring the social side of CrossFit: a qualitative study', Mental Health and Social Inclusion, Vol. 25 No. 1, pp. 63–75. https://doi.org/10.1108/MHSI-08-2020-0051.

popular 'unofficial mascot': CrossFit's Dirty Little Secret, Eric Roberston, Medium, 20 Sept 2013.

Another mascot-clown: CrossFit Glossary: 71 Terms You Should Know, https://wodreview.com/crossfit-glossary.

CrossFit groups: https://www.livestrong.com/article/13730816-crossfit-statistics/.

tribal subgroups in which we spent most of our time numbered perhaps twenty-five to thirty: Fact-checking note, William Buckner.

happiness isn't closely linked to our socioeconomic status . . . 'respect and admiration within one's local group': 'The Emotional Underpinnings of

Social Status', Conor Steckler and Jessica Tracy, *The Psychology of Social Status*, pp. 347–362, 10.1007/978-1-4939-0867-7_10.

'the greatest rush of positive emotions': *Why We Fight*, Mike Martin (Hurst & Company, 2018). Kindle location 704.

'political values played a very minor part in sustaining their motivation for combat': *Not Born Yesterday*, Hugo Mercier (Princeton University Press, 2020), p. 130.

'Competition' is defined as happening when people's outcomes . . . Research on this matter is mixed: 'Driven to Win: Rivalry, Motivation, and Performance', G. J. Kilduff, *Social Psychological and Personality Science*, 2014, 5 (8) 944–952.

moderate levels are thought to increase diligence and productivity: *The Weirdest People in the World*, Joseph Henrich (Penguin, 2020), p. 348.

Rivalry emerges over time between parties who've jostled repeatedly: 'Driven to Win: Rivalry, Motivation, and Performance', G. J. Kilduff, *Social Psychological and Personality Science*, 2014, 5 (8): 944–952.

Research shows that when players compete with someone they consider a rival, they 'feel their status is at stake': 'Do status hierarchies benefit groups? A bounded functionalist account of status', C. Anderson and R. Willer, 2014, in *The Psychology of Social Status*, edited by J. T. Cheng, J. L. Tracy and C. Anderson (Springer, 2014), pp.47–70.

Rivalry between companies is highest when they're competing in the same domain: 'The Psychology of Rivalry: A Relationally Dependent Analysis of Competition', Gavin Kilduff, Hillary Elfenbein and Barry Staw, *Academy of Management Journal*, 2010, 53, 943–969. 10.5465/AMJ.2010.54533171.

when Apple CEO Steve Jobs encounters a senior executive from Microsoft: https://www.youtube.com/watch?v=yleJZ3hVcyM

CHAPTER 10

world's 3.6 billion users of social media: www.statista.com/statistics/278414/number-of-worldwide-social-network-users/.

A 2019 survey of nearly two thousand US smartphone users: https://www.asurion.com/about/press-releases/americans-check-their-phones-96-times-a-day/.

another survey, of 1,200 users: https://rootmetrics.com/en-US/content/rootmetrics-survey-results-are-in-mobile-consumer-lifestyles.

ten-week class . . . his students had amassed sixteen million users: 'The Class That Built Apps, and Fortunes', Miguel Helft, *New York Times*, 7 May 2011.

aged 10 . . . 'I learned names': *Persuasive Technology*, B. J. Fogg (Morgan Kaufmann, 2003). Kindle location 169.

'Someday in the future': *Persuasive Technology*, B. J. Fogg (Morgan Kaufmann, 2003). Kindle location 2154.

'Traditional media, from bumper stickers to radio spots': *Persuasive Technology*, B. J. Fogg (Morgan Kaufmann, 2003). Kindle location 286.

'When you pack a mobile persuasive technology': *Persuasive Technology*, B. J. Fogg (Morgan Kaufmann, 2003). Kindle location 2180.

'a toll booth': 'The Formula for Phone Addiction Might Double As a Cure', Simone Stolzoff, *Wired*, 1 February 2018.

The model said a person is compelled to act when three forces: 'A behavior model for persuasive design', B. J. Fogg, 2009, 40. 10.1145/1541948.1541999.

'there was nothing useful you could do with LinkedIn': 'The Binge Breaker', Bianca Bosker, *The Atlantic*, 8 October 2016.

'To strengthen an existing behaviour': *Persuasive Technology*, B. J. Fogg (Morgan Kaufmann, 2003). Kindle location 750.

Eleonora 'Lele' Pons was reportedly charging . . . fellow YouTuber Zach King: Instagram Rich List 2020, www.hopperhq.com/blog/instagram-rich-list/niche/influencer/.

According to the *Washington Post*, top YouTube stars earn: 'Tiptoeing on Social Media's Tightrope', Sarah Ellison, *Washington Post*, 3 October 2019.

Notices about ethical concerns were woven carefully: 'The Facts: BJ Fogg & Persuasive Technology', B. J. Fogg, Medium, 3 August 2018.

Facebook's former vice president of user growth, Chamath Palihapitiya: 'The Tech Industry's War on Kids', Richard Freed, Medium, 12 March 2018.

CHAPTER 11

His 1976 live album, *Wings Over America*, featured five Beatles songs. He credited them to McCartney-Lennon: 'The Ballad of Paul and Yoko', Gilbert Garcia, *Salon*, 18 June 2009.

Yoko Ono said no: 'We can work it out, Sir Paul tells angry Yoko', Adam Sherwin, *The Times*, 18 December 2002.

Back in the U.S. featured nineteen Beatles songs: 'The Ballad of Paul and Yoko', Gilbert Garcia, *Salon*, 18 June 2009.

Ono wasn't having it. She instructed her lawyer to release a statement. McCartney's actions, it said, were 'ridiculous, absurd and petty': 'Ono! You Can't Do That Paul!', Uncredited author, *NME*, 16 December 2002.

reportedly removed his name from the Plastic Ono Band's: 'Beatles Credit Feud Continues', Gil Kaufman, *Rolling Stone*, 16 December 2003.

It wasn't until 2003 that Ono and McCartney reached a truce: 'McCartney makes up with Ono', BBC News, 1 June 2003.

But even in 2015 he was still grumbling about it: 'Paul McCartney', Alex Bilmes, *Esquire*, 2 July 2015.

'There was no point': *Status*, Cecilia L. Ridgeway (Russell Sage Foundation, 2015), p.59.

survey of more than seventy thousand people: *Possessed*, Bruce Hood (Penguin, 2019), p. 29.

Professor Michael Norton . . . 'All the way up the income-wealth spectrum': 'The Reason Many Ultrarich People Aren't Satisfied With Their Wealth', Joe Pinsker, *The Atlantic*, 4 December 2018.

Tom Cruise . . . Madonna: 'The Most Outrageous Celebrity Diva Demands', Sarah Biddlecombe, *Daily Telegraph*, 16 November 2014.

'From Ariana Grande to Beyonce, Which Star is the Biggest Diva of Them All?', Kate Wills, *The Sun*, 27 April 2019.

The Czarina, Anna of Russia, insisted: 'Fashion, Sumptuary Laws, and Business', Herman Freudenberger, *Business History Review*, 1963, vol. 37, issue 1–2, pp. 37–48.

Imelda Marcos: 'Shoes, Jewels, and Monets: The Immense Ill-Gotten Wealth of Imelda Marcos', Catherine A. Traywick, *Foreign Policy*, 16 January 2014.

'The Weird World of Imelda Marcos', David McNeill, *Independent*, 25 February 2006.

'11 Bizarre Things You Didn't Know About Imelda Marcos', Valerie Caulin, *Culture Trip*, 14 November 2017.

The Kingmaker, documentary, 2020.

Prince Andrew was attacked for spending tens of thousands: 'Andrew Wasted

Thousands Using Helicopters Like Taxis, say Officials', Andrew Johnson, *Independent*, 23 January 2005.

a preposterous feast in Westminster Hall: *Old Court Customs and Modern Court Rule*, Hon. Mrs Armytage (Richard Bentley & Son, 1883), pp. 37–47.

George IV . . . determined his celebration: https://brightonmuseums.org.uk/discover/2015/02/26/george-ivs-coronation/.

When the CEOs of Ford, Chrysler and General Motors: *The Dark Side of Transformational Leadership*, Dennis Tourish (Routledge, 2013), p. 92.

he'd had the director's kitchens relocated: 'Ex-RBS chief Goodwin Faces Legal Challenge to £693k Pension', Graeme Wearden, Jill Treanor, *Guardian*, 26 February 2009.

'Lifting the Lid on Fred "The Shred" Goodwin's Greed and Recklessness', Julie Carpenter, *Daily Express*, 27 August 2011.

people in lower corporate ranks tend to 'habitually exaggerate': *The Dark Side of Transformational Leadership*, Dennis Tourish (Routledge, 2013), p. 81.

difficult, overly negative or not 'team players': *The Dark Side of Transformational Leadership*, Dennis Tourish (Routledge, 2013), p. 79.

85 per cent of employees: *The Dark Side of Transformational Leadership*, Dennis Tourish (Routledge, 2013), p. 79.

'frequently shocked': *The Dark Side of Transformational Leadership*, Dennis Tourish (Routledge, 2013), p. 78.

'perfumed trap': *The Dark Side of Transformational Leadership*, Dennis Tourish (Routledge, 2013), p. 77.

A study of 451 CEOs: *The Dark Side of Transformational Leadership*, Dennis Tourish (Routledge, 2013), p. 81.

'During workshops, many have swapped': *The Dark Side of Transformational Leadership*, Dennis Tourish (Routledge, 2013), p. 89.

those with the 'least compliant' followers: *The Dark Side of Transformational Leadership*, Dennis Tourish (Routledge, 2013), p. 87.

psychologists persuaded fifteen highly identifiable American celebrities: 'Being a Celebrity: A Phenomenology of Fame', Donna Rockwell and David Giles, *Journal of Phenomenological Psychology*, 2009, 40, 178–210. 10.1163/004726 609X12482630041889.

CHAPTER 12

'egalitarian lifestyles of the hunter-gatherers exist because': Paul Bloom, *Just Babies* (Bodley Head, 2013), p. 68.

One recent study: 'Status does not predict stress: Women in an egalitarian hunter–gatherer society', P. Fedurek, L. Lacroix, J. Lehmann, et al., *Evolutionary Human Sciences*, 2, 2020, E44. doi:10.1017/ehs.2020.44.

highly sensitive to signs of 'big shot' behaviour and hotly policing it: Paul Bloom, *Just Babies* (Bodley Head, 2013), p. 68.

Our Inner Ape, Frans de Waal (Granta, 2005), p. 74.

The term 'big shot behaviour', in this context, is from Polly Wiessner, quoted in *Moral Origins*, Christopher Boehm (Basic Books, 2012), p. 70.

'militant egalitarianism': *The Goodness Paradox*, Richard Wrangham (Profile, 2019). Kindle location 3552.

Dr Elizabeth Cashdan writes that: *The Goodness Paradox*, Richard Wrangham (Profile, 2019). Kindle location 2587.

asking of his kill, 'What is it?': *Just Babies*, Paul Bloom (Bodley Head, 2013), p. 69.

In Inuit camps: *The Goodness Paradox*, Richard Wrangham (Profile, 2019). Kindle location 2600.

'norm violations by high-status individuals': *Behave*, Robert Sapolsky (Vintage, 2017), p. 302.

Studies in the developed world find we too prefer tattle: *The Oxford Handbook of Gossip and Reputation* (Oxford University Press, 2019), p. 179.

finding participants took pleasure in the felling of a 'tall poppy': *Evolutionary Psychology*, David Buss (Routledge, 2015), p. 373.

often centred around villages, called chiefdoms: *The Weirdest People in the World*, Joseph Henrich (Penguin, 2020), p. 116.

increasingly defined by kin and lineage: you could be born into: *The Weirdest People in the World*, Joseph Henrich (Penguin, 2020), pp. 380-470

They'd often forbid intermarriage with lower clans: *The Weirdest People in the World*, Joseph Henrich (Penguin, 2020), p. 117.

They'd lead the chiefdom, either via a council of elders or a single ruler: *The Weirdest People in the World*, Joseph Henrich (Penguin, 2020), p. 116.

immeasurably greater than that which existed in earlier eras: Note from fact-check, William Buckner: 'hunter-gatherers did have accumulations of resources, just less so'.

3,500-year-old tombs in Greece . . . Over in Chile, elite mummies: *The Rise and Fall of the Third Chimpanzee*, Jared Diamond (Vintage, 1991). Kindle location 3283–3295.

an experiment in which participants played in three online worlds: *Blueprint*, Nicholas Christakis (Little Brown, 2019), p. 108.

Possessed, Bruce Hood (Penguin, 2019), pp. 111–112.

around half of his British subjects holding a positive opinion: https://yougov. co.uk/topics/politics/articles-reports/2018/11/14/prince-charles-first-line-throne-only-seventh-popu.

CHAPTER 13

It is 1974 and the anthropologist Professor Jerome Barkow: *Darwin, Sex and Status*, Jerome Barkow (University of Toronto Press, 1989), pp. 217–227.

One study into 'national narcissism' asked thousands of students: 'We Made History: Citizens of 35 Countries Overestimate Their Nation's Role in World History', Franklin M. Zaromb, James H. Liu, Dario Páez, Katja Hanke, Adam L. Putnam, Henry L. Roediger, *Journal of Applied Research in Memory and Cognition*, Volume 7, Issue 4, 2018, pp. 521–528.

A study tracking happiness in Britain over the last two centuries: 'Historical analysis of national subjective wellbeing using millions of digitized books', T. T. Hills, E. Proto, D. Sgroi et al., *Nature Human Behaviour* 3, 2019, 1271–1275.

author Laurie Lee who recalled in his 1920s classroom, 'a wall of maps': *Down in the Valley*, Laurie Lee (Penguin, 2019), chapter 6.

In one study, 5-year-olds were given a coloured T-shirt: 'Consequences of "Minimal" Group Affiliations in Children', Y. Dunham, A. S. Baron and S. Carey, *Child Development* 82, 2011, 793–811.

CHAPTER 14

At the time of writing: https://www.lse.ac.uk/News/Latest-news-from-LSE/2021/g-July-21/A-fresh-look-at-the-origins-of-moralising-religions.

3,000 castes and 25,000 subcastes: 'What is India's caste system?', Soutik Biswas, bbc.co.uk, 19 June 2019.

Caste didn't only define a player's occupation but their: *Private Truths, Public Lies*, Timur Kuran (Harvard University Press, 1998), p. 159.

found in the Laws of Manu, which date: *Private Truths, Public Lies*, Timur Kuran (Harvard University Press, 1998), p. 240.

'grave anxiety' and 'horror' at having 'any kind of contact': 'A Historical Analysis of Segregation of Untouchable Castes in North India from circa AD600–1200', Malay Neerav, *Amity Business Review*, Vol. 17, No.2, July–December 2016.

if the shadow of an untouchable fell over a teacher's meal: *A Little History of Religion*, Richard Holloway (Yale University Press, 2016), p. 170.

lived in separate colonies and didn't share wells: 'What is India's caste system?', Soutik Biswas, bbc.co.uk, 19 June 2019.

In Mehrana, a village near New Delhi: *Private Truths, Public Lies*, Timur Kuran (Harvard University Press, 1998), p. 158.

According to the *National Geographic*: 'India's "Untouchables" Face Violence, Discrimination', *National Geographic*, Hillary Mayell, 2 June 2003.

novelist V. S. Naipaul writes of a businessman: *Private Truths, Public Lies*, Timur Kuran (Harvard University Press, 1998), p. 163.

'by ostracising a peer': *Private Truths, Public Lies*, Timur Kuran (Harvard University Press, 1998), p. 163.

about a third accepting they'd earned untouchability: *Private Truths, Public Lies*, Timur Kuran (Harvard University Press, 1998), p. 237.

untouchable writer Hazari speaks the words of a true player: *Private Truths, Public Lies*, Timur Kuran (Harvard University Press, 1998), p. 237.

more than 65 per cent of people not wanting the 'highest status rank': *The Psychology of Social Status*, Joey T. Cheng, Jessica L. Tracy, Cameron Anderson (Springer, 2014), p. 172.

What creates revolutionary conditions: *Revolutions*, Jack A. Goldstone (Oxford University Press, 2013), pp. 16–17.

'indeed,' writes Goldstone, 'in most revolutions': *Revolutions*, Jack A. Goldstone (Oxford University Press, 2013), p. 10.

Such dynamics drove Tunisia's 'Jasmine Revolution': *Revolutions*, Jack A. Goldstone (Oxford University Press, 2013), pp. 117–119.

Goldstone finds a predictable precursor to societal collapse to be 'elite-overproduction' . . . Goldstone finds these dynamics in: http://peterturchin.com/cliodynamica/intra-elite-competition-a-key-concept-for-understanding-the-dynamics-of-complex-societies/.

those who rule them can become tamed and toppled by status play . . . Professor Yuval Noah Harari describes this as the 'imperial cycle': *Sapiens*, Yuval Noah Harari (Vintage, 2015), p. 246.

'bewildering mosaic of warring kingdoms': *Sapiens*, Yuval Noah Harari (Vintage, 2015), pp. 247–248.

Most humans alive today are playing by the rules and symbols: *Sapiens*, Yuval Noah Harari (Vintage, 2015), p. 235.

CHAPTER 15

Nobody gets to choose exactly what kind of mind they have: For a great overview of the science of personality, see: *Personality*, Daniel Nettle (Oxford University Press, 2009).

Researchers find 'the jobs in which we spend a large portion of our lives': *Personality Psychology*, Larsen, Buss and Wisjeimer (McGraw Hill, 2013), p. 147.

'not just statistically significant, it is massive': *Blueprint*, Robert Plomin (Penguin, 2018), p. viii.

'tend to be ambitious' and 'are prepared to work very hard': *Personality*, Daniel Nettle (Oxford University Press, 2009), p. 83.

'most reliable personality predictor of occupational success across the board': *Personality*, Daniel Nettle (Oxford University Press, 2009), p. 143.

'because of all the broken crack vials littering the streets': *American Individualisms*, Adrie Kusserow (Palgrave Macmillan, 2004), p. 4.

a 'safe and neat community' with a 'great deal of pride': *American Individualisms*, Adrie Kusserow (Palgrave Macmillan, 2004), pp. 71–72.

'spoiled', 'fresh', 'whiny': *American Individualisms*, Adrie Kusserow (Palgrave Macmillan, 2004), p. 26.

'you shouldn't pay too much attention': *American Individualisms*, Adrie Kusserow (Palgrave Macmillan, 2004), p. 37.

a 4-year-old spilled her grape juice: *American Individualisms*, Adrie Kusserow (Palgrave Macmillan, 2004), p. 55.

'Examples of the child's lower status were manifested in': *American Individualisms*, Adrie Kusserow (Palgrave Macmillan, 2004), pp. 51–52.

'holding their own in a jungle': *American Individualisms*, Adrie Kusserow (Palgrave Macmillan, 2004), p. 4.

'try things out,' 'stand out,': *American Individualisms*, Adrie Kusserow (Palgrave Macmillan, 2004), p. 73.

'I want my kids to definitely strive for everything': *American Individualisms*, Adrie Kusserow (Palgrave Macmillan, 2004), p. 76.

'opened out into the world, into a successful career': *American Individualisms*, Adrie Kusserow (Palgrave Macmillan, 2004), p. 82.

Parents emphasised 'the delicacy of the child's self': *American Individualisms*, Adrie Kusserow (Palgrave Macmillan, 2004), p. 171.

on reading a story in which a 12-year-old was admonished: *American Individualisms*, Adrie Kusserow (Palgrave Macmillan, 2004), p. 103.

'gives her a certain status': *American Individualisms*, Adrie Kusserow (Palgrave Macmillan, 2004), p. 106.

Kusserow noted various techniques . . . 'My basic feeling': *American Individualisms*, Adrie Kusserow (Palgrave Macmillan, 2004), pp. 103–104.

'I'm not interested in the normal': *American Individualisms*, Adrie Kusserow (Palgrave Macmillan, 2004), p. 82.

'What seems lacking for some Parkside children': *American Individualisms*, Adrie Kusserow (Palgrave Macmillan, 2004), p. xii.

a result of alterations to a region of the brain: *The Popularity Illusion*, Mitch Prinstein (Ebury, 2018). Kindle location 826.

'become increasingly aware': *Inventing Ourselves*, Sarah-Jayne Blakemore (Transworld, 2018), p. 25.

the presence of an 'imaginary audience': I first read this term in Blakemore's book. She, in turn, credits the psychologist David Elkind.
Inventing Ourselves, Sarah-Jayne Blakemore (Transworld, 2018) p. 26.

'remains quite high even in adulthood': *Inventing Ourselves*, Sarah-Jayne Blakemore (Transworld, 2018), p. 27.

'By the time we are thirteen': *The Popularity Illusion*, Mitch Prinstein (Ebury, 2018). Kindle location 861.

'critical window for acquiring status': *The Psychology of Social Status*, Joey T. Cheng, Jessica L. Tracy, Cameron Anderson (Springer, 2014), p. 191.

teeth are yanked out: *Virtuous Violence*, Alan Fiske and Tage Shakti Rai (Cambridge University Press, 2014), p. 180.

Initiates into the Bimin-Kuskusmin . . . 'struggle and shriek': *Virtuous Violence*, Alan Fiske and Tage Shakti Rai (Cambridge University Press, 2014), p. 181.

'the mutilated individual is removed': *Virtuous Violence*, Alan Fiske and Tage Shakti Rai (Cambridge University Press, 2014), p. 184.

'all those sticks that you were beaten with': *Virtuous Violence*, Alan Fiske and Tage Shakti Rai (Cambridge University Press, 2014), p. 183.

Students can be kicked . . . 'The claim to belonging to a superior "elite"': *Virtuous Violence*, Alan Fiske and Tage Shakti Rai (Cambridge University Press, 2014), p. 182.

'Social mammals are status seeking': *Blueprint*, Nicholas Christakis (Little Brown, 2019), p. 283.

a team led by anthropologist Professor Don Merten: 'Burnout as Cheerleader: The Cultural Basis for Prestige and Privilege in Junior High School', D. Merten, *Anthropology & Education Quarterly*, 1996, 27 (1) 51–70.

paper by Patrick J. Schiltz: 'On Being a Happy, Healthy, and Ethical Member of an Unhappy, Unhealthy, and Unethical Profession', Patrick J. Schiltz, *Vanderbilt Law Review*, 1999, 52, 871.

CHAPTER 16

Maranda Dynda knows this: Interview with author and additional sources: www.voicesforvaccines.org/i-was-duped-by-the-anti-vaccine-movement/ www.npr.org/transcripts/743195213?t=1611143785309 www.publicradioeast.org/post/when-it-comes-vaccines-and-autism-why-it-hard-refute-misinformation.

members of our group are more intelligent: 'How group identification distorts beliefs', Maria Paula Cacault, Manuel Grieder, *Journal of Economic Behavior & Organization*, Volume 164, 2019, pp. 63–76.

harder to reason logically over arguments that contradict our group's beliefs: '(Ideo)Logical Reasoning: Ideology Impairs Sound Reasoning', A. Gampa,

S. P. Wojcik, M. Motyl, B. A. Nosek, P. H. Ditto, *Social Psychological and Personality Science*, 2019, 10 (8): 1075–1083.

processes opinions we already agree with as if they're facts: 'That's My Truth: Evidence for Involuntary Opinion Confirmation', M. Gilead, M. Sela, A. Maril, *Social Psychological and Personality Science*, 2019, 10 (3) 393–401.

stupider, more biased and less moral and less trustworthy: 'Taking the High Ground: The Impact of Social Status on the Derogation of Ideological Opponents', Aiden Gregg, Nikhila Mahadevan and Constantine Sedikides, *Social Cognition*, 2017, 36, 10.1521/soco.2018.36.1.43.

When psychologists study how people's religious, political and social identities: *The Intelligence Trap*, David Robson (Hodder, 2020). Kindle location 999–1016.

'Coalition mindedness': 'Coalitional Instincts', John Tooby, *Edge*, 22 November 2017.

84 per cent of the world's population identifies as religious: https://www.pewforum.org/2012/12/18/global-religious-landscape-exec/.

it's why a study of 11,672 organ donations: *The Consuming Instinct*, Gad Saad (Prometheus, 2011), p. 100.

people were more likely to believe God could change physical laws: 'Immutable morality: Even God could not change some moral facts', Madeline Reinecke and Zach Horne 2018, 10.31234/osf.io/yqm48.

For the Malagasy people in Madagascar: *Taboo: A Study of Malagasy Customs and Beliefs* (Oslo University Press, 1960), pp. 89, 117, 197.

Adolescent boys of the Marind: *Mixed Messages*, Robert Paul (University of Chicago Press, 2015), pp. 46–49.

'institutionalised sodomy': *The Origins and Role of Same-Sex Relations in Human Societies*, James Neill (McFarland, 2011), p. 48.

Among the people of the Moose . . . 'all concerned': *Evolutionary Psychology*, David Buss (Routledge, 2015), p. 8.

who was voted Woman of the Millennium: 'There's Something About Marie', Ros Coward, *Guardian*, 25 January 1999.

honoured on special Royal Mail stamps in 2008: 'Royal Mail Criticised for Stamp Honouring "Racist" Marie Stopes', John Bingham, *Daily Telegraph*, 14 October 2008.

'our race is weakened': *Married Love*, Marie Stopes (Oxford University Press, 2004), p. xv.

'it is the urgent duty of the community': *Radiant Motherhood*, Marie Stopes, via: https://www.gutenberg.org/files/45711/45711-h/45711-h.htm.

'Ours is one continued struggle against a degradation': *Subliminal*, Leonard Mlodinow (Penguin, 2012), p. 157.

'To say that one had "seen the light" is a poor description': *The God That Failed*, Richard Crossman (editor) (Harper Colophon, 1963), p. 23.

CHAPTER 17

Louise Armstrong, has since written of the 'staggering array': *The Day Care Ritual Abuse Moral Panic*, Mary de Young (McFarland, 2004), p. 16.

Pazder told journalists, 'in the beginning I wondered': *We Believe The Children*, Richard Beck (PublicAffairs, 2015), p. 27.

A survey of more than two thousand: *The Day Care Ritual Abuse Moral Panic*, Mary de Young (McFarland, 2004), p. 55.

Dr Roland Summit described as, 'the most serious threat to children': *The Day Care Ritual Abuse Moral Panic*, Mary de Young (McFarland, 2004), p. 8.

the 'Rule of P's': *The Day Care Ritual Abuse Moral Panic*, Mary de Young (McFarland, 2004), p. 47.

'the more illogical and incredible' . . . 'very few children, no more than two or three per thousand': 'The child sexual abuse accommodation syndrome', R. C. Summit, *Child Abuse and Neglect*, 1983, 7, 177–193.

'became the banner of that decade': *The Day Care Ritual Abuse Moral Panic*, Mary de Young (McFarland, 2004), p. 18.

fear of the dark: *The Day Care Ritual Abuse Moral Panic*, Mary de Young (McFarland, 2004), p. 33.

with a 'wink response test' . . . 'microtraumas': *We Believe The Children*, Richard Beck (PublicAffairs, 2015), pp. 58–59.

charging $455 a time: *We Believe The Children*, Richard Beck (PublicAffairs, 2015), p. 60.

Heger told a young girl, 'I don't want to hear any more "no's"': *We Believe The Children*, Richard Beck (PublicAffairs, 2015), p. 60.

the repeated and clear denials of a boy called Keith: *We Believe The Children*, Richard Beck (PublicAffairs, 2015), p. 46.

'You're an absolute trooper'... 'We know there were naked games': *Conviction: American Panic*, podcast, 2020, episode 3.

being rewarded with praise for lying: *Conviction: American Panic*, podcast, 2020, episode 5.

Children had had their eyes stapled shut: This paragraph is a compilation from all noted sources.

'Abundant with clinical terms': *The Day Care Ritual Abuse Moral Panic*, Mary de Young (McFarland, 2004), p. 93.

In 1984 the Justice Department financed: *Satan's Silence*, Debbie Nathan and Michael Snedeker (iUniverse, 2001), pp. 126–129.

former officer Robert Hicks, 'attend a few cult seminars': *The Day Care Ritual Abuse Moral Panic*, Mary de Young (McFarland, 2004), pp. 52–53.

In one single case, in Wenatchee, Washington: *We Believe The Children*, Richard Beck (PublicAffairs, 2015), p. xxii.

ten million viewers . . . 'used in worshipping the devil': *Conviction: American Panic*, podcast, 2020, episode 5.

the highest-rated televised documentary ever: 'The History of Satanic Panic in the US – and Why it's Not Over Yet', Aja Romano, *Vox*, 30 October 2016.

David Shaw, would go on to win a Pulitzer Prize: 'Is Shaken Baby Syndrome the New Satanic Panic?' Amy Nicholson, *LA Weekly*, 9 April 2015.

one daycare centre was pelted with eggs: *We Believe The Children*, Richard Beck (PublicAffairs, 2015), p. 62.

Parents dug in its grounds: *The Day Care Ritual Abuse Moral Panic*, Mary de Young (McFarland, 2004), p. 35.

'definitely or probably guilty': *The Day Care Ritual Abuse Moral Panic*, Mary de Young (McFarland, 2004), p. 36.

When she was bailed . . . Peggy was shunned: *The Day Care Ritual Abuse Moral Panic*, Mary de Young (McFarland, 2004), p. 36.

Their case alone cost 15 million dollars: *The Day Care Ritual Abuse Moral Panic*, Mary de Young (McFarland, 2004), p. 41.

writes de Young, 'took to the national conference': *The Day Care Ritual Abuse Moral Panic*, Mary de Young (McFarland, 2004), p. 44.

'to this small cadre of moral entrepreneurs': *The Day Care Ritual Abuse Moral Panic*, Mary de Young (McFarland, 2004), p. 44.

190 people were formally charged . . . at least eighty-three convicted: *We Believe The Children*, Richard Beck (PublicAffairs, 2015), p. xxi.

almost entirely on the testimony of a 3-year-old: *We Believe The Children*, Richard Beck (PublicAffairs, 2015), p. 115.

Frances and Dan Keller of Austin, Texas: 'The History of Satanic Panic in the US – and Why it's Not Over Yet', Aja Romano, *Vox*, 30 October 2016.

'triumph of ideology over science': *The Day Care Ritual Abuse Moral Panic*, Mary de Young (McFarland, 2004), p. 51.

'may actually be difficult to overestimate': *The Day Care Ritual Abuse Moral Panic*, Mary de Young (McFarland, 2004), p. 51.

Political scientist Dr Ross Cheit has even gone so far: *The Witch-Hunt Narrative*, Ross Cheit (Oxford University Press, 2014).

But Cheit's thesis has come under serious criticism: 'A Critical Evaluation of the Factual Accuracy and Scholarly Foundations of *The Witch-Hunt Narrative*', J. M. Wood, D. Nathan, R. Beck, K. Hampton, *Journal of Interpersonal Violence*, March 2017, 32 (6): 897–925.

'The Methodology of *The Witch-Hunt Narrative*: A Question of Evidence – Evidence Questioned', K. M. Staller, *Journal of Interpersonal Violence*, March 2017, 32 (6) 853–874.

We Believe The Children, Richard Beck (PublicAffairs, 2015), pp. 248–252.

in 2013 Mouw testified . . . 'no doubt' her hymen was normal: 'A Critical Evaluation of the Factual Accuracy and Scholarly Foundations of *The Witch-Hunt Narrative*', J. M. Wood, D. Nathan, R. Beck, K. Hampton, *Journal of Interpersonal Violence*, March 2017, 32 (6) 897–925.

'Sometimes it takes time to figure out what you don't know': *We Believe The Children*, Richard Beck (PublicAffairs, 2015), p. 248.

'When a group of people make something sacred': *The Righteous Mind*, Jonathan Haidt (Penguin, 2012), p. 28.

CHAPTER 18

lunch by the beach in La Jolla, California: https://worldhatchlearning. wordpress.com/2018/09/22/the-origins-of-web-community-the-well/.

'one of the bibles of my generation' . . . 'like Google in paperback form': Steve Jobs, Commencement address at Stanford University, 12 June 2005.

It was launched to the public in 1985, on April Fools' Day: *The Well*, Katie Hafner (Carroll & Graf, 2001), p. 18.

'The idea was just about as simple': *The Well*, Katie Hafner (Carroll & Graf, 2001), p. 7.

'baby boomers in their late thirties and early forties': 'The Epic Saga of The Well', Katie Hafner, *Wired*, 1 May 2005.

when user-numbers approached five hundred: *The Well*, Katie Hafner (Carroll & Graf, 2001), pp. 33–34.

His log-in was Grandma: *The Well*, Katie Hafner (Carroll & Graf, 2001), p. 34.

Smith had been homeless for around twenty years: 'Censorship In Cyberspace', Mark Ethan Smith, www.angelfire.com/bc3/dissident/.

living in near-poverty in Berkeley: *The Well*, Katie Hafner (Carroll & Graf, 2001), p. 34.

'white male clan': 'Censorship In Cyberspace', Mark Ethan Smith, www.angelfire.com/bc3/dissident/.

Smith would start brutal 'flamewars': 'The Epic Saga of The Well', Katie Hafner, *Wired*, 1 May 2005.

'Smith had a knack for finding people's': *The Well*, Katie Hafner (Carroll & Graf, 2001), p. 42.

'penis bearing morons': http://shikan.org/bjones/Usenet.Hist/Nethist/0020.html.

'the same kind of guys who take time off': 'Complaint and the World-Building Politics of Feminist Moderation', Bonnie Washick, *Signs: Journal of Women in Culture and Society*, 2020, 45:3, 555–580.

'Somebody has to defend the rapists': http://shikan.org/bjones/Usenet.Hist/Nethist/0020.html.

He threatened to track down and sue: 'Complaint and the World-Building Politics of Feminist Moderation', Bonnie Washick, *Signs: Journal of Women in Culture and Society*, 2020, 45:3, 555–580.

'sadists and bigots will not stop torturing people': https://groups.google.com/g/misc.legal/c/NLUs2u11X_s/m/NJbxBjEWbEAJ.

'Suck AIDS and DIE!': https://www.linux.it/~md/usenet/legends3.html.

One complained Smith was being 'patently offensive for the sheer pleasure': https://groups.google.com/g/soc.women/c/6gj8voK9ZHQ/m/_Qj5U8woK1gJ.

'I never became a man, nor do I wish to be known as a man': Censorship In Cyberspace, Mark Ethan Smith, www.angelfire.com/bc3/dissident/.

'diminutive', insisting on the 'right to equal terms': 'Complaint and the

World-Building Politics of Feminist Moderation', Bonnie Washick, *Signs: Journal of Women in Culture and Society*, 2020, 45:3, 555–580.

were respected by many women of The Well and a few of the men: 'Censorship In Cyberspace', Mark Ethan Smith, www.angelfire.com/bc3/dissident/.

One wrote: 'According to Mark, you have to call me by a name': 'Complaint and the World-Building Politics of Feminist Moderation', Bonnie Washick, *Signs: Journal of Women in Culture and Society,* 2020, 45:3, 555–580.

'The more defined The Well became': *The Well*, Katie Hafner (Carroll & Graf, 2001), pp. 42–43.

'You are a sick individual': https://groups.google.com/g/soc.women/c/6g-j8voK9ZHQ/m/_Qj5U8woK1gJ.

Some tried to introduce special code: 'Complaint and the World-Building Politics of Feminist Moderation', Bonnie Washick, *Signs: Journal of Women in Culture and Society*, 2020, 45:3, 555–580.

'Just because she was obnoxious': *The Well*, Katie Hafner (Carroll & Graf, 2001), p. 37.

In October 1986, Smith was told by a new manager: *The Well*, Katie Hafner (Carroll & Graf, 2001), p. 43.

According to Smith, hundreds of thousands of his words: 'Censorship In Cyberspace', Mark Ethan Smith, www.angelfire.com/bc3/dissident/.

described his foes as a 'mob': 'Censorship In Cyberspace', Mark Ethan Smith, www.angelfire.com/bc3/dissident/.

In an undated essay: 'Censorship In Cyberspace', Mark Ethan Smith, www.angelfire.com/bc3/dissident/.

When neuroscientist Professor Sarah Gimbel presented forty people: 'Neural correlates of maintaining one's political beliefs in the face of counterevidence', Jonas Kaplan, Sarah Gimbel and Sam Harris, *Scientific Reports*, 2016, 6. 39589. 10.1038/srep39589.

'you were walking through the forest and came across a bear': 'The Neuroscience of Changing Your Mind', *You Are Not So Smart*, David McRaney, Episode 93, 13 January 2017.

participants who were offered more points for discriminating blues: *The Case Against Reality*, Donald Hoffman (Penguin, 2019), p. 70.

Psychologists had participants decide if protestors in a video: '"They Saw a Protest": Cognitive Illiberalism and the Speech-Conduct Distinction',

February 5, 2011, Dan M. Kahan, David A. Hoffman, Donald Braman, Danieli Evans Peterman and Jeffrey John Rachlinski, *Cultural Cognition Project Working Paper* No. 63, *Stanford Law Review*, Vol. 64, 2012, Temple University Legal Studies Research Paper No. 2011–17.

become '"another manifestation of the rich peasant mentality"': *Red Guard*, Gordon A. Bennett and Ronald N. Montaperto (Allen & Unwin, 1971), p. 5.

'the extroverts don't disguise their disdain': *Snoop*, Sam Gosling (Profile, 2008), p. 127.

we often demand unreasonably high evidence: A fuller exploration into these biases features in my book *The Heretics* (Picador, 2013), in chapter 6: 'The Invisible Actor at the Centre of the World'.

'People do great wrong': 'Questioning the Banality of Evil', Steve Reicher and Alex Haslam, *The Psychologist*, January 2008, Vol. 21, pp. 16–19.

anthropologists Professors Alan Page Fiske and Tage Shakti Rai find that 'when people hurt or kill someone': *Virtuous Violence*, Alan Fiske and Tage Shakti Rai (Cambridge University Press, 2014), p. xxii.

'perceived as a potential threat or contaminant to the in-group', such acts are seen as 'morally praiseworthy': *Virtuous Violence*, Alan Fiske and Tage Shakti Rai (Cambridge University Press, 2014), p. 19.

The Marind of South New Guinea: *Mixed Messages*, Robert Paul (University of Chicago Press, 2015), pp. 46–49.

The women of the Marind engaged in extremely frequent sexual: 'The dialects of sex in Marind-anim culture', Jan van Baal, in *Ritualized Homosexuality in Melanesia*, edited by Gilbert H. Herdt, (Berkeley, Los Angeles, London, 1984), p. 128.

'identities within a Blackness that I had no right to claim' for the 'better part' of her adult life: 'The Truth, and the Anti-Black Violence of My Lies', Jessica A. Krug, Medium, 3 September 2020.

'I have never met anyone more racist than her': 'Musician went on a "Tinder date from hell" with race faker Jessica Krug', Ben Ashford, *Daily Mail*, 10 September 2020.

One of the first major cross-cultural studies of intergroup conflict: 'The Evolutionary Anthropology of War', Luke Glowacki, Michael L. Wilson, Richard W. Wrangham, *Journal of Economic Behavior & Organization*, Volume 178, 2020, pp. 963–982.

according to anthropologist Professor Richard Wrangham, 'exceptionally' violent: *The Goodness Paradox*, Richard Wrangham (Profile, 2019). Kindle location 373.

the nearly four hundred re-education camps: 'Xinjiang: Large Numbers of New Detention Camps Uncovered in Report', Uncredited author, bbc. co.uk, 24 September 2020.

more than two hundred thousand souls incarcerated by the East German Stasi: *Stasi*, documentary, 2016.

In thirteenth-century France, when the heretical Cathars refused to convert: *Brain and Culture*, Bruce Wexler (MIT Press, 2008), p. 215.

For political psychologist Dr Lilliana Mason, part of the reason we continually attempt at warring for victory is: *Uncivil Agreement*, Lilliana Mason (University of Chicago Press, 2018), p. 49.

Sociologist Professor Nicholas Christakis writes, this finding 'depresses me even more': *Blueprint*, Nicholas Christakis (Little Brown, 2019), p. 267.

CHAPTER 19

analysis of social ties between World War II veterans . . . 'more intense the social threat': *Personality Psychology*, Larsen, Buss and Wisjeimer (McGraw Hill, 2013), p. 199.

Chinese participants having their brains scanned: *Rule Makers, Rule Breakers*, Michele J. Gelfand (Robinson, 2018). Kindle location 1005.

'opportunity to acquire resources': *Personality Psychology*, Larsen, Buss and Wisjeimer (McGraw Hill, 2013), p. 199.

weren't typically ruled by a lone 'big man' figure . . . 'sometimes a wise individual': *Moral Origins*, Christopher Boehm (Basic Books, 2012) p. 109.

we've killed them: For a great analysis, see *Moral Origins*, Christopher Boehm (Basic Books, 2012).

what anthropologists call the 'tyranny of the cousins': Richard Wrangham credits Ernest Gellner with this phrase: *The Goodness Paradox*, Richard Wrangham (Profile, 2019). Kindle location 2439.

'when a band coalesces to bring down a tyrant': *Moral Origins*, Christopher Boehm (Basic Books, 2012), p. 86.

a band of males who then fired poison arrows: *The Goodness Paradox*, Richard Wrangham (Profile, 2019). Kindle location 2411.

Players could be executed for: *Moral Origins*, Christopher Boehm (Basic Books, 2012), p. 83.

The Goodness Paradox, Richard Wrangham (Profile, 2019). Kindle location 3517.

'social cage of tradition': *The Goodness Paradox*, Richard Wrangham (Profile, 2019). Kindle location 2439.

deadly consensus-making amongst the Gebusi: *The Goodness Paradox*, Richard Wrangham (Profile, 2019). Kindle location 2467.

the group could exact punishments of shame: *Behave*, Robert Sapolsky (Vintage, 2017), p. 323.

member of the Mbuti in the Congo was caught cheating: *Moral Origins*, Christopher Boehm (Basic Books, 2012), p. 39.

an iconic 1951 experiment: 'Effects of group pressure upon the modification and distortion of judgments', Asch, S. E. (1951), in *Groups, Leadership and Men: Research in Human Relations* edited by H. Guetzkow (Carnegie Press, 1951), pp. 177–190.

prefer to play with a puppet they've seen punishing: *The Domesticated Brain*, Bruce Hood (Pelican, 2014), p. 195.

Children start enforcing rules spontaneously at around age 3: *Enigma of Reason*, Dan Sperber and Hugo Mercier (Penguin, 2017), p. 71.

A study into the reasons schoolchildren: 'Understanding Rejection between First-and-Second-Grade Elementary Students through Reasons Expressed by Rejecters', Francisco J. Bacete García, Virginia E. Carrero Planes, Ghislaine Marande Perrin, Gonzalo Musitu Ochoa, *Frontiers in Psychology*, Vol. 8, 2017, 462.

'what actually leads to rejection': 'A New Study Looks at Why Kids Reject Other Kids', Susie Neilson, *Science of Us*, 17 May 2017.

John Perry Barlow, published a 'Declaration': https://www.eff.org/cyberspace-independence.

One such case is that of Karen Templer: https://fringeassociation.com/2019/01/07/2019-my-year-of-color/.

a follow-up blog entitled 'Words Matter': https://fringeassociation.com/2019/01/12/words-matter/.

a food truck: 'Portland Burrito Cart Closes After Owners Are Accused Of Cultural Appropriation', Carolina Moreno, *Huffington Post*, 25 May 2017.

a yoga studio: 'Kindness Yoga Called Out', Jennifer Brown, *Colorado Sun*, 29 June 2020.

British journalist Helen Lewis: 'Ubisoft Says It Will Patch Out a Watch Dogs Actor Who Made "Controversial Remarks" about Gender', Andy Robinson, *Video Games Chronicle*, 7 November 2020.

Vanity Von Glow was banned: 'Vanity Von Glow: the Left Eats its Own', Andrew Doyle, *Spiked*, 6 June 2017.

Tabitha Moore-Morris, a Kentucky hospital worker: 'Baptist Health: Woman in Videos No Longer on Staff', Uncredited author, *West Kentucky Star*, 11 June 2020.

brilliant Silicon Valley technologist, Austen Heinz: I told the story of Austen Heinz in *Selfie* (Picador, 2017).

activists, predominantly millennials: This account comes from *Like War*, P. W. Singer and Emerson T. Brooking (Mariner, 2018), pp. 4–11, 150–154.

one of the largest ever studies of Britain's social psychology: 'Britain's Choice: Common Ground and Division in 2020s Britain', October 2020, report conducted by More in Common.

Additional information via private communication with study co-author Tim Dixon.

In the US, a similar study: *American Fabric: Identity and Belonging*, December 2020, MiC Report.

in 1958, just 4 per cent of Americans: 'In U.S., 87% Approve of Black-White Marriage, vs. 4% in 1958', Frank Newport, Gallup, 25 July 2013.

3 per cent of Britons believe being 'truly British': 'Culture wars risk blinding us to just how liberal we've become in the past decades', Kenan Malik, *Guardian*, 23 June 2020.

73 per cent agree hate speech is an issue: 'Britain's Choice: Common Ground and Division in 2020s Britain', October 2020, MiC Report.

transphobia is 'somewhat' or 'a great deal' of a problem: https://yougov.co.uk/topics/politics/explore/issue/Political_correctness.

80 per cent believe 'political correctness is a problem in this country': 'Who are the real Shy Trumpers?' Eric Kaufmann, *Unherd*, 6 November 2020.

72 per cent believe political correctness has become a problem: 'Britain's Choice: Common Ground and Division in 2020s Britain', October 2020, MiC Report.

A sizeable minority, 29 per cent: https://www.dailymail.co.uk/news/article-9583001/Sir-Keir-Starmers-Labour-Party-touch-public-opinion-poll-finds.html

polling company YouGov drilled into some specific positions: https://yougov.
co.uk/topics/politics/explore/issue/Political_correctness.

CHAPTER 20

In 2013, at the University of Wyoming, an anonymous Facebook page: 'Meg
Lanker-Simons, UW Student, Accused Of Threatening Herself With Rape
In Facebook Hoax', Rebecca Klein, *Huffington Post*, 5 March 2013.
'Meg Lanker-Simons Cited for Making UW Crushes Post', Trevor T.
Trujillo, kowb1290.com, 30 April 2013.
'UW Student Cited in Facebook Post Investigation', Uncredited author,
uwyo.edu, 30 April 2013.
actor Jussie Smollett . . . 'wanted to promote his career': 'Jussie Smollett's
image takes new hit with revived charges', Tammy Webber, Associated
Press, 12 February 2020.
a campaign of offensive graffiti at Vassar College: *The Rise of Victimhood
Culture*, Jason Manning and Bradley Campbell (Palgrave Macmillan, 2018).
Kindle location 3417.
'Bias incidents at Vassar were a hoax as one of the culprits was "the
transgender student leading the investigations into the offensive graffiti",
Uncredited author, *Mail Online*, 5 December 2013.
Kerri Dunn, described by the *Los Angeles Times* as 'a hero to many students':
'Claremont Professor's Past Is a New Puzzle', Nora Zamichow, *Los Angeles
Times*, 5 April 2004.
'Teacher Gets Prison in Hate Crime Hoax', Wendy Thermos, *Los Angeles
Times*, 16 December 2004.
delivering a lecture on hate speech: *The Rise of Victimhood Culture*, Jason
Manning and Bradley Campbell (Palgrave Macmillan, 2018). Kindle loca-
tion 3308.
'Kike Whore', 'NiggerLover', 'Bitch', 'Shut Up' and a half-finished swastika:
'From Hate to Hoax in Claremont', Tom Tugend, *Jewish Journal*, 1 April
2004.
Republican campaign volunteer Ashley Todd faked an attack: 'Ashley Todd
Fake "Mutilation" Exposed', Uncredited author, *Huffington Post*, 24
November 2011.

in 2007, Princeton student Francisco Nava falsely claimed: 'The Tale of an Ivy-League Hoaxer', Laura Fitzpatrick, *Time*, 18 December 2007.

An analysis of warriorship in premodern societies: 'The Role of Rewards in Motivating Participation in Simple Warfare', Luke Glowacki and R. Wrangham, *Human Nature* 24, 2013, 444–460.

more likely to be collective narcissists . . . 'predictor of hypersensitivity': 'Collective Narcissism Predicts Hypersensitivity to In-group Insult and Direct and Indirect Retaliatory Intergroup Hostility', A. Golec de Zavala, M. Peker, R. Guerra and T. Baran, *Eur. J. Pers.*, 2016, 30: 532–551.

Warriors are also likely to strongly identify . . . 'When a group's status is threatened': *Uncivil Agreement*, Lilliana Mason (University of Chicago Press, 2018), p. 23.

In one study, participants watched the film *Rocky IV*: *Uncivil Agreement*, Lilliana Mason (University of Chicago Press, 2018), p. 84.

analyses of tweets that find those most likely to be retweeted: 'Attentional capture helps explain why moral and emotional content go viral (in press)', W. J. Brady, A. P. Gantman and J. J. Van Bavel, *Journal of Experimental Psychology*: General.

A study of seventy million messages: *LikeWar*, P. W. Singer and Emerson T. Brooking (Mariner, 2018), p. 162.

studies of mobbing events on Twitter find shamers increase their follower counts: 'Online Public Shaming on Twitter: Detection, Analysis, and Mitigation', R. Basak, S. Sural, N. Ganguly and S. K. Ghosh, in *IEEE Transactions on Computational Social Systems*, Vol. 6, No. 2, pp. 208–220, April 2019.

are guilty of a 'disgusting crime': 'Like My Good Friend Jameela Told Me At The Chateau Marmont', Kristin Iversen, *Nylon,* 12 December 2018.

the Kardashians, Cardi B: 'Calling time on Jameela Jamil and her toxic brand of feminism', Diyora Shadijanova, *The Tab*, 3 May 2019.

Rihanna: 'Put It Away RiRi!', Jameela Jamil, *Company*, April 2013.

Miley Cyrus, Nicki Minaj, Iggy Azelea: 'Calling time on Jameela Jamil and her toxic brand of feminism', Diyora Shadijanova, *The Tab*, 3 May 2019.

Caroline Calloway: 'Caroline Calloway might be controversial, but for Jameela Jamil to publicly vilify her exposes complete hypocrisy', Olivia Petter, *Independent*, 3 April 2020.

Beyoncé: 'Beyonce's Drawing A Line Under That "Is She A Feminist Question" Once And For All', Sophie Wilkinson, *The Debrief*, 2 February 2014.

J. K. Rowling: 'J.K. Rowling criticized once again for anti-trans comments', Clark Collis, *Entertainment Weekly*, 7 June 2020.

presented by Caroline Flack . . . engaged in a hostile Twitter exchange: 'Jameela Jamil reignites feud with Caroline Flack as the stars get into war of words', Ellie Phillips, *Mail Online*, 23 October 2019.

A journalist then released a private message: 'Stinking Hypocrisy!', Piers Morgan, *Mail Online*, 3 October 2020.

He later complained the inclusion of Sikh soldiers: 'Laurence Fox issues apology to Sikhs for his "clumsy" 1917 comments – but stands by everything else he's said', Emma Kelly, *Metro*, 24 January 2020.

boycott of the supermarket chain Sainsbury's: 'Laurence Fox says he is boycotting Sainsbury's for "promoting racial segregation and discrimination" after it announced support for Black History Month', Katie Feehan, *Mail Online*, 4 October 2020.

Before his *Question Time* appearance: Via The Wayback Machine.

those most likely to circulate 'hostile political rumours': 'A "Need for Chaos" and the Sharing of Hostile Political Rumors in Advanced Democracies', Michael Petersen, 2018, 10.31234/osf.io/6m4ts.

Dr Justin Tosi and Dr Brandon Warmke: *Grandstanding*, Justin Tosi and Brandon Warmke (Oxford University Press, 2020), p. 53.

A study led by psychologist Professor Robb Willer: 'The False Enforcement of Unpopular Norms', Robb Willer, Ko Kuwabara and Michael W. Macy, *American Journal of Sociology*, 2009, 115:2, 451–490.

call a 'purity spiral' in which players 'strive to outdo one another': *The Rise of Victimhood Culture*, Jason Manning and Bradley Campbell (Palgrave Macmillan, 2018). Kindle location 4576.

The European witch-hunts . . . usually took place in times of severe pressure: Contemporary scholars note that hostile climatic conditions alone aren't sufficient to predict witch trials and executions in any location. What often tipped affected regions into frenzy was the additional arrival of ambitious status warriors who represented the rival games of Catholicism and Protestantism, who were, at that time, warring hard. An analysis by economists Professor Peter Leeson and Professor Jacob Russ found trials occurred most often in regions where these rivals were in greater competition for neural territory in the minds of the populace. 'More intense religious-market contestation led to more intense witch-trial activity.' Their trials acted as powerful advertisements for their particular game. 'Both Catholic and Protestant religious suppliers vigorously prosecuted witches,' they write. 'Religious suppliers could evidence their commitment and power to protect consumers from worldly manifestations of Satan's evil through their commitment and power to prosecute such people for witchcraft.' Their executions were often huge public events drawing hundreds, sometimes thousands.

'Witch Trials', P. T. Leeson and J. W. Russ, *Economic Journal*, 128: 2066–2105.

'a heightened sense of the need for societal purity and uniformity': *The Reformation*, Peter Marshall (Oxford University Press, 2009), p. 112.

Henri Boguet, 'Witchcraft is a crime apart' . . . For Jean Bodin, 'proof of such evil': 'Taxes, Lawyers, and the Decline of Witch Trials in France', N. Johnson and M. Koyama, *The Journal of Law & Economics*, 2014, 57(1), 77–112. https://doi.org/10.1086/674900.

at least eighty thousand people were tried, around half of whom were executed: 'Witch Trials', P. T. Leeson and J. W. Russ, *Economic Journal*, 2018, 128: 2066–2105.

Most were poor women, often widows. In one German town: 'Witchcraft, Weather and Economic Growth in Renaissance Europe', Emily F. Oster, *Journal of Economic Perspectives*, Winter 2004, Available at SSRN: https://ssrn.com/abstract=522403.

In 1478, Spain's monarchs approved: This account comes from *The Spanish Inquisition*, Henry Kamen (Yale University Press, 2014).

under canon law, anonymous denunciations had been forbidden, now: 'The Spanish Inquisition, 1478–1492', Ruth Johnston, ruthjohnston.com/AllThingsMedieval/?p=2272.

CHAPTER 21

She finds nations that have suffered events such as disease: *Rule Makers, Rule Breakers*, Michele Gelfand (Robinson, 2018). Kindle location 817.

'Groups that deal with many ecological and historical threats': *Rule Makers, Rule Breakers*, Michele Gelfand (Robinson, 2018). Kindle location 812.

'The greater the threat, the tighter the community': *Rule Makers, Rule Breakers*, Michele Gelfand (Robinson, 2018). Kindle location 1379.

In tight cultures – that include Pakistan: *Rule Makers, Rule Breakers*, Michele Gelfand (Robinson, 2018). Kindle location 382.

Their citizens are more punctual: *Rule Makers, Rule Breakers*, Michele Gelfand (Robinson, 2018). Kindle location 125.

Even the time shown on public clocks: *Rule Makers, Rule Breakers*, Michele Gelfand (Robinson, 2018). Kindle location 610.

greater respecters of hierarchy and authority: *Rule Makers, Rule Breakers*, Michele Gelfand (Robinson, 2018). Kindle location 1229.

During the 2020 coronavirus pandemic: 'The relationship between cultural tightness-looseness and COVID-19 cases and deaths: a global analysis', Michele Gelfand, Joshua Jackson, Xinyue Pan, Dana Nau, Dylan Pieper, Emmy Denison, Munqith Dagher, Paul Lange, Chi Yue Chiu and Mo Wang, *The Lancet Planetary Health*, 2021.

precisely correct moral behaviour: *Rule Makers, Rule Breakers*, Michele Gelfand (Robinson, 2018). Kindle location 1229.

one resident complained about a barking dog: *Rule Makers, Rule Breakers*, Michele Gelfand (Robinson, 2018). Kindle location 592.

more interested in moral purity: *Rule Makers, Rule Breakers*, Michele Gelfand (Robinson, 2018). Kindle location 1229.

more likely to have the death penalty: *Rule Makers, Rule Breakers*, Michele Gelfand (Robinson, 2018). Kindle location 538.

less welcoming to outsiders: *Rule Makers, Rule Breakers*, Michele Gelfand (Robinson, 2018). Kindle location 718.

prefer dominant leaders: *Rule Makers, Rule Breakers*, Michele Gelfand (Robinson, 2018). Kindle location 784.

An analysis of tightness – looseness across the US states: *Rule Makers, Rule Breakers*, Michele Gelfand (Robinson, 2018). Kindle location 1224.

'Neither one of us felt that we were part of this world': *Heaven's Gate Cult* documentary – History TV, https://www.youtube.com/watch?v=ca2Lh JdlK3U.

'alienated, hopeless, incomplete and utterly unsatisfied': *Heaven's Gate: America's UFO Religion*, Benjamin E. Zeller (NYU Press, 2014), p. 53.

'believed that their status as the two witnesses': *Heaven's Gate: America's UFO Religion*, Benjamin E. Zeller (NYU Press, 2014), p. 33.

Former member Swyody recalls: *This "Little Book" Provides the "Backside" Evidence Showing How All Jesus' Prophecy Revelations are Fulfilled By Those* who were known as: Ti & Do The Father and "Jesus" Heaven's Gate UFO Two Witnesses . . . Sawyer (Authorhouse, 2017).

'They all ordered the exact same thing': 'Heaven's Gate 20 Years Later: 10 Things You Didn't Know', Michael Hafford, *Rolling Stone*, 24 March 2017.

their deaths 'resulted from a deliberate decision': 'Making Sense of the Heaven's Gate Suicides', R. Balch and D. Taylor, in *Cults, Religion, and Violence* edited by D. Bromley and J. Melton (Cambridge University Press, 2002), pp. 209–228.

'I loved them dearly. We were a tight group': *Heaven's Gate: America's UFO Religion*, Benjamin Zeller (NYU Press, 2014), p. 55.

CHAPTER 22

successful organisations 'help keep their most talented employees': 'Is the Desire for Status a Fundamental Human Motive? A Review of the Empirical Literature', C. Anderson, J. A. D. Hildreth, L. Howland, *Psychological Bulletin*, 16 March 2015.

'overwhelming evidence': *Status*, Cecilia L. Ridgeway (Russell Sage Foundation, 2019), p. 13.

One analysis of their glossy magazine *Dabiq*: *The Reputation Game*, David Waller (Oneworld, 2017). Kindle location 2058.

rivalrous anger, when combined with optimistic enthusiasm: *Uncivil Agreement*, Lilliana Mason (University of Chicago Press, 2018), p. 122.

'they want to jump into the ring': *Uncivil Agreement*, Lilliana Mason (University of Chicago Press, 2018), p. 123.

'Without a threat to a social group': *Uncivil Agreement*, Lilliana Mason (University of Chicago Press, 2018), p. 124.

'few, if any, twentieth-century political leaders enjoyed greater': *The Hitler Myth*, Ian Kershaw (Oxford University Press, 2001), p. 1.

wealthiest and most highly developed . . . 'capitalist enterprise had reached': *The Coming of the Third Reich*, Richard Evans (Penguin, 2004). Kindle location 289.

Germany produced two-thirds of all the steel: *The Coming of the Third Reich*, Richard Evans (Penguin, 2004). Kindle location 790.

'No one was prepared for the peace terms': *The Coming of the Third Reich*, Richard Evans (Penguin, 2004). Kindle location 1491.

compelled to accept 'sole guilt': *The Coming of the Third Reich*, Richard Evans (Penguin, 2004). Kindle location 1535.

surrendering vast tracts of land in Europe ... 'These provisions': *The Coming of the Third Reich*, Richard Evans (Penguin, 2004). Kindle locations 1491, 1560.

The government had been expecting reparations and wealth: *The Coming of the Third Reich*, Richard Evans (Penguin, 2004). Kindle location 2211.

a gramophone costing five million: *The Coming of the Third Reich*, Richard Evans (Penguin, 2004). Kindle location 2263.

A coffee at a cafe might cost: *The Coming of the Third Reich*, Richard Evans (Penguin, 2004). Kindle location 2290.

by December 1923 that same dollar cost 4,200,000,000,000 marks: *The Coming of the Third Reich*, Richard Evans (Penguin, 2004). Kindle location 2247.

when Germany fell behind on its reparations of gold and coal: *The Coming of the Third Reich*, Richard Evans (Penguin, 2004). Kindle location 2211.

'The sense of outrage and disbelief that swept through': *The Coming of the Third Reich*, Richard Evans (Penguin, 2004). Kindle location 1568.

'secret, planned, demagogic campaign': *The Coming of the Third Reich*, Richard Evans (Penguin, 2004). Kindle location 1491.

'remained on a continued war footing': *The Coming of the Third Reich*, Richard Evans (Penguin, 2004). Kindle location 1679.

thirteen million people: *The Coming of the Third Reich*, Richard Evans (Penguin, 2004). Kindle location 4561.

around 600,000 practising Jews: *The Coming of the Third Reich*, Richard Evans (Penguin, 2004). Kindle location 833.

Generally speaking, they were a high-status group: *The Coming of the Third Reich*, Richard Evans (Penguin, 2004). Kindle locations 822, 847.

a 'Jewish-Bolshevik conspiracy': *The Coming of the Third Reich*, Richard Evans (Penguin, 2004). Kindle location 3129.

new scientific ideas about heredity: *The Coming of the Third Reich*, Richard Evans (Penguin, 2004). Kindle locations 1099, 1113, 1127.

relatively few endorsed brutal actions against them: *The Hitler Myth*, Ian Kershaw (Oxford University Press, 2001), p. 235.

'among ordinary Party activists in the 1920s and early 1930s': *The Coming of the Third Reich*, Richard Evans (Penguin, 2004). Kindle location 4239.

Prior to 1922 he'd been ranting about the Jews: *The Hitler Myth*, Ian Kershaw (Oxford University Press, 2001), p. 230.

he raised the 'Jewish Question' relatively rarely in his speeches: *The Hitler Myth*, Ian Kershaw (Oxford University Press, 2001), pp. 231–241.

unfortunate but understandable flare-ups of overenthusiasm, and not endorsed by Hitler: *The Hitler Myth*, Ian Kershaw (Oxford University Press, 2001), p. 234.

Hitler's party positioned itself as young and forward-thinking: *Marketing the Third Reich*, Nicholas O'Shaughnessy (Routledge, 2017), pp. 71–72.

O'Shaughnessy notes that by 1931, almost 40 per cent of members of the Nazi Party were under 30.

'the Prometheus of mankind . . .': *Selling Hitler*, Nicholas O'Shaughnessy (C. Hurst & Co, 2016), p. 160.

'there are no such things as classes: they cannot be': Speech, April 1921, https://web.viu.ca/davies/H479B.Imperialism.Nationalism/Hitler.speech. April1921.htm.

'greatest villainy of the century' . . . 'everything went black': *The Coming of the Third Reich*, Richard Evans (Penguin, 2004). Kindle location 3333.

'Finally a practical proposal for the renewal of the people!': *The Coming of the Third Reich*, Richard Evans (Penguin, 2004). Kindle location 4354.

'to think as one, to react as one': *The Coming of the Third Reich*, Richard Evans (Penguin, 2004). Kindle location 7315.

the Malicious Practices Act . . . 'every nationally minded': *The Hitler Myth*, Ian Kershaw (Oxford University Press, 2001), p. 56.

nonconformists would be 'purged': *The Third Reich in Power*, Richard Evans (Penguin, 2006), p. 134.

professors, artists, writers, journalists and scientists: *The Third Reich in Power*, Richard Evans (Penguin, 2006), p. 15.

'atmosphere of intimidation and vigilance': *The Hitler Myth*, Ian Kershaw (Oxford University Press, 2001), p. 57.

Communist Party was formally banned . . . numbering at least in the tens of thousands: *The Coming of the Third Reich*, Richard Evans (Penguin, 2004). Kindle location 6447.

Evans quotes Communist Party figures of 130,000 arrested and imprisoned and 2,500 killed but adds these figures are 'probably something of an exaggeration.'

'massive, brutal and murderous assault': *The Coming of the Third Reich*, Richard Evans (Penguin, 2004). Kindle location 6454.

Soon, all other political parties were banned: *The Hitler Myth*, Ian Kershaw (Oxford University Press, 2001), p. 60.

the 'Heil Hitler' compulsory for state employees . . . 'anyone not wishing to come under suspicion': *The Hitler Myth*, Ian Kershaw (Oxford University Press, 2001), p. 60.

a then-teenager reported: *The Third Reich in Power*, Richard Evans (Penguin, 2006), p. 266.

first address to the media: https://research.calvin.edu/german-propaganda-archive/goeb62.htm.

'There are two ways to make a revolution': *Selling Hitler*, Nicholas O'Shaughnessy (C. Hurst & Co, 2016), p. 100.

the 'vast majority of professors' being 'strongly nationalist': *The Coming of the Third Reich*, Richard Evans (Penguin, 2004). Kindle location 2744.

were replaced by 'often mediocre figures': *The Coming of the Third Reich*, Richard Evans (Penguin, 2004). Kindle location 7826.

'an elite to which racism, antisemitism': *The Coming of the Third Reich*, Richard Evans (Penguin, 2004). Kindle location 2763.

'organized campaigns against unwanted professors': *The Coming of the Third Reich*, Richard Evans (Penguin, 2004). Kindle location 7813.

Hitler Youth accommodated over two million adolescents: *The Third Reich in Power*, Richard Evans (Penguin, 2006), p. 271.

The Nazis staffed their enormous social welfare administration: *The Coming of the Third Reich*, Richard Evans (Penguin, 2004). Kindle location 2962.

Voluntary associations in every village: *The Coming of the Third Reich*, Richard Evans (Penguin, 2004). Kindle location 7165.

'staffed with loyal and energetic functionaries' . . . 'and for many other constituencies': *The Coming of the Third Reich*, Richard Evans (Penguin, 2004). Kindle location 4131.

The party finessed their message to suit the values of every game: *Marketing the Third Reich*, Nicholas O'Shaughnessy (Routledge, 2017), p. 71.

'the Nazis offered something for everyone': *Marketing the Third Reich*, Nicholas O'Shaughnessy (Routledge, 2017), p. 70.

party membership tripled . . . 'at least one-half and most likely two-thirds': Public display, NS-Dokumentationszentrum Muenchen (as per September 2020).

'until they have become addicted to us': *The Coming of the Third Reich*, Richard Evans (Penguin, 2004). Kindle location 7275.

the motorway: *The Third Reich in Power*, Richard Evans (Penguin, 2006), pp. 322–328.

5 billion marks . . . subsidies for house . . . substantial amounts in deprived areas: *The Third Reich in Power*, Richard Evans (Penguin, 2006), p. 330.

interest-free loans . . . nearly a quarter of a million: *The Third Reich in Power*, Richard Evans (Penguin, 2006), pp. 330, 331.

theatre tickets (accounting for more than half: *The Third Reich in Power*, Richard Evans (Penguin, 2006), pp. 466–467.

package holidays . . . Libya, Finland, Bulgaria and Istanbul: *The Third Reich in Power*, Richard Evans (Penguin, 2006), p. 467.

accounting for as many as 11 per cent: *The Third Reich in Power*, Richard Evans (Penguin, 2006), p. 474.

140,000 passengers: *The Third Reich in Power*, Richard Evans (Penguin, 2006), p. 467.

annual Winter Aid drive raised hundreds of millions of marks: *The Third Reich in Power*, Richard Evans (Penguin, 2006), p. 487.

foreign debt was stabilised: *The Third Reich in Power*, Richard Evans (Penguin, 2006), p. 409.

wide range of advanced public health measures . . . 'decades ahead' . . . definitively link: *The Reputation Game*, David Waller (Oneworld, 2017). Kindle location 1251.

6.1 million people: www.bbc.co.uk/bitesize/guides/zpvhk7h/revision/1.

2.2 million, by 1937 it was under a million: *The Third Reich in Power*, Richard Evans (Penguin, 2006), p. 333.

by 1939 full employment was claimed: www.bbc.co.uk/bitesize/guides/zqrfj6f/revision/3.

the agricultural economy grew by 71 per cent: *The Third Reich in Power*, Richard Evans (Penguin, 2006), p. 349.

gross national product soared by 81 per cent: *The Third Reich in Power*, Richard Evans (Penguin, 2006), p. 409.

wood pulp and 'long lines of sullen people before the food shops': *Berlin Diary: The Journal of a Foreign Correspondent, 1934–1941*, William L. Shirer (Ishi Press, 2010), p. 85.

'the overwhelming majority of the population clearly': *The Hitler Myth*, Ian Kershaw (Oxford University Press, 2001), p. 122.

'soaring to a new pinnacle': *The Hitler Myth*, Ian Kershaw (Oxford University Press, 2001), p. 126.

'frenzied acclaim' with hundreds of thousands: *The Hitler Myth*, Ian Kershaw (Oxford University Press, 2001), p. 127.

'the spirit of Versailles is hated by all Germans': *The Hitler Myth*, Ian Kershaw (Oxford University Press, 2001), p. 129.

'unprecedented heights': *The Third Reich in Power*, Richard Evans (Penguin, 2006), p. 663.

'Hitler is a great and clever statesman': *The Hitler Myth*, Ian Kershaw (Oxford University Press, 2001), p. 132.

'symbolically wiping out the humiliation': *The Hitler Myth*, Ian Kershaw (Oxford University Press, 2001), p. 155.

'the symbol of the indestructible life-force': *The Hitler Myth*, Ian Kershaw (Oxford University Press, 2001), p. 48.

'In the personality of Hitler, a million-fold longing': *The Hitler Myth*, Ian Kershaw (Oxford University Press, 2001), p. 58.

'Germany is Hitler, and Hitler is Germany': *The Hitler Myth*, Ian Kershaw (Oxford University Press, 2001), p. 151.

'Hitler-Oaks' and 'Hitler-Lindens': *The Hitler Myth*, Ian Kershaw (Oxford University Press, 2001), p. 55.

squares were renamed 'Adolf-Hitler Platz': *The Third Reich in Power*, Richard Evans (Penguin, 2006), p. 122.

Hitlerine, Adolfine, Hitlerike and Hilerine: *How to be a Dictator*, Frank Dikötter (Bloomsbury, 2019). Kindle location 921.

portraits and busts of Hitler adorned with flowers: *The Hitler Myth*, Ian Kershaw (Oxford University Press, 2001), p. 58.

became known as 'Hitler weather': *Marketing the Third Reich*, Nicholas O'Shaughnessy (Routledge, 2017), p. 119.

thousands of letters, gifts and poems . . . 'My fervently adored Führer!': *The Hitler Myth*, Ian Kershaw (Oxford University Press, 2001), p. 73.

gazed at Hitler's image for hours to 'gain strength': *Marketing the Third Reich*, Nicholas O'Shaughnessy (Routledge, 2017), p. 116.

the walls of bombed houses holding Hitler's portrait: *Marketing the Third Reich*, Nicholas O'Shaughnessy (Routledge, 2017), p. 125.

swastika sausages were sold: *How to be a Dictator*, Frank Dikötter (Bloomsbury, 2019). Kindle location 926.

swastika manicures: *Marketing the Third Reich*, Nicholas O'Shaughnessy (Routledge, 2017), p. 116.

a butcher sculpted Hitler in lard: *Marketing the Third Reich*, Nicholas O'Shaughnessy (Routledge, 2017), p. 19.

'vowed to Heil Hitler and give the Nazi salute at the point of orgasm': *Marketing the Third Reich*, Nicholas O'Shaughnessy (Routledge, 2017), p. 116.

'perhaps even millions': *The Coming of the Third Reich*, Richard Evans (Penguin, 2004). Kindle location 6604.

'caught in a mob of ten thousand hysterics': *Berlin Diary: The Journal of a Foreign Correspondent, 1934–1941*, William L. Shirer (Ishi Press, 2010), p. 17.

CHAPTER 23

One study of ninety-four wars since 1648: *Virtuous Violence*, Alan Fiske and Tage Shakti Rai (Cambridge University Press, 2014), p. 94.

frequently, 'decision-makers': *Virtuous Violence*, Alan Fiske and Tage Shakti Rai (Cambridge University Press, 2014), pp. 94–95.

the more a nation feels humiliated: *Virtuous Violence*, Alan Fiske and Tage Shakti Rai (Cambridge University Press, 2014), p. 96.

between 500,000 and two million people were killed: 'The Cultural Revolution', Tom Phillips, *Guardian*, 11 May 2016.

Leader Mao Tse Tung was notoriously grandiose: For more on Mao's narcissism, see: *How to be a Dictator*, Frank Dikötter (Bloomsbury, 2019), chapter 4.

'the man who leads planet Earth into Communism': 'The Cultural Revolution', Tom Phillips, *Guardian*, 11 May 2016.

'dictatorship of the bourgeoisie' . . . 'representatives': 'The Cultural Revolution', Tom Phillips, *Guardian*, 11 May 2016.

recalled being surprised . . . 'I was unwilling': *Red Guard*, Gordon A. Bennett and Ronald N. Montaperto (Allen & Unwin, 1971), pp. 42–44.

'always very intense', Dai has said . . . 'We forced the teachers': *Red Guard*, Gordon A. Bennett and Ronald N. Montaperto (Allen & Unwin, 1971), p. 41.

'enormous cardboard replica of a cow's head': *Red Guard*, Gordon A. Bennett and Ronald N. Montaperto (Allen & Unwin, 1971), p. 53.

When the revolution spilled into the streets . . . 'Some of us would tear down the walls': *Red Guard*, Gordon A. Bennett and Ronald N. Montaperto (Allen & Unwin, 1971), pp. 70–80.

'What America is tasting now': 'Shame, guilt, and violence', James Gilligan, *Social Research: An International Quarterly* 70 (4):1149–1180.

'the shame and humiliation': *Why We Fight*, Mike Martin (Hurst & Company, 2018). Kindle location 2964.

Dr Eyad El-Sarraj: 'Shame, guilt, and violence', James Gilligan, *Social Research: An International Quarterly* 70 (4):1149–1180.

An academic interviewing a Muslim extremist in Indonesia: *Virtuous Violence*, Alan Fiske and Tage Shakti Rai (Cambridge University Press, 2014), p. 105.

Theodore Roosevelt, 'the settler': *Virtuous Violence*, Alan Fiske and Tage Shakti Rai (Cambridge University Press, 2014), p. 211.

When Algerians killed 103 French people: *The Rise and Fall of the Third Chimpanzee*, Jared Diamond (Vintage, 2002). Kindle location 4933.

'The most potent weapon of mass destruction': 'Genocide, Humiliation, and Inferiority: An Interdisciplinary Perspective', Evelin Gerda Lindner, in *Genocides by the Oppressed: Subaltern Genocide in Theory and Practice*, edited by Nicholas A. Robins and Adam Jones (Indiana University Press, 2009), chapter 7, pp. 138–158.

'experiences a decline in or threat' . . . 'rises or attempts to rise in status': *The Geometry of Genocide*, Bradley Campbell (University of Virginia Press, 2015), p. 16.

'genocide is highly moralistic': *The Geometry of Genocide*, Bradley Campbell (University of Virginia Press, 2015), p. 31.

'outright zeal in humiliating' . . . during the Armenian genocide: *The Geometry of Genocide*, Bradley Campbell (University of Virginia Press, 2015), p. 3.

during the Gujarat genocide: *The Geometry of Genocide*, Bradley Campbell (University of Virginia Press, 2015), p. 74.

Tutsi were symbolically 'cut down to size': 'Genocide, Humiliation, and Inferiority: An Interdisciplinary Perspective', Evelin Gerda Lindner, in *Genocides by the Oppressed: Subaltern Genocide in Theory and Practice*, edited by Nicholas A. Robins and Adam Jones, 2009, chapter 7, pp. 138–158.

For survivor Marian Turski: '"Humiliation was the worst"; Holocaust survivor at UN, asks world to act with "empathy and compassion"', Uncredited author, UN News, 28 January 2019.

cut their hair, shaved their beards, paraded them: Public display, Topography of Terror, Berlin (visited November 2018).

dangerous quantities of castor oil: *The Coming of the Third Reich*, Richard Evans (Penguin, 2004). Kindle location 7898.

ordered them to carry out pointless tasks: Public display, Topography of Terror, Berlin (visited November 2018).

In Vienna, William Shirer witnessed: *Berlin Diary: The Journal of a Foreign Correspondent, 1934–1941*, William L. Shirer (Ishi Press, 2010), p. 110.

a singing, laughing, accordion-playing crowd: *The Geometry of Genocide*, Bradley Campbell (University of Virginia Press, 2015), pp. 159–160.

a prominent rabbi: *The Geometry of Genocide*, Bradley Campbell (University of Virginia Press, 2015), p. 150.

CHAPTER 24

defined the tenor of existence for thousands of years. We'd be born into a kin-based: *The Weirdest People in the World*, Joseph Henrich (Penguin, 2020), p. 27.

marriage took place mostly within networks of kin: *The Weirdest People in the World*, Joseph Henrich (Penguin, 2020), p. 167.

advised maidens to always 'marry into their own estate': *The Politico's World*, Joan Wildeblood and Peter Brinson (Oxford University Press, 1965), p. 21.

one in ten global marriages are between relatives: *The Weirdest People in the World*, Joseph Henrich (Penguin, 2020), p. 157.

Partly it has to do with lucky geography: This argument was made in *Guns, Germs, and Steel*, Jared Diamond (Vintage, 1998).

the roots of Western individualism: This argument was made in *The Geography of Thought*, Richard E. Nisbett (Nicholas Brealey, 2003) and explored further in my 2017 book *Selfie*.

for the Catholic Church's weird preoccupation with incest: This argument was made in *The Weirdest People in the World*, Joseph Henrich (Penguin, 2020).

starting in AD 305, the Church instituted a series of rule changes: 'The Origins of WEIRD Psychology', Jonathan Schulz, Duman Bahrami-Rad, Jonathan Beauchamp and Joseph Heinrich, 22 June, 2018.

The Weirdest People in the World, Joseph Henrich (Penguin, 2020), pp. 165–199.

these changes 'systematically broke down': 'Western Individualism Arose from Incest Taboo', David Noonan, *Scientific American*, 7 November 2019.

Learning to 'navigate a world with few inherited ties': *The Weirdest People in the World*, Joseph Henrich (Penguin, 2020), p. 28.

the longer a population lived by them: 'Western Individualism Arose from Incest Taboo', David Noonan, *Scientific American*, 7 November 2019.

is partly thanks to a tweak: *Sapiens*, Yuval Noah Harari (Vintage, 2015), p. 242.

religious belief doesn't fall upon populations . . . 'psychological and emotional condition': *Not Born Yesterday*, Hugo Mercier (Princeton University Press, 2020), p. 123.

God couldn't be worshipped by sacrifice, like pagan gods, but by 'proper belief': *Inside the Conversion Tactics of the Early Christian Church*, Bart D. Ehrman, History.com, 29 March 2018.

'eternally burned, without being consumed' . . . this, from Saint Leonard: *Sin and Fear*, Jean Delumeau (St Martin's Press, 1990), pp. 365, 380.

in some Muslim communities, paid higher taxes: 'Medieval Muslim societies', Uncredited author, Khanacademy.org.

'Religion had never promoted such an idea before': *Inside the Conversion Tactics of the Early Christian Church*, Bart D. Ehrman, History.com, 29 March 2018.

the most powerful institution on earth . . . a crime against God: *A Little History of Religion*, Richard Holloway (Yale University Press, 2016), pp. 124–150.

the largest landowner in Europe, owning 44 per cent: *The Weirdest People in the World*, Joseph Henrich (Penguin, 2020), pp. 182, 185

the wealthy could enjoy their riches . . . the wealthy gave so much to the Church: *The Weirdest People in the World*, Joseph Henrich (Penguin, 2020), pp. 183–184.

'What is a man by himself, without grace?': *Sin and Fear*, Jean Delumeau (St Martin's Press, 1990), p. 2.

'The tricky thing': *The Reformation*, Peter Marshall (Oxford University Press, 2009), pp. 43–44.

for sins including cousin marriage: *The Weirdest People in the World*, Joseph Henrich (Penguin, 2020), p. 185.

forgiveness for future sins: *The Renaissance*, Jerry Brotton (Oxford University Press, 2006), p. 69.

nuclear families with two to four children: *The Weirdest People in the World*, Joseph Henrich (Penguin, 2020), p. 189.

with more than fifty established by 1500, producing lawyers: *The Weirdest People in the World*, Joseph Henrich (Penguin, 2020), p. 319.

learned a trade, joined the game, before moving on to another master: *The Weirdest People in the World*, Joseph Henrich (Penguin, 2020), p. 447.

'work ethic' . . . 'the beginning of a work-centred society': *Work*, Andrea Komlosy (Verso, 2018). Kindle locations 213, 229.

less conformist and less in awe of tradition, ancestry: *The Weirdest People in the World*, Joseph Henrich (Penguin, 2020), p. 314.

Tetzel the Persuader: *The Reformation*, Peter Marshall (Oxford University Press, 2009), p. 13.

'Why does not the Pope': *The Renaissance*, Jerry Brotton (Oxford University Press, 2006), p. 69.

between 1517 and 1520, more than three hundred thousand copies of his books:
The Renaissance, Jerry Brotton (Oxford University Press, 2006), p. 71.

Believers were to look for clues of 'assurance': *The Reformation*, Peter Marshall (Oxford University Press, 2009), p. 47.

'we are all equally priests', wrote Luther: *The Reformation*, Peter Marshall (Oxford University Press, 2009), p. 80.

reading wasn't merely encouraged, it was a foundational rule: *The Weirdest People in the World*, Joseph Henrich (Penguin, 2020), pp. 9–10.

'fastest in countries where Protestantism was most deeply established': *The Weirdest People in the World*, Joseph Henrich (Penguin, 2020), p. 10.

monks as wolves, friars as demons and the Pope as a dragon: *The Reformation*, Peter Marshall (Oxford University Press, 2009), pp. 19, 80.

a priest with a freshly shaven head 'took up a cow's dung': *The Reformation*, Peter Marshall (Oxford University Press, 2009), p. 81.

high-value goods such as: *The Renaissance*, Jerry Brotton (Oxford University Press, 2006), pp. 90–91.

They dictated: *Empire of Things*, Frank Trentmann (Allen Lane, 2016), pp. 38–40.

in 1363, legislation was introduced to curb: 'The 1363 English Sumptuary

Law: A comparison with Fabric Prices of the Late Fourteenth-Century', Sarah Kelly Silverman, PhD thesis 2011.

'outrageous consumption of meats' . . . 'no knight under the estate of a lord': 'Sumptuary Laws of the Middle Ages', www.lordsandladies.org/sumptuary-laws-middle-ages.htm.

In 1574, one Londoner was imprisoned: *Empire of Things*, Frank Trentmann (Allen Lane, 2016), p. 39.

'a family without as much as an old broom': *Empire of Things*, Frank Trentmann (Allen Lane, 2016), p. 47.

roughly comparable with modern day USA: *Empire of Things*, Frank Trentmann (Allen Lane, 2016), p. 32.

painters, sculptors, architects, potters and makers of hair extensions and false teeth: *Empire of Things*, Frank Trentmann (Allen Lane, 2016), p. 30.

Giovanni Pontano, even wrote a treatise: 'The Economic and Social World of Italian Renaissance Maiolica', R. Goldthwaite, *Renaissance Quarterly*, 1989. 42(1), 1–32.

'for it is not vomiting but holding the vomit in your throat that is foul': *The Civilizing Process*, Norbert Elias (Blackwell, 2000), p. 51.

In 1475 one Florence banker ordered a set of: *Empire of Things*, Frank Trentmann (Allen Lane, 2016), p. 29.

a single banquet in 1565: 'The Economic and Social World of Italian Renaissance Maiolica', R. Goldthwaite, *Renaissance Quarterly*, 1989, 42 (1), 1–32.

East adopted relatively few Western technologies and notions: *A Culture of Growth*, Joel Mokyr (Princeton University Press, 2016), p. 146.

the Hindu-Arabic numeral system: *The Renaissance*, Jerry Brotton (Oxford University Press, 2006), pp. 26–27.

At first in Italy in the 1500s: *A Culture of Growth*, Joel Mokyr (Princeton University Press, 2016), p. 152.

In the beginning, this manifested as 'an upper class fascination': *A Culture of Growth*, Joel Mokyr (Princeton University Press, 2016), p. 153.

Showing knowledge had become a status symbol: *A Culture of Growth*, Joel Mokyr (Princeton University Press, 2016), p. 154.

patronage by dukes, princes and kings: *A Culture of Growth*, Joel Mokyr (Princeton University Press, 2016), p. 204.

Mokyr writes: 'In early modern Europe, intellectuals as such (with the exception perhaps of a handful of superstars) still had fairly low social status. Powerful and high status patrons supplied them with an opportunity for a secure existence as well as elevated social status; thus, patronage provided powerful incentives to creative and learned people to exert themselves.' (p. 183).

As Mokyr writes, 'reputation based on peer evaluation was what counted': *A Culture of Growth*, Joel Mokyr (Princeton University Press, 2016), p. 181.

Players could win major status: *A Culture of Growth*, Joel Mokyr (Princeton University Press, 2016), pp. 201, 214.

Rather than jealously protecting their ideas: *A Culture of Growth*, Joel Mokyr (Princeton University Press, 2016), pp. 189, 192, 199.

'teaches men humility and acquaints them': *A Culture of Growth*, Joel Mokyr (Princeton University Press, 2016), p. 198.

The Council was colonised by a hereditary aristocracy: *Why Nations Fail*, Daron Acemoglu and James A. Robinson (Profile, 2012), pp. 155–156.

not only of nobles, knights and aristocrats, but: *Why Nations Fail*, Daron Acemoglu and James A. Robinson (Profile, 2012), p. 185.

Soon afterwards, the Bank of England was founded: *Why Nations Fail*, Daron Acemoglu and James A. Robinson (Profile, 2012), pp. 102–103.

in 1675, it's thought not a single household in London: *Empire of Things*, Frank Trentmann (Allen Lane, 2016), p. 60.

Britons 'became innovators because they adopted an improving mentality', writes historian Dr Anton Howes: 'The Spread of Improvement: Why Innovation Accelerated in Britain 1547–1851', Anton Howes, Working Paper April 2017. Quoted with permission.

an 'associational world': *British Clubs and Societies 1580–1800: The Origins of an Associational World*, Peter Clark (Oxford University Press, 2000).

by 1700, there were around two thousand in London alone: *A Culture of Growth*, Joel Mokyr (Princeton University Press, 2016), p. 222.

economist James Dowey, numbered less than fifty: 'The Spread of Improvement: Why Innovation Accelerated in Britain 1547–1851', Anton Howes, Working Paper April 2017.

The Society for the Encouragement of Arts: 'Age of Invention: England's Peculiar Disgrace', Anton Howes, Newsletter 14 April 2020.

Dowey finds: 'Mind over Matter: Access to Knowledge and the British

Industrial Revolution', Dissertation, J. Dowey, London School of Economics and Political Science, 2017.

speech by a mathematician, Dr Olinthus Gregory: 'Age of Invention: Higher Perfection', Anton Howes, Newsletter 19 December 2019.

'Humanity does not desire to be great, but to be beloved': 'Adam Smith and Thorstein Veblen on the Pursuit of Status Through Consumption versus Work', Jon Wisman, *Cambridge Journal of Economics*, 2019, 43, 17–36. 10.1093/cje/bey015.

By the end of the nineteenth century: All the statistics from this section are from *Enlightenment Now*, Steven Pinker (Allen Lane, 2019).

CHAPTER 25

This chapter is based on my 2017 book *Selfie*.

topping out at 90 per cent in America: *The Rise and Fall of American Growth*, Robert J. Gordon (Princeton University Press, 2016), p. 617.

'What's irritated me about the whole direction of politics': 'Mrs Thatcher: The First Two Years', Ronald Butt, *Sunday Times*, 1 May 1981.

One study of over three hundred million births: 'Fitting In or Standing Out: Trends in American Parents' Choices for Children's Names, 1880–2007', Jean M. Twenge et al., *Social Psychological and Personality Science*, 2010, 1(1), 19–25.

a Gallup poll for *Newsweek* in 1992: 'Hey, I'm Terrific!', Jerry Adler, *Newsweek*, 17 February 1992.

a 1987 advert for a Gold MasterCard: *The Age of Entitlement*, Christopher Caldwell (Simon & Schuster, 2020), p. 128.

high-school children in the 1970s: *Generation Me*, Jean Twenge (Atria, 2006), p. 99.

'very best thing in the world': 'Children say being famous is best thing in world', Andrew Johnson and Andy McSmith, *Independent*, 18 December 2006.

intended for use in business meetings: 'Front-facing cameras were never intended for selfies', Anne Quito, qz.com, 26 October 2017.

93 million selfies: 'Taking Selfies Destroys Your Confidence and Raises Anxiety, a Study Shows. Why Are You Still Doing It?', Minda Zetlin, *Inc.*, 31 May 2019.

Robert Putnam has charted their collapse: *Bowling Alone*, Robert D. Putnam (Simon & Schuster, 2001), pp. 27, 16, 183.

Arthur Miller described its tragic hero: *The South Bank Show*, 9 November 1980.

busy people were viewed as having 'more status': 'Conspicuous Consumption of Time: When Busyness and Lack of Leisure Time Become a Status Symbol', Silvia Bellezza, Paharia Neeru and Keinan Anat, *Journal of Consumer Research* 44, June 2017, no. 1, 118–138.

There are various forms of perfectionism: Interviews, Professor Gordon Flett, Professor Rory O'Connor.

a study of more than forty thousand: 'Perfectionism Is Increasing Over Time: A Meta-Analysis of Birth Cohort Differences From 1989 to 2016', Thomas Curran and Andrew Hill, *Psychological Bulletin*, 2017, 145. 10.1037/bul0000138.

sixty-nine of the hundred largest economies on earth: '69 of the richest 100 entities on the planet are corporations', Uncredited author, *Global Justice Now*, 17 October 2018.

In the first quarter of 2021 alone, technology company Apple: https://twitter.com/olifranklin/status/1354547507574034432?s=03.

'Apple surpasses $100 billion in quarterly revenue for first time in its history', Chris Welch, *The Verge*, 27 January 2021.

'Apple Becomes First U.S. Company Worth More Than $2 Trillion', Sergei Klebnikov, *Forbes*, 19 August 2020.

Between 1978 and 2014, inflation-adjusted CEO pay: 'Top CEOs make more than 300 times the average worker', Paul Hodgson, *Fortune Magazine*, 22 June 2015.

1975 to 2017, inflation-adjusted US GDP nearly tripled: *The Value of Everything*, Mariana Mazzucato (Allen Lane, 2018), p. xiii.

in the UK: the richest one per cent: 'Britain must close the great pay divide', Danny Dorling, *Guardian*, 28 November 2010.

'been on a broadly downwards trend': 'Real wages have been falling since the 1970s and living standards are not about to recover', Institute of Employment Rights, 31 January 2014.

Over a million Britons: www.statista.com/statistics/414896/employees-with-zero-hours-contracts-number/.

Academic Professor Guy Standing argues: *The Precariat*, Guy Standing (Bloomsbury, 2016). Kindle location 112.

evidence of a tightening: Jean M. Twenge, Sara H. Konrath, A. Bell Cooper, Joshua D. Foster, W. Keith Campbell, Cooper McAllister, 'Egos deflating with the Great Recession: A cross-temporal meta-analysis and with-in-campus analysis of the Narcissistic Personality Inventory, 1982–2016', *Personality and Individual Differences*, volume 179.

CHAPTER 26

he was 'apt to suspect': *The Enlightenment*, John Robertson (Oxford University Press, 2015), p. 63.

Gustave Le Bon wrote: *The Ape that Understood the Universe*, Steve Stewart-Williams (Cambridge University Press, 2018), p. 64.

Intellectuals such as Hume and Le Bon experienced a reality: Such views were common. David Sloan Wilson writes, 'It's hard to find a major figure who didn't arrange humans into a hierarchy of races with Europeans at the top.' *This View of Life*, David Sloan Wilson (Pantheon, 2019). Kindle location 285.

published use of the word 'rights' quadrupling: *Inventing Human Rights*, Lynn Hunt (W. W. Norton & Company), p. 135.

Torture increasingly fell out of fashion: *Inventing Human Rights*, Lynn Hunt (W. W. Norton & Company), p. 76.

Public executions in the UK . . . 'remorseless multitude': *Inventing Human Rights*, Lynn Hunt (W. W. Norton & Company), p. 95.

In 1868 Parliament abolished them. It wasn't even eighty years: *Inventing Human Rights*, Lynn Hunt (W. W. Norton & Company), p. 77.

'Since pain' . . . 'the traditional framework of pain': *Inventing Human Rights*, Lynn Hunt (W. W. Norton & Company), p. 97.

by a majority of 385 to 55: www.historyextra.com/period/20th-century/what-was-the-1918-representation-of-the-people-act/.

put to death for masturbating: *The Goodness Paradox*, Richard Wrangham (Profile, 2019). Kindle location 2346.

until 1834 Britain was still gibbeting the corpses: *Inventing Human Rights*, Lynn Hunt (W. W. Norton & Company), p. 77.

One major investigation of more than 200,000 job applications: 'The persistence of racial discrimination in hiring', Lincoln Quillian, Devah Pager, Ole Hexel, Arnfinn H. Midtbøen, *Proceedings of the National Academy of Sciences*, September 2017, 201706255; https://doi.org/10.1073/pnas.1706255114.

Sociologist Professor Lincoln Quillian argued: 'Do Some Countries Discriminate

More Than Others?', Uncredited author, Institute for Policy Research, 18 June 2019.

introducing 'additional legitimate and unambiguous status information': *Status*, Cecilia L. Ridgeway (Russell Sage Foundation, 2019), p. 119.

A similar effect was found in a study in which white players: 'The neural substrates of in-group bias: a functional magnetic resonance imaging investigation', J. J. Van Bavel, D. J. Packer, W. A. Cunningham, *Psychological Science*, November 2008, 19 (11):1131–9. doi: 10.1111/j.1467-9280.2008.02214.x. PMID: 19076485.

'There's a name for that': social identity theory', Emily Moon, *Pacific Standard*, 3 December 2018.

One survey across the G7 nations: The Reykjavik Index for Leadership survey on behalf of the World Economic Forum, www.weforum.org/agenda/2018/12/women-reykjavik-index-leadership/.

One study, taking in 200,000 respondents: 'Men and things, women and people: a meta-analysis of sex differences in interests', R. Su, J. Rounds, P. I. Armstrong, *Psychological Bulletin* November 2009, 135 (6):859–884. https://doi.org/10.1037/a0017364. PMID: 19883140.

Steven Pinker, 'there's an enormous average': 'The Science of Gender and Science: Pinker vs. Spelke', *Debate*, 16 June 2005, transcript: www.edge.org/event/the-science-of-gender-and-science-pinker-vs-spelke-a-debate.

Nancy Mitford, the aristocratic daughter: 'The English Aristocracy', Nancy Mitford, accessed at: www.unz.com/print/Encounter-1955sep-00005.

Eton provides a glossary as part of its 'New Boy Guide': This was publicly available at www.etoncollege.com/glossary.aspx during my research but appeared to have been removed as of January 2021.

find 'subtle ways': *Posh Boys*, Robert Verkaik (OneWorld, 2018), p. 141.

'an instant sense of belonging': *Posh Boys*, Robert Verkaik (OneWorld, 2018), p. 21.

the writer Alan Bennett said, 'Private education': *Engines of Privilege*, David Kynaston (Bloomsbury, 2019), p. 15.

Around 7 per cent of Britons have been privately educated: 'Private school and Oxbridge "take top jobs"', Sean Coughlan and David Brown, BBC News, 24 June 2019.

over 70 per cent of the nation's barristers: *Engines of Privilege*, David Kynaston (Bloomsbury, 2019), p. 4.

60 per cent of its Oscar winners: *Engines of Privilege*, David Kynaston (Bloomsbury, 2019), p. 6.

Less than one per cent of the population attended Oxford or Cambridge: 'Oxbridge uncovered: More elitist than we thought', Hannah Richardson, BBC News, 20 October 2017.

71 per cent of senior judges: 'Private school and Oxbridge "take top jobs"', Sean Coughlan and David Brown, BBC News, 24 June 2019.

both taken exactly the same degree: *Social Class in the 21st Century*, Mike Savage (Pelican, 2015), p. 222.

Eton maintains a database: *Posh Boys*, Robert Verkaik (OneWorld, 2018), p. 140.

survey led by the sociologist Professor Mike Savage: *Social Class in the 21st Century* (Pelican, 2015), p. 204.

Savage's team interviewed Gita: *Social Class in the 21st Century* (Pelican, 2015), p. 213.

the most successful UK ethnic groups by income: Chinese ethnic group biggest earners in the UK', Uncredited author, BBC News, 9 July 2019.

69 per cent of Chinese-background state school pupils: Entry rates into higher education, 24 August 2020, www.ethnicity-facts-figures.service.gov.uk/.

in the USA, the most successful demographic by income: 'Asian women and men earned more than their White, Black, and Hispanic counterparts in 2017', 29 August 2018, www.bls.gov.

CHAPTER 27

Analysis from the UK: 'Britain's Choice: Common Ground and Division in 2020s Britain', October 2020, More in Common Report.

more qualified than the baby boomers and yet 20 per cent less wealthy: 'The Emerging Millennial Wealth Gap: Divergent Trajectories, Weak Balance Sheets, and Implications for Social Policy', Report, Reid Cramer et al., *New America*, October 2019.

average personal deficit of $32,700 in the US: 'Average Student Loan Debt in America: 2019 Facts & Figures', Justin Song, Value Penguin, 4 January 2021.

£40,000 in England: Student loan statistics, Paul Bolton, House of Commons Library, 9 December 2020.

from the wealthiest households and being the most highly educated: 'Britain's

Choice: Common Ground and Division in 2020s Britain', More in Common Report, October 2020. Additional information via private communication with study co-author Tim Dixon.

In 2019, 31 per cent of UK graduates: 'Almost a third of graduates "overeducated" for their job', Uncredited author, BBC News, 29 April 2019.

A 2020 survey of 215,000 recent graduates: Graduate wellbeing recorded in the Graduate Outcomes survey, Office for Students report, 8 December 2020.

13 per cent of adults have a PhD, MSc: About 13.1 Percent Have a Master's, Professional Degree or Doctorate, American Counts Staff, census.gov, 21 February 2019.

34 per cent of college graduates: '41% of Recent Grads Work in Jobs Not Requiring a Degree', Elizabeth Redden, insidehighered.com, 18 February 2020.

graduates in the arts, humanities and media are among the most underemployed: 'Almost a third of graduates "overeducated" for their job', Uncredited author, BBC News, 29 April 2019.

'41% of Recent Grads Work in Jobs Not Requiring a Degree', Elizabeth Redden, insidehighered.com, 18 February, 2020.

between 2015 and 2018, support for capitalism: 'Keynes was wrong. Gen Z will have it worse', Malcom Harris, *MIT Technology Review*, 16 December 2019.

approve of Communism: 'US Attitudes Toward Socialism, Communism and Collectivism', YouGov, October 2019.

'anti-capitalism has become': 'Intellectuals and Resentment Toward Capitalism', T. Cushman, *Sociology*, 2012, 49, 247–255.

satisfaction with democracy among millennials fell below 50 per cent: 'Youth and Satisfaction with Democracy: Reversing the Democratic Disconnect?', R. S. Foa, A. Klassen, D. Wenger, A. Rand and M. Slade, 2020, Cambridge, United Kingdom: Centre for the Future of Democracy.

'higher debt burdens, lower odds of owning a home': 'Democracy: Millennials are the most disillusioned generation "in living memory"' – global study, News release, University of Cambridge, 19 October 2020.

Between 1979 and 2005, the average real hourly wage: *Red, Blue and Purple America: The Future of Election Demographics*, Alan Abramowitz and Roy Teixeira (Brookings Institution Press, 2008), p. 110.

Katherine Cramer describes: 'A new theory for why Trump voters are so angry – that actually makes sense', Jeff Guo, *Washington Post*, 8 November 2016.

'grew up seeing themselves at the respected centre': *Status*, Cecilia L. Ridgeway (Russell Sage Foundation, 2019), p. 53.

'fuelled a strong sense of relative deprivation': *National Populism*, Roger Eatwell and Matthew Goodwin, (Pelican Books, 2018), p. xxii.

'hyper ethnic change': *National Populism*, Roger Eatwell and Matthew Goodwin (Pelican Books, 2018), p. 129.

'prioritize the culture and interests of the nation': *National Populism*, Roger Eatwell and Matthew Goodwin (Pelican Books, 2018), p. ix.

'absolutely central' to the movement: *National Populism*, Roger Eatwell and Matthew Goodwin (Pelican Books, 2018), p. 32.

'impacted strongly on people's perceived levels of respect': *National Populism*, Roger Eatwell and Matthew Goodwin (Pelican Books, 2018), p. 212.

a sequence of tweets by a US journalist, Rani Molla: https://twitter.com/rani-molla/status/1024680943666257922.
https://me.me/i/rani-molla-ranimolla-follow-oh-shut-the-fuck-up-how-0ac67c62de214f79af249d3c17487ab4.

Molla has written for the *Wall Street Journal*: https://www.vox.com/authors/rani-molla (accessed 10 November 2020).

When the New Right look upwards: *National Populism*, Roger Eatwell and Matthew Goodwin (Pelican Books, 2018), p. 106.

41 per cent of white millennials: *National Populism*, Roger Eatwell and Matthew Goodwin (Pelican Books, 2018), p. 10.

white non-college voters comprised around three-fifths: *National Populism*, Roger Eatwell and Matthew Goodwin (Pelican Books, 2018), p. 26.

74 per cent: *National Populism*, Roger Eatwell and Matthew Goodwin (Pelican Books, 2018), p. 26.

'culturally liberal mindset': *National Populism*, Roger Eatwell and Matthew Goodwin (Pelican Books, 2018), p. 28.

New Left have been found to be less proud of being British: 'Britain's Choice: Common Ground and Division in 2020s Britain', More in Common Report, October 2020.

Starbucks . . . promoting controversial trans rights charity Mermaids: 'Starbucks new limited-edition Mermaids Cookie is making a splash!', Press Release, 2 February 2020.

Gillette . . . 'it's been going on far too long': www.youtube.com/watch/k0PmuEyP3ao.

'If you're dressing up for #Huluween this year': 'Hulu deletes tweet about wearing "respectful" Halloween costume', Audra Schroeder, *The Daily Dot*, 17 October 2018.

Chief Librarian of the British Library Liz Jolly: 'British Library's chief librarian says "racism is the creation of white people" as bosses call for changes to displays in wake of BLM movement after colleagues were "urged to support work of Labour MP Diane Abbott"', Katie Feehan, *Mail Online*, 30 August 2020.

Edinburgh Comedy Awards director Nica Burns: 'I am looking forward to comedy's future in the woke world', Nica Burns, chortle.co.uk, 5 August 2018.

the American Psychological Association who approvingly press-released: 'APA calls for true systemic change in U.S. Culture', Zara Abrams, apa.org, 1 September 2020.

Sarah Jeong, a journalist with a history of racist tweets: 'When Racism Is Fit to Print', Andrew Sullivan, *New York Magazine*, 3 August 2018.

The University of Michigan's DEI mission: 'The Campus Diversity Swarm', Mark Pulliam, *City Journal*, 10 October 2018.

Yale has more than one hundred and fifty staff: 'The Downside of Diversity', Anthony Kronman, *Wall Street Journal*, 2 August 2019.

study of 669 US universities: 'The rise of universities' diversity bureaucrats', B.S., *The Economist*, 8 May 2018.

'booming, creating new career paths and roles': 'The Big Business of Unconscious Bias', Nora Zelevansky, *New York Times*, 20 November 2019.

risen 18 per cent between 2017 and 2018, with 130 per million postings: *Diversity Inc.*, Pamela Newkirk (Bold Type, 2019). Kindle location 2608.

between 2018 and 2019 it jumped a further 25 per cent: 'The Big Business of Unconscious Bias', Nora Zelevansky, *New York Times*, 20 November 2019.

A survey of 234 companies in the S&P 500: *Diversity Inc.*, Pamela Newkirk (Bold Type, 2019). Kindle location 2621.

Universities, including Yale, Cornell: 'The Big Business of Unconscious Bias', Nora Zelevansky, *New York Times*, 20 November 2019.

charging up to $2,400 just for registration: *Diversity Inc.*, Pamela Newkirk (Bold Type, 2019). Kindle location 2660.

Google spent: *Diversity Inc.*, Pamela Newkirk (Bold Type, 2019). Kindle location 2737.

eight billion dollars every year on diversity training: *Diversity Inc.*, Pamela Newkirk (Bold Type, 2019). Kindle location 2608.

between 2006 and 2020, one consultant alone: 'Obscene federal "diversity training" scam prospers – even under Trump', Christopher F. Rufo, *New York Post*, 16 July 2020.

Elsewhere, it's reported the charity Time's Up: 'Star-studded Time's Up charities spent big on salaries, little on helping victims', Isabel Vincent and Paula Froelich, *New York Post*, 28 November 2020.

In both places, the white working class felt outnumbered by minority groups, excluded from the political process and subject to racial prejudice: *The New Minority*, Justin Gest (Oxford University Press, 2016), pp. 20–23.

'Many white working-class individuals view the struggle for equal treatment': *The New Minority*, Justin Gest (Oxford University Press, 2016), p. 22.

average income of just $14,996: *The New Minority*, Justin Gest (Oxford University Press, 2016), p. 92.

'It's the American Nightmare': *The New Minority*, Justin Gest (Oxford University Press, 2016), p. 159.

When Gest asked members of the white working class who looked out for their interests: *The New Minority*, Justin Gest (Oxford University Press, 2016), p. 113.

A mother of two told Gest: *The New Minority*, Justin Gest (Oxford University Press, 2016), p. 136.

'driving around in new cars': *The New Minority*, Justin Gest (Oxford University Press, 2016), p. 95.

African, Afro-Caribbean, South Asian and Eastern European origin: *The New Minority*, Justin Gest (Oxford University Press, 2016), p. 47.

Gest visited the home of 59-year-old Nancy Pemberton: *The New Minority*, Justin Gest (Oxford University Press, 2016), pp. 44–45.

'If there's a job interview': *The New Minority*, Justin Gest (Oxford University Press, 2016), p. 162.

'a mute button pressed': *The New Minority*, Justin Gest (Oxford University Press, 2016), p. 73.

Across forty interviews, Gest heard the 'I'm not racist, but . . .': *The New Minority*, Justin Gest (Oxford University Press, 2016), p. 72.

'I am proud to be English': *The New Minority*, Justin Gest (Oxford University Press, 2016), p. 61.

'make it like it used to be fifty years ago': *The New Minority*, Justin Gest (Oxford University Press, 2016), p. 52.

CHAPTER 28

This notion is thought to have its roots in Ancient Greece: *Communism*, Richard Pipes (Weidenfeld & Nicolson, 2001), p. 1.

Plato argued for an ideal state in which: *Communism*, Richard Pipes (Weidenfeld and Nicolson, 2001), p. 2.

The word itself was invented in 1840s Paris: *Communism*, Richard Pipes (Weidenfeld & Nicolson, 2001), pp. ix–xi.

80 to 90 per cent of the world's economy had been based on agriculture: *Communism*, Richard Pipes (Weidenfeld & Nicolson, 2001), p. 9.

resented the rise in status of these nouveaux riches: *Communism*, Richard Pipes (Weidenfeld & Nicolson, 2001), p. 10.

'society regulates the general production': *Communism*, Richard Pipes (Weidenfeld & Nicolson, 2001), p. 12.

forced people away from their natural state of cooperation: *Marx*, Peter Singer (Oxford University Press, 2000), p. 35.

'A house may be large or small': *Marx*, Peter Singer (Oxford University Press, 2000), p. 63.

It was ownership that created social classes, ownership that led to the 'pauperization': *Communism*, Richard Pipes (Weidenfeld & Nicolson, 2001), p. 13.

'The human species, the sluggish Homo sapiens': *Communism*, Richard Pipes (Weidenfeld & Nicolson, 2001), p. 68.

many contemporary historians see its genesis: *Communism*, Leslie Holmes (Oxford University Press, 2009), p. 399.

'laughably amateur' but nearly successful: *Lenin The Dictator*, Victor Sebestyen (Weidenfeld & Nicolson, 2018), p. 45.

'the mass of Simbirsk province's' . . . tossed back to the 'margins of society': *Lenin*, Robert Service (Macmillan, 2000), p. 59.

Dignitaries who'd once been guests stopped visiting: *Lenin The Dictator*, Victor Sebestyen (Weidenfeld & Nicolson, 2018), p. 47.

'Respectable Simbirsk' . . . Every member of the family was held responsible: *Lenin*, Robert Service (Macmillan, 2000), p. 59.

including the children, and faced 'unending social ostracism in Simbirsk': *Lenin*, Robert Service (Macmillan, 2000), p. 62.

'This triggered the vitriolic, sometimes uncontrollable': *Lenin The Dictator*, Victor Sebestyen (Weidenfeld & Nicolson, 2018), p. 47.

'radicalised almost overnight': *Lenin The Dictator*, Victor Sebestyen (Weidenfeld & Nicolson, 2018), p. 47.

not concern for the poor, but hatred: *Communism*, Richard Pipes (Weidenfeld & Nicolson, 2001), p. 28.

more than a third of the global population: *Communism*, Leslie Holmes (Oxford University Press, 2009). Kindle location 522.

they won under a quarter of the vote: *How to be a Dictator*, Frank Dikötter (Bloomsbury, 2019). Kindle location 1332.

After seizing power violently in a coup d'état: *Revolutionary Russia 1891–1991*, Orlando Figes (Pelican, 2014). Kindle location 1484.

the 'dictatorship of the proletariat': *Communism*, Leslie Holmes (Oxford University Press, 2009), p. 379.

'the looting of the looters': http://www.orlandofiges.info/section6_TheOctoberRevolution1917/RevolutionandRevenge.php.

'for centuries our fathers and grandfathers': *Revolutionary Russia 1891–1991*, Orlando Figes (Pelican, 2014). Kindle location 1674.

They were classed as 'former people' . . . 'They were forced to sell': *Revolutionary Russia 1891–1991*, Orlando Figes (Pelican, 2014). Kindle location 1674.

Lenin banned other political parties: *Communism*, Leslie Holmes (Oxford University Press, 2009). Kindle location 543.

thousands of priests and nuns: *How to be a Dictator*, Frank Dikötter (Bloomsbury, 2019). Kindle location 1328.

The press demanded revenge: *Revolutionary Russia 1891–1991*, Orlando Figes (Pelican, 2014). Kindle location 1891.

having their hands boiled until a glove of skin: *Revolutionary Russia 1891–1991*, Orlando Figes (Pelican, 2014). Kindle location 1854.

'The *kulaks* are the rabid foes': *Lenin The Dictator*, Victor Sebestyen (Weidenfeld and Nicolson, 2018), p. 394.

in this 1918 telegram: *Lenin The Dictator*, Victor Sebestyen (Weidenfeld & Nicolson, 2018), p. 396.

https://www.marxists.org/archive/lenin/works/1918/aug/11c.htm.

'favored policies that strongly discriminated against': *Everyday Stalinism*, Sheila Fitzpatrick (Oxford University Press, 1999), p. 5.

'just enough bread so as not to forget the smell of it': *Revolutionary Russia 1891–1991*, Orlando Figes (Pelican, 2014). Kindle location 1854.

By 1920, 5.4 million were directly employed by the government: *Revolutionary Russia 1891–1991*, Orlando Figes (Pelican, 2014). Kindle location 1850.

'There can be little doubt that': *Communism*, Leslie Holmes (Oxford University Press, 2009), p. 562.

essay by author Arthur Koestler: *The God That Failed*, Richard Crossman (editor), (Harper Colophon, 1963), pp. 15–75.

some small businesses would be permitted: *Revolutionary Russia 1891–1991*, Orlando Figes (Pelican, 2014). Kindle location 2184.

taking of grain from peasants would be replaced with taxation: *How to be a Dictator*, Frank Dikötter (Bloomsbury, 2019). Kindle location 1328.

The economy grew rapidly: *Revolutionary Russia 1891–1991*, Orlando Figes (Pelican, 2014). Kindle location 2272.

'new exploitation of the proletariat': *Revolutionary Russia 1891–1991*, Orlando Figes (Pelican, 2014). Kindle location 2193.

'We are advancing full steam ahead': *Revolutionary Russia 1891–1991*, Orlando Figes (Pelican, 2014). Kindle location 2411.

once produced nearly three-quarters of the nation's commercial grain: *Harvest of Sorrow*, Robert Conquest (Vintage, 2002). Kindle location 1822.

'liquidation of the *kulaks* as a class': *Communism*, Richard Pipes (Weidenfeld & Nicolson, 2001), p. 58.

first two months of 1930 alone, about sixty million peasants: *Revolutionary Russia 1891–1991*, Orlando Figes (Pelican, 2014). Kindle location 2452.

Around 1.4 million were sent to 'special settlements': *Revolutionary Russia 1891–1991*, Orlando Figes (Pelican, 2014). Kindle location 2475.

Records show one single train leaving the small regional station of Yantsenovo: *Harvest of Sorrow*, Robert Conquest (Vintage, 2002). Kindle location 3020.

'used to seeing corpses there in the morning': *Harvest of Sorrow*, Robert Conquest (Vintage, 2002). Kindle location 3038.

In 1933 around five thousand *kulaks* and 'déclassé elements': *Cannibal Island*, Nicolas Werth (Princeton University Press, 2007), p. 129.

'the liver, the heart, the lungs': *Cannibal Island*, Nicolas Werth (Princeton University Press, 2007), p. 139.

One witness remembered a 'pretty girl': *Cannibal Island*, Nicolas Werth (Princeton University Press, 2007), p. 141.

'The boy was out of luck': *Cannibal Island*, Nicolas Werth (Princeton University Press, 2007), p. xiv.

'Throw your bourgeois humanitarianism out of the window': *Revolutionary Russia 1891–1991*, Orlando Figes (Pelican, 2014). Kindle location 2449.

Lev Kopelev scolded himself: *Revolutionary Russia 1891–1991*, Orlando Figes (Pelican, 2014). Kindle location 2487.

'they are not human beings, they are *kulaks*': *Harvest of Sorrow*, Robert Conquest (Vintage, 2002). Kindle location 2807.

A decree in 1932 ordered ten years' hard labour: *Communism*, Richard Pipes (Weidenfeld & Nicolson, 2001), p. 59.

peasants began grass and tree bark: *How to be a Dictator*, Frank Dikötter (Bloomsbury, 2019). Kindle location 1515.

around six million peasants starved to death: *Communism*, Richard Pipes (Weidenfeld & Nicolson, 2001), p. 60.

a 'catastrophe for the Soviet economy': *Revolutionary Russia 1891–1991*, Orlando Figes (Pelican, 2014). Kindle location 2504.

At the start of the 1930s goods began disappearing from shops in the towns and cities; severe shortages of foods, clothes and other essentials began: *Everyday Stalinism*, Sheila Fitzpatrick (Oxford University Press, 1999), p. 2.

'the most precipitous peacetime decline in living standards': *Communism*, Richard Pipes (Weidenfeld & Nicolson, 2001), p. 57.

The party didn't accept the concept . . . 'Everything people did in private was': *Revolutionary Russia 1891–1991*, Orlando Figes (Pelican, 2014). Kindle location 2328.

commented on the 'extraordinary uniformity: *Caviar with Champagne*, Jukka Gronow (Berg, 2003), p. 2.

'The purges began here': *Revolutionary Russia 1891–1991*, Orlando Figes (Pelican, 2014). Kindle location 2352.

'open and secret violators' of the party who 'cast doubt': *Everyday Stalinism*, Sheila Fitzpatrick (Oxford University Press, 1999), p. 19.

over half a million party members were: *Revolutionary Russia 1891–1991*, Orlando Figes (Pelican, 2014). Kindle location 2719.

'isolated from everybody' . . . 'Can everything be collapsing in this way?': *Everyday Stalinism*, Sheila Fitzpatrick (Oxford University Press, 1999), pp. 19–20.

elites and former elites came under heavy suspicion: *Everyday Stalinism*, Sheila Fitzpatrick (Oxford University Press, 1999), p. 7.

smeared as 'bourgeois specialists': *Everyday Stalinism*, Sheila Fitzpatrick (Oxford University Press, 1999), p. 5.

priests, *kulaks* and the so-called 'Nepmen': *Everyday Stalinism*, Sheila Fitzpatrick (Oxford University Press, 1999), p. 7.

'"Going through the Purge" meant confessing your sins': *Everyday Stalinism*, Sheila Fitzpatrick (Oxford University Press, 1999), p. 20.

'the shameful example of my fall': *Everyday Stalinism*, Sheila Fitzpatrick (Oxford University Press, 1999), p. 19.

There were millions of informants: *Revolutionary Russia 1891–1991*, Orlando Figes (Pelican, 2014). Kindle location 3208.

People denounced celebrities: *Everyday Stalinism*, Sheila Fitzpatrick (Oxford University Press, 1999), p. 208.

denounced her husband's academic rival as 'a vulgarian' . . . 'letters from leading actors': *The Rise of Victimhood Culture*, Jason Manning and Bradley Campbell (Palgrave Macmillan, 2018). Kindle location 1634.

One poet was denounced for not signing . . . for being the drinking companion: *Everyday Stalinism*, Sheila Fitzpatrick (Oxford University Press, 1999), p. 198.

having *kulak* fathers or being 'brought up by a merchant': *Everyday Stalinism*, Sheila Fitzpatrick (Oxford University Press, 1999), p 204.

When a photographer complained: *Everyday Stalinism*, Sheila Fitzpatrick (Oxford University Press, 1999), p. 208.

'super-denouncers': *Everyday Stalinism*, Sheila Fitzpatrick (Oxford University Press, 1999), p. 209.

One later described how he and a partner would go to meetings with 'ready-made lists' . . . 'I do not know': *Revolutionary Russia 1891–1991*, Orlando Figes (Pelican, 2014). Kindle location 3242.

the police were issued quotas: *Communism*, Richard Pipes (Weidenfeld & Nicolson, 2001), p. 63.

165,200 priests were arrested, 106,800 of whom were shot: *Communism*, Richard Pipes (Weidenfeld & Nicolson, 2001), p. 65.

one and a half thousand people were executed daily: *Revolutionary Russia 1891–1991*, Orlando Figes (Pelican, 2014). Kindle location 3080.

One and a half million ordinary Russians were arrested by the secret police:

How to be a Dictator, Frank Dikötter (Bloomsbury, 2019). Kindle location 1546.

executed for 'counter-revolutionary activities': *Revolutionary Russia 1891–1991*, Orlando Figes (Pelican, 2014). Kindle location 3066.

All of Stalin's close political rivals were wiped out: According to Pipes: 'In his 'Testament,' Lenin listed six leading Communists as his potential successors; all but one – Stalin – perished.' *Communism*, Richard Pipes (Weidenfeld & Nicolson, 2001), p. 64.

created new vacancies, which meant new opportunities for millions: *Caviar with Champagne*, Jukka Gronow (Berg, 2003), p. 11.

'proletarianizing' . . . former low-status players: *Everyday Stalinism*, Sheila Fitzpatrick (Oxford University Press, 1999), p. 6.

'All over the Soviet Union, at every level': *Everyday Stalinism*, Sheila Fitzpatrick (Oxford University Press, 1999), p. 86.

there were actually three: workers, peasants and intelligentsia: *Caviar with Champagne*, Jukka Gronow (Berg, 2003), p. 5.

Old symbols of hierarchy . . . In the military: *Everyday Stalinism*, Sheila Fitzpatrick (Oxford University Press, 1999), pp. 106–107.

He called it 'equality mongering': *Why Nations Fail*, Daron Acemoglu and James A. Robinson (Profile, 2012), p. 129.

'egalitarianism' . . . was an 'ultra-left' idea: *Communism*, Richard Pipes (Weidenfeld & Nicolson, 2001), p. 57.

'a person is a person': *Revolutionary Russia 1891–1991*, Orlando Figes (Pelican, 2014). Kindle location 2844.

once been a 'Party Maximum' wage cap: *Revolutionary Russia 1891–1991*, Orlando Figes (Pelican, 2014). Kindle location 2755.

Stalin 'vigorously demanded that individual skills': *Caviar with Champagne*, Jukka Gronow (Berg, 2003), p. 12.

'The authorities clearly understood': *Caviar with Champagne*, Jukka Gronow (Berg, 2003), p. 13.

the Soviet champagne industry was born . . . two thousand roubles per month: *Caviar with Champagne*, Jukka Gronow (Berg, 2003), p. 22.

in 1934 1,400 tonnes of cocoa beans: *Caviar with Champagne*, Jukka Gronow (Berg, 2003), p. 50.

'New Year's trees': *Caviar with Champagne*, Jukka Gronow (Berg, 2003), p. 36.

fifty kinds of bread . . . 'including twenty new types': *Everyday Stalinism*, Sheila Fitzpatrick (Oxford University Press, 1999), p. 90.

Americans made five thousand hamburgers . . . 'in Germany ice cream is sold': *Caviar with Champagne*, Jukka Gronow (Berg, 2003), pp. 74–75.

a folding umbrella and thermos plates: *Caviar with Champagne*, Jukka Gronow (Berg, 2003), p. 94.

Restaurants . . . promoting themselves as superior: *Caviar with Champagne*, Jukka Gronow (Berg, 2003), pp. 109–115.

sociologists found at least ten: 'Social Stratification and Mobility in the Soviet Union: 1940-1950', A. Inkeles, *American Sociological Review*, 1950, 15(4), 465–479.

His regime 'introduced systematic discrimination': *Everyday Stalinism*, Sheila Fitzpatrick (Oxford University Press, 1999), pp. 11–12.

A person's social class was even listed on their passport: *Caviar with Champagne*, Jukka Gronow (Berg, 2003), p. 12.

admissions procedure included . . . College admissions were similarly policed: *Everyday Stalinism*, Sheila Fitzpatrick (Oxford University Press, 1999), p. 16.

In the arts . . . 'They give medals to Armenians': *Everyday Stalinism*, Sheila Fitzpatrick (Oxford University Press, 1999), p. 168.

Engineers and the new, approved, correct-thinking intelligentsia: *Everyday Stalinism*, Sheila Fitzpatrick (Oxford University Press, 1999), p. 96.

Industrial workers comprised about 40 per cent of the workforce: *Caviar with Champagne*, Jukka Gronow (Berg, 2003), p. 123.

'the most important workers of the most important factories': *Caviar with Champagne*, Jukka Gronow (Berg, 2003), p. 125.

The new elites gained access to special apartments and had the best goods automatically reserved for them: *Everyday Stalinism*, Sheila Fitzpatrick (Oxford University Press, 1999), p. 98.

Their children were sent to exclusive summer camps: *Everyday Stalinism*, Sheila Fitzpatrick (Oxford University Press, 1999), pp. 101–102.

It became 'normal' for them to have live-in servants . . . 'They are even worse': *Everyday Stalinism*, Sheila Fitzpatrick (Oxford University Press, 1999), pp. 99–100.

they were a *vanguard*: *Everyday Stalinism*, Sheila Fitzpatrick (Oxford University Press, 1999), p. 105.

luxury trains: *Caviar with Champagne*, Jukka Gronow (Berg, 2003), p. 127.

'The *nomenklatura* is on another planet': *Communism*, Richard Pipes (Weidenfeld & Nicolson, 2001) p. 65.

'kingdom of equality': *Communism*, Richard Pipes (Weidenfeld & Nicolson, 2001), p 7.

had been corrected by his student, Aristotle: *Communism*, Richard Pipes (Weidenfeld & Nicolson, 2001), p. 3.

CHAPTER 29

Professor Susan Fiske argues that: 'The role of morality in social cognition', J. L. Ray, P. Mende-Siedlecki, A. P. Gantman and J. J. Van Bavel (in press), in *The Neural Bases of Mentalizing*, K. Ochsner and M. Gilead (Eds.) (Springer Press).

warmth and competence: 'Universal dimensions of social cognition: Warmth and competence', S. T. Fiske, A. J. Cuddy and P. Glick, *Trends in Cognitive Sciences*, 11, 77–83.

'not only a critical and separable dimension'...Elsewhere, 'perceived sincerity': 'Impression mismanagement: People as inept self-presenters', J. Steinmetz, O. Sezer, C. Sedikides, *Social and Personality Psychology Compass*, 2017: 11:e12321.

This fascinating paper concerns 'hubris, humblebragging, hypocrisy, and backhanded compliments' as strategies people use to curry a positive image that 'often end in failure'. The researchers concluded that 'people are fairly inept impression managers'. One routine problem is we're just not great at predicting the emotional effects of self-status boosting on our audience. We think what's made us happy will naturally make others happy. It won't. It also represents a basic misunderstanding of the game: prestige-based status is granted by others, not declared by a victor.

But a couple of interesting wrinkles are added. Firstly, people aren't so harsh if we claim our success is due to hard work rather than natural talent, the latter perhaps seeming less deserved and therefore more infuriating. Secondly, and pleasingly, we're also bad at predicting how confessions of our failures will land: people tend to believe an observer 'will judge them more harshly for mishaps or debacles than is actually the case'. But unless we're boasting to someone like a parent or romantic partner, and a golden droplet of our newfound status might feasibly wash back in their direction via the principle of leaky status, the chances our audience will delight at our victories is minimal.

change especially as we move from West to East: 'Cross-Cultural Investigation of Compliance Without Pressure: The "You Are Free to" Technique in France, Ivory Coast, Romania, Russia, and China', A. Pascual, C. Oteme, L. Samson et al., *Cross-Cultural Research*, 2012, 46 (4):394–416.

'evoking freedom': 'I'm free but I'll comply with your request: generalization and multidimensional effects of the "evoking freedom" technique'. N. Guéguen, R. V. Joule, S. Halimi-Falkowicz, A. Pascual, J. Fischer-Lokou and M. Dufourcq-Brana (2013), *Journal of Applied Social Psychology*, 43: 116–137.

those with 'complex', multiple self-identities: *Happiness*, Daniel Nettle (Oxford University Press, 2005), pp. 156, 175.

'minor acts of nonconformity: *Status*, Cecilia L. Ridgeway (Russell Sage Foundation, 2019), p. 114.

INDEX

development as communities
settled, 100; and dominance behaviour, 62; of the family, 121–2;
health differentials due to status,
16–17; as inevitable, 291–300; in
prison, 10; Renaissance success
games, 237–8; and revolutions,
114–15; role of the leader, 201–2; in
schools, 64, 73, 125–7; as shallow in
hunter-gatherer societies, 97–8,
102–3, 168, 169–70; in Soviet
Russia, 286, 295–6; and subconscious processes, 4–5, 25, 33; and
tight cultures, 192–3, 217 see also
social class/structure
'hikikomori,' Japanese, 38
Hinduism, 137; caste system, 111–13,
170; Gujarat genocide, 223
Hitler, Adolf, 203–4, 207–16, 223–4
Ho, David Yau Fai, 35
Hogan, Robert, 16
Holmes, Leslie, 287
Holocaust, 223–4
honour killings, 71, 204
Hood, Bruce, 25
Hooke, Robert, 242
Houston, Whitney, 249
Howes, Anton, 242–3
Hoxha, Enver, 165
Hulu, 274
human archetypes, 40
human rights concept: and anti-colo-
nial movements, 117; in collective
cultures, 35; emergence of, 255,
256–7
Hume, David, 53, 256
humiliation, 64–70, 115, 204; humiliated grandiosity, 69–75, 204–7,
217–23, 284–5; and Lenin's background, 283–5; and Mao's Cultural
Revolution, 219–20; national, 204–7,
214, 218; and terrorism, 220–21; use
of as weapon, 65–6, 299
Hunt, Lynn, 257
hunter-gatherer societies, 13–14, 32,
43, 102, 138–9, 164, 302; and lead-

ership, 168–70; shallow hierarchies
in, 97–8, 169–70

identity, human: and beliefs, 106–7;
and cults, 193–200; dishonest identity games, 163–4; as fluid and
creative, 129, 163, 254; identity
politics, 4; need for a variety of
games, 306; our idols as versions of
us, 99; and progressive activists,
179; rise of National Populism,
272, 273–4; 'social perfectionists,'
251; status games as forming, 2, 30,
211, 300
immigration, 265, 271, 272, 273,
277–9, 308
imperialism/colonialism, 105–7, 108,
116–17, 165, 221
India, 48, 71, 108, 117, 170, 173–6;
Gujarat genocide, 223; Hindu caste
system, 111–13, 170
individualism, 6, 226, 231–2, 245,
248–52, 304; individual/human
rights, 117, 255, 256–7; neoliberal
hyper-individualism, 247, 308; in
Western culture, 34
Industrial Revolution, 242–5, 255;
inequality created by, 281–2
inequality: and development of
communism, 280–1; and display of
wealth, 101–2; humans as not
natural seekers of equality, 299–300
as increasing in neoliberal era, 252;
and Industrial Revolution, 281–2;
and need for games to function
properly, 114–16; and new
merchant/banking societies, 236;
and Plato, 280–1; shallow hierarchies in premodern age, 97–8,
102–3, 169–70 and 'status detection
system,' 25–6
influence, 53–5, 59–60; and social
media, 49–50, 85–7, 88
innovation: in Britain of 1700s/1800s,
242–4; and Industrial Revolution,
242–6; our instinct for rewarding